Making ~~D~~ ~~￼~~ *ℯ*

Making Religion, Making the State

The Politics of Religion in Modern China

EDITED BY YOSHIKO ASHIWA

AND DAVID L. WANK

Stanford University Press
Stanford, California

Stanford University Press
Stanford, California

Printed in the United States of America
on acid-free, archival-quality paper

Library of Congress Cataloging-in-Publication Data

Making religion, making the state : the politics of religion in
modern China / edited by Yoshiko Ashiwa and David L. Wank.
    p. cm.
Includes bibliographical references and index.
ISBN 978-0-8047-5841-3 (cloth : alk. paper)
ISBN 978-0-8047-5842-0 (pbk. : alk. paper)
  1. Religion and state—China. 2. Religion and politics—
China. 3. China—Religion. I. Ashiwa, Yoshiko, 1957–
II. Wank, David L., 1957–
BL65.S8M35 2009
322'.10951090511—dc22

                        2008043090

Contents

Acknowledgments

WE ARE INDEBTED to many people whose commitment to this work, both intellectually and practically, made the publication of our book possible. The chapters you are about to read draw upon anthropology, history, political science, religious studies, and sociology. We were fortunate enough to bring all of these perspectives together at Stanford University in 2004 with the support of an Association of Asian Studies China and Inner Asia Research Conference Grant. We would like to thank Jean Oi for giving us access to Stanford's superb facilities, and to Connie Chin and the staff of Stanford's Center for East Asian Studies for their tireless and efficient help. Alison Jones provided us with an excellent summary of the discussions that took place.

We are grateful to the scholars whose work appears in this volume for their flexibility in looking beyond disciplinary boundaries to explore the broad issues addressed in the book. Though their writing is not represented here, Eriberto Lozada, David Palmer, and Ning Qiang made important contributions to the development of the ideas expressed.

We are also grateful to Muriel Bell at Stanford University Press for her strong support in bringing the results to publication, to Stacy Wagner and Jessica Walsh who oversaw the project through to completion, and to Richard Gunde for his careful copyediting.

Yoshiko Ashiwa and David L. Wank

Making Religion, Making the State

CHAPTER 1

Making Religion, Making the State
in Modern China: An Introductory Essay

YOSHIKO ASHIWA AND DAVID L. WANK

AN ASTOUNDING REVIVAL of religion has occurred in China since the late 1970s. China now has the world's largest Buddhist population, fast-growing Catholic and Protestant congregations, expanding Muslim communities, and active Daoist temples.[1] According to state statistics there are 100 million religious believers, 85,000 religious sites (churches, mosques, temples), 300,000 clergy, and 3,000 religious organizations. Buddhism has more than 13,000 temples and monasteries and 200,000 monks and nuns, while, additionally, Tibetan Buddhism has over 3,000 monasteries, 120,000 lamas, and 1,700 living Buddhas. Daoism has 1,500 temples and 25,000 masters. In Islam there are 30,000 mosques, 40,000 imams, and 18 million believers. Catholicism has over 4,000 churches, 4,000 clergy, and 4 million believers. Protestantism has 12,000 churches, over 25,000 meeting places, 18,000 clerics, and 10 million believers (Information Office of the State Council 1997).[2]

These statistics on the revival of religion in China, which is ruled by a communist party that is avowedly atheist, stimulate various interpretations. They could be seen as signifying the victory of religious believers over the state. Attempts by the Chinese Communist Party (Party) to eradicate religion during the Cultural Revolution (1966–76) failed; belief can never be conquered by political ideologies such as communism. The statistics could also be seen as part of the Chinese state control of religion; they are inaccurate numbers based on officially registered religious sites. Many of these religious sites are fronts for tourism and museums and contain few "real" temples and churches, while the numerous unregistered churches that are thriving are not visible in the state's official statistics.

We see the statistics in a rather different way, which is the main theme of this volume. The statistics reflect the state representation of the extent of religion in China today in terms of the state's definition of "modern religion" as well as the efforts of believers, clergy, and worshippers to accommodate the modern definition of religion. Our point, therefore, is that the situation of religion in China is not simply a history of conflict between state and religion but rather processes of interactions among multiple actors that comprise the making of modern religion and the modern state over the course of the past century.

To understand these processes, it is fruitful to briefly leave the Chinese context and think about the state and religion in the broader context of modernity. Recently, some arguments have been raised about the concepts of modernity and religion. It has been argued that "religion" is a modern concept that is seen most sharply in colonial interactions from the late nineteenth century (Asad 1993; van der Veer 2001). Talal Asad's discussion is in the context of Christianity and Islam while Peter van der Veer focuses on India and England. In these interactions colonizers presented ideal images of themselves as modern because state power was separate from religion. The state was defined as the political authority and religion as individual belief. To enlightened elites in non-European countries, "being modern," therefore, required the simultaneous reform of indigenous practices to appear as "religion" and the institutionalization of religion as a category within the state's constitution and administration.

In this volume, we maintain that this happens not only in the context of colonized regions, but also in Asian countries that have struggled against colonization and to create their own modern state. In this struggle they have been pursuing an enlightened "modern" civilization of their own design by changing their frameworks of thought, ideology, and political systems. Thailand, Japan, and China have been on this historical track since the late nineteenth century. Stanley Tambiah has described how Thailand's King Chulalongkorn modernized the monarchical state and centralized the Buddhist temple and clergy system to support this new state power. He renewed the mutually supportive system of legitimation of the king and Buddhism as the central core of political authority and model of the modern Thai polity in the new, modern context (1977). Yoshio Yasumaru has described how Japan's new Meiji state system broke down the old religious social and cultural bases that were an historical amalgam of Buddhism and Shinto to create a new ideology of "state Shintoism," which led to the formation of new religious sects, such as Tenrikyō (1987, 2002). In China, Charles Brewer Jones traces the changing organization of Buddhism in Taiwan from community halls to national associations, a change that was both a response to pressures from the Japanese colonial and Chinese republican states, and a way for Buddhists to work with these centralizing state powers to secure recognition for Buddhist activities (1999).

The chapters in this volume examine the processes of the making of "religion" and the "state" in China's modernity up to contemporary times. They share an historical awareness that "religion" is a category that came to China in the late nineteenth century as part of modern state formation. They focus on the processes of politics as seen in the negotiations and interactions of actors to control discourses, representations, and resources to fit situations and practices into the modern category of "religion." They illustrate this with ethnographic observations from fieldwork and other primary sources derived from specific locales and contexts. These issues are primarily discussed in the context of the five religions that are officially recognized as "religion" by the Party—Buddhism, Catholicism, Daoism, Islam, and Protestantism—as well as the Black Dragon King Temple and qigong.

Approaches to State and Religion in China

The issue of state and religion has been a growing topic among social scientists specializing in China (e.g., Dean 2003; Gladney 1991; Eng and Lin 2002; Fan 2003; Flower and Leonard 1997; Hillman 2005; Jing 1996; Lozada 2001; Madsen 1998). Many studies see state and religion in dichotomous frameworks of antagonism and conflict. Dichotomous frameworks are useful for elucidating a situation in order to highlight specific tendencies. But this very simplification often obscures complexities of the reality. In this section we contrast assumptions of extant dichotomous frameworks with our institutional framework of multiple actors and political processes. We claim that our framework is a closer approximation of the reality of state and religion in the space of the reviving religions in China.

One dichotomous framework emphasizes reoccurring patterns of state control over religion throughout Chinese history (Bays 2004; Hunter and Chan 1993; Overmyer 2003; Yu 2005). Daniel Bays writes that "one finds little new about today's pattern of relations between the state and religion in China. Government registration and monitoring of religious activities . . . has been a constant reality of organized religious life in both traditional and modern times" (2004: 25). Oft noted similarities include: legitimating selective rituals by applying negative and positive dichotomies—"orthodoxy/heterodoxy" in the dynastic period and "religion/superstition" in the modern era; labeling proscribed religious activities as crimes of "disloyalty" then and "unpatriotic" now; controlling religions through dedicated state bureaucracies—the imperial Bureau of Rites and the communist State Administration for Religious Affairs (*Guojia zongjiao shiwu ju*).[3] Historical similarities in state ideologies toward religion are noted by Anthony Yu. He argues that the Party's categorical definitions of legitimate and illegitimate beliefs are similar to the "imperial state . . . mentality . . . [of a] cultic obsession with state power and legitimacy propped up by a particular form of ideology" (2005: 145).

Another dichotomous framework emphasizes the Party's fight to maintain control over the rapidly expanding religious activities (Hunter and Chan 1993; Leung 1995; Overmyer 2003; Potter 2003). Jason Kindopp writes, "The government's external constraints and internal manipulations conflict with religious groups' own norms of operation, beliefs, and values. . . . Religious faith commands an allegiance that transcends political authority, whereas the Communist Party's enduring imperative is to eliminate social and ideological competition" (2004: 3, 5). The Party eliminates competition by such measures as: co-opting clergy and believers into state-approved religious associations; confining religious activities to such registered sites as churches and temples; recognizing only clergy trained in state-approved seminaries; vetting sermons and monitoring the foreign contacts of religions. Within these state constraints religions still manage to thrive. They forge new networks and activities outside of the state that are the seeds of a nascent civil society (Madsen 1998). Other believers reject state-controlled religious activities and, despite threats of violence, participate in "underground churches" that are unregistered by the state (Bays 2004; Hunter and Chan 1993: 66–71). These arguments constitute a key perspective within Western scholarship on religion in China. It is undeniable that parts of these arguments overlap with the neo-liberal activist agenda of foreign media, human rights groups, governments, and some scholars to "advance religious freedom in China" (Hamrin 2004). They criticize the Chinese state for persecuting religious believers and violating their human rights (Spiegel 2004) and are confident that religious freedom will grow because of the "collapse of communist ideology," the people's "spiritual hunger," and so on (e.g., Aikman 2003; Chan 2004). Unconsciously or otherwise, the influence of this tendency also directs some scholarly analysis toward certain questions and conclusions.

There are several differences between these state-control frameworks and the institutional framework of this volume. First, the state-control framework is a two-actor interaction of state and religion, whereas we emphasize multiple actors. These various actors include different levels and agencies within the state, religious associations, clergy, religious adherents, overseas Chinese, foreign religious groups, and such sectors as tourism, business, education, and philanthropy. Second, the state-control frameworks view the state-religion interaction as inherently antagonistic whereas we see multiple political processes, including competition, adaptation, and cooperation, as well as conflict. Third, the state-control frameworks have an essentialist definition of religion as "individual belief" and see the space of religion as distinct from the state, whereas we view "religion" as a constructed category and its definition as "individual belief" arising through modern state formation. Our analytic concern therefore is not the degree of freedom of religions or whether or not the state respects individual belief but how the various actors attempt to implement the modern category of "religion" and the consequences of this both within religions and in the state.

Another dichotomous framework locates conflict between state and religion in the context of the state's "modern" hegemonic discourses of nation, science, and development (Anagnost 1994; Duara 1995; Feuchtwang 2000; Fulton 1999; Gillette 2000; Xu 1999; Yang 2004). Prasenjit Duara argues that an Enlightenment narrative of history came to China in the late nineteenth century that depicted a universal transition from tradition to modernity. Political, bureaucratic, and intellectual elites sought to build a nation-state to effect the transition. To do so, they marginalized or co-opted so-called bifurcated histories that had alternative representations of the people and history. Popular religion was one such bifurcated history that was suppressed as "superstition" by new laws. "By means of these laws, the nationalist state was able to proclaim its modern ideals, which included the freedom of religion, and simultaneously consolidate its political power in local society by defining legitimate believers in such a way as to exclude those whom it found difficult to bring under its political control" (Duara 1995: 110).

Despite the similar view of "religion" as an imported category of modernity, there are significant differences between this dichotomous hegemony framework and this volume's institutional framework. The key difference concerns agency in implementing "religion." The hegemony framework reduces implementation to the forceful exercise of state power that religions either resist or reactively conform to. In contrast, this volume also sees "religion" as enacted by the religions themselves. For many religious elites, the modern discourse of "religion" is meaningful because they, too, oppose "superstition," advocate the professional training of clergy, and so on. Therefore, we see institutionalization as proceeding not through an imposed state hegemony but rather through interactions among multiple actors in the state and religions. A second difference is the failure of the hegemony framework to question the category of "religion" itself. For example, Duara describes how new state regulations against "superstition" distinguished it from "proper religion." But he does not explain how a powerful modern concept of "proper religion" was defined, possessed, and propagated in the state and among officials and clerics. In contrast, this volume focuses on the institutionalization of "religion" in both the state and religions through processes that are mutually constitutive. A third difference is the portrayal of the state. Whereas the hegemony framework portrays the state as hegemonic discourses, we also consider its organizational aspects. And whereas the hegemony framework focuses on the violent coercive power of the state, especially through campaigns to smash superstition to implement "religion," we also consider the institutional effects of the routine operation of the state's bureaucratic-legal structures in implementing "religion."

Making Religion, Making the State: An Institutional Framework

Our starting point is Talal Asad's argument that the modern category of religion defined as individual belief emerged through the politics of modern state formation in Europe. In the seventeenth century, European rulers facing the chaos of the Reformation embraced the political philosophy of secularism. This philosophy defined the state as sovereign and delimited religion as individual belief, thereby supporting rulers' acquisition of political authority. However, to avoid appearing to attack Christianity, rulers made the state the protector of Christianity as individual belief. During the eighteenth and nineteenth centuries this protection took shape as the constitutional right of individual belief (Asad 2003). Also, during the nineteenth century a theory of religion was created by scholars of philosophy and emerging social sciences who were influenced by the universalism, rationalism, and positivism of scientific thinking. The theory maintained that religion is symbolic meanings expressed through rites and doctrines with generic functions and features distinct from any specific historical and cultural instances. Non-Western belief and religion first became objects of scientific study in the West, and this ultimately led to the scientific study of Christianity as one of the religions and as the ideal type of "religion" (Asad 1993). This modern concept of "religion" and its place in a modern "state" that had emerged through two centuries of tumultuous political change in Europe gradually came to be widely acknowledged and influential.

In the late nineteenth century, colonialism and capitalism spread the modern categories of "religion" and "state" to other parts of the world. To enlightened elites in Asian countries, these two categories appeared as necessary components of the doctrine of modernity. "Religion" was one of the categories that, alongside "market," "nation," "rational bureaucracy," "police," "education," "science," and so on, was considered necessary in a modern state. These categories were visible in aspects of modern towns and capital cities, such as Shanghai, Tokyo, and Delhi, as well as in such sites as city halls, banks, schools, post offices, railroad stations, police stations, clock towers, and churches. Both on large and small scales, these were the accoutrements that symbolized modernity. But for non-Western elites churches were ambiguous and had to be replaced by non-Christian "modern" sites such as temples, mosques, or shrines. This is because, while non-Western enlightened elites voluntarily accepted modernity, they rejected the idea, in their history and thought, of being conquered by Christianity. They also quickly realized that religions other than Christianity could support the essential ethos of their own non-Western ethnic and national identities that they were creating as the foundation of their modern states. While they wanted modern religion, it had to be neither Christianity nor "unscientific" and "irrational" "superstition" that could hinder their efforts and make them appear as backwards. Elites worked to define modern "religion" in scientific terms to exclude "superstition" and to delimit religion in secular terms as individual belief. This took institutional form in constitutions, laws, and policies that defined religion and its place in the centralizing state.

Since the early twentieth century Chinese political, bureaucratic, religious, and intellectual elites have struggled to position the idea of modern religion in the state ideology. In pursuit of this goal they both attacked religion and destroyed temples that were not considered "modern," and promoted "modern" religious activities and organizations acknowledged by the state. This has been occurring through the efforts of successive political authorities to create their own modern definitions of "religion" and position them as a constitutional right and administrative category within the state system. The positioning of religion is not simply an issue of religion itself but reflects the elites' total idea of the state system that they wish to create. Even now the Party has a very strong awareness of "socialist modernization" and "religion." It now claims that the existence of religion, alongside capitalism, is a part of the necessary Marxist historical process of the transition to communism.

This volume seeks to explain the processes of institutionalizing the modern concept of religion in the state and in religion. The processes by which situations are adapted to the modern definition of religion are political, as explained by Talal Asad.

True, the "proper domain of religion" is distinguished from and separated by the state in modern secular constitutions. But formal constitutions never give the whole story. On the one hand, objects, sites, practices, words, representations, even the minds and bodies of worshipers, cannot be confined within the exclusive space that secularists name "religion." They have their own ways of being. The historical elements of what come to be conceptualized as religion have disparate trajectories. On the other hand, the nation-state requires clearly demarcated spaces that it can classify and regulate: religion, education, health, leisure, work, income, justice, and war. The space that religion may properly occupy in society has to be continually redefined by the law because the reproduction of secular life within and beyond the nation-state continually affects the discursive clarity of that space. (Asad 2003: 200–201)

The politics of modern "religion," therefore, is constituted by ongoing negotiations, among multiple actors, including state officials, intellectuals, religious adherents, and businesspersons, to adapt religion to the modern state's definitions and rules even as they are continuously being transgressed. Religions can accommodate the state institutions as modern "religion" in order to ensure their existence in the new order while the presence of religion in state institutions shows that the state is a modern, enlightened state that acknowledges religion.

The common focus of this volume's chapters is the institutionalization of religion through political processes. We define institutions as rules that "constitute community, shaping how individuals see themselves in relation to others, and providing a foundation for purposive action" (Sweet, Sandholtz, and Fligstein 2001; see also Powell and DiMaggio 1991). We emphasize formal institutions, mostly in the state, that are codified in constitutions, laws, and policies, although the chapters also consider such informal institutions as networks, practices, and ideas in society as dynamically interacting with formal state institutions.

Institutionalization is the process by which situations adapt to institutions. These processes are political because "institutional symbols and claims can be manipulated and their meaning and behavioral implications contested, [and] any activity . . . can carry multiple meanings or motivations" (Friedland and Alford 1991: 255). Therefore "some of the most important struggles between groups, organizations, and social classes are over the appropriate relationships between institutions, and by which institutional logic different activities should be regulated and to which categories of persons they apply" (Friedland and Alford 1991: 256). Institutionalization is also unpredictable: "Once institutions—rules and procedures—are in place, they can be exploited or developed in ways that the founding powers did not foresee and cannot control. Other actors . . . apply, interpret, and clarify the rules in ways that alter the context for subsequent action" (Sweet, Sandholtz, and Fligstein 2001: 13). In this volume we take up the challenge of examining the process of implementing institutions of modern religion, and how this constitutes organizations, communities, thought, and ideology within and beyond the state.

Institutions of Modern Religion in China

Institutions of modern religion were foreshadowed in the New Policy Reform (*xinzheng*) in the final years of the imperial state. In 1904 a project to turn local temples and shrines into schools for promoting the education of the ordinary people was proposed but not fully implemented. In the Republic of China, established in 1912, initiatives were launched to establish local self-government and other modern institutions, such as the police, banking, and educational systems during the term (1912–16) of Yuan Shikai, first president of the Republic of China. These reforms drew on advisors and models of modernity, most of which reflected the Japanese achievements in the Meiji era. One model was "religion," which was referred to by the new Japanese term of *shūkyō*, pronounced *zongjiao* in Chinese. This model distinguished religion from "superstition" (*mixin*) in a dichotomy of "primitive/modern." Yuan Shikai used it as part of his efforts to modernize Chinese society by eliminating those aspects that he saw as backward. The label of "superstition" became an institutionalized term in the *Regulations for the Supervision of Monasteries and Temples* (*Guanli simiao tiaolie*) issued in 1915. This distinction between "religion" and "superstition" was furthered imposed during the Smashing Superstition campaign in 1929. However, coterminous with this campaign, the Nationalist Party issued the *Standards for Preserving and Abandoning Gods and Shrines* that characterized Buddhism and Daoism as "pure faith" and gave them legal protection. This shows the fluidity and contextuality of the boundary between superstition and religion.

After the founding of the People's Republic of China in 1949 the Party developed a comprehensive modern definition of religion. Religion was scientifically defined as having universal features, such as a logical theosophy, scriptures, a professional clergy, and fixed religious sites. The five aforementioned religions were acknowledged as fitting this definition. Their followers were covered by the constitutional right of freedom of belief in the 1954 constitution, which declares: "citizens of the People's Republic of China enjoy the freedom of . . . religious belief" (Luo 1991: 12). An administrative bureaucracy to control religion was created that reflected the distinction in the state between the Party, which is responsible for ideological development and policy formation, and the government, which is responsible for policy implementation and enforcement. In 1954 the Bureau of Religious Affairs, precursor of the current State Administration for Religion Affairs, was established as a central ministry under the State Council (*Guowuyuan*), the highest level of government, and local offices were created. Its main task was to develop and implement a comprehensive state policy toward religion. The state also established representative associations for each of the five religions. These associations were under the authority of the United Front Work Bureau (*Tongyi zhanxianbu*), the Party organ that supervises all non-Party social groups. The task of associations included: communicating state religious policies to their members and reporting their thinking and activities to the state; mobilizing members in such state campaigns as the elimination of corruption, identifying spies, and increasing production; supporting state diplomacy toward predominately Buddhist countries (Welch 1972).

These institutions of religion, the Party maintained, fully accorded with the Party's modern ideology of Marxism and dialectical materialism (Luo 1991: 7–8). This is explained in a 1950 *People's Daily* editorial.

So long as a part of mankind is technologically backward and hence continues to be dependent on natural forces and so long as part of mankind has been unable to win its release from capitalist and feudal slavery, it will be impossible to bring about the universal elimination of religious phenomenon from human society. Therefore with regard to the problem of religious belief as such, any idea about taking coercive action is useless and positively harmful. This is the reason why we advocate protecting freedom of religious belief, just as we advocate protecting freedom to reject religious belief. (*People's Daily* 1950, cited in Welch 1972: 4)

Subsequently, religion came to be severely questioned from the late 1950s. This questioning began during the Anti-Rightist Campaign (1957), which targeted ideological nonconformists, and the Great Leap Forward (1958–60), which mobilized the population for a rapid transition to communism. Radical Party leaders loudly proclaimed that religion had "lost its basis for existence in the socialist society" and that it was necessary to "abolish the system of feudal exploitation in the form of religion" (Luo 1991: 144). Popular movements arose to "wipe out religion by encouraging the seizure of church or temple properties by the government during the 'Great Leap Forward' and people's commune movements, suspending religious activities: and, in a few places, 'advising' believers to back out from religion" (Luo 1991: 144). Attacks on religion escalated. In 1965 Party leaders declared, "the task of the Communists is to exterminate religions" (Luo 1991: 145). During the Cultural Revolution (1966–76) religion was considered one of the "four olds" (*sijiu*) (old beliefs, customs, traditions, and thought) that needed to be eliminated to make way for communism. Destruction and confiscation of religious sites was widespread, visible religious activity ceased, clergy were forced to laicize, and the Bureau of Religious Affairs and religious associations were shut down.

After the Cultural Revolution ended in 1976, the Party began emphasizing a market economy and once again acknowledged religion. Gradually institutions of religion were revived and reorganized and new ones were created in the central state. The constitutions of 1975 and 1982 reaffirmed freedom of belief and placed a new stress on nonbelief. The 1975 constitution stipulates, "Citizens enjoy freedom to believe in religion and freedom not to believe in religion and to propagate atheism" (Leung 1995). This showed that the state was very modern because it protected the right of belief of both religious followers and atheists. In the 1982 constitution the space of religion was further elaborated to position it with state security concerns.

—Citizens of the People's Republic of China enjoy freedom of religious belief. No organs of state, public organizations or individuals shall compel citizens to believe in religion or disbelieve in religion, nor shall they discriminate against citizens who believe or do not believe in religion.

—The state protects legitimate religious activities. No one may use religion to carry out counter-revolutionary activities or activities that disrupt public order, harm the health of citizens or obstruct the educational systems of the state. No religious affairs may be dominated by any foreign country. (Leung 1995)

New policies and regulations defining religion and its place in society have been promulgated since the early 1980s. The Party's theory and approach toward religion was set out in a 1982 document, *On the Basic Viewpoint and Policy on the Religious Question during Our Country's Socialist Period* (*Document 19*). The Party's reason for reviving religion is to unite people for the task of economic modernization so as "to construct a modern, powerful, socialist state" (Chinese Communist Party Central Committee 1987 [1982]: 435). "Normal" religious activities are permitted as long as they are confined to registered "religious activity sites" (*zongjiao huodong changsuo*). The document also defines the key regulatory actors— the Bureau of Religious Affairs, renamed the State Administration for Religious Affairs in 1998, and religious associations—and their duties. Since the issuance of *Document 19* further rules for religion have being promulgated regarding the registration of religious sites, contacts with foreign religious groups, and so on, and an effort has been made to standardize local state regulations and laws (Chan and Carlson 2005: 1–24).

However, the institutionalization in locales has not proceeded uniformly, as they differ greatly in regard to their conditions, such as history, contours of religion, economic circumstances, and ethnic and political issues. Another reason that institutionalization has not been uniform is that each religion has different issues. The situation of Islam cannot be discussed without the issues of borders and ethnicity in the peripheries, where many of the Muslims live, as well as the presence of major mosques in big cities. Of course, for Catholicism the foreign authority of the Vatican is a major issue. Catholicism, along with Protestantism, faces issues of Sinicization, Chineseness, and indigenization, and the creation of new Christian groups and teachings. Daoism is very embedded in local communities and is between the definition of "local culture" and religion. The situation of Buddhism is connected with its positioning as a part of Han Chinese civilization and a majority Han Chinese religion, and the state's concern with relations with other predominantly Buddhist countries.

The Politics of Religion in Modern China: Contributions of This Volume

The chapters in this volume highlight several different political processes of institutionalizing rules and definitions of "religion" in China. They reflect the varied situations of diverse locales and of each religion. They identify the multiple actors and interactions that are institutionalizing modern religion.

POLITICS WITHIN THE STATE

One process is politics within the state. This occurs in debates and competition among politicians and bureaucrats over the interpretation of the institutions of "religion" and their application to actual activities and entities. The competition reflects the interests and agendas of specific agencies and levels of the state. Timothy Brook's historical perspective on Buddhism and Daoism notes the problems that confronted local state officials in applying the centrally defined conceptual categories of the imperial state. According to the state's Confucian ideology, the "teachings of the two masters"—Buddhism and Daoism—were unorthodox, thereby precluding a category in the gazetteers to record their temples. Brook examines the attitudes and tactics of local officials in the Qing dynasty toward Buddhism and Daoism as they coped with this classification problem. The coming of the modern concept of religion (zongjiao) shattered their classifying tactics. After the collapse of the Qing dynasty in 1911, Confucianism was no longer the state ideology, while Buddhism and Daoism achieved greater legitimacy through their redefinition by political, intellectual, and religious elites as "religion."

In Chapter 2 Yoshiko Ashiwa examines the institutionalization of "modern" religion through central-local politics in two periods in the twentieth century. In the 1920s and 1930s institutionalization proceeded through a state campaign to eliminate superstition and appropriate temple assets that was embedded in intrastate politics. Radical members of local Nationalist party branches sought to undermine the local gentry who supported the conservative bureaucrats in the central state by attacking as "superstition" the deities and shrines that the gentry managed as a symbol of their status and power. Ashiwa then describes how Buddhists raised legal challenges to the appropriation of temple land and buildings during the campaign, resulting in legal decisions on temple property. This institutionalized "religion" in laws and the strong norm that religions should serve a public purpose. Since the 1980s "religion" is once again being institutionalized in Buddhism and the state through local political processes that invoke central authority to resolve disputes, as seen in conflicts regarding temple property and leadership. In her conclusion, Ashiwa points to aspects of Buddhism in people's daily lives that are framed by the state institution of "culture" as "local tradition," "history," and so on, and considers their relation to religion.

Utiraruto Otehode's chapter examines the shifting definitions of *qigong* and their links to different interests in the state's modern medical, science, and sports sectors. In the 1950s a health official in the northern city of Tangshan obtained state recognition of certain body cultivation techniques that he termed *qigong*. He made qigong palatable to the state by expunging Daoist and other "religious" elements to represent it as a physical therapy practice of health maintenance rooted in the history of the Chinese working people. Suppressed during the Cultural Revolution, qigong was vigorously promoted in the 1980s by nationalistic members of China's military, scientific, and medical establishments. This led to a contentious debate about whether or not qigong is a "science." Utiraruto describes how this debate has proceeded through attempts to frame qigong by such modern principles as "science," "superstition," "nation," and "medicine" and how this politics both reflects and creates interests in different sectors of the state.

STATE IMPOSITION OF "RELIGION" ON RELIGIONS

Several chapters highlight the process of imposing the state's discursive category of modern religion on practices and beliefs. They illustrate how unpredictable institutionalization can be: it can generate perceptions and politics that depart from the state's goal of control and regularity. Carsten Vala examines "patriotic education" in state-recognized Protestant seminaries. Concerns of patriotism in regard to Protestantism first arose in the 1930s as Chinese Protestants replaced Western missionaries as heads of the church and questioned their foreign origins. Since 1949 the state has been concerned about foreign control of Protestantism and has sought to instill loyalty to the Party in pastors through "patriotic education" in state-approved seminaries. However, the institutionalization of "patriotic education" ends up undermining state control. First, the political screening that it entails weeds out candidates most committed to the rigors of ministry, causing a severe shortage of pastors. This shortage, in turn, devolves administrative responsibility in state-recognized churches to deacons and elders who are not educated in state seminaries. They are less equipped to combat heresies and prevent congregation members from defecting to unregistered churches. Second, the heavy-handedness of patriotic education stimulates new links between the state-recognized and unregistered churches. Seminarians come to see the unregistered churches as offering a more authentic belief. As pastors, they also minister to congregations in unregistered churches, in some cases even resigning their positions in state-approved churches.

Dru Gladney highlights unintended consequences of Islam's positioning by the state in multiple modern institutions. Historically, Chinese states have feared rebellions among Muslims in the borderlands of central Asia, while for Muslims accommodation to dominant Han Chinese culture is a long-standing source of tension. In the twentieth century, these situations have been complicated by the imposition of the modern categories of "religion" and "ethnicity." The state classifies Muslims as an "ethnic minority" that is defined by belief in the "religion" of Islam. This generates further tensions because it lumps together many peoples with little or no historical interaction and linguistic affinity, and with widely differing accommodations to Han culture. Also, labeling these "ethnic" groups as Islamic stimulates their transnational links in the global Islamic ecumene of groups dedicated to cultural nationalism and independent statehood. Such nationalist movements and the state monitoring of them have intensified with China's policies to develop its western regions, China's rising role in central Asia, and the global war on terrorism. These chapters underscore the unpredictability of institutionalization, because the process itself produces effects.

ACCOMMODATION OF STATE INSTITUTIONS BY RELIGIONS

Actors within religions also work to position themselves within the state's discursive institution of "religion." This gives the religions the legitimacy of state recognition, letting them openly conduct activities, and reinforces their claims for resources. David Wank examines the institutional consequences of this positioning in the Buddhist community of Xiamen city, Fujian province. He describes the politics of organizational actors to control temple property and wealth. Their actions reflect competing and contradictory principles in the state discourse of "religion" in *Document 19* and other institutions, such as "self-management," "patriotism," "religious freedom," and "administrative guidance." By framing their multiple claims for control in terms of these discrete principles, the Xiamen Religious Affairs Bureau,[4] Xiamen Buddhist Association, and temples shape their organizational attributes and interests. Their escalating conflict drew in the central state authority, which reoriented relations among the local actors and created new links to the central state. Paradoxically, efforts by Xiamen's major temple, Nanputuo, to invoke the central state in order to enhance its autonomy from local politics brought the temple more firmly under central state control and conformity to "religion" and other state discursive institutions.

Adam Chau describes the Black Dragon King Temple, a well-known divination shrine in Shaanxi province that did not fit the state definition of a "religion." Community activists promoted the shrine by suppressing blatantly "superstitious" activities that would attract state scrutiny and positioning its activities within state institutions of "market," "education," and "environmentalism." The crowds of worshippers who flocked to the temple generated a large income that was used in ways to create significant support for the temple. Some income was used to pay off officials in a variety of local state agencies to tolerate the temple. Other income was invested in a school for children of the villages whose members served on the temple committee, thereby ensuring community support. Finally, funds were invested in a reforestation project around the temple, gaining it national recognition and even international environmental acclaim. Eventually the Shaanxi Province Daoist Association recognized the Black Dragon King Temple as a Daoist temple, securely positioning it within the state category of "religion." These two chapters illustrate how actors seek legitimacy by positioning themselves within discursive institutions of modern religion, and by doing so also define their attributes and interests.

POPULAR INSTITUTIONS AND THE POLITICS OF "RELIGION"

The politics of the religious revivals is also shaped by popular institutions in society. Several chapters illuminate relations between these popular institutions and the state's formal institutions of modern religion. Richard Madsen and Lizhu Fan examine the different representations of Sheshan, a Catholic shrine in Shanghai dedicated to the Virgin Mary. Since the mid-nineteenth century, different state regimes have represented Sheshan in distinct ways to support their authority. The French developed Sheshan's imagery in the nineteenth century as a "civilizing project" to support their colonial authority. In the twentieth century, the Nationalist Party and the Chinese Communist Party remade Sheshan's imagery to represent the nation. Among believers, Sheshan has long had an image of a benevolent protectress. Since 1949 it has also signified to some Catholics opposition to the state-approved Catholic Church. These multiple meanings that have adhered to the shrine prevent it from being dominated by any single one. It is visited by Catholics from both the state-registered and unregistered churches, and can help diffuse tensions between Catholics inside and outside the People's Republic of China. Sheshan is considered a "tame" shrine because it poses no problems for the state in contrast to the "unruly" Dong Lü shrine in a nearby rural area, which is dominated by the underground church and is a site of resistance to the state.

Utiraruto Otehode's portrays distinct intrastate elite and intrasocietal processes in the institutionalization of qigong. The intrastate process is traceable to attempts by intellectuals and officials to position traditional body cultivation techniques within the modern institutions of medicine, science, and nation, as described above. The intrasocietal process, visible since the 1980s, is the revival of qigong in practitioner groups. Many groups are headed by self-styled qigong masters because the earlier generation that had received state-approved training was subsequently persecuted in the Cultural Revolution and did not play a leading role after 1980. Instead, a popular revival has been led by younger self-styled qigong masters who mix Buddhist and folk religious imagery. These inter- and intrastate processes overlap. Actors in the state research institutes have invited self-styled qigong masters to participate in scientific experiments, thereby giving the qigong masters access to the state's organizational and legitimacy resources. This has enabled some masters to vastly expand their audiences in mass gatherings and to create national networks, such as Falungong.

Finally, Kenneth Dean shows the limited effects of "religion" in the popular institutions of Daoism, which are deeply embedded in local communities. Since the late nineteenth century modern ideas of organizational rationality and scriptural authority have put pressure on Daoist traditions, even threatening to eliminate them at certain times. These tensions exist today in the problematic fit between the discursive clarity of the Party's modern definition of "religion" and Daoist rituals and modes of expression. The scriptural emphasis of the rationalized Daoist education in state-recognized Daoist seminaries strips away the ritual experience of Daoism that emphasizes local communities served by masters who transmit ritual methods to their initiated disciples and provides a framework for local rituals. Therefore, the state's modern institution of "religion," as well as "culture," only adheres to the surface of Daoism. This veneer of institutionalization is also strategically enacted by Daoists to satisfy state expectations while letting them conduct rituals as they see fit.

All of the chapters describe processes of institutionalizing the state's discursive institution of "religion." They show how institutionalization is affected and shaped by the histories and forms of capital of specific religions, how this interaction shapes the characteristics of organizational actors and the relations of the field, and how institutionalization is also linked to the expansion of such other modern categories in the state as science, superstition, environment, medicine, education, nation, market, tourism, and law. Yet at the same time these chapters also acknowledge, explicitly (Ashiwa; Dean) or otherwise, the existence of numerous beliefs and rituals outside the modernist framing of "religion" that are enacted as part of the daily lives of people and rituals of communities. The issue of beliefs and their relation to "religion" lies outside this volume's scope, but it is, nevertheless, important to acknowledge in order to underscore that the chapters are concerned with those aspects of religion that are enacted within the state's modern institutions.

Conclusion

Modernity treats religion as a matter of individual belief in the context of secularism. At least within the modern social sciences, since Max Weber, individual belief and secularism have been key concepts of the study of religion in modernity. Social scientists have been challenging these concepts of individual belief and secularism through fieldwork in and monographs on non-Western societies. However, as Talal Asad points out, even social scientists such as Clifford Geertz, who are extremely sophisticated advocates of the interpretation of cultures to capture their complexity, are often ignorant of their own ambiguous use of the analytical as well as descriptive concepts of religion and belief when they analyze what they observe in religious practices in everyday life in non-Western societies. This is because the concepts of religion and belief are embedded in the modern way of thinking. Any understanding, therefore, that these concepts appear to impart is derived from their basis in the modern concept of religion. In this volume, although we acknowledge that the issue of individual belief is becoming crucial for the state and society in China, we have chosen not to discuss belief, but rather decided to delineate how the concept of modern religion has been, and is being, made within the process of state making in China. It is important to note that institutions both reflect ideas and are ideas in themselves. In this sense, the approach of this volume is to analyze the framework that reflects the beliefs of the people and individuals in China's modernity.

The categories behind the statistics on religion in China are part of the process of making religion and making the state that has been ongoing at all levels of the state and people's relationship through the continuous efforts to institutionalize modernity. Every chapter in this volume argues that China is in the throes of this process.

Notes

1. We would like to thank Ken Dean and Carsten Vala for comments on drafts of this chapter.

2. These statistics first appeared in a white paper, "Freedom of Religious Belief," and have been cited in subsequent white papers: "Fifty Years of Progress in China's Human Rights" (2000) and "Progress in China's Human Rights Cause in 2003." However, based on a survey conducted between 2005 and 2007, university-based researchers maintain that there are 300 million religious believers above the age of sixteen. Buddhists, Daoists, Catholics, Muslims, and Protestants account for 67.4 percent of these believers. About 200 million are Buddhists, Daoists, or worshippers of the Dragon King, God of Fortune, and other figures, while about 40 million are Protestants (*Wenweipo* 2007; Wu 2007).

3. The state bureaucracy of religious management was called the Religious Affairs Office from 1951 to 1954 and the Bureau of Religious Affairs from 1954 until 1998. The current name—State Administration for Religious Affairs—was adopted in 1998. For ease of reference this volume uses the current name to refer to the post-1949 bureaucracy at the national level. Local level offices of religious administration from the provincial level on down often use the word "bureau," and therefore the term "Religious Affairs Bureau" will refer to the local levels, unless otherwise indicated.

4. The official name of the bureau is the Bureau of Ethnic and Religious Affairs of Xiamen (*Xiamen shi minzu yu zongjiao shiwu ju*). In this chapter it is shortened to Xiamen Religious Affairs Bureau. For the use of one bureau to manage both ethnic and religious affairs see Ashiwa and Wank (2006: 344n12).

References

Aikman, David. 2003. *Jesus in Beijing: How Christianity Is Transforming China and Changing the Global Balance of Power.* Washington, DC: Regnery.

Anagnost, Ann S. 1994. "The Politics of Ritual Displacement." In *Asian Visions of Authority: Religion and the Modern States of East and Southeast Asia*, edited by Charles F. Keyes, Laurel Kendall, and Helen Hardacre, pp. 221–54. Honolulu: University of Hawai'i Press.

Asad, Talal. 1993. *Genealogies of Religion: Discipline and Reasons of Power in Christianity and Islam.* Baltimore: Johns Hopkins University Press.

———. 2003. *Formations of the Secular: Christianity, Islam, Modernity.* Stanford, CA: Stanford University Press.

Bays, Daniel H. 2004. "A Tradition of State Dominance." In *God and Caesar in China: Policy Implications of Church-State Tension*, edited by Jason Kindopp and Carol Lee Hamrin, pp. 25–39. Washington, DC: Brookings Institution.

Chan, Kim-kwong. 2004. "Accession to the World Trade Organization and State

Adaptation." In *God and Caesar in China: Policy Implications of Church-State Tension*, edited by Jason Kindopp and Carol Lee Hamrin, pp. 58–74. Washington, DC: Brookings Institution.

Chan, Kim-kwong, and Eric R. Carlson. 2005. *Religious Freedom in China: Policy, Administration and Regulation; a Research Handbook*. Santa Barbara, CA, and Hong Kong: Institute for the Study of American Religion and Hong Kong Institute for Culture, Commerce and Religion.

Chinese Communist Party Central Committee (Zhonggong zhongyang). 1987 [1982]. "Guanyu woguo shehuizhuyi shiqi zongjiao wentide jiben guandian he jiben zhengce" (Regarding the basic viewpoint and policy on the religious question during our country's socialist period). In *Shiyijie sanzhong quanhui yilai zhongyao wenxian xuandu* (Collection of important documents since the third plenum of the Eleventh Party Congress), v. 1., pp. 428–48. Beijing: Renmin chubanshe.

Dean, Kenneth. 2003. "Local Communal Religion in Contemporary South-east China." *China Quarterly* 174 (June): 338–58.

Duara, Prasenjit. 1995. *Rescuing History from the Nation: Questioning Narratives of Modern China*. Chicago: University of Chicago Press.

Eng, Irene, and Yi-min Lin. 2002. "Religious Festivities, Communal Rivalry, and Restructuring of Authority Relations in Rural Chaozhou, Southeast China." *Journal of Asian Studies* 61, 4: 1259–85.

Fan, Lizhu. 2003. "The Cult of the Silkworm Mother as a Core of Local Community Religion in a North China Village: Field Study in Zhiwuying, Baoding, Hebei." *China Quarterly* 174 (June): 359–72.

Feuchtwang, Stephan. 2000. "Religion as Resistance." In *Chinese Society: Change, Conflict and Resistance*, edited by Elizabeth J. Perry and Mark Selden, pp. 161–77. London: Routledge.

Flower, John, and Pamela Leonard. 1997. "Defining Cultural Life in the Chinese Countryside: The Case of the Chuan Zhu Temple." In *Cooperative and Collective in China's Rural Development: Between State and Private Interests*, edited by Eduard B. Vermeer, Frank N. Pieke, and Woei Lien Chong, pp. 273–90. Armonk, NY: M. E. Sharpe.

Friedland, Roger, and Robert A. Alford. 1991. "Bringing Society Back In: Symbols, Practices, and Institutional Contradictions." In *The New Institutionalism in Organizational Analysis*, edited by Walter W. Powell and Paul J. DiMaggio, pp. 232–63. Chicago: University of Chicago Press.

Fulton, Brent. 1999. "Freedom of Religion in China: The Emerging Discourse." In *Civic Discourse, Civil Society, and Chinese Communities*, edited by Randy Kluver and John H. Powers, pp. 53–66. Stamford, CT: Ablex.

Gillette, Maris Boyd. 2000. *Between Mecca and Beijing: Modernization and Consumption among Urban Chinese Muslims*. Stanford, CA: Stanford University Press.

Gladney, Drew C. 1991. *Muslim Chinese: Ethnic Nationalism in the People's Republic*. Cambridge, MA: Council on East Asian Studies and Harvard University Press.

Hamrin, Carol Lee. 2004. "Advancing Religious Freedom in Global China: Conclusion." In *God and Caesar in China: Policy Implications of Church-State Tension*, edited by Jason Kindopp and Carol Lee Hamrin, pp. 165–85. Washington, DC: Brookings Institution.

Hillman, Ben. 2005. "Monastic Politics and the Local State in China: Authority and Autonomy in an Ethnically Tibetan Prefecture." *China Journal* 54: 29–52.

Hunter, Alan, and Kim-kwong Chan. 1993. *Protestantism in Contemporary China*. Cambridge, UK: Cambridge University Press.

Information Office of the State Council of the People's Republic of China. 1997. "White Paper on Freedom of Religious Belief in China." www.china.org.cn/e-white/Freedom/f-1.htm (last accessed 10-10-05).

Jing, Jun. 1996. *The Temple of Memories: History, Power, and Morality in a Chinese Village*. Stanford, CA: Stanford University Press.

Jones, Charles Brewer. 1999. *Buddhism in Taiwan: Religion and the State, 1660–1990*. Honolulu: University of Hawai'i Press.

Kindopp, Jason. 2004. "Policy Dilemmas in China's Church-State Relations: An Introduction." In *God and Caesar in China: Policy Implications of Church-State Tension*, edited by Jason Kindopp and Carol Lee Hamrin, pp. 1–22. Washington, DC: Brookings Institution.

Leung, Beatrice. 1995. "Religious Freedom and the Constitution in the People's Republic of China: Interpretation and Implementation." *DISKUS* (Web edition) 3,1: 1–18. www.uni-marburg.de/religionswissenschaft/journal/diskus/leung.html.

Lozada, Eriberto P., Jr. 2001. *God Aboveground: Catholic Church, Postsocialist State and Transnational Processes in a Chinese Village*. Stanford, CA: Stanford University Press.

Luo, Zhufeng (ed.). 1991. *Religion under Socialism*, translated by Donald E. MacInnis and Zheng Xi'an. Armonk, NY: M. E. Sharpe.

Madsen, Richard P. 1998. *China's Catholics: Tragedy and Hope in an Emerging Civil Society*. Berkeley: University of California Press.

Overmyer, Daniel L. 2003. "Religion in China Today: An Introduction." In *Religion in China Today*, edited by Daniel L. Overmyer, pp. 1–10. Cambridge, UK: Cambridge University Press.

Pittman, Potter. 2003. "Belief in Control: Regulation of Religion in China." In *Religion in China Today*, edited by Daniel L. Overmyer, pp. 11–31. Cambridge, UK: Cambridge University Press.

Powell, Walter W., and Paul J. DiMaggio (eds.) 1991. *The New Institutionalism in Organizational Analysis*. Chicago: University of Chicago Press.

Spiegel, Mickey. 2004. "Control and Containment in the Reform Era." In *God and Caesar in China: Policy Implications of Church-State Tensions*, edited by Jason Kindopp and Carol Lee Hamrin, pp. 40–57. Washington, DC: Brookings Institution.

Sweet, Alec Stone, Wayne Sandholtz, and Neil Fligstein. 2001. "The Institutionalization of European Space." In *The Institutionalization of Europe*, edited by Alec Stone Sweet, Wayne Sandholtz, and Neil Fligstein, pp. 1–28. New York: Cambridge University Press.

Tambiah, Stanley. 1977. *World Conqueror and World Renouncer: A Study of Buddhism and Polity in Thailand against a Historical Background*. Cambridge, UK: Cambridge University Press.

Van der Veer, Peter. 2001. *Imperial Encounters: Religion and Modernity in India and Britain*. Princeton, NJ: Princeton University Press.

Welch, Holmes. 1972. *Buddhism under Mao*. Harvard East Asian Series 69. Cambridge, MA: Harvard University Press.

Wenweipo (online edition). 2007. "Sanyi Guomin jie xinyang, minjian sushen cheng xinglong" (300 million citizens' belief in religion, popular beliefs are flourishing). March 3. http://paper.wenweipo.com/2007/03/03/NS0703030001.htm (last accessed 11-15-07).

Wu, Jiao. 2007. "Religious Believers Thrice the Estimate." *China Daily* (February 7) (online edition). www.chinadaily.com.cn/china/2007-02/07/content _802994.htm (last accessed 11-15-07).

Xu, Jian. 1999. "Body, Discourse, and the Cultural Politics of Contemporary Chinese Qigong." *Journal of Asian Studies* 58, 4: 961–91.

Yang, Mayfair Mei-hui. 2004. "Spatial Struggles: Postcolonial Complex, State Disenchantment, and Popular Reappropriation of Space in Rural Southeast China." *Journal of Asian Studies* 65, 3: 719–55.

Yasumaru Yoshio. 1987. *Deguchi Nao*. Tokyo: Asahi shinbunsha.

———. 2002. *Kamigami no Meiji ishin: Shinbutsubunri to haibutsukishaku* (The Meiji revolution of gods: separation of Shintoism and Buddhism, and the abandonment of Buddhism). Tokyo: Iwanami shoten.

Yu, Anthony C. 2005. *State and Religion in China: Historical and Textual Perspectives*. Chicago: Open Court.

CHAPTER 2

The Politics of Religion:
Late-Imperial Origins of the Regulatory State

TIMOTHY BROOK

THE SOCIALIST STATE's relationship with established religions is no longer as simple as we assumed it to be in its early interventionist phase. Religious policies that the state adopted in the years between 1949 and 1979 gave the impression that the state understood its historical role to be to restrict, dismantle, and finally eradicate religious belief systems and the organizations that sustained communities of believers. After 1979, the teleology that assumed that the people would give up their opiate once the social relations of production had been revolutionized was abandoned. The subsequent relationship between religion and the state has become so complex, so nonlinear, and so implicated with other political goals that the story told before 1979 is no longer the one we tell now. The old posture of prohibition has been replaced by a new posture that accepts the presence of religion in society so long as it remains subject to the supervision of the state: the posture of regulation, in other words. It is only if we view things from the perspective of the three decades before 1979 that the posture appears new. In fact, as this chapter will show, the Chinese state has a long tradition of regulating organized religion. The regulatory state has in fact been the norm throughout the late-imperial and Republican periods. Even so, as this chapter again will show, the prohibitionist state that emerged in the 1950s was not an aberration borrowed from the atheist strain in nineteenth-century European socialism that so appealed to Marx and Engels. It drew just as surely on late-imperial traditions as did the accommodationist posture that has reasserted itself over the past quarter-century. This is not to say that nothing changes in China; rather, it is to say that change usually takes its contours from the shapes of the past.

The intellectual challenge of understanding how the position of religion in the Chinese polity has changed up to and through the socialist period is usually handled by appealing to a logic of modernization. This logic understands that state policies and official/elite attitudes toward religion develop in response to the adjustments that people make through their religious organizations to the stresses and opportunities that arise as capital reshapes economic relations, complexifies political interests, and projects these interests into multiple social fields. As these changes happen, "enlightenment" discourses of many political hues emerge to reform religions according to modernist imperatives or even challenge the bases on which they exist. This is certainly part of the story that can be told about the history of religion in twentieth-century China. But alongside this logic has to be placed a second, the logic of historical precedent. It hardly requires profound historical research to point out, for example, that the Chinese state's response to Falungong has been continuous with the responses of the late-imperial state to dissenting Buddhist sects.[1] How the contemporary state conceives of its role in relation to religious groups is heavily shaped by precedents for regulatory intervention undertaken by earlier Chinese states. Of course, the history of the state-religion relationship prior to 1911 cannot account for everything that has happened since then, but it can help us to recognize the key in which state policies are being played now, and perhaps even to anticipate chord changes yet to come.

The late-imperial state did not maintain a static posture with regard to religion, for all the continuity that I shall demonstrate. Among the range of responses that can be reconstructed from Ming and Qing sources, three main postures can be observed: patronage, prohibition, and regulation. Patronage is the state-religion relationship that Buddhists upheld as their ideal. The patron state is one that chooses to identify its moral pedigree or legitimacy by aligning itself with one or more religions, and that extends financial and symbolic support to religious institutions and personnel in exchange for religious ratification of its regime. Prohibition stands at the opposite extreme. The prohibitionist state strives to ban religious institutions and religious practice as inimical to good social, political, and moral order. It regards religion as a hotbed of refusal and dissent that threatens its right to rule. Between these two positions of patronage and prohibition lies the posture of regulation. The regulatory state neither promotes religion nor seeks to abolish it, but acts to supervise, control, or limit the scale and form of religious practices in relation to its own goals for the maintenance of public order and the supervision of associational life.

All three postures can be traced in the first half-century of Ming rule. The founding emperor, Hongwu (r. 1368–98), inaugurated his reign as an emperor who adopted the pose of Buddhist patron. After a dozen years in power, however, he shifted to a regulatory posture that was so stringent as to amount almost to prohibition (Brook 1997: 161–69). As soon as his son took power as the Yongle emperor (r. 1403–22), however, the state's relationship to Buddhism shifted from prohibition into a more moderate, though still firm, regulatory mode. Later Ming emperors often listed to the side of patronage, but their patronal gestures drew more from their capacity and resources as head of the imperial household than as head of state. None would veer off in the direction of outright prohibition, as the founding emperor had done; yet none dared return fully to the official pose of patron with which the founder had started his reign. Regulation thus became entrenched as the dominant (though not invariable) posture of the Ming state, and of all subsequent Chinese states, toward religion. This entrenchment was not new. The Chinese state had for the previous millennium assumed that religion was appropriately within its purview, that the work of good government included keeping religious institutions under supervision and even limitation, and that it had a legitimate right to regulate religion in the public interest as well as its own. But it was only in the Ming that the institutional effects of all three postures were made manifest within one dynasty.

That said, the maintenance of the state's policies toward religion did not begin and end with decisions the emperor made. The regulatory regime that the Ming state built was not sustained purely as a one-way project coming down from the capital. It took shape and developed the full extent of its social articulation through interaction with local elites. The gentry—self-appointed guardians of the Confucian order at the local level—were not empowered to regulate religion on the state's behalf, but they often took an active interest in the sometimes threatening vitality of religious activities going on around them. The few individuals among them who served as local officials elsewhere had even greater opportunities to align their religious preferences with the authority of the state, of which they were legitimate proxies. While the first part of this chapter addresses the formation of central state policies toward religion, the bulk of it is devoted to examining the tensions and arguments in local society about what religious activity signified and what the state's agencies and representatives should do about it.

The Regulatory State

We can begin to trace the outlines of the Ming regulatory state by examining the laws touching on religion in the Ming Code. The code was the core legal document of the dynasty, providing the framework for judicial decisions at all levels of government. Its statutes were published, read, and regularly referred to by judges and accused alike. The laws affecting the categories of action and institution that would today be considered religion appear in the first, fourth, eleventh, and eighteenth chapters of the code. The first chapter, on the laws governing state officials, includes a provision that Buddhist monks and Daoist priests serving as officials not only be liable for punishment if found breaking the law, but be forced to revert to lay status (*Da Ming lü* 1999: 8; Jiang 2005: 28). This law shows that the state accepted that members of the ordained clergy could serve the state, as well as that clerics invested with state office were not immune from the jurisdiction of the laws governing all other officials. Any appointment was conditional on there being monks in good standing. Furthermore, those appointed as officials at the county level were "not within officialdom" (*wei ru liu*): they held their posts at the pleasure of the local government and could not claim eligibility for promotion or transfer to service at any higher level of government. Nonetheless, licensed religious professionals were within the reach of the state and fully subject to its authority.

The fourth chapter of the code deals with household registration and taxable property. Buddhism comes up in this place in the state's legal framework because a monastery was a fiscal tax-paying household like any other, and clerical status entailed defined fiscal exemptions from corvée labor (*Da Ming lü* 1999: 46–47; Jiang 2005: 71). The regulations here, which originated with the Hongwu emperor, expressly ban the founding of religious institutions, other than when the emperor himself personally permitted it, and forbid individuals from entering into monastic life without obtaining a state license. The state claimed a prerogative to limit the scale of religious institutions and exert exclusive control over access to religious life. At least formally, religious communities lay fully within the state's regulatory grasp.

The eleventh chapter of the Ming Code, on sacrificial rites, includes two articles relevant to the state's relationship to religion. One forbids individuals from sacrificing to heaven, the other from forming private devotional societies and conducting collective sacrifices before secret images. The first article is particularly anxious about what men and women might get up to under the pretense of going together to temples to burn incense. It also indicts monks who hold *jiao* masses or other devotional services aimed at addressing heaven or calling down destruction (that, at least, is the state's hostile interpretation of appeals to alternative spiritual authority). The second article specifically names Maitreyanism, White Lotus, Manichaeanism, and the White Cloud sect as examples of the sort of lay devotional associations the law prohibits. The penalty for "pretending to practice virtuous deeds but actually inciting and misleading people" is strangulation (*Da Ming lü* 1999: 89; Jiang 2005: 112). The regulatory Ming state was thus concerned to control not just institutions but the ritual practices that religious professionals might perform outside their walls, especially in social spaces that were out of sight of state representatives. Linked to the concern about mass delusion is a provision in the eighteenth chapter of the code, dealing with treason, which forbids the writing or distributing of seditious writings that "confuse people" (*Da Ming lü* 1999: 135; Jiang 2005: 155). This law, which could be invoked to prosecute anyone who circulated popular religious tracts such as "precious scrolls," complements the preceding article in the eleventh chapter by providing the state with legislation confirming its control over texts as well as social activities organizing according to religious affiliations.

The presence of religious regulation in the Ming Code falls short of making a general statement outlining the dynastic state's overall orientation toward the entities and activities we identify as religious. One can, however, find something of the sort, very briefly stated, in the supplementary compendium of imperial legislation, the *Da Ming huidian* or *Statutory Precedents of the Ming Dynasty*. It is in the *Huidian* rather than the code that we find important imperial edicts on institutional religion. The closest we get to a general statement on the relationship between the state and religion appears in this short anonymous introduction to the second section of the 104th chapter in the 1587 edition:

Buddhism and Daoism have been popular among the people since the Han and Tang dynasties, and [would be] difficult to do away with completely. All one can do is to be strict about [maintaining] the restrictions and agreements and not let the two spread further. The relevant regulations are all there, detailed and thorough in the extreme. (*Da Ming huidian* 1588: 104.2a–b)

The author of this text appears to work from the proposition that the ideal relationship of the Ming state to religion should be not regulation, but prohibition. He also recognizes the impossibility of imposing prohibition in practice, as he goes on to celebrate the regulatory state as an adequate second-best imposing the conditions under which Buddhism might be allowed to exist. He also regrets that Buddhism is popular, suspecting that, left unregulated, it would become even more widely practiced among the people.

Should we take this statement at face value and accept that the Ming state's ideal was prohibition? Given the long record of accommodation to religious institutions after 1398, if this was an ideal, it was not one that anyone ever realistically expected the state to put into practice. Who then was the author of this passage speaking for? My hypothesis, which the readings from local gazetteers that are about to become this chapter's primary sources substantiate, is that he represents a faction within the Confucian establishment that feared for its authority and privilege as the class deserving to rule the ideal Confucian state. The Hongwu emperor's early prohibitionist stance was one that this faction approved of; anything less made them nervous that a competing moral authority, as Buddhism was under the Yuan dynasty, might erode their right to monopolize power. Where this faction's voice can be mostly strongly heard is not in central government documents, though Confucian activists occasionally made their voices heard at court by damning Buddhism as a tax dodge or an opportunity to defraud the ignorant and calling on the court to shut down monasteries and return monks and nuns to lay life. Rather, it is in the local political arena, where Buddhism's institutional presence as an alternative social collectivity was most keenly felt. The *Huidian* editor who wrote the introductory passage quoted above was not accurately describing the place of Buddhism within the constitution of the Chinese state, however much he may have wished it were like that. He nonetheless felt authorized to do so by his commitment to social analysis that polarizes the state and the people. From this perspective, the people are Buddhist as the state cannot be. Buddhism is something in which the people might "seek refuge," in Buddhist parlance, but not the state. Since the state's project is to control the people, so it must control Buddhism.

Missing from the *Huidian* editor's analysis is any mention of the gentry, the local Confucian-trained families who saw themselves as standing for the Confucian moral order and by proxy for the Confucian state. When we move our gaze down to the county-level society, the gentry do not show themselves to be always in perfect accord with the state's desires with regard to Buddhism, however, though many share the *Huidian* editor's desire for a more prohibitionist stance. There was good reason for this, for their everyday experience of religion and political power in often strife-ridden local contexts showed them that Buddhism was integrally involved in the ordering of public life in ways that were indifferent to state regulations. As we will see shortly, ordinary people accepted Buddhist monasteries as legitimate institutions within and around which other legitimate forms of social action took place. When prohibitionism tugged on gentry hearts, it did so for reasons having everything to do with their own power. The *Huidian* editor's complaint signals that popular religion was a troubling element in local society among those who sought to assert the class dominance of the gentry. Religious institutions and festivals too often, in their eyes, became occasions for conflict between local leaders and proxies of the state. As self-appointed guardians of a Confucian moral order that was also politically advantageous to themselves, the gentry were often caught between a permissiveness that allowed Buddhist and Daoist institutions to exist and even on occasion flourish under their patronage, and a longing for a greater degree of regulation, even prohibition, that would allow society to revert to entirely Confucian norms and resecure their own authority as its leaders. To the extent that the gentry looked to the state for their legitimacy as a local ruling class, they had to regard Buddhism as a potential challenge to their authority. The Ming-Qing state took a position vis-à-vis religion that was more often regulatory than patronal or prohibitionist, yet it largely relied on the agreement and initiative of local elites to see that Buddhist and Daoist institutions and personnel were prevented from doing what the state most feared: posing a threat to its own hegemony.

Gazetteers as Sites for Representing Buddhism

The most extensive evidence of Confucian uncertainty about the appropriate place of religion in society can be found in local gazetteers. Gazetteers were major publications that every county hoped to produce roughly every sixty years. Produced under the supervision of the county magistrate, they were compiled by local scholars to record local topographical and administrative data and celebrate the practical and literary achievements of county residents. Gazetteer compilers usually strove to highlight the best of local society, projecting an image of local conformity to Confucian standards, though many compilers—whom I would identify as conservative Confucians—were willing to point out lapses in local society that needed to be addressed to bring local life into full conformity with state designs. For these conservative Confucians, the presence of Buddhist and Daoist practices and institutions was one such lapse, one such failure to conform to state norms. How the compiler of a gazetteer dealt, or declined to deal, with the Buddhist institutions in his locality; how much information about religious practices he included, and of what sort; into what categories he sorted or concealed this information; what comments he might or should append by way of introduction or conclusion to expose or cover up the extent of popular religion: these were the sorts of intricate editorial issues over which compilers had to struggle, both with themselves and with their colleagues. Those decisions could imply much about the character and role of local Confucian order—and were read by contemporaries this way.[2]

To phrase what was at stake in a simple fashion: did information about the flourishing condition of the institutions and practices of the Two Masters (*er shi*, as the Buddha and Laozi were commonly known) in local society belong in a book that could be construed as, if not a Confucian publication, then at least a publication that acknowledged the ideals of Confucian social order? How a gazetteer compiler answered that question could imply an answer to another, more loaded question: were the institutions and practices of the Two Masters "within the Way"—that is, if Confucius stood for the true Way, could Buddhists and Daoists be squeezed under his moral umbrella, or should they be left out? As we shall see, some editors thought one way, some the other. Some argued that the spirit of imperial state regulations should be prohibitionist; others, accommodationist. Some argued that the ideals of Chinese historiography going back to Confucius required vigilant selectivity; others, that the ideals going back instead to Sima Qian, the celebrated court historian of the Han dynasty and preeminent authority on all matters concerning official history, demanded inclusiveness.[3] Some were sure that religion degraded state authority and the public interest; others, that it advanced and secured it.

This difference of opinion excited a restless flow of political and social commentary in local gazetteers of the late-imperial period, from which I shall siphon off what I consider a few telling examples of how the regulatory state operated in practice down at the county level. The worrying of puzzled Confucian authors on these points should not, however, inspire us to find the right solution to their bewilderment; their concerns are not ours. But it can serve as an invitation to take their lack of resolution as evidence of a fundamental tension in the constitution of the late-imperial Chinese state. I shall limit my survey to the gazetteers of the metropolitan region in which Beijing lay, known in turn as North Zhili in the Ming, Zhili in the Qing, and Hebei province thereafter. The views expressed in Hebei gazetteers are not necessarily representative of China as a whole, but nor do they represent a peculiarly northern view. Still, those who lived or worked in proximity to the capital tended to share a conservatism on cultural matters, compounded by the sense that they, as tiny elites in less prosperous counties, had to work harder to bring their locales into line with the strictest interpretation of state programs and rules. Hebei magistrates were anxious to keep their administrations within whatever expectations they presumed prevailed in the capital; and compilers of Hebei gazetteers were concerned to confine their county's appearances to the models mandated by Beijing.

Every Hebei compiler was conscious of the late Hongwu restrictions, especially the ban on the founding of new monasteries in 1391. This edict created two categories of monasteries: those permitted to exist by virtue of already existing, and those not. A compiler hostile to Buddhism could take Hongwu's antipathy toward Buddhism as an indication of best practice and exclude all monasteries from his gazetteer, though in fact that was to go further than the emperor himself. The more moderate conservative position was to record only those monasteries enjoying a legal right to exist, and leave the rest out. They might continue to exist, but were not worthy of entering the official record of local life. An editorial decision in this vein was often accompanied by a negative editorial comment to the effect that post-1391 monasteries could only be sites devoted to "licentious sacrifices" (*Yongping fu zhi* 1501: *fanli*.2b). The extreme position—that all references to religion should be totally excluded from the gazetteer—nonetheless found periodic favor, notably in the early decades of the Qing dynasty. As one compiler declared tendentiously in 1676, since "our kingly government has continued the [Hongwu] prohibition on the setting up of Buddhist monasteries and Daoist temples," all monasteries should be treated as illegal institutions and left out of the gazetteer (*Guangping xian zhi* 1676: 1.28a).[4] More often, Confucian conservatives took a less extreme position, acknowledging the legitimacy of the state's restrictions on monasteries but wanting still to hold them to the severest letter of the law. This is what a compiler in 1749 does when he declares that, although privately founded monasteries exist within his county, they should not be recorded as they fall within "the present dynasty's meritorious ban on monastic founding" (*Nanhe xian zhi* 1749: 3.7a). A more lenient editorial stance during the early-Qing period was to include any monastery founded before the Qing and not worry overly about whether the founding had taken place before or after 1391, which was sometimes impossible to determine in any case (*Qingyuan xian zhi* 1873: 18.*siguan*.1a). The exceptions, of course, were those "illegal" monasteries to which a Ming or Qing emperor had shown imperial favor by visiting or presenting a gift.

State Regulation as Insufficient Confucian Prophylaxis

From the editorial comments that compilers inserted into their gazetteers, it is clear that the Hebei gentry liked to complain about the power and influence of religious communities and institutions in their local societies. Their complaint is of a piece with the northern gentry's reputation as a dourly Confucian lot who were unsympathetic to the cultural and political enthusiasms of their southern counterparts. The southern taste for abbatial friendships and monastic patronage so strong among the gentry in the Yangzi River valley was not something most of them shared, except during the heady days of the late Ming (Brook 1993: 94–96). A distrust of such cultural indiscretion dovetailed with their grumpy attitude toward the richly non-Confucian world humming around them, a world in which popular religious practices went on out of their sight and made them anxiously dream of restoring a staunchly Confucian dominion of rites and deference. That dominion may never have existed, but appealing to it was a way of putting themselves between the people and the state, and giving themselves the illusion of having a more secure place in the order of things.

The anti-religious, and more specifically anti-Buddhist, comments to be found in Hebei gazetteers are generally phrased in the language of Confucian self-discipline and moral prophylaxis. That self-discipline committed the conservative gentry to act as the defenders of orthodoxy, which most wanted to see enforced as broadly as possible. Buddhism could not be left to the masses, who might mobilize it to promote their interests. It was the first zone that lay in the path of the vigilant Confucian trekking his way into the cultural wilds of popular religious life. Among other things, that vigilance meant reminding other Confucians, whether they be local gentry or local officials, of what distinguished them from the common people. "We Confucians," the compiler of the Jinzhou gazetteer of 1690 states, "do not talk about the Two Teachings and are strict about heterodox ways." He cannot declare Buddhism and Daoism to be heterodox, since he knows they are tolerated by the state and permitted within the code, but he can warn that they might become hotbeds from which heterodox thinking arises (*Jinzhou zhi* 1690: 10.*siguan*.4a). In general, compilers appeal more to Confucian values than dynastic regulations to justify restricting their records of the Buddhist presence in their counties, although the unfinished promise of the Chinese state to conduct itself as the exclusive patron of the Confucians never lurks far from the foreground of the Confucian mind.

This is the position that magistrate Zhang Xun takes in the earliest surviving Ming gazetteer in Hebei, the 1373 gazetteer of Zhuozhou subprefecture south of Beijing, when he observes, "Confucians do not talk about things related to Buddha or Laozi. Using their propaganda about sin and fortune to transform ignorant customs is like using a torch to brighten the sunlight" (*Zhuozhou zhi* 1373: 9.2b). In 1373, this pitting of Confucians against Buddhists and Daoists had a particular edge, for during the recently overthrown Yuan dynasty, Mongol emperors had treated all three alike as technicians of the invisible realm and equally worthy of support. Confucians did not like to think of themselves within the same category as Buddhist monks, but that is how the Mongol occupiers regarded them, no better and perhaps only a little worse than monks. Zhang's objection may have had a doctrinal logic, but it more likely stemmed from his sense of the local market for state patronage among religious professionals. At this early point in his reign, the Hongwu emperor was still Buddhism's patron. Buddhists and Confucians both may have assumed that each would have to compete for opportunities to participate in local manifestations of the state's presence. That could not have pleased Zhang.

The Ming state was on Zhang's side. It elected to redifferentiate the cultic streams in Chinese society and mark off Confucians for official state patronage and, after 1380, Buddhists and Daoists for state supervision. It rehabilitated Confucianism as the conduit of state orthodoxy, extended formal recognition to cults connected to Confucians or exemplars whose moral virtue complemented Confucianism, and made these central to its official regulations governing sacrifices, the "sacrificial corpus" (*sidian*) or "ritual corpus" (*lidian*). This corpus did not include any Buddhist rituals. Accordingly, the compiler of the Wuqiang county gazetteer of 1694, who begins by announcing that "we Confucians spurn the Two Teachings," concedes that Buddhist and Daoist rituals were in wide use but observes that these were not the rituals conducive to propagating the "moral teachings" that Confucianism, through state sponsorship, brought to the world (*Wuqiang xian xinzhi* 1694: 2.24b). Many compilers make direct reference to Buddhism's absence from the state's corpus of officially sanctioned sacrifices, usually to justify their unwillingness to "indiscriminately mix them" with officially sanctioned state-cult institutions (*Shahe xian zhi* 1757: 20.10b; see also *Gaocheng xian zhi* 1698: 2.10a; *Luanzhou zhi* 1810: 9.1a). Some exploit the prohibitionist implication of this absence to justify cutting down the scale of reporting of local monasteries (*Xinhe xian zhi* 1679: 2.21a), a few to cut them out of the published record altogether (*Lingshou xian zhi* 1685: 2.6b).

Confucian competition thus combined with state restrictions to cast a shadow over the legitimacy of Buddhist monasteries, at least in the eyes of the gazetteer compilers. It did so in the face of considerable popular support for popular religion, as the compiler of a 1679 county gazetteer admits when he professes to be at a loss to account for the greater popularity of Buddhism over Confucianism:

Buddhist and Daoist monasteries, chapels, and cloisters properly have no relationship to the official sacrificial corpus. Yet rural bumpkins and ignorant folk all go around to the monasteries to pray on their knees, and to the chapels and cloisters to burn incense and beg for good fortune. Why is this? Is it perhaps because the Teaching of the Sage isn't as easy to comprehend as Buddhism and Daoism? Or is it because the ancestral tablets aren't brightly colored as are their clay statues? (*Xinhe xian zhi* 1679: 2.21a)

The author chooses to wrestle with the fact that Confucianism had neither a reassuring message or "curb appeal" for non-elites, nor reflected the conditions of the lives of most people that left them vulnerable to disease, want, and unattended old age—and at a much higher rate than himself and his gentry friends. This allows him to parse their Buddhism as a lapse of intelligence, discrimination, and good taste, just as twentieth-century modernizers across the political spectrum would also be prone to do in their turn.

A linked argument against Buddhist institutions and rituals was that they were not just gaudy but wasteful. Some compilers found it an easy matter to jump from brightly colored statues to expensively decorated ones, then declare the project of monastic patronage to be an unjustifiable drain on local resources. To offer an example from 1604: "Today the realm has reached an extreme of poverty. If we wish to economize, nothing is better than cutting out extraneous expenses; among such expenses, nothing is more wasteful than constructing palatial buildings; and among palatial buildings, nothing is more wasteful than monasteries." The compiler goes on to concede that doctrinally Confucian arguments against Buddhism, though sound, get him nowhere with popular opinion. What people should do is not what they do, he complains:

> How can we use clear and readily understood principles to criticize them [Buddhism and Daoism]? The delusions of this generation cannot be dispelled. The first delusion is not respecting parents at home but respecting spirits and Buddhas outside the home. The second is not trembling before state regulations but secretly fearing to go against the Buddhist dharma. The third is not mending what is right in front of your eyes but instead trying to mend what is off in the next life. The fourth is fighting over wealth with kinsmen while giving riches to priests and monks. Why don't even one or two ignorant men and women see this and return to orthodoxy? (*Huairou xian zhi* 1604: 1.42b–43a)[5]

The writer despairs about whether the state's message of order and frugality will ever get through to the people. He wants the state to be tougher, since the free operation of religious collectivities was endowing them with a local priority over state institutions as the context within which public authority could be asserted, and therefore as the prime force delineating the terms within which people organized their lives. The regulatory state, he feared, was not in touch with this social reality. His only way to undermine this authority was by pointing out the costs involved—which made no dent in the devotion of those who willingly gave.

Conservative Confucians constantly returned to the argument that it was necessary that they or the local magistrate (occasionally one and the same person) should step in to impose prohibitionary measures, often in the context of bemoaning the tide of heterodoxy they felt rising from below. Yet there were distinct limits to what they could actually carry out. "Suppressing heterodoxy and lifting up orthodoxy is the great prophylactic task of government," one prohibitionist compiler-magistrate insisted. He was able to boast that "therefore no Buddhist or Daoist monasteries have I deigned to list" (*Lingshou xian zhi* 1685: *fanli*.1b), but he had little other room for action. At the end of the section in the second *juan* of his gazetteer, the section on temples where one would expect to find the standard list of monasteries, he observes that in the hills and upland

valleys of his county, "the shrines of the Two Teachings are found in pro-
fusion, awe-inspiring and magnificent, where rituals are conducted daily
without pause." What distressed him was that people were visiting these
shrines and carrying out their rituals to the neglect of temples mandated
in the official ritual corpus. He regarded this situation as a "great imbalance" and called on the gentry to "promote the one and dispense with
the other" (*Lingshou xianzhi* 1685: *fanli*.2.6b).[6] Prohibition should prevail,
thought those at the extreme conservative wing of the local gentry, but it
could only prevail on paper, not in reality.

Most within the conservative wing of Confucian compilers adopted a
more accommodative stance. They were aware that cutting out a significant sector of local society from the published record might be morally
correct but was "excessively narrow," as another editor puts it. He complains in good state-Confucian fashion that monasteries should not be allowed to exist "in the villages and along the roads" where they can siphon
off people's wealth and lead them into heterodox ways, but he does not
allow his disapproval to convince him that Confucian prophylaxis justifies
removing references from the gazetteer or even eradicating the religious
sites in the mountains to which people go, often simply for the pleasure of
sight-seeing (*Fuping xian zhi* 1874: 2.35a). Religion might well be suspect,
but regulation was all that could reasonably be hoped for. Compilers of
an anti-Buddhist bent might fantasize about a final solution for the power
of Buddhist institutions in local society, which would obviate the need to
record them (*Yongning xian zhi* 1602: 47b), but until their statutory legitimacy was revoked, it was not within the gentry's prerogative to cut them
out. What the Hongwu emperor had allowed, however grudgingly, no
scholar could forbid. As one resigned Ming compiler put it, reading about
Buddhist institutions in the local gazetteer allowed one to "witness the
doings of the Great Sage," that is, the Hongwu emperor. "Therefore I
have listed them in the pages of this book to show what existed in the past
and is of no harm to the people" (*Fengrun xian zhi* 1570: 12.4b).

A few compilers were willing to go even further, allowing that
Confucian mores were not always easy to propagate, and that popular religion, with its zeal to promote the good and punish the evil, might well
complement Confucianism. As one compiler phrased his reasoning for including monasteries in his gazetteer, "If people in fact constantly worried
about life and death and about fortune and misfortune, then few would
go against their superiors or make trouble. Thus the Way of the gods can
firm up the proper Teachings" of Confucius (*Shulu xian zhi* 1671: 2.20a).
The visible "remnants" of Buddhism, according to another, should not
be ignored, for their survival "simply encourages the ignorant folk who
believe in them to be good, not because [the state] really reveres them"

(*Xincheng xian zhi* 1617: 12.1b). Another went further, arguing not only that Buddhism and Daoism are not in contradiction with the Confucian order, but that they are essential to its maintenance:

In the age of Yao and Shun, one had only to open sluices gates and let the water flow off. Today, if it weren't for thick dikes and towering seawalls, there would be no way to protect ourselves from the devastations of flood. Given the ways of this world, how are the ignorant lower classes any different from this? The Two Masters are truly the dikes that hold back the flood. (*Anping xian zhi* 1687: 3.3a)

Rather than raising a flood of heterodoxy from below, as many gentry feared, Buddhism and Daoism could in fact serve to quell the greater tide of licentiousness and insubordination that always seemed to lurk beneath the order over which they presided.

Buddhism in the Chinese Constitution

The disinclination among the magistrates and gentry of Hebei to provide full reports on the Buddhist institutions and practices in their counties could be taken as a sign of a widespread antipathy among the elite to religious institutions and practices. Seen in terms of the gazetteer genre, however, this may not be a complete explanation of what was going on. The purpose of making a gazetteer was not to produce a documentary that transcribed the complex reality of local society, after all; it was to render that reality into a textual form that conformed to the principles by which the state governed the realm. I would therefore like to suggest that disagreement over how to report monasteries reflects more than religious tastes, and points instead to what I see as a debate within the elite over the late-imperial constitution. As a field supporting norms and institutions that could compete with, or at least be indifferent to, state hegemony as Confucians imagined it, Buddhism posed a latent challenge to that hegemony, especially in periods when that hegemony appeared to be under siege.

There was no question of declaring Buddhism or Daoism illegal, in the sense of something that the code criminalized. Throughout most of the imperial period and beyond, the Chinese state recognized Buddhist and Daoist temples as legitimate religious institutions. Whether Buddhism protected the Confucian order or threatened it was not a question that this recognition could be taken to satisfactorily resolve. Within that irresolution laid the possibility of ongoing debate among state elites about whether the state was doing enough, or too much, to restrict the field within which organized religions might operate. Put starkly, these two tendencies represent the range of responses that state elites could imagine, and continue to imagine, as the appropriate place of religion in the Chinese constitution: on one side, as corroding the norms and institutions that should govern public life; on the other, as at least indifferent to them, perhaps even contributing to them.

Underneath this splay of choices laid a starker social reality. The late-imperial gentry were keenly aware of the power that Buddhism enjoyed in local society. The compiler of the 1732 gazetteer of Wan county understood Buddhism was anything but inconsequential to the production of local order. He enumerates one dismaying sign after another that Buddhist institutions were in full flower in his county: Buddhist temples ubiquitous and beyond counting; the "gold and azure sparkle" of Buddhist statuary dazzling onlookers; fund-raisers able to collect vast sums to support these institutions. Most conspicuously, he is horrified by the uncontrollable and vibrantly human activity that Buddhist institutions house:

How do people dare illicitly build structures that are not on the list of canonical shrines? Still, lay people of this generation set up temples and make statues by the side of the high roads or at the edge of markets without justification, [places that] appear reverent and yet are rife with cacophony and confusion, without even a wall around the outside, while the stench [of incense] billows. How potent are their arts! (*Wanxian zhi* 1732: 2.27a–b)

This is not a religion on the margin or in decline. The Buddhism under the compiler's scrutiny was richly integrated into the networks of social participation and communication that extended from market to market along Wan county's main roads. It is not surprising to discover an anxious compiler a decade later explaining that he had to exclude from publication the numerous Buddhist sites that could be found scattered "in the rural wastes and the village markets" (*Wanquan xian zhi* 1742: 2.44a), as these were the very places that the people who animated the network ties in local society crossed and thronged. The world of movement and activity beyond the capacity of the state to police in which this popular Buddhism was implicated was separate from the one the elite self-consciously inhabited, but it was not the irredeemable chaos that the compiler liked to imagine. Despite the impression of "cacophony and confusion" that Buddhist institutions gave to this gazetteer compiler, these institutions actively sustained an order that was visible and reasonable to those who participated in it.

Anxiety over the vital presence of Buddhism in local society exposed the fissures of class, privilege, and interest in the power relations animating political life from the locality to the center. These relations and fissures were not uniformly corrosive of elite or state power, however. Indeed, they might be better thought of as supporting the success with which the

Chinese sociopolity has reproduced itself as something like an equilibrium: regulatory legal systems working from above, community networks brokering local interests from below. Between these two, the gentry were uncertainly poised, eager to consolidate their position vis-à-vis the state, even sometimes exploiting monasteries to do so, yet always ready to back toward state systems and use them as bulwarks of enlightened discipline against the chaos that seemed poised to erode their local ground of privilege every time commoners gathered for their religious activities. For most everyone else, though, monasteries were part of the making and strengthening of the social networks through which they made their decisions about what to do, whom to associate with, and where to invest in public and private goods. By giving people a place in the cosmic order that was also a place in the order of public authority and social exchange by which they lived, Buddhism could be regarded as grounding local social life in a reproducible equilibrium, but it could also be seen as posing a radical alternative to secular power. Whether religion was treated as orthodox—something that the state and Confucianism could tolerate—or heterodox—something that could not be tolerated—depended on how people understood the composition and purpose of public life. By the same token, whether the state chose to act against religion had far more to do with local class tensions and competition for authority than with any characteristic or capacity that we might want to designate as "religious."

The Republican Continuation

The ongoing adjustment that local elites were constantly having to make between what existed in local society and what they believed should exist did not end with the close of the imperial era. The context and direction of change shifted as other factors and ideologies intervened to challenge existing social and political arrangements, but the regulatory posture—as well as the ever lurking threat of prohibition—continued unbroken. This continuity we can track by turning, again, to the gazetteers that local scholars continued to produce during the Republican period (1911–49). The genre underwent its own transformation as it adjusted to new political and cultural realities, abandoning its pretense of being an official administrative record and shifting to becoming more a compendium of statistical data and social surveys. Even so, the same ambivalence about religion, the same urge to bring it within secure categories from which its natural urge to err may be brought under control, can be detected.

Republican compilers rarely write about religion in quite the same language that their late-imperial predecessors used, yet their earnest adherence to modernity readily tempted them into continuing much the same postures of scrutiny and disapproval. The morally dismissive epithet of "the Two Masters" that we found in Ming and Qing gazetteers was allowed to fade from the record, but what replaced it—the Japanese neologism invented to translate the European term "religion" (*shūkyō*, which was read as *zongjiao* in Chinese)—could be made to do much the same classifying work and carry some of the same intellectual baggage. The modern-sounding "superstition" might now substitute for the old charge of "heterodoxy," for instance, and yet the same anxieties about the people's resistance—albeit to modernity and enlightenment rather than to deference and Confucian ritual—poke through the descriptive entries.

One effect of the arrival of the category of "religion" was to place the religious collectivities already present in local society in a continuum within new institutions that included Christian congregations. This alignment between native and non-native religions had contradictory effects. On the one hand, categorizing Buddhism and Daoism alongside Catholicism and Protestantism (with Islam placed ambiguously between them) endowed the former with a legitimacy different from any conceived for them in the past. As one compiler commented who introduced a *zongjiao* chapter into his county gazetteer early in the 1930s, he neither supports nor understands Buddhism, but he allows that it has a place in his record (*Daming xian zhi* 1934: 25.7a–b). For another compiler at this time, their new status as *zongjiao* set them up to play the role of culturally marking a "Chinese" religious tradition that was distinct from but parallel to Islam, Protestantism, and Catholicism, which became the other three of China's new "five religions" (*Nanpi xian zhi* 1932: 13.37b–38a). On the other hand, the association set Chinese religions up as targets of the modernist critique of religion as superstition, and as culprits in the doping of the Chinese people. By being moved into a neutral sociological category and placed under a different style of intellectual surveillance, Buddhism and Daoism could still be regarded with suspicion—no longer hotbeds of "heterodoxy" and "lavishness," perhaps, but reservoirs of modern vices that the new enlightenment could label "superstition" and "corruption." The condescension with which Confucian compilers regarded institutional religion migrated with little modification into the new discourses of sociology and state management.

The coming of *zongjiao* and its attendant concept of superstition had another curious effect, and that was to lower the tension between Confucianism on the one hand and Buddhism and Daoism on the other. The reframing of Confucianism within this new conceptual environment is a complex story with roots that go back to the Jesuit encounter with China in the seventeenth century, but it had an immediate impact on gazetteer compilers, who had not only Buddhism and Daoism but also the state-cults of Confucianism to make sense of. In his insightful 1938 handbook on the tasks involved in producing a local gazetteer, Li Jinxi reflects on the difficulty of submerging the older categories of "rites" and "temples" into the new category of "religion." While accepting that a new category is in play, he still has to ask, "Are there not shrines and rites that are outside of *zongjiao*? The [imperial] ritual corpus concerned with honoring virtue and repaying goodness, attested by grand buildings and abundant steles, is most certainly not mere superstition, but is Confucian. Therefore, these are also combined into the same section [*zongjiao*]."[7] In other words, the new language of *zongjiao* not only claimed Buddhism and Daoism, but the ritual and ideological tradition that upheld the authority of the state somewhat in opposition to them. All were now religions. Confucianism could no longer motivate criticism of Buddhism or Daoism, because it had been collapsed into the same category of things bearing the same characteristics. Effectively, recategorizing Confucianism as a religion stripped it of its capacity for moral critique.

Even though the new categories rearranged old values, the new terminology recycled old rhetoric. Reading late-imperial compilers complain about financial waste ("how is it that their teachings can still convince the ignorant laity that donation is good and parsimony is bad?"), vent their frustration over popular support ("people's minds are easily deluded"), harbor suspicions about the anarchic congregating of the lower classes and the chaos they produce ("bringing people together in unbroken succession"), and express the urge to set themselves apart ("What can I say? I pray only at the shrines to living officials"), one can hear the very same anxieties and prejudices of modernizing Republican elites who regarded Buddhism as a hopeless superstition unworthy of their attention (*Guangping xian zhi* 1676: 1.28a; *Nanhe xian zhi* 1749: 3.6b; *Jinzhou zhi* 1690: 10.*siguan*.4a; *Wanxian zhi* 1732: 2.27b; *Xinhe xian zhi* 1679: 2.20a). The language of disapprobation changed, but not its intent, which was to marginalize Buddhism as a source of public authority that might interfere with the next reincarnation of elite dominance.

What rescued this critique of Buddhism from becoming itself marginal in the new social order was the introduction of a framework of state supervision that was different from what the Ming or Qing state had imposed, and to which the elites of the new era allied themselves. No longer was the founding of new monasteries prohibited, yet tax laws were introduced that would do more than prohibitions to weaken Buddhist institutions. A new educational system hostile to religious training came in and undercut the old relationship between ritual and the state, and local officials no longer voiced the opinion that Buddhism be allowed to inculcate in the people a passive acceptance of their lot. Buddhism was written into Republican constitutions in the form of freedom of religion, but as a "right" of individuals, not as a component integral to the new order.[8] The constitutions of the 1950s forward brought the Confucian condemnation of Buddhism to completion by compromising the newly endowed "right" to believe in Buddhism with the equal "right" to propagate atheism, though of course without any backward glance at Confucianism.[9]

Conclusion

The People's Republic of China quickly assumed the role of the regulatory state in its policies toward religion, veering at times to the prohibitionist extreme. Indeed, no Chinese state since the end of the fourteenth century has asserted such powerful oversight from the center over religious personnel and institutions. Much of the 1950s legislation replicated the regulations that the Hongwu emperor introduced in the 1380s and 1390s, the main difference with that era being the socialist state's capacity to impose its regulatory purposes.[10] When that state moved toward religious prohibition during the Cultural Revolution, it seemed as though the Confucian prophylaxis, unwittingly taken on board and rephrased by Republican modernizers as resistance to superstition, and rephrased as "feudal superstition" within Communist ideology, was about to find final completion under socialism.

The congruence between Communist and Confucian hostilities to religion and their capacity to influence state policy is not haphazard coincidence, of course. Late-imperial history has mattered enormously to the options that Chinese states have considered, and the choices they have made, in fashioning their regulatory frameworks. Without that history, neither the Republican nor the Communist state would have acted as it did, nor continue to act as it does. What I cannot decide, and I leave this puzzle for the reader to ponder, is whether the power of the regulatory state since the fourteenth century belongs to the state itself, or whether it should be ascribed to local elites (say, activists among the Confucian gentry in the Ming and Qing, and members of the Chinese Communist Party in the People's Republic of China) who, in aligning themselves to state power, found the hostility to religion at the core of both Confucian and Communist ideologies a convenient weapon in their briefly successful struggles to dominate local society. Whether that power belongs to the state at the center or to its service elites in the locality, the history of Chinese religion after the 1970s, like the history of religion in China after the 1390s, suggests that communities and individuals will continue to create networks of religious activity beyond the framework of state regulation, regardless of the laws of the state or the activism of prohibitionist state elites, and that religion, indifferent to the logic of the state, will continue to have a dynamic presence in local society.[11]

Notes

1. The classic account of the late-imperial state's anxieties over the political potential of private sectarian organizing is Overmyer (1976). The continuities with the contemporary state's analysis of Falungong and its sanctions against it are striking.

2. I explore the intricacies of these editorial decisions in Hebei gazetteers in "Buddhism in the Chinese Constitution," in Brook (2005).

3. Arguing that "the section on Buddhist and Daoist monasteries is intrinsic to the gazetteer genre," one Wanli-era compiler names Sima Qian to bolster his argument for inclusiveness as a fundamental principle of historical writing; *Nanchang fu zhi* 1588: *fanli.* 2a.

4. The Qing repetition of Hongwu's ban on private founding is in *Da Qing huidian shili* 1886/1899: 501.2b, 3b–4a, 7b–8a, 14b.

5. For another comment on the wasteful extravagance of monastic construction, see *Nanpi xian zhi* 1680: 3.14a.

6. The latter passage is repeated verbatim in the 1874 edition.

7. Li Jinxi, *Fangzhi jinyi* (Contemporary proposals for local gazetteers), reprinted in Zhu (1983: 105).

8. On the written constitutions of the twentieth century, see Nathan (1986). Nathan gives freedom of religion only passing attention, reflecting the relative unimportance of this "right" in Chinese political thought.

9. Espousing atheism was not a borrowed convention. The compiler of *Qingxian zhi* (1673) denied the existence of Buddha by citing Fan Shen's treatise of the fifth century, "Wofo lun" (That there is no Buddha), as part of his argument against supporting Buddhist institutions, though he included them in his gazetteer nonetheless (2.2a).

10. I have speculated elsewhere that the other influence on the state regulation of religion in the 1950s is the regulatory framework that the Japanese imposed in the occupied areas of East China during the war; see Brook (1996).

11. On the capacity of local religion to evade state logic, see Dean (1997, this volume).

References

Brook, Timothy. 1993. *Praying for Power: Buddhism and the Formation of Gentry Society in Late-Imperial China.* Cambridge, MA: Council on East Asian Studies, Harvard University.

———. 1996. "Toward Independence: Christianity in China under Japanese Occupation, 1937–1945." In *Christianity and China: From the Eighteenth Century to the Present,* edited by Daniel Bays, pp. 317–37. Stanford, CA: Stanford University Press.

———. 1997. "At the Margin of Public Authority: The Ming State and Buddhism." In *Culture and State in Chinese History: Conventions, Conflicts, and Accommodations*, edited by Theodore Huters, R. Bin Wong, and Pauline Yü. Stanford, CA: Stanford University Press. Reprinted in Timothy Brook, 2005, *The Chinese State in Ming Society*, pp. 139–67, London: Routledge.

———. 2005. *The Chinese State in Ming Society*. London: Routledge.

Da Ming huidian (Collected precedents of the Ming dynasty). 1588.

Da Ming lü (The Ming code). 1999. Edited by Huai Xiaofeng. Beijing: Falü chubanshe.

Da Qing huidian shili (Administrative precedents and substatutes of the Qing dynasty). Promulgated 1886, printed 1899.

Dean, Kenneth. 1997. "Ritual and Space: Civil Society or Popular Religion?" In *Civil Society in China*, edited by Timothy Brook and B. Michael Frolic, pp. 172–92. Armonk, NY: M. E. Sharpe.

Jiang, Yonglin (trans.). 2005. *The Great Ming Code / Da Ming lü*. Seattle: University of Washington Press.

Nathan, Andrew. 1986. "Political Rights in Chinese Constitutions." In *Human Rights in Contemporary China*, edited by R. Randle Edwards, Louis Henkin, and Andrew Nathan. New York: Columbia University Press.

Overmyer, Daniel. 1976. *Folk Buddhist Religion: Dissenting Sects in Traditional China*. Cambridge, MA: Harvard University Press.

Zhu Shijia (ed.). 1983. *Fangzhi xue liangzhong* (Two texts in the field of local gazetteers). Changsha: Yuelu shushe.

CHAPTER 3

Positioning Religion in Modernity:
State and Buddhism in China

YOSHIKO ASHIWA

Modernity and the Creation of the Space of Religion

The late nineteenth and early twentieth centuries were a time in Asia of shaping modernity by, actively or passively, reshaping Western modernity. This dynamic transformation involved various projects that demanded the abandonment or reform of previous ideologies, systems, institutions, and consciousness. One of the projects of this modernity was religion. The term "religion" was translated from European languages into Asian ones, creating such neologisms as *shūkyō, zongjiao,* and *agama* that spread among intellectuals and political elites in Asia, who quickly adapted "religion" into their modern thinking as a necessary space for the making of a modern state. Therefore, in seeking a modern state, a space of religion newly emerged as part of this indispensable apparatus of modernity. The space of religion was constituted mainly by two actors. One was politicians and state officials, who promulgated modern constitutions, laws, and regulations regarding religion, often through conflicts and tensions linked to local politics and value systems. The other was reformist religious leaders and laypersons, who advocated the making of modern teachings, disciplines, and organizations within the established world religions, such as Buddhism and Christianity, in cooperation with or opposition to state elites.

Hence, a space of religion emerges through modern state formation. This dynamic process involves the efforts to position religion undertaken by both religious reformers and state elites. In considering this process, this chapter explores several questions. How do the state and modern nation system relate to and mutually compose each other? How does the space of religion emerge through this process and what are its attributes? What influence does the process have on the beliefs of individuals? In the context of China the state elite has sustained a strong self-consciousness of modernizing from the late nineteenth century. Even today the state elite in the People's Republic, including officials of the Chinese Communist Party (Party) and the government, has a strong consciousness of China as being "in the process of developing toward socialist modernization" and forcefully imposes it on the people. An examination of the efforts to impose the modern concept of religion on Buddhism during the 1920s and 1930s and then in the 1980s and 1990s illuminates the historically ongoing process of the creation of a space of religion and the process of state formation.

According to Henri Lefebvre (1991), space is constituted by the integration of physical, institutional, and semiotic aspects. In the Chinese context of modernity, the physical space of religion refers to sites, including land, buildings, and monuments, that have been repeatedly destroyed and rebuilt throughout history, especially from the latter half of the nineteenth century, when China entered modernity during a period of extreme political turmoil. Repeated destruction and reconstruction reflects contestation over the modern concept of religion and attempts to impose it. Institutional space refers to religion in law and regulations controlled or defined by the state, and also religion as defined by associations, devotee societies, temple administration, and seminaries. Semiotic space refers to the meanings and discourses of religion through the practice of rituals and religious activities, which include beliefs. This chapter focuses on the institutional aspects linked to the physical and semiotic aspects, a focus expressed through the phrase "positioning of religion in space." A major attribute of modernity is that the space of religion emerges and is positioned on the platform of the modern state through projects to institutionalize certain principles that create, reshape, and allocate situations, peoples, and organizations. Thus, modernity is not a one-sided project of the state to discipline people's thoughts but is a reciprocal project of religions and states reshaping themselves and each other.

PROJECTS OF MODERNITY

Earlier modernization theorists such as Talcott Parsons, Daniel Lerner, and Clifford Geertz posited a paradigm of an abstracted single path of Western modernization as an ideal, universal process. However, this paradigm, which maintained that Asian countries are in earlier stages of this linear, universal modernization, has been acutely questioned and criticized. For example, Talal Asad (1993) has pointed out Clifford Geertz's confusion, or rather ambiguities, of linear Western history of modernization and indigenous histories and cultures. Contemporary social theories increasingly recognize "modernity" as multiple projects or "a series of interlinked projects" that, as Asad writes, can be attained through various routes and processes in both Western and Asian societies.

> It is right to say that "modernity" is neither a totally coherent object nor a clearly bounded one, and that many of its elements originate in relations with the histories of peoples outside Europe. Modernity is a project—or rather, a series of interlinked projects—that certain people in power seek to achieve. The project aims at institutionalizing a number of (sometimes conflicting, often evolving) principles: constitutionalism, moral autonomy, democracy, human rights, civil equality, industry, consumerism, freedom of the market—and secularism. (Asad 2003: 13)

Asad's definition of modernity has two significant points. First, it is noteworthy that he defines the essential characteristics of modernity as something furthered by specific persons wielding subjective power. Modernity is not something that emerges spontaneously from the everyday lives of people who are embedded in enduring styles and values, but instead is an amalgamation of ongoing projects furthered by politicians, intellectuals, capitalists, state bureaucrats, and other power elites. Second, he stresses that these projects of modernity intentionally aim at institutionalizing such modern "new" principles as constitutionalism, industry, nationalism, civil rights and market economy human rights, civil society, and secularism. These projects are intertwined with modern state formation and the institutionalization of these principles.

Modernity is multiple projects or, rather a series of interlinked projects, of which religion is a part. Initiated by power holders, religion is directly linked to state formation through the institutionalization of such principles as secularism. Asad mostly emphasizes the institutionalization of principles of secularism as the foundation of the state. In this chapter I will argue that this institutionalization and counterinstitutionalization of religion are achieved through allocations and configurations of people, power, organizations, physical land, and property ownership through which the principles are represented.

SPREAD OF RELIGIOUS SPACE TO ASIA

Asia entered modernity through the collapse and reorganization of previous political regimes in the context of multiplying contacts with the West. These contacts consisted of new interstate relations, commodity exchanges, and popular flows (of immigrants, adventurers, ideologues, businesspeople) made possible by advances in transportation and domestic political turmoil. This period saw the beginnings of movements of large-scale globalization that connected the societies of the West and Asia through the expansion of colonialism, capitalism, and mass migration. This triggered the emergence of unprecedented spaces. It also led to the establishment in Asia of many spaces that were constituted by conflicts, contradictions, resistance, and amalgamation, such as the absolutizing and relativizing of Western values and their refusal and acceptance, and imitation and transformations, that were occurring under the coercive power of colonization, imperialism, capitalism, and efforts at modern state formation in Asia.

This process can be described as the fermentation of modernity, as Asian elites haphazardly formed myriad ideologies from pieces that incorporated a wide range of modern Western thought: Enlightenment history, scientism, rationalization, evolutionism, imperialism, anti-imperialism, socialism, pan-Asianism, Marxism, democracy, ethnicity, secularism, asceticism, spiritualism, and so on. These pieces of thought and ideologies, in other words sets of value systems, were combined and woven in integrated and contradictory fashions into numerous indigenous slogans, writings, and policies that composed the activities and disciplines of movements. Prasenjit Duara (1994) writes that some of these ideologies and movements triggered bifurcated histories that were then variously suppressed, absorbed, or ignored by the state as it made a master narrative of modernization. It is through this process that religious space was formed.

An active space of religion constituted by these multiple ideologies and movements rapidly emerged in this period. However, it appeared not only in Asian countries that were struggling to form modern states but also through the expansion of such discursive spaces in the West as: Oriental studies, the study of Eastern religions, and the separation of religious studies from theology at Chicago, Oxford, and Heidelberg universities; the salons of politicians, intellectuals, and entrepreneurs; the 1893 World Parliament of Religion at the Chicago Exposition; the numerous ecumenical encounters of missionaries and scholars organized by Christians, which included meetings of entrepreneurs, bureaucrats, intellectuals, and revolutionaries from the West and Asia. On the one hand, in this space of religion in the West there can be seen emerging a powerfully resonant orientalism and relativization of the values of Christianity to encompass non-Christian religions. On the other hand, in Asia the activities of capitalists, bureaucrats, intellectuals, clergy, and revolutionaries constructed and institutionalized the space of religion alongside such other new spaces as a modern economy, politics, and science.

Over this period movements in Sri Lanka, Thailand, Burma, Japan, China, and other Asian countries created an indigenous conceptual term of "religion" that was equivalent to the English word "religion." This subsequently promoted the representation and acceptance of the concept and the classification and reform of extant beliefs to fit the category of "religion." In the case of Buddhism, its fit to the category of "religion" developed through imitating and adapting Christian missionary ethics and techniques, and through attempts to position and institutionalize Buddhism within the process of state building. This led Buddhism, as a modern religion, to accommodate ethnocentrism, modernist clergy and devotees, rationalism, and anti-imperialism, and then to internalize them. Furthermore, in this historical process the depth of the rationalism, pan-Asianism, and cosmopolitanism of the emerging space of religion was as remarkable as its novelty. Intersections among the Sri Lankan reformer of Buddhism Anagarika Dharmapala, the Chinese Buddhist devotee Yang Wenhui, who proposed the modern reform of Chinese Buddhism, the monk Taixu, who actively pursued the modernization of Chinese Buddhism, and the Japanese scholarly monk Nanjō Fumio, who assisted Max Muller and other Asianists, were constituted by ideas, networks, and encounters in Japan, Sri Lanka, North America, and Europe. The thoughts and understandings nourished in these interactions were mutually catalytic, and inspired the emergence and growth of new movements in these regions. These movements were a driving force of numerous projects that constituted modernity.

SPREAD OF RELIGIOUS SPACE TO CHINA

Religion in contemporary China has been involved in a continuous series of such projects of modernity. Religion was in decline during the troubled state-building of the Republican era and the first decade of the People's Republic of China. It was decisively suppressed during the decade-long Cultural Revolution (1966–76). Then, following the major shift toward a market economy from the late 1970s, religious activities were officially sanctioned and swiftly reemerged (Luo 1991; MacInnis 1989). According to a survey by university-based researchers, China has 300 million religious believers above the age of sixteen. Buddhists, Daoists, Catholics, Muslims, and Protestants account for 67.4 percent of these believers. About 200 million are Buddhists, Daoists, or worshippers of the Dragon King, God of Fortune, and other figures, while about 40 million are Protestants (*Wenweipo* 2007; Wu 2007).

There are various explanations for this rapid revival of religion. One is that the change in state policy toward religion from 1979 has released people's suppressed desire for religion, and enabled them to find in religion an alternative to communist ideology (Overmyer 2003). Another explanation, reflecting the role of the Catholic Church in the collapse of communist party-states in Eastern Europe, sees the revival as a shift to a more liberal state with an emerging civil society brought about by a newly tolerant religious policy (Madsen 1998). However, these interpretations are inadequate because they presuppose a sharp disjuncture of the circumstances surrounding religion before and after 1979. A close examination of the empirical details of the religious revival after 1979, such as the interaction between the state and religious organizations, and the conflicts and accommodations of religion and political ideologies, shows that the more long-term accumulation of cultural, historical, and social forms of capital before what appears as a conspicuous change around 1979 prepared a multilayered foundation and ideological basis for the emergence of the space of religion. Furthermore, these capital forms have emerged almost unnoticed in local fields of revival with significant political meanings.

An explanation of the contemporary revival of religion should go beyond a focus on the period since the new state religious policies that were introduced in 1979 or even from the founding of the People's Republic of China. The revival is imbricated in aspects of religious organization and teachings that predate not only the 1979 policy changes but also the 1949 establishment of the new state. Therefore, an explanation of the revival needs to be grounded in the seeds of the projects of modernity sown around the turn of the twentieth century from which the space of religion emerged.

As Asad points out, modernity is neither coherent nor totally bounded from other phenomena. If we assume that modernity is a continuum of interlinked multiple projects or if, as Duara (1995) says, bifurcated histories are hidden behind the linear history that constructs the master narrative, then the contemporary revival of religion, especially Buddhism, can be seen as the resulting integration of parts of all these multiple projects or bifurcated histories. Religion in China has to be viewed as a thread of the fabric of modernity, the design of which began to take distinctive and visible form around the end of the nineteenth century.

Stirrings toward the Modern State and the Space of Religion

By the late nineteenth century the Qing dynasty was collapsing from challenges both internal (such as from the Taiping Rebellion) and external (such as from the Opium War). There began at this time reform and institutionalization by the religions themselves to become modern and fit the space of religion, which the modern state was also struggling to create. From the state powerholders' point of view, which had been inconsistent in regard to the positioning of religion in the state system and ideology, the work of positioning religion in the system was, in fact, part of a very careful arranging that was directly linked to the building of the modern state itself. This generated various arguments and debates about religion that were linked to power struggles within the state but that also enabled the state to recognize the existence of religion, underscoring how the placement of religion within the state system is a crucial part of the process of modern state formation.

Among the modernist political and cultural elites were many who sought a subjective amalgamation of technology and the Chinese spirit. These persons included intellectuals and elite government bureaucrats, some of whom were also political activists and revolutionaries, and most of whom had the experience of living and traveling in Western countries as well as Japan. They used the knowledge they acquired abroad to achieve a breakthrough in China's confrontation with the chaotic situation. Many had a keen interest in Buddhism, because they saw the possibility of reforming it to be a modern religion to express an essential core of Chineseness as an alternative to Christianity. However, Buddhism in the late Qing dynasty had reached a nadir as many temples were abandoned or inhabited by self-ordained monks and other self-styled practitioners. During this time Buddhist teachings were barely kept alive among scattered lay-intellectual devotees (*jushi*) who collected, studied, and edited Buddhist sutras.[1] Buddhism faced further challenges from Christian missionaries who were vigorously proselytizing among people from all walks of life—from the worldly and powerful to the parochial and poor.

In the early twentieth century, the Republican state launched the Convert Temples to Schools Movement (*miaochan xingxue yundong*) and the Smashing Superstition Movement (*mixin dapo yundong*). These movements deepened Buddhism's dire straits, accelerating modern reform efforts within Buddhism by active and enlightened monks and devotees.

THE SMASHING SUPERSTITION MOVEMENT: DEMOLISHING SUPERSTITION AND DISPOSITIONING LOCAL POWER

When the Nationalist Party took power in the provinces around Shanghai in the 1920s, a movement to ban "superstition" and "sorcery" by destroying temples and idols was underway. Called the Smashing Superstition Movement, it was initiated by political reformists in local Nationalist Party branches at the county level and below. A study by Mitani Takashi (1978) shows how this movement reflected not only the antipathy of "science" toward "superstition" but also the complexity of politics at that time. The movement's key promoters were younger members of local party branches influenced by the May Fourth Movement of 1919 to uphold democracy and science, and who were also interested in communism. After receiving a modern education in urban centers after

1919 that promoted belief in democracy and science, they returned to their hometowns as schoolteachers and local intellectuals. They became the majority in local Nationalist Party branches and were the local leaders of the movement to smash the shrines and idols that the people worshipped. Their consciousness is evident in one of their publications.

We must make the people thoroughly understand the exercise of the rights of the people and propel them toward the rational way so as to completely free them from the trap of old conventions. Divine authority is an obstacle to the development of the people's rights and the societal evolution. A society based on divine authority can never coexist with the new society based on the Three Principles of the People. (Chou 1927)

These young party members viewed the masses as obstinately believing in divine oracles and prophets, obeying traditional authority and conventions, failing to comprehend individual rights, and accepting subjugation by local landowners. Therefore, they viewed the destruction of temples and idols as necessary to enlighten, train, and guide the people, in order to direct them away from their false ideas and subjugation toward democracy and science.

Mitani points out that the political aspects of the Smashing Superstition Movement reflected the contemporary political split between the Nationalist and Communist parties. First, the movement was an explicit action by young Nationalist Party members to resist the conservatism among some central bureaucrats in the national capital of Nanjing. The central state, led by Chiang Kai-shek, desperately needed the support of capitalists and warlords. But the young members of local Nationalist Party branches were idealists who, influenced by communism, sought to awaken the masses for radical revolution. Their condemnation of what the conservatives stood for led them to launch the Smashing Superstition Movement.

Second, the Smashing Superstition Movement aimed to undermine the power and prestige of the landowners and gentry class who, as major local power holders, were in charge of the festivals, gods, and temples that the movement attacked. As a result, the new authority established in the center was expanding its control over the old power of local society. The state was attempting to reorganize the government administration but its weak local control made even tax collection difficult, while entrenched landowners and gentry still held power in county governments. Therefore, the destruction of the traditions controlled by these local power holders symbolically expressed the new power of the central government and the invasion of ideology, smashing and conquering the ideology and social structure of local entrenched authorities. The destruction of local beliefs, organizations, and sites controlled by these old entrenched authorities exposed symbolically and revealed practically the destruction of the old order and the power of the new regime.

In the early stage of the Smashing Superstition Movement all religious activities were considered premodern, unenlightened superstition. Buddhist and Daoist temples were included as targets of attack along with local deities. Buddhists complained to the Nanjing government about the attacks, and in response the central state issued *Standards for Preserving and Abandoning Gods and Shrines* (*Shenci cunfei biaojun*) that decreed what could and could be not be attacked and destroyed. The major criteria for determining whether a site should be destroyed or preserved were historical importance and scientific significance. The criteria had two categories defining sites to be preserved. One was the sage category (*xianzhelei*), which consisted of deities that had contributed to the nation, state, and society, possessed scholarly knowledge that had benefited the people, or had exhibited a loyalty, devotion, filial piety, and justice that inspired pride among the masses, such the agriculture god (Shennong), Confucius, and Guanweng. The second category to be preserved was the religious category (*zongjiaolei*): it consisted of "pure and true" teachings that ordinary people could believe in, such as Buddhism and parts of Daoism. The next two categories designated sites to be destroyed. The old gods category (*gushenlei*) referred to the gods that had been worshipped before the development of science but had since become meaningless, such as the gods of the sun, moon, and stars. The minor spirits category (*yincilei*) consisted of plant and animal spirits, such as the cow goblin and the snake god, that could also be destroyed (Mitani 1978: 10). However, these guidelines were not observed. They had been devised by upper class intellectuals on the basis of science and rationalism, but were interpreted locally as justifying the destruction of all religion. This was understandable because in the chaotic circumstances of Buddhism many temples were derelict and self-styled practitioners abounded, making it difficult to distinguish between Buddhist temples and those of the old gods and minor spirits. Furthermore, it is probable that the local people were not conscious of any clear-cut distinction between the categories. Therefore, the Smashing Superstition Movement launched in 1928 angered the masses of people and turned them against the central state being formed by the Nationalist Party and toward the Communist Party.

Two things are clear as a result of the Smashing Superstition Movement. One is that the actions and behavior toward religion created a space for it in which rationalism, scienticism, and enlightenment thinking—disciplines of modernity—clearly appeared in the space of religion. Second, the space of religion is highly vulnerable, and its manipulation and institutionalization had large influences on the process of reforming and organizing the political structure of the new regime and exhibiting its power.

THE CONVERT TEMPLES TO SCHOOLS MOVEMENT: THE UTILITY OF RELIGIOUS FACILITIES

A new movement was launched at the same time as the Smashing Superstition Movement to confiscate temple property for the construction of vocational schools and libraries to educate the masses. This use of temples for public education had first been advocated in a essay "Exhortation to Study" (*Quan xue bian*) written in 1901 by Zhang Zhidong, an enthusiastic proponent of adapting Western thought and technology to China. At that time it led to a movement to appropriate temples for schools that shook Buddhist indifference to the drastic changes occurring in society. The movement was revived in the late 1920s by Tai Shuangqiu, a modern rationalist with a doctorate in education from Columbia University who taught at Jiangsu University. In an article titled "The Converting Temples to Schools Movement" he called for the rapid dissemination of compulsory education. He saw the entry of children into temples to become clerics as a serious obstacle to modern education, and viewed temple property and wealth as a huge reservoir of capital for the construction of a modern education system as the foundation of the state. The Convert Temples to Schools Movement encouraged local education bureaus and universities to occupy temple lands and buildings, expel the clergy and confiscate their wealth, and reconstitute the temples as modern schools. This movement spread concurrently with the Smashing Superstition Movement.

However, the Convert Temples to Schools Movement contradicted the *Regulations for the Supervision of Monasteries and Temples* issued earlier, in 1915, by Yuan Shikai, then president of China, which stipulated that "Temples should not be abandoned and eliminated" and "Temple wealth and property should not be subject to occupation, confiscation, and fines based on pretexts" (Ohira 2002). The contradiction reflects two contesting themes of modern ideology. One is that the enlightened modern state guarantees freedom of religion while the second is that it promotes rational religion and the abandoning of premodern superstition. This contradiction led to several legal cases. Ohira summarizes one such case that was reported in the *Jiangsu Provincial Government Communiqué* (*Jiangsu sheng zhengfu gongbao*). The abbot of Yuntaishan Faqi Temple, Guanyun county, in Zhejiang province, was sued and arrested for his "wrong behavior." The Nationalist Party county branch ordered the temple's property and wealth to be used for educational purposes. Central University (*Zhongyang daxue*) applied to the county government to do so, and the temple's property was duly confiscated. The county government allocated 40 percent of the temple's wealth for education and 60 percent for temple maintenance. However, the Jiangsu Buddhist Federation (*Jiangsu Fojiao lianhehui*), which took legal ownership of the temple after the abbot's arrest, refused to accept this and demanded the return of the property, upon which now stood a school and agriculture research center. This caught the county government between the Convert Temples to Schools Movement and the *Regulations*, the former decreeing the utilization of temple property for education, and the latter prohibiting the occupation and confiscation of temple property. The local government appealed to higher levels of the government for a resolution to this case. However, the provincial government only gave an ambiguous response, which restrained hasty confiscations but did not touch on the issue of the ownership of temple property. Nevertheless, in restraining confiscations, the provincial government determined that the Convert Temples to Schools Movement enlarged the interests of the government organizations, such as the university and Ministry of Education, whereas the Smashing Superstition Movement was based on the Nationalist Party's guidance (*zhidao*). The Nationalist Party criticized this decision with the counter argument that, "The Smashing Superstition Movement is not related to temple land and property. The provincial declaration to stop the movement and protect religion is contrary to the party's policy principles" (Ohira 2002). The Nationalist Party criticized the government for its inadequate study of the party's spirit. Despite a subsequent amendment to the *Regulations*, the contradiction still remained over the legitimacy of smashing religions labeled as "premodern superstition" and the confiscation of temple property for the public good, while, as a modern state, guaranteeing freedom of religion.

With regard to modernity, the Convert Temples to Schools Movement generated three important consequences. First, Buddhists voluntarily started to make their own organizations. In 1912 the Chinese Buddhist Association (*Zhonghua Fojiao zonghui*) was established by the monk Jing'an, as the first nationwide organization in China for the purpose of protecting temple wealth and property. However, the state soon forced it to dissolve, leaving only local organizations, such as the aforementioned Jiangsu Buddhist Federation. During the Convert Temples to Schools Movement in the late 1920s, the first national meeting of the All-China Buddhist Representative Conference (*Quanguo Fojiao daibiao huiyi*) was convened to oppose the movement and reform Buddhism. The conference inaugurated a new national Chinese Buddhist Association that had the support of Chiang Kai-shek. The Convert Temples to Schools Movement compelled Buddhists to organize as a collective entity that could negotiate with other forces in society to oppose confiscation of temple property. This is the

moment when Buddhism entered a new venue of political institutionalization during the process of modern state formation; Buddhism dressed
up as "religion" that could cooperate and resist the power of the central
authorities who were making a modern state.

Second, the Convert Temples to Schools Movement created a shared
recognition among the new state, Buddhists, and the masses that the public interest was a significant criterion and discourse for evaluation and legitimacy. With regard to who and what constituted the "public interest,"
however, there were differences in the modern state system according to
which subject was making the claim. Most intellectuals viewed temples
as feudal remnants that harmed people's livelihood and urged that the labor of clergy and temple wealth be put to public use. The state declared
that religion could not passively orient itself to the public interest through
rituals and beliefs but had to commit temple resources to benefit society
through social welfare and philanthropic projects. Thereupon, Buddhists
began to use temple property to promote the public benefit and, furthermore, to undertake a reform of Buddhist teachings that emphasized the
benefit for people in this world rather than in the other world after death.
Putting aside differences in the interpretations of public benefit, the rise
of the concept of public interest underscores the significance of temple
property, facilities, and wealth as a public space. The modern state principle, "public, collective bodies that do not contribute to the public interest should not be recognized" became established as a norm with absolute
legitimacy, even within the reformist ideas to modernize Buddhism.

Third, the Convert Temples to Schools Movement furthered a new recognition of religion and religious sites as a key arena of contestation over
the institutionalization of property rights, ideology, and authority in the
modern state system. The aforementioned examples illuminate the struggles over power and ideology between the center and local state, government and party, and enlightened young elites and conservative landowners. At issue were the interpretation and handling of religious issues that
were created by juridical and administrative decision-making regarding
property rights that reached from the local to national levels. Regarding
religion, there were conflicts between, for example, the Ministry of
Education and the Nationalist Party. Moreover, the conflicts involved not
only a clash between premodern and modern ideologies but even disputes
within the ideology of modernity. A tension between the modern principles of individual freedom of belief and upholding the public interest
occurred in the context of the Convert Temples to Schools Movement
and the *Regulations for the Control of Monasteries and Temples*. The Convert
Temples to Schools Movement was a modernizing project that sought a
position for religion vis-à-vis the central state, which was in the process of

modern state formation. In this moment of crises, there arose a group of Buddhists who subjectively participated in state formation.

THE REFORM MOVEMENT OF BUDDHISM: MODERNIZATION FROM WITHIN

Although Buddhism was in decline in the late nineteenth century, a modern reform movement was growing among a small number of Buddhists. Two of the movement's representative leaders were the lay devotee Yang Wenhui and the monk Taixu, both of whom were deeply aware of the changes in the world outside China. Yang Wenhui had lived in Europe as a member of the Chinese legation in the late Qing dynasty. There he met many people working on Buddhism, including Max Müller at Oxford University and Nanjio Bunyiu (Nanjō Bunyū), the scholar-monk of the Honganji sect who assisted Müller in editing and translating Buddhist sutras. In Europe Yang witnessed how Christianity was positioned within the system of the modern state and also how Buddhism, which had almost disappeared in China, was a newly established academic discipline in such prominent universities as Oxford. Upon his return to China, he resigned his government post to concentrate on collecting Buddhist texts. He met Anagarika Dharmapala, a prominent reformer of Buddhism in Sri Lanka, when Dharmapala visited China after attending the 1893 World Parliament of Religions in Chicago. He was impressed by Dharmapala's efforts to return Buddhism to India, spread Buddhism throughout the world, and promote the modern reform of Buddhism. Yang edited and printed the scattered Buddhist sutras he was collecting, and established the Jetavana Hermitage (*Zhihuan jingshe*) for the innovative, modern Buddhist education of monks and devotees. His emphasis on Buddhist education, the modernization of Buddhism, and Buddhism's contribution to society influenced enlightened devotees who became thinkers, political activists, and reformers. One of the first students of the Jetavana Hermitage was the young monk Taixu. A disciple of the monk Jing'an, who advocated the reform of Buddhism along traditional lines, Taixu dedicated himself to the modernization of Buddhist teachings, pedagogy, and the monastic system in the troubled years when Buddhism was under attack by the Smashing Superstition and Convert Temples to Schools movements during the turbulent emergence of the modern state (Ohira 2000; Pittman 2001).

Taixu made three major contributions.[2] First, the he advocated a Buddhist reform movement that would be guided by "three revolutions": a "revolution of teaching and doctrines" (*jiaoli*), a "revolution of institutions" (*jiaozhi*), and a "revolution of religious property" (*jiaochan*). Regarding the doctrinal revolution, Taixu believed that Buddhism should be concerned not with problems after death but with those of the living world. Thus he advocated social salvation, studying the truth of human life, and contributing to the progress of human beings. Regarding the institutional revolution, Taixu worked to reform the monastic system and established monastery schools that were organized along modern lines. Instruction was to be in classrooms with standardized grading and a curriculum that included not only Buddhist texts but also secular subjects, some of which were also just newly emerging in the West, such as Western history, Asian history, the history of Theravada and other Buddhist traditions, literature, mathematics, psychology, and sociology. His essay "Reorganization of the Sangha System" (*Zhengli cengjia zhidu lun*), written between the two waves of the Convert Temples to Schools Movement, advocated the rationalization of temple management and the economic self-sufficiency of the clergy. By the revolution of religious property he meant that temple property should not be privately owned by abbots but rather collectively shared by all the monks residing in a temple. Through these three revolutions Taixu envisioned the emergence of a new type of Buddhism that could be active in the real world: he called it "human Buddhism" (*renjian Fojiao*), contrasted it with the Buddhism that was focused on rituals and meditation, and he devoted his life to it.

Second, Taixu was oriented toward a "world Buddhism." Influenced by Yang Wenhui, he had a strong vision of Buddhism as a universal religion that was equivalent to Western Christianity. He saw China as the center of Buddhism for promoting its worldwide spread.[3] However, his orientation to world Buddhism was limited, because his apparent cosmopolitanism was contradicted by strong Chinese nationalism and he confined his appeal to Chinese audiences domestically and overseas (Ashiwa 2002).

Third, Taixu cultivated a large web of personal connections, among Buddhists as well as in secular fields. In his youth he had steeped himself in new intellectual streams by reading Tolstoy, Marx, Bakunin, and Kotoku Shusui (a socialist anarchist), and had been involved in socialist activities and discussions with anarchists. His acquaintances included Christian missionaries, Japanese Buddhists, politicians, scholars, lay devotees in business communities in China and abroad, and revolutionaries. At a later stage of his life he developed and maintained collaborative ties with central political leaders including a close relationship with Chiang Kai-shek. Chiang dispatched him as special envoy to India and other South Asian countries during World War II to promote solidarity with Buddhist countries and gain allies against the Japanese and communists.

During the domestic political turbulence of modern state formation, the meaning and very existence of Buddhism was questioned and passed through the sieve of modernity. Some Buddhists worked for the survival of Buddhism by seeking to adapt it to the new conditions and ideologies of the modern state. Trained by intellectuals and enlightened lay devotees, they started to recognize the shape of religion that the modern state system requires. The modern state system itself, too, was taking shape through many projects, one of which was positioning religion within it. Buddhists' recognition of their situation was the starting point for a project to further the modern reform of the monastic system and Buddhist teachings by promoting a human Buddhism that sought to integrate Buddhist contributions to the lay world with Buddhist teachings.

However, the ongoing political turbulence from the Japanese invasion in the 1930s to the founding of the People's Republic of China hindered the reform of Buddhism. Taixu died in 1947, only two years before the creation of a communist country. After 1949 the Party issued new regulations that severely restricted all religions, including Buddhism, except when religion suited state purposes. The space for religion that had just started to emerge in China was cast aside.

I stress that in this early period of modern state formation, Buddhism had an opportunity to reform itself by modernizing and gain a legitimate space to expand inside the modern state. A space for Buddhism emerged through such multiple projects as the Convert Temples to Schools Movement and reform movements within Buddhism that comprised networks of practical activities among Buddhist clerics and devotees, expansion of social reform movements, the position of Buddhism in the laws and regulations enacted by the state, and the expansion of human Buddhism and imagination. The integration of this space with other newly emerging spaces of modernity, such as the economy, education, and diplomacy gradually took shape.

This space of religion, created by the critical condition of religion in China, was not limited to the domestic order. Clergy who were escaping the suppression and crackdown on Buddhism joined the flow of people and capital that had been moving abroad since the late nineteenth century and established temples in overseas Chinese communities. Many of these clerics were supporters of modern reform Buddhism influenced by Taixu yet their interpretations and practices were diverse. After a half century this space of Buddhism abroad based on overseas Chinese networks came to play a significant role in the movement for the revival of Buddhism in China from the 1980s (Ashiwa and Wank 2005).

Revival of Buddhism since the Open Economic Policy

The constitution of the newly established state of the People's Republic of China recognized freedom of religion, despite the Party's embrace of the atheistic ideology of Marxism-Leninism (Leung 1995). Article 99 of the 1954 constitution says, "Citizens of the People's Republic of China enjoy freedom of religious belief." This principle has remained unchanged in successive constitutions. However, during the Cultural Revolution (1966–76) the state eliminated the space of religion. Religion came under attack during the national campaign to eradicate the "four olds" (*sijiu*)—old habits, ideas, customs, and beliefs—that were considered cultural barriers to realizing socialism. Unlike the Smashing Superstition Movement, this time the destruction of temples was complete. There was no room for Buddhism to resist or negotiate with the state. The physical space of religion ceased to exist.

From the early 1980s and the open economic policy, religion started to revive. In the southeast coastal areas the revival has been especially remarkable (Birnbaum 2003; Duara 1994; Luo 1991; MacInnis 1989; Waldron 1998). Buddhism entered a new, vigorous stage. The 1982 constitution proclaims, "The state protects legitimate religious activities. No person is permitted to use religion to conduct counterrevolutionary activities or activities which disrupt social order, harm the people's health, or obstruct the educational system of the country." In this section I discuss the attributes of the new religious space that suddenly reopened due to the changes in state policy, and the continuity and discontinuity of the space of religion between the time of Yang Wenhui and now.

STATE CONTROL OF RELIGIOUS SPACE

The state established an ideological and administrative space of religion in the early 1980s for the purpose of promoting religious activities within limits. At first the state needed to legitimate the logic of this radical change of direction. The Party issued a document in 1982, *The Basic Viewpoint and Policy on the Religious Question during Our Country's Socialist Period*, that, consistent with Marxist historical materialism, maintains that China is developing toward communism and that religion will naturally disappear once communism is attained: until that time religion must be acknowledged and tolerated to prevent the emergence of splits among the people that would hinder the development of a powerful socialist state.

A classification system was introduced that distinguished religion from superstition, popular belief (*minjian xinyang*), and feudal superstition. It defined religion as having such attributes as a logical system of thought oriented to the afterlife that is contained in scriptures, specially trained clergy, and fixed sites for religious activities (temples, churches, etc.) managed by clergy. Based on this modern concept, the state recognized five religions—Buddhism, Catholicism, Islam, Protestantism, and Daoism. The basic condition that the state imposes on religion is "love the state, love religion" (*aiguo aijiao*), which means loyalty to the Party and government above all else: it should never be "love religion, love the state" (*aijiao aiguo*). Religious observances should be performed within designated "religious activity sites" and be financially self-sufficient. In addition, Party members are prohibited from believing in religion. Superstition consists of oracles and shamans, which have none of the characteristics of religion and are banned. In between religion and superstition there are many gods and deities that do not belong to the five recognized religions but are worshipped by people in locales: these are considered "popular belief" (*minjian xinyang*). They often have fixed sites, but lack a logical system of thought and scriptures, and usually a professional clergy. However, activities involving popular beliefs that are acknowledged as having "historical" and "cultural" value are permitted so long as they are defined as "cultural" rather than "religious."

The space of religion in the Chinese state proceeds through the dual Party/government structure: the Party provides ideological guidance while the government furnishes administrative guidance. Religious matters are handled by both the State Administration for Religious Affairs in the government and the United Front Work Department (*Tongyi zhanxian bu*) in the Party.[4] The State Administration for Religious Affairs has offices the center, provincial, and county/city levels to implement the state's religious policy. The United Front Work Department is the Party agency that handles relations with non–Party social groups and members and supervises the religious associations of the five recognized religions, whose members are prominent clergy, devotees, and scholars.

Religious associations were created by the state in the 1950s to be a bridge between the various religions and the state. The basic tasks of the Buddhist Association of China are to support the implementation of religious policy, heighten Buddhists' awareness of socialism and patriotism, represent the legal rights and interests of Buddhists, and organize "normal" religious activities. In practice the Buddhist Association of China functions to avoid direct confrontation between Buddhists and the state, and is the key channel for coordinating the coexistence of state and religion (Ashiwa and Wank 2006). During the first stage of the revival of Buddhism, local Buddhist associations worked with the local United Front Work Department offices to identify clerics who could represent Buddhists in dealings with the state and overseas Chinese, and coordinate efforts to reclaim temple land and rebuild temples that had been used by the state in the 1950s and 1960s as military posts, tourist sites, government offices, schools, factories, and community centers.

Buddhist temples have considerable autonomy when it comes to religious activities, such as rituals, teachings, and monastery regulations, although the space for religious activities is restricted to the temple site. While the clergy occasionally need advice from local Buddhist associations regarding formalities, they have the authority to control teaching and temple management. Rituals are the main performances at temples. Early morning and evening chanting is conducted daily, large rituals and festivals are performed according to the annual calendar, and numerous rituals for sending merit to ancestors are frequently conducted at the request of lay persons. Even the "relief of fiery mouths" (*fangyankou*)[5] ritual that, anthropologically speaking, contains many elements of exorcism and popular belief, is performed in temples without any questions being asked. The curriculum and management of Buddhist academies, which educate persons to be nuns and monks, are decided by the clergy. The curriculum for educating monks consists of Buddhist teachings as well as such secular subjects as mathematics, philosophy, foreign languages, sociology, psychology, and accounting. The daily routine of temples is controlled by the abbot or prior and based on the *baizhang qinggui*—the traditional regulations for monks drawn up by the monk Baizhang Huaihai (720–814) in the Tang dynasty.

Some temples have a large network overseas. The relationship of monks and donors abroad with specific temples in China has been reactivated since the late 1970s (Ashiwa and Wank 2005). There are now flows of donations to temples in China and exchanges of people. Young clerics in temples in China migrate to overseas temples as caretakers and many believers from abroad visit Buddhist sites in China as pilgrims and tourists. In this fashion the interaction between believers in China and with those abroad is expanding the space for networks of Buddhism (Ashiwa and Wank 2005).

Religion is performed to the maximum extent possible within the limits set by the state. However, there is considerable flexibility in those limits depending upon the needs and power relations for implementing and improvising useful interpretations of regulations. By this collaboration and contestation, both the state and religion are actually making the space of "religion."

REVIVAL OF NANPUTUO TEMPLE

The mutual constitution of the space of "religion" can be viewed in the revival of Nanputuo Temple (*Nanputuosi*) in Xiamen city, Fujian province. The following account of the temple's revival is based on research conducted between 1989 and 2002.[6] It illuminates how religious space is institutionalized and acquires attributes through cooperation and contestation between religions and the state, and how this process has furthered China's economic development policies (see also Wank, this volume).

Nanputuo Temple is one of the first major Buddhist temples in China to have recovered after the Cultural Revolution. The temple compound has been restored and today there many more buildings than before the Cultural Revolution, many worshippers and tourists visit every day, and rituals are performed frequently. The temple's vitality can be traced to Fujian province's long history of Buddhism: as early as the Tang dynasty, one thousand years ago, the province was called "the land of Buddhism." Xiamen was one of the first treaty ports opened to foreign trade following China's defeat in the Opium War (1840–42) and its entrepot economy flourished. Emigration from Fujian increased and today the province is the ancestral homeland of many overseas Chinese. For emigrants embarking from Xiamen it was customary to visit Nanputuo Temple to pray for one's ancestors, a safe passage, and good fortune overseas. During the Cultural Revolution the temple was sealed off and escaped major destruction, although a military observation post, factory, and school were established on the temple's land. By the late 1970s only a few monks remained, many fewer than the two hundred monks in the 1930s, at the temple's earlier peak. However, by the year 2002 there were about six hundred clergy in residence.

Several factors account for the temple's rapid revival. First, it has thick historical networks with overseas Chinese and clergy that have been reactivated since the late 1970s. Early in the twentieth century the temple's abbot, Huiquan, visited Chinese communities in Singapore, Hong Kong, and Malaya and established temples there (Ashiwa and Wank 2005). In 1980 a leading monk in Nanputuo Temple wrote letters to the clergy residing in these temples overseas. Clergy and devotees overseas, many with personal ties to Nanputuo Temple, were pleased to hear of the revival of Buddhism in the temple and donated funds for its restoration, as well as the rebuilding of other of Xiamen's temples.

Second, Nanputuo Temple was also a major site of Taixu's modern Buddhist reform movement in the early twentieth century. At that time Xiamen was a key locus of modernity in China with many foreign residents and numerous banks, universities, churches, and the marked presence of Western culture. The temple attracted patrons among new bourgeois youth who were interested in modernizing Buddhism and concerned about the spread of Christianity, which was especially visible in the treaty ports. By the 1920s the temple was a spearhead of modern Buddhist reform. Originally of the Linji sect, it became ecumenical (*shifang conglin*) in 1924 and instituted a system for the democratic election of the abbot by the temple's clergy. The following year the Minnan Buddhist Academy (*Minnan Foxueyuan*) with Taixu as its head was established for the modern education of clergy. Reform was facilitated by the lack of a strong historical tradition of Buddhism in Xiamen. By the 1920s the temple showed much vitality and was a center of modern reform.

The temple's historical link to Taixu has enhanced its legitimacy since the late 1970s. State religious policy has similarities to Taixu's human Buddhism with its emphasis on patriotism, societal contributions, and anti-superstition.[7] In his day, Taixu had sought to persuade the Nationalist Party elite that Buddhism could make a useful contribution to state building. Now the Nanputuo clergy invoke the image of Taixu to present the temple as having a thoroughly modern face to both the state and the people through such actions as reopening the Minnan Buddhist Academy, celebrating the hundredth anniversary of Taixu's birth, publishing special issues of the *Minnan Buddhist Academy Journal* on Taixu, and restoring the Taixu memorial stone and his meditation hut behind the temple. Clearly, Nanputuo Temple's historical links with Taixu have been effectively used by the temple to gain legitimacy to revive and expand in the context of the current state as a modern temple of "human Buddhism" for the public welfare. The modern reform Buddhism that Taixu promoted matches the need of the Party to make the state a modern one that acknowledges a space of religion.

The third reason for Nanputuo's rapid revival is that the temple started to reproduce its human capital early on. As soon as the restoration of the temple compound got underway in the early 1980s, the head monk revived the Minnan Buddhist Academy and the first class graduated in 1989. The same year Fujian province's first ordination ceremony since the Cultural Revolution was held at Guanghua Temple. Over five hundred monks and nuns were ordained, most of whom were elderly clerics from rural areas who had been forced to return to lay life during the Cultural Revolution and intended to return to their rural temples after ordination. But in the ordination ceremony, the fresh faces of the young nuns and monks from the Minnan Buddhist Academy stood out. Full of eagerness to be clerics, they had also studied such secular subjects as accounting and foreign languages and were assuming important roles in rituals and administration in Nanputuo Temple. This caused the power of actual management of the temple to shift from the Xiamen Religious Affairs Bureau to the young clerics. The rapidly growing number of young trained clerics also considerably raised the reputation of Nanputuo Temple by enabling it to conduct more rituals and send more young clergy to assume leading positions in overseas temples.

REDISPOSITION OF THE SYSTEM

The reemergence and growth of the market economy in China since 1979 has stimulated religion while the revival of Buddhism has also spurred the economy. This is especially apparent in Xiamen city, which was designated a Special Economic Zone by the central state in 1980 to attract business investment, particularly from Taiwan and overseas Chinese in Southeast Asia. The state also expected that the visible presence of religion would impress overseas Chinese with the openness of Chinese society, spurring them to invest. Expectations were especially high for Buddhism due to officials' assumption that many overseas Chinese businesspersons were Buddhists. Also, Nanputuo Temple itself was viewed by the Xiamen city government as an economic resource for the local tourist industry. However, the temple's success in addressing these various expectations soon strengthened it politically, which in turn led to conflicts between its clergy and the city government over the management of the temple. The ensuing confrontation redistributed power among the temple, city government, and other organizations.

At the start of the revival in the early 1980s when there were only a few monks in Xiamen, the monks and the Xiamen Religious Affairs Bureau worked closely with an elderly cleric named Miaozhan to revive the temple. The Xiamen Religious Affairs Bureau handled the temple's financial accounts and developed its commercial resources.[8] However, as the number of administratively capable clerics increased during the 1980s tensions emerged between the clergy and the Xiamen Religious Affairs Bureau. The flashpoint was a highly profitable vegetarian restaurant in the temple that was managed by a layperson who had been appointed as temple accountant through his close tie with the chief of the Xiamen Religious Affairs Bureau. This lay manager had hired several hundred kin and friends of bureau officials to work in the restaurant, and distributed profits among them as bonuses while giving virtually nothing to the monks. In 1989 Miaozhan asserted the clergy's authority over the restaurant by appointing a recent graduate of the Minnan Buddhist Academy to manage the temple's commercial activities. But the Xiamen Religious Affairs Bureau, worried about losing control of the restaurant's rich income and employment, refused to acknowledge the appointment of this monk. In 1990, Miaozhan appealed to the Buddhist Association of China in Beijing. The association dispatched an investigative team to Xiamen to gather testimony for consideration back in Beijing by leading members of the Party and government. These officials affirmed the temple's ownership of the restaurant but recommended that it be leased to the lay manager, so as to avoid, in accordance with Buddhist precepts, the direct involvement of the clergy. This judgment supported the temple in principle while leaving the practical situation relatively unchanged. However, the appeal to the central authorities to resolve a local problem unexpectedly created a new direct link between the temple and the center that enhanced the latter's local control.

The implications of this new link became apparent when Miaozhan died in 1994. The issue of his successor as abbot created further conflict between the clergy and the officials of the Xiamen Religious Affairs Bureau, frightening other monks at Nanputuo Temple who were possible successors. The Buddhist Association of China in Beijing used this as an opening to nominate its own candidate, who had no connections to Xiamen or Nanputuo Temple. Both the Xiamen Religious Affairs Bureau and Nanputuo Temple had no choice but to accept this candidate, despite the fact that the local election of the abbot was a major symbol of the temple's autonomy stemming from Taixu's time. This new abbot was in his forties and a member of the first graduating class of the China Buddhist Academy in Beijing since the Cultural Revolution as well as vice chair of the Buddhist Association of China. As a new-generation cleric he had an excellent grasp of temple management and the position of religion in China's socialist state; in fact, his graduating master's thesis was said to be on temple management. The replacement of the elderly Miaozhan, who had devoted much of his later life to reestablishing the vigor of Nanputuo Temple and rekindling ties with overseas Chinese, by the younger monk, Shenghui, who had a modern education in the center and fully accepted the position of religion in the communist state, symbolized the temple's realignment from a locally embedded temple to one closer to the central authorities. In this way, the involvement of the center in local politics reallocated local power relations and further implanted central control.

Nanputuo has developed itself subjectively, by utilizing its capital accumulated from the late nineteenth century, including its history as an enlightened temple and an important link in overseas networks, to coordinate interpretations of both the state and the temple, and to endeavor to duplicate the religious space defined by the state in the space of Buddhism, which the temple wants to expand. However, as a result Nanputuo is now being transformed into a temple that is closer to the state ideal of a model temple, and moving away from the local context and believers.

The Question of Belief and Religion

The policy of religious freedom in contemporary China is a part of the continuing process of state building and subjective modernization that stretches back to the beginning of the twentieth century. It is a new stage in the state's approach to religion that has been decided by the Party to complement its rejuvenation within the framework of the open economic policy. In this continuing project of modernity, which includes modern state building, the space of religion and its demarcation have been evolving, ever changing, and shifting according to the context of the times.

THE CONTINUING SPACE OF MODERNITY

The revival in Taixu and Yang Wenhui's time and the revival occurring since 1980 show both continuities and discontinuities. The most evident difference is that there now exists a stronger central state structure. The Party-state clearly intends to acknowledge religion as a necessary condition of a secular, modern state such as the People's Republic of China, and to include it in the state structure. The Chinese state has a clear and pragmatic purpose for linking the vital power of religion that has reemerged due to the open religious policy: to stimulate the economy. It expects that domestic and international tourism to temples will enrich local service industries and that overseas Chinese devotees will bring business opportunities. These contexts of reorienting the modern centralized state and the open economy through waves of globalization did not exist during the time of Taixu and Yang Wenhui.

However, the formation of the space of religion that has emerged since the early 1980s reveals certain continuities and similarities with the space of religion that began to take shape at the end of the nineteenth century. First, the late nineteenth century marked the beginning of a period of turmoil that stimulated flows of people abroad, including Buddhist clerics and devotees who had accumulated status and wealth overseas. These transnational flows went hand in hand with the expansion of the space of religion to overseas Chinese communities. This history constitutes capital for contemporary Buddhism. It has been reactivated through networks of people and money that have been flowing back to China (Ashiwa and Wank 2005). As noted above, this link between Buddhism and overseas Chinese is a major reason the state sees economic potential in Buddhism. A second continuity is that the institutionalizing of religion that involved the Chinese Buddhist Association in the 1920s and 1930s through its challenges to and negotiations with the state is proceeding now through the Buddhist Association of China. Both associations are significant linkages between the state and Buddhism. However, in the contemporary revival the Party and Buddhists are careful to avoid the kinds of earlier confrontations between Buddhism and the state by paying great attention to the formulation, interpretation, and implementation of laws regarding religion. Third, a century after Taixu's birth, his "human Buddhism" has been revived and is again being held up by both the Party and Buddhist clergy as an ideal modern Buddhism that contributes to the formation of a modern society and state (ruled by the Party). One of the intentions of the Party in reactivating the space of Buddhism is to provide support for the state's foreign diplomacy. This aim proceeds through cultural and academic exchanges with other Buddhist states, such as Japan and Myanmar, and with academic and religious institutions abroad. In this phase of efforts by the state and religion to rebuild the space which had once been devastated, the emphasis of contemporary Buddhism on continuity with the modern Buddhist reform advocated by Taixu is a collaboratively enacted heritage of intentional modernity agreed on by the state on the one hand, and Buddhist clergy and devotees on the other.

In addition, there are new dynamics in the contemporary revival. The reform of Buddhism toward a "religion under state guidance" is proceeding not by the exercise of the state's violent power as before, but rather by gradual transformations guided by the state and the Buddhist Association of China, as well as partly from within Buddhism. A centralized educational system based on the China Buddhist Academy in Beijing was established to train clerics who could fit the needs of the modern period. The academy is subject to strong political guidance by the Party and collaborates closely with it. The academy produces elite young clerics who are motivated to promote Buddhism in China's communist society. In the 1990s most of the elderly leaders of the religion who had survived the Cultural Revolution and contributed greatly to the revival of Buddhism in the 1980s were passing from the scene. These clergy had survived tumultuous times and contributed to the revival of Buddhism despite their old age. As living links with the past, they had enabled Buddhists to activate networks of overseas Chinese and to wield techniques for confronting the state that they had acquired through their earlier experiences. Among them was the aforementioned Miaozhan, leader of Nanputuo Temple's revival, who was eighty years old when he became abbot in 1990. The great respect and support he received from local believers and overseas Chinese enabled his temple to rapidly recover and expand. It also enabled him to appeal to the central authorities to help solve the temple's problems with the local government. However, his successor, Shenghui, represents a generation, in their twenties to forties, that was mostly educated in the aforementioned China Buddhist Academy and understands completely the position of "normal" religion in the state system and ideology. They are now becoming young abbots in local major temples and heads of Buddhist academies, and reproducing "modern" style Buddhism in China.

In contrast to the dynamics in the major temples described above, the efforts of lesser temples to gradually develop themselves by cultivating local as well as overseas devotees and believers through their own unique approaches cannot be overlooked. Xiamen's lesser temples pursue various strategies; some play on the concern of the local government to promote tourism and local leisure spots by establishing vegetarian restaurants with a panoramic views, photo booths, and gift shops. Others are developing new sources of income by building large halls to perform masses for souls in hell or holding services to send merit to the spirits of the ancestors. One temple for lay-nuns (*zhaigu*) has become a weekend community center for female devotees who are factory workers. In Xiamen most of the secondary temples are maintained by clergy who come from southern Fujian province. They can communicate with the believers in the local Minnan dialect, which is highly effective in creating intimate relationships among clergy and local believers. At these other temples, the local believers can enjoy group activities such as pilgrimages and festivals organized together with the clerics, something that they cannot do at Nanputuo temple because most of the clergy are from rural areas in north and central China and speak Mandarin with a heavy accent that is difficult for local believers to understand. These lesser temples are under the control of the local Religious Affairs and Buddhist Association offices, and are inspected annually. The everyday lives of people are more closely woven into the "popular Buddhism" practiced in these lesser temples, such as funerals conducted with the help of the devotee associations, rituals for sending merit for ancestors, and praying for success in school exams and business deals. Even during the political turbulence of the first decades of the People's Republic of China this popular Buddhism that was tightly woven into the people's everyday life and customs continued to exist on a small scale and in underground activities, such as chanting accompanied by offerings of food and flowers (Welch 1968, 1972).

Problems with Falungong in 1999 caused the government to launch a "movement to suppress heterodoxy." Buddhist clergy, even in such major temples as Nanputuo, were very fearful that this movement would trigger the suppression of Buddhism because the label of heterodoxy that the state applied to Falungong was partly based on the fact that its teachings and practices were an amalgamation of Buddhist idioms and elements. Therefore, after the state campaign against Falungong began, Nanputuo promptly decided to issue booklets and put up wall posters in the temple claiming that Buddhism is not Falungong but rather a pure and legitimate religion recognized by the state that is firmly committed to the slogan "love the state, love religion." Small temples followed suit and started to pay more attention to keeping good relations with the local Religious Affairs and Buddhist Association offices in order to reinforce their status as practicing "pure" Buddhism.

THE PLACE OF BELIEF

According to Ann Anagnost (1987), in its drive for modernity the Chinese state continues to deploy the classifications of religion and superstition in order to legitimate the leading role of the Party. This echoes the movement initiated in the 1930s by the Nationalist Party to

Communism, Science, religion, Superstition

stamp out superstition. However, the contemporary situation under the Party is different. The Party is far less concerned with the "modernity/nonmodernity" of religion than was the state in the 1930s. In addition the Party's concern with "religion/superstition" merely follows the framework of the official definition and law regarding religion. With regard to Falungong, the Party's greatest fear is its power to mobilize and organize large numbers of people through its widespread and deep roots among the masses. The object of this fear is people's "belief," which is the source of Falungong's power and is stronger than the Party's ideology. This is evident in Falungong's power to drive its adherents to challenge the Party. When Falungong was still small and local and just starting to grow, its application to the Buddhist Association of China for official recognition as a Buddhist organization was rejected (Utiraruto, this volume). Yet the fact that Falungong could keep expanding its power to threaten state power despite the rejection as a legitimate religion shows that there is a space that "religion" as a system of legitimate institutions and organizations cannot control. This is the space of belief.

Although this chapter has not discussed the issue of belief, it is precisely belief that differentiates religion from all other projects of modernity that construct the state in terms of institutionalization and organization. In general, in the theory of modernity, belief is removed from the public space and sealed in an individual private space. In its aim to construct a modern state, the Chinese state is attempting to achieve precisely this sealing off of belief. The issue that the Chinese state is most concerned about and seeks to avoid is confrontation with "belief" because the state knows full well that "belief" can be a huge source of energy that can shake the state to its foundations as, for example, the Taiping Rebellion demonstrated. Therefore, any arguments about modernity and religion that focus only on institutions and state formation and avoid discussing belief are, perforce, deficient.

In the process of striving to be modern, both in the West and in the non-West, a crucial question is whether the state can successfully enclose belief within private space while expanding the institutionalization of the space of religion. At the same time, continuing waves of religious movements, such as religious fundamentalism, have emerged in modern contexts. In fact, religious fundamentalism is not a product of nonmodernity; religious fundamentalism and such modernized religions as reformed Buddhism, are both products of modernity. Valentine (2002) argues that both religious fundamentalism and modernized religion lead people to be cognizant of oneself and the world, and to consciously choose one "religion" and to become a "believer" of it with rational understanding and practice. He analytically distinguishes two types of consciousness of religion—epistemological and ontological. Epistemological religion is the aforementioned creation of modernity that compels people to rationally and cognitively choose one religion rather than another. Ontological religion is the belief of "being" as a part of the culture and customs into which a person is born: people are "in" the religion by living their everyday lives. Valentine argues that the introduction of epistemological religion into ontological religion in Asia during the colonial period through numerous projects of modernity caused, by the late nineteenth century, a reaction among the "awakened" believers of the non-Christian traditions that took shape in the reform movements of Buddhism and Hinduism. Since then, ontological belief has diminished and has been left out of the public scene. It has been either forgotten or has only existed in the everyday customs of popular religions, such as the discursive space of "popular Buddhism," "superstition," and "culture and customs."

It is very illuminating to see how the Chinese state institutionally deals with beliefs that do not fit its definition of religion. Good examples are the Mazu belief, which has many enthusiastic adherents in southern China, Taiwan, and overseas, and the Three-in-One (*Sanyijiao*), which has a long history in Fujian province (Dean 1998). As Chau (this volume) shows, negotiations among the local Religious Affairs Bureau offices and other state agencies and believers' groups enable these beliefs to legitimate their activities within state discursive institutions by positioning them as "popular belief" and "local customs" (*difang chuantong*), or in other words, as "cultural" phenomena that have tourist and historical value. In this formulation, the domestic and foreign pilgrims and participants who visit the sites revered by these beliefs are considered tourists contributing to the local economy or persons expressing patriotism.[9]

However, the populace continues to have an ontological consciousness of being Buddhist and they are familiar with Buddhism as social and domestic customs of everyday life (which institutionalizes popular belief as "culture"). This leads to confrontations between people's popular beliefs and the Buddhism practiced in temples. A telling example is the attempt to prevent people from burning paper money in Nanputuo Temple on Guanyin's Birthday because the clergy and state officials consider it a "superstition." The temple has banned burning paper money in the main compound, requiring it be burned outside the temple. Such confrontations of "belief" with modern "religion" may generate extreme mass behavior without any flexibility to negotiate. It could cause people to question and challenge the Party's inviolable principle of "love the state, love religion." This questioning could then confront people with the choice of choosing between "love religion" and "love the state," and place the former over the latter. To avoid a situation where this choice comes to be seen as absolutely inevitable, religions and the state will have to make on-going efforts. While not yet visibly expressed, the question of the strength or pureness of belief will eventually emerge.

Conclusion

The creation of modernity is represented in the formation of the space of the modern state and the space of religion. In other words, the formation of each space mutually constrains and promotes the other through multiple projects of modernity. In this process, both religion and the state seek to define themselves. This process is constituted by an inclusion that defines oneself, an exclusion that defines the other, and occasionally the creation of new third parties. These projects are never coherent, the spaces are not stable, and boundaries are being continuously created and re-created by both subjects to demarcate the other. This mutual characterization of space is an ongoing process of conflict, negotiation, collaboration, accommodation, resistance, and compromise. Because religion, more than other spaces, has attributes of unstable fluidity due to its specific basis of belief, thought, and teachings, the space of religion requires multiple interpretations as well as multiple legitimacies depending on contexts and circumstances. The two periods discussed in this chapter, from the end of the Qing dynasty until 1949, and from the late 1970s to today, are remarkable for the great efforts to legitimately include religion within the state system, both as organizations as well as ideologies of practice. In these moments both the state and religion have aggressively moved to create their systems and position themselves vis-à-vis the other through the establishment of "religion" as concepts, institutions, teachings, and organizations.

The apparatus of the modern state takes shape and is forming by processes of selection and evaluation that institutionalize religion. Through projects of modernity, religions have adjusted their shape many times and in various ways. Religions both demand and necessitate the rearrangement of the state apparatus. In China, where modernization was promoted as the powerful master narrative for building the state, the state and religion are creating modernity by relating themselves to the creation of the space of religion.

Notes

1. The importance of lay devotees in keeping Buddhism alive is reflected in the term "lay devotee Buddhism" (*jushi Fojiao*) that is often used to describe the Buddhism of this period.

2. The study of Taixu's contribution has grown over the past decade (see Pittman 2001).

3. Complex domestic politics, fierce criticism from Buddhist traditionalists, and conflicts among Buddhist reformers in China further stoked Taixu's eagerness to spread Buddhism abroad.

4. The state bureaucracy of religious management was called the Religious Affairs Office from 1951 to 1954 and the Bureau of Religious Affairs from 1954 until 1998. The current name—State Administration for Religious Affairs—was adopted in 1998. For ease of reference this chapter uses the current name to refer to post-1949 bureaucracy at the national level.

5. Hungry ghosts have very small throats and cannot drink water. Whenever they open their mouths fire comes out and burns the food in front of them so they are always hungry. Only magic can open up their throats, extinguish the flames, and relieve their suffering.

6. An account of the fieldwork can be found in Wank (this volume).

7. On the historical links between Taixu and the state in the first years of the People's Republic, see Welch (1972).

8. The official name of the bureau is the Bureau of Ethnic and Religious Affairs of Xiamen (*Xiamen shi minzu yu zongjiao shiwu ju*). In this chapter the name is shortened to Xiamen Religious Affairs Bureau. For a discussion of the use of the same bureau to manage ethnic and religious affairs see Ashiwa and Wank (2006: 344n12).

9. Ontological belief can be seen in the chapter by Utiraruto (this volume). Falungong contains elements of fundamentalism from Buddhism and is a production of modernity but is also linked to *qigong*, which is constituted by many folk beliefs that are outside the state's medical establishment but widely held by the common people.

References

Anagnost, Ann. 1987. "Politics and Magic in Contemporary China." *Modern China* 13, 1: 40–61.

Asad, Talal. 1993. "The Construction of Religion as an Anthropological Category." In *Genealogies of Religion: Discipline and Reasons of Power in Christianity and Islam*, pp. 27–54. Baltimore: Johns Hopkins University Press.

———. 2003. *Formations of the Secular: Christianity, Islam, Modernity*. Stanford, CA: Stanford University Press.

Ashiwa Yoshiko. 2000. "Chūgoku ni okeru Bukkyō Bukkō no dōtai: kokka shakai to toranzunashonarizumu" (The dynamics of the Buddhism Revival Movement in southern China: state, society and transnationalism). In *Kokka-shakai tono kyōsei kankei: gendai Chūgoku no shakai kōzō no henyō* (The symbiotic relationship of state and society: transformation of social structure in contemporary China), edited by Hishida Masaharu et al. Tokyo: Tōkyō daigauku shuppankai.

———. 2002. "Shūkyō no seiritsu to minzoku: Suriranka to Chūgoku no kindai Bukkyōkaikakusha nimiru kosumoporitanizumu no yukue" (The formation of religion and nation: on cosmopolitanism seen in modern reformists of Buddhism in Sri Lanka and China). In *Minzoku no undō to shidōshatachi* (Ethno-movements and their leaders), edited by Etsuko Kuroda. Tokyo: Yamakawa shuppansha.

Ashiwa, Yoshiko, and David L. Wank. 2005. "The Globalization of Chinese Buddhism: Clergy and Devotee Networks in the Twentieth Century." *International
Journal of Asian Studies* 2, 2: 217–37.

————. 2006. "State, Association, and Religion in Southeast China: The Politics of a
Reviving Buddhist Temple." *Journal of Asian Studies* 65, 2: 337–59.

Birnbaum, Raoul. 2003. "Buddhist China at the Century's Turn." *China Quarterly*
174 (June): 428–50.

Chinese Communist Party Central Committee (Zhonggong zhongyang). 1987
(1982). "Guanyu woguo shehuizhuyi shiqi zongjiao wentide jiben guandian
he jiben zhengce" (Regarding the basic viewpoint and policy on the religious
question during our country's socialist period). In *Shiyijie sanzhong quanhui yilai
zhongyao wenxian xuandu* (Collection of important documents since the third
plenum of the Eleventh Party Congress), vol. 1. Beijing: Renmin chubanshe.

Chou Wei. 1927. "Geming de Jiangsu nongmin" (Revolutionary farmers of Jiangsu).
Buersaiweike 1 (October).

Dean, Kenneth. 1995. *Taoist Ritual and Popular Cults of Southeast China*. Princeton,
NJ: Princeton University Press.

————. 1998. *Lord of the Three in One: The Spread of a Cult in Southeast China*.
Princeton, NJ: Princeton University Press.

Duara, Prasenjit. 1995. "Campaigns against Religion and the Return of the Repressed." In *Rescuing History from the Nation: Questioning Narratives of Modern
China*, pp. 85–113. Chicago: University of Chicago Press.

Information Office of the State Council of the People's Republic of China. 1997.
"White Paper on Freedom of Religious Belief in China." www.china.org.cn/
e-white/Freedom/f-1.htm (last accessed 10-10-05).

Lefebvre, Henri. 1991. *The Production of Space*, translated by Donald Nicholson-
Smith. Oxford: Basil Blackwell.

Leung, Beatrice. 1995. "Religious Freedom and the Constitution in the People's
Republic of China: Interpretation and Implementation." *DISKUS* 3, 1: 1–18.

Luo, Zhufeng. 1991. *Religion under Socialism in China*. Armonk, NY: M. E. Sharpe.

MacInnis, Donald E. 1989. *Religion in China Today: Policy and Practice*. Maryknoll, NY:
Orbis.

Madsen, Richard. 1998. *China's Catholics: Tragedy and Hope in an Emerging Civil Society*. Berkeley: University of California Press.

Mitani Takashi. 1978. "Nankinseifu to meishindaha undō, 1928–1929" (The Nanjing
government and the Smashing Superstition Movement, 1928–1929). *Rekishigaku
kenkyū* (Journal of history) 455: 1–14.

Ohira Kōji. 2000. "Chūgoku Bukkyō no kindaika wo saguru: Taikyo no shoki
Bukkyō kaika undō" (A study of the modernization of Chinese Buddhism: the
early period of Taixu's Chinese Buddhism reform movement). *Ritsumeikan tōyō
shigaku* (Ritsumeikan journal of oriental studies) 23.

————. 2002. "Nankin kokuminseifu seirituki no byōsankogaku undō to
Bukkyōkai" (The Convert Temples to Schools Movement and Buddhist society during the formative period of the Nanjing government: on utilizing the
property of temples and monks). *Ritsumeikan gengo bunka kenkyū* (Ritsumeikan
journal of language and cultural studies) 13, 4: 21–38.

Overmyer, Daniel. 2003. *Religion in China Today*. Cambridge, UK: Cambridge University Press.

Pittman, Don A. 2001. *Toward a Modern Chinese Buddhism: Taixu's Reforms*. Honolulu: University of Hawai'i Press.

Sakamoto Hiroko. 1998. "Yō Bunkai" (Yang Wenhui). In *Kindai Chūgoku no shisakushatachi* (Modern Chinese thinkers), edited by Satō Shinichi. Tokyo: Taishukan shoten.

Sueki Fumihiko, and Cao Zhangqi. 1996. *Gendai Chūgoku no Bukkyō* (Buddhism in contemporary China). Tokyo: Hirakawa shuppansha.

Valentine, Daniel. 2002. "The Arrogation of Being by the Blind-Spot of Religion." In *Discrimination and Toleration*, edited by K. Hastrup and G. Ulrich, pp. 31–53. London: Kluwer International.

Waldron, Andrew. 1998. "Religious Revivals in Communist China." *Orbis* 42, 2 (Spring): 325–34.

Wank, David L. 2000. "Bukkyōfukkō no seijigaku: kyōgō suru kikō to seitōsei" (The politics of the revival movement of Buddhism: competing institutions and legitimacy). In *Kokka-shakai tono kyōsei kankei: gendai Chūgoku no shakai koōzō no henyō* (The symbiotic relationship of state and society: the transformation of social structure in contemporary China), edited by Hishida Masaharu et al., pp. 275–304. Tokyo: Tōkyō daigaku shuppankai.

Welch, Holmes. 1967. *The Practice of Chinese Buddhism, 1900–1950*. Cambridge, MA: Harvard University Press.

———. 1968. *The Buddhist Revival in China*. Cambridge, MA: Harvard University Press.

———. 1972. *Buddhism under Mao*. Cambridge, MA: Harvard University Press.

Wenweipo (online edition). 2007. "300 Million Citizens' Belief in Religion, Popular Beliefs Are Flourishing." March 3. http://paper.wenweipo.com/2007/03/03/NS0703030001.htm (last accessed 11-15-07).

Wu, Jiao. 2007. "Religious Believers Thrice the Estimate." *China Daily*, February 7 (online edition). www.chinadaily.com.cn/china/2007-02/07/content_802994.htm (last accessed 11-15-07).

CHAPTER 4

The Catholic Pilgrimage to Sheshan

RICHARD MADSEN AND LIZHU FAN

ON THE TOP OF SHESHAN, a hill on the outskirts of Shanghai, sits a shrine to the Virgin Mary that is one of the major pilgrimage destinations for Chinese Catholics. The shrine has been a major focus of Catholic devotion in the Shanghai area since it was established by French Jesuit missionaries in the nineteenth century. With the passage of time, it has gained national and international significance. Currently, during the month of May (which in the Catholic Church is dedicated to the Virgin Mary), at least 60,000 Catholics visit the shrine, and a steady stream of pilgrims continues throughout the rest of the year. Although the majority of these visitors are from the Shanghai area, there are pilgrims from all parts of China and from overseas Chinese communities around the world. Since the shrine's establishment, pilgrims have reported miracles and apparitions of the Virgin Mary.

Mary is seen as an agent with great power and authority. She uses her power to heal believers and to protect Catholics from harm. She uses her authority to guide Catholics on morally correct paths. Catholics believe that this power and authority are manifested in a special way in the shrine. It is understandable that ambitious people would want to get control of Mary's power and wrap themselves in the mantle of her authority. One way to do so is to control access to the sacred power incarnated in the shrine. Since the shrine was established, a variety of political leaders have tried to do this, including French colonialists, Vatican diplomats, Nationalist Party (Guomindang) officials, and Communist cadres. All of them had partial success, yet none has ever been able to monopolize the sacred power and authority that believers attribute to Mary, and none has been able to maintain even their partial hegemony for an extended time. In this chapter we will show how various leaders tried to gain control over the sacred power of the Sheshan shrine and why the shrine has eluded control.

The Pilgrimage Described

First, however, let us give a fuller account of the origin of the pilgrimage and a fuller description of how it is carried out today. Located about an hour's ride outside the center of Shanghai, Sheshan is only about three hundred feet high, but it is the highest place near Shanghai. It is named after a Master She, who may have been a Daoist hermit there. Since the Song dynasty, it has been a pilgrimage site. Until the late nineteenth century there were many Buddhist and Daoist temples on the hill. As the highest spot in the region it was a natural place to construct temples that would connect heaven and earth. Pilgrims came to partake of the benefits of this connection, and undoubtedly to enjoy the beautiful bamboo groves and scenic views. In 1720, the Kangxi emperor visited the place and renamed it "Blue Bamboo Shoots Mountain" (*Sheshan sheji* 1931; Charbonnier 1993: 334).

Taking advantage of the new freedoms made possible by the unequal treaty of Tianjin, the Jesuits started buying land on the mountain in 1863. The priests steadily replaced the Buddhist and Daoist temples with Catholic shrines. Their main shrine consisted of a painting of Mary housed in a pavilion on the mountaintop. The picture depicts the Virgin Mary wearing a crown and holding her infant Son, who also wears a crown. The picture has been associated with miraculous protection of the Shanghai Catholic community from harm as well as with miraculous healing of individual Catholics. In 1935, the original church and pavilion were replaced with a large baroque-style church, which can seat about three thousand. This church, and the sacred picture it contains, are the main goal of the Sheshan pilgrimage.

The main pilgrimage, in May, reaches its culmination on May 24, the feast day of Our Lady Help of Christians. There is a smaller wave of pilgrims in October (the month of the Holy Rosary). Pilgrims come from as far as Inner Mongolia and Xinjiang—and also from abroad—Hong Kong, Taiwan, the Philippines, and even from Europe and North America. Most domestic Chinese pilgrims from outside of the Shanghai area travel to Sheshan on buses chartered by their local churches. Most of them sleep and eat in their buses because they cannot afford hotels in Shanghai. They take no more than a day for the devotions on the mountain, and then return home. (It takes about three days each way for the bus trip from Inner Mongolia.)

To give a sense of what the pilgrimage today looks and feels like, we present in the following section a summary of field research by a research team directed by Fan Lizhu, who did participant observation research on the pilgrimage in May 2004.

Together with Fan Lizhu, the five researchers (undergraduate and graduate students in the sociology of religion at Fudan University) reserved places on a bus caravan sponsored by the Cathedral of Saint Ignatius in Xujiahui in Shanghai. Their first challenge was getting the tickets. Each day the church sold tickets for one bus on the Saturday on which the research team wanted to attend the pilgrimage. The office that sold the tickets (for a nominal price of seven yuan) opened at 6:30 AM and was sold out within half an hour. In the end, there were twelve buses chartered for that day. Most of the rest of the 120 churches in the Shanghai would have chartered their own bus tours.

The buses left from St. Ignatius Cathedral at 7:30 AM There were no organized activities on the bus, just a lot of loud chatter. Most people attended in family groups—grandparents, parents, children—and family members mostly sat together and talked with one another. Nonetheless, some of them told the interviewers that this trip was a good opportunity to communicate with a wider circle of friends.

A direct bus trip from the Xujiahui district (in the heart of metropolitan Shanghai) to Sheshan would take about an hour. But halfway to the destination, the bus stopped at a cemetery that contains the remains of most Shanghai Catholics. The pilgrims got out and spent a half hour visiting the urns containing the ashes of their family members and praying in the church connected with the cemetery. Continuing on to Sheshan, the bus proceeded up a narrow road up the mountain and stopped at a parking lot near the peak. The pilgrims got out and walked several hundred feet to the church at the top. The church is built out of red brick and "skillfully unites the Romanesque and Gothic styles."

The walk from the parking lot to the church requires climbing up a flight of brick stairs. Some of the pilgrims were too old or feeble to traverse the stairs—some were indeed in wheelchairs—but they were carried up by their family members. It seemed, in fact, that the pilgrimage was most meaningful for the oldest people. As one researcher put it, "From the looks on their faces you can see that this is very significant. For some who are very sick, this may be their last time to come here."

Families sat together (not as in other churches, or as in reports on the Sheshan pilgrimage written in the 1930s, men on one side and women on the other side of the aisle). The church was filled to capacity. Throughout the Mass, one group of people, mostly elderly, knelt in front of a side chapel, in which there is a picture of Mary and her Child, and they seemingly paid no attention to the priest who was saying Mass at the main altar.

In his sermon, the priest noted that most in the congregation were relatively old and female. (As estimated by the research team, on that occasion, about 85 percent seemed to be over forty years old and 70 percent were female.) The priest encouraged the pilgrims to bring more young people along in the future. (Church attendance has been falling off in Shanghai, especially among the younger generation, who seem more interested in consumerism than religion [Madsen 1998: 114–15].) Every person, the priest told them, is the Blessed Mother's Child. He asked them to pray that Mary protect each family and help the "parents to be benevolent and the children to be filial" (*fucizixiao*).

After the Mass, some of the people walked down a path leading to a smaller church on the midlevel of the mountain. This church was built in 1894 and to this day it functions as the main parish church for the Sheshan area. Inscribed around the main door are the words: "Rest a while by the small chapel halfway up the hill and perform your filial homage. The sanctuary is on the mountaintop. Climb a few steps more and implore the mercies of the Mother of God." On a large chalkboard in front of the church are written histories of the pilgrimage and explanations of its significance. This is meant to give instruction to the curious onlookers who also travel to the pilgrimage site.

Next to this midlevel church is a plaza flanked by three large pavilions, about twenty feet high, containing statues of Mary, St. Joseph, and the Sacred Heart of Jesus. These pavilions are shaped like miniature Romanesque churches, with round cupolas on top of sturdy pillars. Bouquets of flowers surround each statue and candles surround each pavilion, covering the ground with wax. All of these structures date from the early years of the twentieth century. In a distinctive chanting style, worshippers recite the rosary over and over again at this place. The people leaving the church have to stand behind a group of worshippers occupying a space just in front of these statues. These are members of the "underground church," who accept the authority of Bishop Fan Zhongliang, a cleric who is unrecognized by the Shanghai government, instead of the officially approved Bishop Jin Luxin. The underground Catholics refuse to enter the midlevel church, because this church is under the (for them) illegitimate authority of Bishop Jin. They do enter the basilica on top of the mountain, to pray in front of the Marian picture enshrined therein. Even though the basilica is under the control of the illegitimate authorities of the diocese, the holy picture embodying the Marian presence transcends that control. The underground Catholics do not, however, attend

Mass in the Marian basilica, because they do not accept the legitimacy of the priests celebrating the Mass. They instead express their Marian devotion by praying the rosary, over and over again, in front of the "Three Holy Statues." According to a member of the Shanghai Public Security Bureau with responsibility for maintaining order at the shrine, the percentage of underground Catholics attending the pilgrimage is relatively small—less than 20 percent of the total.

Some of the people who had just left the Mass, along with some of the underground Catholics, also carried out the devotion of the Stations of the Cross. On the path leading from the Three Holy Statues toward the Marian basilica, there are fourteen carved images of the sufferings endured by Jesus on the way to Calvary, each encased in a five-foot-high cement structure. The faithful knelt to pray in front of each of the fourteen stations.

After completing their devotions, people gathered in family groups to eat together, mostly with homemade lunches they had brought with them on the bus. Then they walked around enjoying the beautiful scenery (the hill is still covered with bamboo forests and most of it is actually a public park) until it was time to board the return buses at 4:00 PM. Before getting on the bus, some also stopped at one of the stalls that sell rosaries, statues and pictures of Mary, prayer books, candles, and other devotional objects.

The pilgrimage today thus brings together a very wide range of China's Catholics. An administrator of the Shanghai Catholic diocese remarked with a certain degree of critical disapproval about the range of appeal of the pilgrimage: "This Marian devotion is very popular in all sectors of society—somewhat too much, because the doctrine of the Church emphases Jesus more than Mary. In Shanghai during May, practically everyone goes at least once. They come from all walks of life. Even very lax Catholics, who hardly ever go to church, go on the pilgrimage. It's a custom." When asked whether intellectuals did not take the pilgrimage as seriously as uneducated people, he replied, "When carrying out devotion to the Virgin Mary, everybody is equal."

Despite drawing together such a wide range of people, including Catholics in the officially recognized and the underground factions of the Church, the pilgrimage today is an orderly affair. The diocesan administrator said that "although so many people come, there are very few incidents [probably referring here to demonstrations of opposition of the underground church against the official church, such as those which have marred public celebration in other parts of China]. We ask that the city send a few police to keep order, but there are no big problems." This was confirmed by an interviewee from the Shanghai Public Security Bureau. "There is no conflict between official church members and the underground in public settings," he says. "The conflict takes place in more private ways."

This orderliness represents a certain victory for the Chinese government. Working through the officially approved church leaders of Shanghai, it has helped to rebuild the shrine and to facilitate access to it, while selectively emphasizing those aspects of Marian devotion that encourage private solutions to personal problems rather than collective action for public purposes. This has helped make the Shanghai diocese a place of relative harmony among Catholics rather than a source of social instability as in other regions. The success of the local Chinese government in making the Marian shrine serve its agenda is the latest in a long line of efforts to make the shrine serve political purposes. Like the efforts before it, however, it is only a partial success. The meanings ascribed to the shrine are multidimensional and fluid and have always been open to dissident interpretation by groups opposed to the dominant authorities. Let us now review those previous efforts to assert control over the shrine, so we can see the continuities and differences with the current government's efforts.

French Colonialism and the Establishment of the Shrine

The Shanghai Catholic community had its origins in the missionary work of none other than the great Jesuit Matteo Ricci. In 1604 in Beijing, Ricci converted Xu Guangqi, a brilliant Ming scholar-official who eventually became the imperial grand secretary. Xu requested that the Jesuits send a missionary to his native Shanghai. Bolstered by the Xu family's influence, the Catholic community grew steadily. When Xu temporarily returned to Shanghai in 1621, the community flourished. Xu built a great church on land connected with his estate—Xujiahui—to accommodate the Catholics. St. Ignatius Cathedral (built in 1910) stands on the location of this original Catholic center. By 1650, Shanghai had about 20,000 Catholics and was "one of the most splendid Christian centers in the empire" (Hanson 1980: 15–16).

After the rites controversy (in which the pope finally came down on the side of the opponents of the Jesuit approach of reconciling Catholicism with traditional Confucian rituals), the Chinese emperor declared Christianity to be a "heterodox religion" (*xiejiao*) and proscribed it. The Jesuits had to leave Shanghai. Local Catholic communities in the Jiangnan region carried on their faith through lay leadership. The Jesuits returned in 1842 after the First Opium War. They were now backed up by the expansion of French military power into the Shanghai region (Hanson 1980: 17).

Besides having to contend with resentful local officials, the French Jesuits also had to overcome resistance from entrenched Catholic lay leaders, who had ministered to local Catholic communities in the priests' absence. The conflict between Shanghai Catholic localism and outside authorities—whether that of foreign missionaries or central government officials—has shaped much of the history of the Shanghai Church down to the present day.

The nineteenth century French Jesuits often blended a sense of religious mission with a commitment to the French colonial project—and the colonial project meant that, as well as being defended against non-Christian elites, the local Catholic communities had to be placed firmly under the control of French missionaries, not local Chinese Catholics. One group of lay leaders that proved especially troublesome was the "virgins"—unmarried women who had taken informal vows of celibacy (because Chinese women had not been eligible to join formal orders of nuns) and dedicated themselves to religious ministry. They sought to replace the virgins with newly established Chinese congregations of nuns, who would be more firmly under ecclesiastical control and devoted to specialized work—like care of orphans and sewing of priestly vestments—which would not compete with the work of priests (Hanson 1980: 18–20).

During the Taiping Rebellion, the French Jesuits bought their first few acres of land on Sheshan, on which they built a sanitarium for priests to recuperate from the illnesses that became epidemic during that time of turmoil, and to which the missionaries could retreat in relative safety if the Taipings threatened Shanghai itself. They first built a small church on the midlevel of the mountain, next to the sanitarium, and later they erected the pavilion on the mountaintop, in which was placed a statue of the Virgin Mary (*Sheshan shiji* 1931).

At that time, the French form of Marian devotion had a distinctly militant cast. One of the predominant cults was of "Our Lady of Victories"— imagined as a strong woman wearing the crown of a queen and holding her Son, who also wore a crown. It was Our Lady of Victories who had helped the French save European Christian civilization by defeating the Turks (and helped the French Canadians defeat the English). In the nineteenth century, the cult of Our Lady of Victories also became a symbol of the aspiration of the Church to roll back the evil forces of the French revolution and to restore hierarchy, nobility, and authority to a culture ruined by equality, fraternity, and liberty. In the nineteenth century, different French regimes were more or less willing to allow the Church to increase its influence within France, but they all found it useful to allow the Church to propagate religious authoritarianism in the colonies.

It was to Our Lady of Victories that the French Jesuits prayed as the

Taiping menace drew closer, and during a retreat on Sheshan they vowed to build a beautiful church for her if they were spared from the Taipings. The Taipings were defeated in 1864, and the Jesuits dedicated their new church on the top of Sheshan in 1871. But after the Taipings were defeated, the Catholic troubles continued. In the 1870s, major anti-Christian riots began to flare up around the country. It was in this context that the French acquired a large painting of Notre Dame des Victoires from Paris. It is very similar in form to the statue that is placed in the famous Parisian basilica of that name (and to the painting in the Montreal basilica of the same name). The French Jesuits installed this painting in the new church and they prayed before it, imploring Mary to deliver them from persecution. The riots did not reach Shanghai (*Sheshan shiji* 1931). The Jesuits attributed this to Mary's miraculous intervention. They were also helped by the strong presence of French gunboats in Shanghai (Hanson 1980: 20).

The reputation of the miraculous power of Our Lady of Victories grew steadily throughout the rest of the nineteenth century. The power of the Virgin was seen to be somehow concentrated in the picture from Paris. In times of trouble, people came to the mountain to pray before the picture. There were reports of apparitions and miracles.

The establishment of the Sheshan Marian shrine was thus both an expression of a French colonizing project and a means to consolidate that project. The ability to buy up a particularly beautiful and portentous part of the Shanghai region was a demonstration of the wealth and power of the French Jesuits. The installation of a picture with miraculous power was a sign of the French commitment to protect the local church. The iconography of the picture symbolized the supernatural superiority bestowed on French Catholic culture. It could remind Chinese Catholics to be deferential to French authority, even as they relied on French power for their protection. The virginity of Our Lady of Victories was a transcendentally powerful virginity that demanded subordination from the insubordinate Chinese lay virgins. The miraculous image of Our Lady of Victories symbolized all that was beneficial about the religious and political power of the French Church over the Chinese Catholic community.

Although the French could try to define the public identity of the Marian image on Sheshan, they could not stop local Catholics from constructing their own understandings of the image. The Marian shrine might not have inspired the lay Catholic imagination if it had not resonated with the aspirations and expectations of local Chinese Catholics. Like most other Chinese, they would have expected mountaintops to be powerful (*ling*). The major Buddhist and Daoist shrines, after all, were located on mountain peaks, where Heaven and Earth came together. It was natural to expect miraculous happenings to occur there. In popular religious culture, Chinese also expected—and needed—powerful deities to protect them; and they expected that that power could be concentrated in certain images and temples. A disproportionate number of Shanghai Catholics in the nineteenth century were poor fisherfolk, many of them concentrated in the Songjiang River, which flows close to Sheshan (Latourette 1929: 334). Chinese seafarers have traditionally looked to female goddesses like Mazu or bodhisattvas like Guanyin to guide them through troubled waters. But fisherfolk have some difficulty looking to the Buddhist Guanyin because they have to accumulate bad karma through the killing of fish. Mary was the mother of a man who made fishermen his apostles. The Marian cult was especially strong among Shanghai's fishermen. As was suggested to me in an interview with an administrator of the Shanghai diocese, Shanghai's fisherfolk may have been attracted to the image of our Lady of Victories because they knew that she was also Stella Maris, the Star of the Sea.

Perhaps because the French missionaries themselves realized that to captivate the imagination of local Chinese Catholics the image of Mary had to be understood in more inclusive terms than as a protectoress of French interests, they quickly changed the official identification of the image enshrined on Sheshan. When the church housing the image was dedicated in 1871, it was dedicated to Our Lady Help of Christians—the help of all Christians including the Chinese and the French. This gave the image a more open-ended identity that could facilitate further transformations in the meaning of the Marian devotions on Sheshan, even though the picture itself was obviously the same as Notre Dame des Victoires.

Whatever the differences between the French missionaries and Chinese Catholics, both sides were willing prisoners of some powerful common Catholic assumptions. Unlike Protestants, they believed that the supernatural could become powerfully embodied in tangible, localized objects: in a picture inside a particular church on a particular mountaintop. The sacred then took on the particular features of that place. It could be shaped and molded by the natural and historical forces that sculpt mountain peaks and remodel buildings and paint portraits. Grace was embodied in history. This Catholic imaginary resonates, of course, with that of Chinese folk religion.

The localization and incarnation of Mary's supernatural power made that power partially subject to control by those who could provide access to the holy site and build the shrine. As the French missionaries lost their ability to provide such access, they lost their ability—which as we have seen was limited to begin with—to define the meaning of the Marian cult in a way that would bolster their interests.

Our Lady Queen of China

The shrine at Sheshan remained under the tutelage of the French Church and the French government for almost a half century, but the tutelage began to be challenged by the first decades of the twentieth century.

The challenge came from the Vatican. In the nineteenth century, the French government had established a "protectorate" over the Chinese Church (in line with its overall colonial policy and similar to the protectorate it had established over Latin Christians in the Middle East). As Eric Hanson puts it, "During the nineteenth century, all communications between Rome and Constantinople and Rome and Peking had to pass through Paris. France maintained this role in the face of protests from the Vatican itself." In 1886 the Vatican tried to establish direct relations with the Beijing government but was forced to back down by French political pressure (Hanson 1980: 21–22). But after the weakening of France in World War I, the Vatican began to establish direct control over Catholic missionary work in China. In 1919, "Pope Benedict XV issued the encyclical *Maximum Illud*, which deplored the effects of European nationalism on the Catholic Church in China and called for eventual church administration by the Chinese clergy" (Minamiki 1985: 190). In 1922, the Vatican sent a delegation to establish direct communication with ecclesiastical and political leaders. The Vatican delegate, Celso Costantini, convened in Shanghai China's first synod of bishops—an assertion of direct Vatican control over the Chinese Church. At the end of the synod, Costantini together with the other bishops consecrated China to Our Lady of China (Latourette 1929: 727). In 1926, Pope Pius XI personally ordained the first six Chinese bishops, men who could eventually replace the French-dominated foreign missionary leaders.

As the Vatican asserted control over the Chinese Catholic Church, it also established control over the shrine at Sheshan. That control led to a change in the official identity of the Marian image there. The image was now called Our Lady Queen of China.

Part of the demonstration of the Vatican's new control over the Chinese Catholic community came from its ability to sponsor the construction of important new buildings. In 1924, the original church on top of the mountain was torn down to make way for a new church, twice as big as the old. Construction on the new church began in 1925 and was completed in 1935. The architect and engineer of the new church was not a French, but a Portuguese priest (Charbonnier 1993: 335–36). Further development of the shrine was interrupted by the Pacific War, but after the war's end the Vatican raised the shrine to a new level of glory.

In 1946, the Vatican proclaimed the shrine a "basilica." The title of "basilica" can be conferred on a church only by the Vatican and designates a building of special importance, not just for its locality, but for world Catholicism (*Catholic Encyclopedia*). The Sheshan shrine was made a basilica at the same time that the Vatican gave the Chinese Catholic Church the status of a national Church, under the jurisdiction of a national conference of bishops instead of the Vatican office for foreign missions. The designation of the shrine as a basilica was a formal recognition that a powerful holy place had become embedded in Chinese soil and it gave honor and dignity to the whole Chinese Church. It also demonstrated that the Chinese Church was now thoroughly under the authority of the Vatican. In 1947, a ceremony representing the coronation of the Virgin Mary as Queen of China took place in the basilica. All of the main authorities in the Chinese Catholic Church were there: twenty archbishops and bishops, presided over by the Vatican delegate, Archbishop Ribieri, and 60,000 lay Catholics (Hanson 1980: 83; *Catholic Church in Shanghai Today* 2000).

As the Vatican asserted control over the Chinese Catholic Church, it also became entangled with the government. The Vatican established relationships with the Nationalist Party soon after the establishment of the Republic of China in 1927, and in the 1930s, Archbishop Yu Bin of Nanjing became prominent in both Nationalist Party and Catholic Church circles. The basis of this close alliance was both parties' total opposition to communism (Hanson 1980: 25). As Queen of China, Mary would defend China from communism, with the help of the Nationalist Party.

However, even under these circumstances, the Marian cult was by no means simply an instrument of Vatican, much less of Nationalist Party, attempts to maintain control over the Chinese Catholic community. Local Chinese Catholics themselves devoted significant resources to developing the Sheshan shrine and they interpreted the meaning of the Marian cult in ways that transcended the interests of the Vatican or the Nationalist Party.

A significant part of the money for building the Sheshan basilica came from local Shanghai Catholics. The pilgrimages themselves were organized, not so much by clerics, as by lay organizations, such as the "public employees activities committee," which posted notices of upcoming pilgrimage trips, arranged transportation, and sold tickets for 50 cents, part of which was supposed to go to building the new church. A document written in 1931 describes a trip during May organized by this committee. Buses left Shanghai at 3:45 AM, stopping first at the Catholic cemetery, and then at the Songjiang River where the pilgrims boarded a boat to go to Sheshan. They then climbed up the hill, stopping to pray along the Stations of the Cross on the way. Catholics from different churches carried banners representing their churches. When they reached the top of the hill, there was a great cacophony of firecrackers. They returned by boat and bus in the late afternoon, singing and praying together all the way (*Sheshan shiji* 1931).

Such pilgrimages increased in size after the designation of the Sheshan shrine as a basilica and after the coronation of Mary. Perhaps it was because of the increase in glory of the holy space, perhaps it was because of a deeper felt need for Mary's protection in view of the civil war that would soon bring the Communists into power. In any case, the tradition of devotion organized from the bottom up would stand the Shanghai Catholic community in good stead after the Communists defeated the Guomindang and severed the Catholic Church's formal connections with the Vatican.

A Resource for Resistance

After the establishment of the People's Republic of China in 1949, foreign missionaries were expelled, sometimes after being accused of being spies and subjected to show trials. Catholics were pressured into repudiating their connections to foreign imperialism. The Vatican, for its part, demanded that Catholics resist Communist efforts to control the Church. The Chinese government began to arrest Church leaders who refused to comply with its directives. A national "Catholic Patriotic Association" was established to direct Church affairs. One requirement for membership in this association was that members renounce their ties with the Vatican. A few bishops joined this organization, and in 1957, ordained other bishops without approval of the Vatican. The Vatican condemned this. But priests who refused to join the Patriotic Association were forbidden to function as priests. Despite government repression, an underground church began to form (Madsen 1998: 37–38).

Soon after the Communists took over Shanghai (in May 1949), the Vatican appointed a Chinese bishop, Gong Shirong, to replace the French bishop. However, Bishop Gong Shirong fled to Taiwan to join Archbishop Yu Bin, with whom he had been closely connected. In 1950, the Vatican appointed Gong Pinmei as the bishop of Shanghai. The Chinese government had already begun arresting Shanghai priests and laypeople. It put pressure on Gong Pinmei to renounce imperialism and submit to the direction of the new Chinese government. Bishop Gong responded that "he was born in China, had never left it, and would die in China. He detested imperialists. He alone, however, was responsible for the 150,000 Catholics of the diocese and in carrying out this responsibility he conformed to the directives of the Church." Finally, in 1955, the government launched an attack on "the criminal activities of the counterrevolutionary

Gong Pinmei." The bishop was arrested along with other priests and nuns and a large number of lay Catholics. A group of "patriotic" Catholics joined in denouncing Bishop Gong, but this group was relatively small. Although there had been many tensions within the Shanghai Catholic community—between Chinese Catholics and the French, between diocesan priests and the religious orders, especially the Jesuits—the Shanghai Catholics retained a remarkable degree of solidarity against government attempts to control the Church. Because of local resistance, especially from influential extended families in the Shanghai Catholic community who traced their Catholic heritage back for many generations, it took longer than elsewhere—until 1960—for the Shanghai authorities to establish a Shanghai branch of the Catholic Patriotic Association and to put in place a government-approved bishop. The establishment of this association coincided with a mass trial in which the Shanghai Intermediate Court sentenced Bishop Gong and fourteen other Chinese priests to life in prison (Hanson 1980: 72–82).

The Marian shrine at Sheshan played its part in the Catholic defiance. In May of 1953, during a lull in the persecution after the first wave of arrests, Shanghai Catholics flocked to the shrine. On the first Sunday of May alone, 7,000 persons received communion there. The harsher crackdown of 1954 and 1955 then followed. As the government tightened its grip on the Shanghai Church, it restricted mass pilgrimages. But Catholics continued to come to the shrine, individually or in small groups. Rumors circulated about apparitions of the Virgin. There was also a well circulated rumor about a young non-Catholic who died soon after he had posed disrespectfully with the image of Mary (Hanson 1980: 83).

In the eyes of Shanghai Catholics, the image on top of the mountain retained its power, even when Catholics had a harder time visiting her. Though her appearance was still that of Notre Dame des Victoires, an icon of French imperial power, she had become transformed into Our Lady Queen of China, the Patroness and Protector of the Chinese Catholic Church who defied the pretensions of atheist Communist Mao Zedong.

During the Cultural Revolution (1966–76), all religious activity was suppressed, including the pilgrimage to Sheshan. All churches were closed and many of them destroyed. Even those priests who had collaborated with the Patriotic Association were put under house arrest or into prison. The Marian basilica on Sheshan was closed and its interior used as a gymnasium for workers at the adjacent observatory (which had been originally built by the Jesuits, but later taken over by the city). The bronze statue of Our Lady of China atop the steeple was pulled down by Red Guards and broken apart. And the holy picture of Mary was destroyed. "Do not enter" signs were put at the gate leading up to the sanctuary.

At least in the later years of the Cultural Revolution, when lay Christians who expressed interest in religion did not have to fear immediate attacks by Red Guards, small numbers of Catholics quietly ventured up to the sanctuary. There were no guards posted at the gateway. Even if the basilica was locked and even if the holy picture of Mary was gone, they could still gain some consolation by being at the location where the holy things had been (Hanson 1980: 83).

From Collective Militancy to Individual Consolation

The Cultural Revolution era came to an end with Mao's death and the rise to power of Deng Xiaoping. Deng's reform and opening policy included an opening of space for religious activities. In Shanghai, some of the prominent Catholic leaders who had been imprisoned in the 1950s began to be released as early as 1978. Restrictions on public assemblies for religious purposes were lifted. The reforms brought great hope and enthusiasm but also uncertainty, because some important limits on religious freedom remained and religious policy was subject to unpredictable fluctuation.

In Shanghai, the Marian shrine at Sheshan became one of the first sites where the boundaries were tested. Fr. Vincent Zhu Hongsheng, a Jesuit from one of Shanghai's oldest and most prominent Catholic families, was released in early 1979 from the life sentence he had received in 1960, along with Bishop Gong. He became a leader of other newly freed priests in working to revive the Church. In 1981 he was arrested again. The indictment against him claimed that, among other offenses, he had spread dangerous rumors that "doomsday will come in 2000" and the "Virgin Mary will shine and make an appearance on the 15th and 17th of March [1980] on Sheshan." "Deceived by such rumors," the indictment says, "thousands of believers from Shanghai, Jiangsu, Zhejiang, Jiangxi, and Henan flocked to Sheshan. A handful of thugs took advantage of the confusion to rush and smash up the church, beat up our workers [who were using the church as a gymnasium?] and intentionally create disturbances in order to disrupt the political situation of stability and unity." In 1983, Zhu and his "co-conspirators" were sentenced to long prison terms (*Asia Watch* 1993: 41–47).

The government clearly needed to keep Our Lady Queen of China from becoming a symbol of militant resistance. Attempts to destroy the shrine had only sown the seeds of more resistance. Efforts to completely restrict access to the shrine were impractical. The Communist government thus employed the same types of measures that the French, the Vatican, and the Nationalist Party had employed to make the cult serve their particular interests. They tried to get credit for building up and maintaining access to the shrine and to use the prerogative of the builder and maintainer to define the identity of the Marian image venerated there. Like their predecessors, the Chinese government had some real, but only partial, success.

The government's policy toward Sheshan was part of its policy for better controlling the rapid emergence of religious life in general—a policy of co-opting as many religious believers as possible and punishing those who refused co-optation. The basic policy was formulated in Party Central Committee *Document 19*, released in 1982. *Document 19* allowed for the systematic reopening of churches and temples and for the return of some confiscated religious property. It also allowed more freedom to relevant religious bodies—for instance the Catholic Bishops' Council—to make decisions about purely doctrinal and ritual matters. However, it insisted that all religious activity had to be carried out in venues approved by the government and supervised by "patriotic associations" that were controlled by the government (Spiegel 2004: 40–57).

For Shanghai Catholics, this meant that the Catholic Patriotic Association (and ultimately the government's State Administration for Religious Affairs) would have the final word on who could have leadership roles in the Catholic Church. This was the same association that had demanded loyalty to the government over loyalty to the pope, and the same government that had imprisoned, and was continuing to imprison, heroic clergy like Fr. Zhu Hongsheng and Bishop Gong Pinmei for refusing to compromise their loyalty to the pope and their obedience to God. The most devout Shanghai Catholics retained deep suspicion of the new policies.

At the same time, they had been encouraged by the Vatican to develop the Church in defiance of the government's restrictions. In 1978, the Vatican had issued secret instructions for priests and bishops who had maintained their loyalty to the pope in spite of government persecution. To meet the needs of revitalizing Church life in spite of their inability to communicate regularly with the Vatican, the instructions gave "underground" bishops and priests discretion to make important Church policies without having to receive Vatican approval. Underground bishops, for example, could ordain other bishops without having the candidate approved by the Vatican. Priests could set up clandestine seminaries based on whatever teaching materials were at hand, without having curricula approved by Rome. These initiatives led to a rapid development of an underground church that developed outside of Chinese law and without much supervision from the Vatican (Chan 1987: 438–42).

The government nonetheless offered important positive incentives for Shanghai Catholics to submit to the new framework. One of the first gestures of goodwill was aimed at the Sheshan shrine. The Marian basilica was one of the first churches opened (on the feast of Our Lady Help of Christians, May 24, 1981). Throughout the 1980s and 1990s, the Shanghai diocese was able to restore the shrine to much of its former glory. A copy of the old painting of Our Lady was created and placed in the side chapel. The basilica and its surrounding areas were cleaned and refurbished. The economic development of Shanghai led to broad new highways leading out to Sheshan. According to an administrator for the Shanghai diocese, more people now came on the pilgrimage than ever before.

The Catholic leader in charge of this renovation and expansion was Bishop Aloysius Jin Luxian. A Jesuit who received his theological education in Europe, Jin had been ordained to the priesthood in Rome, but returned to China in 1950—at a time when many Chinese priests were heading in the opposite direction. Jin became rector of the Shanghai seminary, was arrested along with Gong Pinmei in 1955 and was given a long prison sentence. After his release from prison in 1978 (his detractors in the Church say that he was released early because he collaborated with his jailors),[1] he chose a path of cooperation rather than confrontation with Shanghai authorities. He sought to get the Catholics of Shanghai to comply with the government's regulations on religion, even as he quietly tried to get officials to loosen the regulations. In 1985, the Catholic Patriotic Association approved his ordination as bishop. The ordination did not have papal approval. In that year the government released Gong Pinmei from prison into house arrest. In 1988, it allowed Gong to go the United States on "medical parole." The Catholic Patriotic Association made Bishop Jin Luxian the head of the Shanghai diocese (Thiessen 2002).

From the point of view of the underground Catholic community in Shanghai, however, the position of diocesan head was not vacant—Bishop Gong Pinmei was still the only rightful bishop, and Jin Luxian was in no way fit to take his place. In 1985 the underground had ordained another bishop, Joseph Fan Zhongliang. In 1988, it declared Bishop Fan to be the coadjutor bishop of Shanghai—the one rightfully in charge of administrating the diocese in Bishop Gong's absence. This appointment had the official approval of the Vatican. Bishop Fan, however, is not recognized as a legitimate bishop by the government authorities and he remains under virtual house arrest. Meanwhile, Bishop Jin has been able to travel around the world appealing for moral and material support for his diocese. The hard core of underground Catholics considers Bishop Jin an illegitimate bishop and a traitor to the Church (Thiessen 2002).

Nonetheless, Shanghai has not been wracked by the intense, even vicious, conflicts between "official" and "underground" segments of the Church that have been seen in other parts of China. This is at least partly due to Bishop Jin's ability to get resources for his diocese. The Shanghai diocese is comparatively wealthy because it owns real estate that has become immensely valuable in the new Shanghai economy. Once some of that property had been returned to it from the government, it was able to make some extremely profitable investments, including the development of an office tower next to St. Ignatius Cathedral in Xujiahui, now the heart of Shanghai's commercial district. Under the leadership of Bishop Jin, the diocese has been able to use its resources to build or reopen 120 churches in Shanghai, more than any other comparable city.

But more important than material development has been Bishop Jin's success in getting expressions of approval from prominent Church leaders abroad. He can get this because, even though the Vatican did not approve of his ordination as bishop, he has genuinely suffered for the Church and he has behaved as someone who is not a completely compliant tool in the hands of the Chinese government authorities. Heads of major religious orders from Europe and the United States regularly come to visit him (and invite him to their countries on visits), and prominent cardinals and bishops, especially from Asia, have come to visit him (*Catholic Church in Shanghai Today* 2000).

From the point of view of the Vatican, however, Bishop Jin's position remains ambiguous. The Vatican still officially recognizes the underground Bishop Fan as head of the Shanghai diocese. Yet since Bishop Fan is unable to carry out any administrative duties and since Bishop Jin seems to have genuinely made good faith efforts, under difficult circumstances, to promote the best interests of the Shanghai Church, the Vatican (or at least some influential factions within it) has been willing to work constructively with Bishop Jin. But since Bishop Jin is not officially recognized by the Vatican, prominent cardinals and bishops have to instill some ambiguity into their meetings with him.

One way to do this is to say that, instead of coming to visit the head of the Shanghai diocese, they can say they are visiting the Marian shrine at Sheshan. This is what Bishop Zen Ze-kiun, the bluntly outspoken bishop of Hong Kong, said when he came to Shanghai in May of 2004, and met with Bishop Jin, on a visit with important political implications. Sheshan is symbolically transcendent ground; a place that Catholics from all levels of the Church hierarchy and within all factions can agree is holy.

Bishop Jin, for his part, tries to keep control over the holy place by attending to its physical development. He oversaw the renovation of the shrine. In the year 2000, he blessed a new bronze statue of Mary for the spire of the basilica to replace the original that had been destroyed during the Cultural Revolution. His diocesan office efficiently organizes the priests, seminarians, and sisters who minister to the pilgrims during the busy month of May. Because of the broad new roads leading to Sheshan, no one in Shanghai has to get up at 3 AM to make a pilgrimage, as they did in the 1930s. The very ease of access to the site brings out large numbers of relatively lax believers who overwhelm zealous adherents of underground or official factions.

Through facilitating the material aspects of the pilgrimage, Bishop Jin tries to lay claim to its spiritual power. He presides over the solemn Masses that begin the pilgrimage month of May and that bring the pilgrimage to its culmination on the feast of Mary Help of Christians. He also tries to define the meaning of the pilgrimage in a way that fosters good relations with the Chinese government and maintains social stability. He has changed the public identity of the Mary who is venerated there. Now, she is no longer the Queen of China, but the Blessed Mother of Sheshan. The new statue atop the basilica does not wear a crown. Unlike the old statue, she does not crush the Serpent of Evil under her feet. As represented in the new statue, Mary, holding her Son over her head, is simply a mother—in fact, a mother who bears a strong resemblance to those sturdy peasant women depicted in socialist realist iconography (*Catholic Church in Shanghai Today* 2000).

By defining Mary primarily as a mother—and a socialist mother at that—the Church authorities of Shanghai encourage pilgrims to come to Mary for gentle healing of their personal problems, not for militant leadership against the forces of evil. The pilgrims pray for good health, for healing from illness, for success in jobs or exams. Some believe that the power of the Virgin really does lead to improvements in their lives, although the Shanghai diocese (in keeping with the government's attempts to instill a rationalistic, scientific worldview into its citizens) discourages them from being too credulous about miracles. "Even at Lourdes, the Church certifies very few of the claimed healings as genuine miracles," says the diocesan administrator. Sheshan has thus been partially co-opted into the government's framework for taming the forces of religious enthusiasm. The mountain becomes more like a public utility than a sectarian arena.

The tamed pilgrimage at Sheshan contrasts with the unruly pilgrimage to another great Chinese Marian shrine, at Dong Lü, a village near Baoding in Hebei province. The differences between Dong Lü and Sheshan are telling. At the center of the Dong Lü cult is a painting of Mary Queen of China. The huge cathedral in which this picture is enshrined was built in the 1980s (to replace an older church that had been destroyed during the Cultural Revolution) with money gathered through unofficial channels, not distributed from above as with Sheshan. Unlike Shanghai, moreover, the major ceremonies at the shrine were led by underground bishops and priests (Madsen 1998: 91–95). By building the shrine and dominating access to it, the underground was able to maintain control of its identity. The image enshrined in the cathedral remained that of a powerful queen. The purpose of the cult was not to provide individual healing but inspiration for collective militancy. During the May pilgrimage in 1995, Dong Lü was the site of a major conflict between underground Catholics, inspired to militancy by a collective apparition of Mary, and the government. The government subsequently arrested the bishops and priests involved in this disturbance and shut down the church.[2]

The potential for Dong Lü style militancy has certainly existed at Sheshan. The burst of collective religious enthusiasm allegedly inspired by Fr. Zhu Hongsheng in 1980 was an indication of that potential. If the government had refused to allow the Shanghai diocese to reopen and refurbish the shrine, the militant potential may have been realized. People would have come to the shrine anyway, as they did at Dong Lü, and, as reportedly happened at Dong Lü, they might have believed that a militant, regal Mary was rewarding them for their collective resistance to government restriction. Under the leadership of Bishop Jin Luxian, however, the Shanghai diocese has generously rebuilt the shrine while channeling its religious enthusiasms toward acceptance of the government's version of public order.

But the potential for militancy has not necessarily been eradicated. The Mary venerated on Sheshan has a multilayered identity. The identity is not only bestowed by the shrine's official patrons, but built up by the accretion of collective memories of generations of ordinary believers. As noted in our description of the present-day pilgrimage at the beginning of this chapter, most of the pilgrims are relatively old. They certainly remember that the Sheshan shrine is dedicated to the Queen of China and they pass this memory on to their children. And the sacred picture that is the center of the cult, the source of its reported miracles, still carries the same features as the picture brought to the mountain by the Jesuits in the nineteenth century—the features of the French Our Lady of Victories. These various layers of meaning are resources for challenging the official understandings of the Marian cult, and they could become more publicly visible if there is a shift in the delicate balance between political power and religious community in Shanghai.

Conclusion

The Roman Catholic tradition stresses God's incarnation, through Christ, in this world. Certain institutions (i.e., the Church) and actions (i.e., the sacraments) embody the presence of the divine. In medieval and early modern Catholic piety, this incarnational vision was extended in popular imagination to an embrace of sacred objects, images, and places. The notion that divine power can be especially present in a certain picture or on a certain mountaintop resonated with powerful strands of Chinese folk religious tradition and helped popularize the pilgrimage to Sheshan. In the course of history, the Catholic incarnational vision has also been used—and abused—by the powerful. Political power tries to represent itself as religious power. Kings rule by divine right. Images like that of Notre Dame des Victoires served to represent and bolster French political power. But evocative Catholic symbols are multivocal. They have layers of meaning that can appeal to and be used by many different constituencies. They cannot be controlled by any single powerful interest—at least not permanently.

When it was first built, the Sheshan shrine gave a religious embodiment to French political power—Our Lady of Victories. But it was always more than that. It embodied hopes and yearnings of local Chinese Catholics, especially poor fisherfolk—Stella Maris. The Vatican attempted to control its identity, crowning it as Queen of China, and local Catholics saw it as their source of refuge from communism. The government in the People's Republic of China tried and failed to destroy it, and in the end could do no more than partially tame it as the Blessed Mother of Sheshan, a representation of the sturdy virtues of good citizens in a socialist market economy. Meanwhile people from throughout China have been seeing in it a source of relief for their individual, private troubles in a complicated world.

The relative success of the diocese of Shanghai in suppressing militant versions of the Marian cult has been due in large part to the local balance of power between official and underground Church factions and to the ecclesiastical and political skills of Bishop Jin Luxian. It may also be connected to the decline of religious enthusiasm among younger generations of Shanghainese due to the distractions of consumer society. In places like Dong Lü, where there is a preponderance of underground Catholics and where more confrontational leaders drove religious politics, and where people are relatively rural and poor, the Marian cult has been more unruly.

But as this chapter has suggested, the Marian cult in China embodies constant change within tradition. The shape of the symbols may remain the same, the sacred space may remain the same, but their predominant meaning changes with historical circumstances. Although the socialist realist statue of the Blessed Mother of Sheshan dominates the steeple of the basilica, many Catholics still focus their primary devotion on the powerful portrait of Our Lady of Victories. In fact some are trying to get a new, authentic version of the painting from France, because they feel that the

Chinese reproduction "is not very good." The tension between different dimensions of the Marian cult could interact with changes in the local balance of power to give new meanings to the pilgrimage.

The pilgrimage to Sheshan represents the capacity of the Shanghai version of the Catholic faith to contain and mediate tensions through a multivalent tradition. Just after meeting with Hong Kong's Bishop Zen in May 2004, Bishop Jin Luxian became gravely ill. Meanwhile, the underground Bishop Fan had become completely incapacitated with Alzheimer's disease. Although Bishop Jin recovered from his life-threatening health crisis, the pressure increased to find a successor who could be acceptable both to the Vatican and the government as well as the different factions of Shanghai Catholics. Bishop Jin promoted the nomination of a forty-two-year-old priest, Joseph Xing Wenzhi, to become an auxiliary bishop with right of succession to be head of the Shanghai diocese. The Vatican approved this and after complicated consultations with priests and laity in Shanghai and with the Chinese government, all parties agreed to this arrangement. Bishop Xing was ordained on June 28, 2005. Although there was no formal acknowledgment during the ordinary ceremony that it had been approved by the Vatican, everyone present knew this to be the case. Shanghai now has a successor bishop that all sides can accept.

The new reconciliation of forces was perhaps made possible by the inclusive spirit of Sheshan. The Marian cult does not straightforwardly reflect anyone's interests. Foreign political powers, the Vatican, the Catholic Patriotic Association, and the underground all at times tried to control the Marian cult, but the control could never be complete. They all are drawn to the mountaintop, but forced to share it, even with their rivals, and perhaps challenged to see their shared space as common ground.

Notes

1. He is accused of making tapes while in prison to persuade Catholics to support the government and of providing information about the underground activities of other Catholics. These accusations come from people connected with the Cardinal Kung Foundation, which is a strongly partisan supporter of the underground factions of the Church (Thiessen 2002).

2. Although the government restricted access to the Marian shrine, people braved hardships to come anyway. On the Feast of Mary Help of Christians in 1995, tens of thousands of underground Catholics gathered for a Mass concelebrated at Dong Lü by four underground bishops and one hundred ten underground priests. At that time, participants claim to have witnessed a miracle. The sun changed colors and moved across the sky. People believed that the "Holy Mother this year has come to comfort her children at Dong Lü, rewarding them for their enormous sacrifice and risk in taking this pilgrimage, with a spectacular, supernatural statement in the sky."

The underground bishop of Baoding, Su Zhimin, expressed his belief that the Holy Mother has "reaffirmed that the Church who is allegiant to the Pope is the true Catholic Church, supported by God." Soon after, the bishop was taken to prison, and the following year, a unit of 5,000 People's Liberation Army soldiers sealed off the area, closed the church, arrested a number of underground Catholics, and took away the picture of Our Lady of China. No one can go to Dong Lü now (Cardinal Kung Foundation 1995).

References

Asia Watch. 1993. *Continuing Religious Repression in China.* New York: Asia Watch.

Cardinal Kung Foundation Online Newsletter. Summer, 1995. www.cardinalkungfoundation.org.

Catholic Church in Shanghai Today. 2000. Shanghai: Guangqi Press (no pagination).

Catholic Encyclopedia, Online Edition. www.newadvent.org/cathen.

Chan, Kim-kwong. 1987. *Towards a Contextual Ecclesiology: The Catholic Church in the People's Republic of China (1979–1983), Its Life and Theological Implications.* Hong Kong: Phototech Systems.

Charbonnier, Jean. 1993. *Guide to the Catholic Church in China, 1993.* Singapore: China Catholic Communication.

Hanson, Eric O. 1980. *Catholic Politics in China and Korea.* Maryknoll, NY: Orbis.

Latourette, Kenneth Scott. 1929. *A History of Christian Missions in China.* New York: Macmillan.

Madsen, Richard. 1998. *China's Catholics: Tragedy and Hope in an Emerging Civil Society.* Berkeley: University of California Press.

Minamiki, George, S.J. 1985. *The Chinese Rites Controversy: From Its Beginnings to Modern Times.* Chicago: Loyola University Press.

Sheshan shiji [History of Sheshan]. 1931. Shanghai Municipal Archives (no pagination).

Spiegel, Mickey. 2004. "Control and Containment in the Reform Era." In *God and Caesar in China*, edited by Jason Kindopp and Carol Lee Hamrin, pp. 40–57. Washington, DC: Brookings Institution.

Thiessen, M. A. 2002. "A Tale of Two Bishops." *Catholic Culture* (internet version: catholicculture.org).

CHAPTER 5

Pathways to the Pulpit: Leadership Training in "Patriotic" and Unregistered Chinese Protestant Churches

CARSTEN T. VALA

ON ANY GIVEN Sunday, more than 24 million Chinese Protestants fill the pews of Three Self Patriotic Movement (TSPM) churches registered with the state while at least as many flock to unregistered churches.[1] In a massive upsurge of Protestantism, the Chinese Communist Party (Party) supports the training of pastors who will lead their registered congregations in "patriotism" (*aiguozhuyi*), defined in terms of "protecting the Party's leadership" and obeying "national laws above religious laws."[2] But instead of bolstering Party authority, the process for training "patriotic" pastors appears to weaken its authority, as pastors-in-training are increasingly likely to reject the TSPM churches as being "false" churches.

The Party's concern with the training of pastors is heightened by the huge numbers of Chinese converting to Protestantism. According to the state's conservative estimates, as they only record believers who are at least eighteen years old and belong to state-registered congregations, the Chinese Protestant population grew from 3 million in 1982 to 10 million in 1995 and 15 million in 1999, a 10 percent annual growth rate. In urban areas, such as Shanghai, the church-going population has ballooned by nearly 15 percent per year since the early 1990s (Li et al. 1999: 204). Membership in rural areas has also grown quickly. For example, Henan province has seen its total Protestant population skyrocket from 100,000 to 5 million since the late 1960s (Lambert 2006 [1999]: 249–50). If Protestants worshipping in unregistered churches were counted as well, the number of Protestants would probably be at least 40 million and maybe over 60 million (Li et al. 1999: 202; Lambert 2006 [1999]: 19).

To handle this burgeoning religious population, the Party attempts to draw Protestants into religious sites approved by the state and then appoints pastors to lead them. By registering groups of believers and then controlling the training of TSPM pastors over them, the Party hopes to influence the beliefs of the Protestants. Theology, the Party recognizes, is key to determining how believers act toward the state. As a director of a provincial Religious Affairs Bureau said, "Practice proves that the kind of theology [one has] determines the kind of political tendency and religious activity [one has]" (Zhou 2002: 62).[3]

But influencing theology requires that adequate numbers of pastors be trained for TSPM churches. Statistics show that while believers are streaming into the pews in greater numbers, few of them are ascending to the pulpit to become pastors. This imbalance is occurring all over China. For example, coastal Jiangsu province has only 98 pastors for almost a million Protestants in 1995 (Zhou 2002: 121). In inland Henan province, 111 pastors serve 5 million believers (Lambert 2006 [1999]: 48, 233), while in northeastern Heilongjiang province the ratio is even starker: there are only 34 pastors for 600,000 TSPM Protestants, or one pastor per 17,600 believers in 2003 (Heilongjiang TSPM 2003).[4] As a TSPM pastor put it, "there are many sheep but few shepherds" (Interview).[5]

Recent scholarship on Chinese Protestantism has neglected to examine the roots and consequences of the imbalance between the number of members and pastors. Tony Lambert observes that the lack of trained pastors has reached crisis proportions, but his focus is the extraordinary growth of the number of Protestants (2006 [1999]: 48, 103). Daniel H. Bays (2003: 496) notes in passing the lack of adequate personnel in TSPM churches, which he attributes to the rapid addition of millions of new members in the 1990s. In explaining the development of varieties of Protestant Christianity, Ryan Dunch does not mention the imbalance, although his analysis reveals how different kinds of Protestantism have different leadership structures (Dunch 2001: 195–216). Jason Kindopp maintains that neglect of theological education during the Mao era caused a paucity of clergy but the result was to energize church volunteers in the TSPM churches (Kindopp 2004: 127). While these analyses have pointed out the remarkable growth in Chinese Protestant numbers, none has examined in detail the interplay of state policies toward religion and the leadership gap.

Given the spectacular growth of the Chinese Protestant population and the stunted development of leadership, this chapter examines how state policy and church politics affect the number of TSPM pastors. It shows that state policies designed to ensure a compliant "patriotic" leadership paradoxically weaken state authority among TSPM pastors. To provide a comparative perspective on leadership pathways, the chapter contrasts the TSPM training with the flexible and informal training in the unregistered churches.

This chapter draws on grassroots fieldwork conducted on both TSPM and unregistered churches. While both Catholic and Protestant churches in China have officially sanctioned churches and "underground" (or house) churches, this research is focused on the Protestant churches alone. Officially sanctioned churches are referred to as registered churches or TSPM churches, because they have official authorization and are staffed by leaders trained or at least approved by the TSPM. I refer to the Protestant house churches as "unregistered churches" to emphasize their lack of formal state approval. For this fieldwork, I conducted interviews with TSPM pastors and higher-level leaders as well as members and leaders in the unregistered churches and seminaries from October 2002 to December 2003 and from May to June 2006 in several cities from Northeast China to Southwest China.

Patriotism and Protestant Churches

From Protestantism's arrival in China in the 1800s to the Communist victory in 1949, popular perceptions of Chinese Protestant churches have shifted from seeing them as a force for modernization to being foreign-controlled organizations. When Protestantism first came to China members of these churches led many Western missionary-founded hospitals, schools, and social relief services that helped modernize the country (Lutz 1988: 38). Other Chinese Protestants played active roles in the 1911 Revolution and later provincial assemblies, finding in Christianity a way to be both patriotic and modern (Dunch 2001). Their nationalism meant that Chinese Protestants did not shrink from criticizing foreign missionaries when Western powers were seen as infringing on China's national interests (Dunch 2001: 60, 186). According to Dunch (2001: 196), "Chinese Protestants, for better or worse, were integral to Chinese society and to the shaping of Chinese modernity."[6]

Starting in the 1920s, however, as the broader population came to equate nationalism with anti-foreign sentiment and Christianity with cultural imperialism, Chinese Protestants began to lose their public role as patriotic modernizers and churches fell under suspicion of being foreign dominated. The shifting winds of public opinion split the mainstream, mission-established churches, as some remained under Western leadership while in others Chinese believers took the lead. Meanwhile, an entirely new stream of indigenous Protestant sects appeared, with a membership that accounted for up to a quarter of all Chinese Protestants (Bays 1996: 307–16).

Soon after the Party took power in 1949, the new regime defined patriotism as declaring loyalty to the Party and severing all ties to Western powers. The next year, Protestant elites penned a "Christian Manifesto" to declare their support for the regime, cut ties to foreign missionary boards, and established a "patriotic" association for Protestants who wanted to be "Three Self": self-governing (*zizhi*), self-supporting (*ziyang*), and self-propagating (*zichuan*). Under Party guidance, these Protestant leaders launched mass campaigns to gather signatures nationwide for the new TSPM association. In the midst of these campaigns, Chinese troops entered the Korean War to fight United States' forces, heightening anti-foreign sentiment and popular support for the regime (Meisner 1999: 70). Protestant congregations confronted a clear choice: reject foreign ties and join the regime-backed TSPM or face closure (Xu 2004: 107–21).

With foreign missionaries forced to leave the country, many mission-founded churches chose to join the TSPM. As Philip L. Wickeri notes in his sympathetic account of the TSPM's origins, Protestant leaders "helped to educate their congregation on the relationship between imperialism and the missionary movement," and guided their flocks to sign on to the regime's patriotic agenda (Wickeri 1988: 132–37). By contrast, leaders of the indigenous Protestant sects, who were also pressured to join the TSPM even though their congregations lacked direct foreign ties, chose church closure and imprisonment. Members of these sects (and some mainstream Protestants) either abandoned their faith or retreated to their homes to worship, solidifying a divide between mainstream TSPM churches and indigenous sects.

By the late 1950s, the Party had merged TSPM churches around the country, reducing the number in Beijing, for example, from sixty-five churches before 1949 to only four by 1958 (Wickeri 1988: 219). Continuing religious repression reached a peak in the Cultural Revolution decade (1966–76) when all churches were shut down and Protestants found even home worship difficult. Zealous Red Guards attacked TSPM leaders and forced them to denounce themselves and each other.[7] Then, in the early 1970s, before the Cultural Revolution ended, Chinese Protestants began to meet quietly in small and large groups in urban and rural areas, drawing believers from the shuttered TSPM churches and the indigenous sects (Wickeri 1988: 177; Lambert 1994: 20–21; Zhao and Zhuang 1997: 228–35).[8] The Party reversed its religious policy in *Document 19*, issued in 1982, to bring this expanding Protestant population inside re-opened TSPM churches, but some of these new Protestant groups have remained suspicious of the Party and rejected church registration. Spread by itinerant evangelists with little formal theological training, churches outside state control have formed in rural areas where no Protestant communities had existed before (just as indigenous sects before 1949 had spread) and in urban areas where new churches attracted new Protestants and believers formerly active in TSPM or earlier mission-founded churches (Dunch 2001: 200).

Defining Patriotism for TSPM Pastors and Members

With too few "shepherds" or pastors, the Party fears the Protestant "sheep" or believers may eventually reject Party leadership. To maintain control over TSPM churches, the Party frequently proclaims the importance of developing a corps of "young, patriotic religious staff," who are expected to fulfill political, religious, and economic tasks (Weng and Wang 2002: 203; Wang 2002: 315–18).

Jiang Zemin spelled out these political tasks in his 1993 "Three sentences" speech, in which "patriotic" religious staff were directed to ensure that believers "love our country, protect the socialist system, [and] protect the leadership of the Communist Party." As part of this patriotic agenda, Jiang asked religious leaders to "mutually adapt religion and socialism" by changing the "religious systems and doctrines that do not fit with socialism, and use the positive elements of religious doctrines, regulations, and morality in the service of socialism" (Jiang 2003: 254–55).

Top TSPM leader Bishop Ding Guangxun responded by launching the Theological Construction Movement in 1998 to reform the "negative elements" of Protestantism (Cao 2001: 163–69). Ding specially promoted "diluting" the traditional doctrine of "justification by [supernatural] faith" with an emphasis on being a "law-abiding, good citizen" (Chen and Gu 2002: 65–66). Protestants, in short, should obey Party-state authority over religious authority. In an effort to summarize how this "mutual adaptation" circumscribes religious doctrines in the name of legal obedience, patriotism, and Party loyalty, the leading professor for religious affairs cadres at the Central Party School explained, "the adaptation of religion to socialism isn't a requirement that religious believers discard their theistic faith but that they warmly love their homeland, protect the socialist system, protect the leadership of the Communist Party, and respect the nation's laws and regulations" (Gong 2003: 262).

In addition to the political and religious tasks assigned to Protestants (indeed to adherents of all religions), believers are also expected to contribute to the country's economic development by repairing roads and bridges, assisting poor households, planting trees, and caring for the elderly (Li et al. 1999: 210). In this way, religious believers led by Religious Affairs Bureau cadres and religious leaders could "do a lot of public welfare works" (Chinai 1999: 233).

In short, even though the official Party line is that economic development will make religion obsolete, in the meantime, training TSPM leaders to guide Chinese Protestants to support the Party politically, follow the TSPM's religious emphasis on being a "good citizen," and contribute to the country's economic development serves many of the Party's purposes.

The Central Role of TSPM Pastors

TSPM pastors play a key role in guiding Chinese Protestants under Party leadership. They serve as the apex of church leadership, congregations' representatives to the state, and the fulcrum of state power in individual churches.

First, a pastor is the head of the church affairs organization, which comprises the internal structure of each TSPM church and runs each church. This organization is known as a "church committee" (*tangwei*) in many areas and is supposed to be elected by members from among their congregation. However, in areas like the Northeast, the city TSPM committee appoints allies to the church affairs organization called a "small group" (*xiaozu*) to gain stronger control over individual TSPM churches. In general, a cashier, an accountant, a pastor, and four lay members constitute the elected or appointed church affairs organizations (Interview).

As the top leader of each church affairs organization, a pastor wields considerable influence over his congregation spiritually (through sermons), organizationally (through planning activities), and relationally (through individual advice and family visits). Pastors are usually the senior church staff members to officiate at major holidays like Easter and Christmas, when churches are filled to overflowing. But pastors do more than spiritual work. One northeastern pastor established literacy classes and recruited a seamstress to provide unemployed congregants with job training (Interviews). Pastoral recommendations are also required for aspiring seminary applicants (as an example below illustrates). In many churches only pastors can baptize new members, and therefore they are gatekeepers for church membership growth. Also, by providing spiritual guidance and organizing job training, well-trained pastors can help individual members better deal with life's problems.

Second, the pastor represents the congregation to TSPM superiors and to Religious Affairs Bureau officials in such matters as when the congregation wants to expand its facilities, an action that needs approval from government real estate departments (Interviews). As church leaders who have received post-secondary education and who have ties with other pastors and TSPM superiors, pastors wield greater authority than lay leaders in negotiations over real estate or in arranging special worship services with state authorities.

Third, as TSPM representatives in individual churches, pastors stand at the bottom of the TSPM hierarchy and act as the fulcrum upon which state power turns in the congregation. A pastor implements instructions from the higher levels of the TSPM and, by enacting state decrees, acts as the "face" of the state toward believers. The interests of the state and the TSPM do not necessarily conflict with those of the pastors, however. For example, the state worries that "cults" will draw members out of TSPM churches where they can no longer be monitored and may transform into a challenge to state power, a phenomenon common in Chinese history.[9] TSPM pastors worry that "cults" will spread incorrect doctrine and lure members away. As a pastor explained, suspected "cult" followers created doctrinal confusion in his TSPM church by persistently questioning church members on their salvation. In order to calm his anxious congregation and prevent their departure, he preached a series of sermons clarifying life-after-death issues that prompted the suspected "cult" followers to leave the congregation (Interview).

At other times, conflict between state and TSPM interests on the one hand, and pastoral interests on the other hand, forces pastors to choose whether to obey the church or the state. When the state decreed that all public gatherings cease in the spring of 2003 to prevent the spread of the SARS virus, all TSPM churches were instructed to cease worship services. The pastor of a TSPM church in a northeastern provincial capital informed his congregation that if they feared infection they could stop coming to church but he would continue to hold services because, as one of his members recalled, "the Bible says we have to keep on meeting" and "we are protected by God." The pastor's interpretation of Biblical injunctions as higher than state decrees meant that he flouted state regulations to continue worship services. Consequently, the pastor incurred a heavy fine from the state but gained respect from his congregation (Interviews).

As head of the church leadership, the church's representative to the TSPM and the state, a bulwark against the emergence of "cults" within congregations, and a respected leader who can transmit state instructions, highly trained pastors can be effective in serving state ends. In the analysis below, however, we will see that not only are too few pastors being trained, but also that the state's management of Protestant training ends up limiting the number and quality of those pastors. In the training and appointing of pastors, individual actors, such as church staff members, local

TSPM leaders, and even the aspiring pastors themselves, exert power to thwart the state's effort to control who enters and completes the process. Finally, there is no guarantee that a pastor who completes pastoral training will end up being a TSPM pastor who is obedient to the state.

High Hurdles in the TSPM Route to Becoming a Pastor

The state erects several hurdles that candidates must clear to become pastors. The difficulty of clearing these hurdles serves to limit the number of pastors produced through the state-controlled process. First, the state curtails the number of pastors and church workers who are trained by providing only limited funding to twenty-four national, regional, and provincial TSPM seminaries (or provincial Bible schools). Though all TSPM training institutions offer three years of instruction, the national seminary and five regional ones have better resources and instruction, and graduation from them confers higher prestige. But inadequate funding hamstrings the provincial seminaries, which must operate on a shoestring budget and can only teach basic Bible literacy alongside state religious policies. Despite limited resources, more and more TSPM seminaries and Bible schools have opened since the religious policy changed in the 1980s. The Nanjing Union Theological Seminary, the only national seminary, was the first to reopen in 1982 with a class of forty-six students (Chinai 1999: 252). By 1989, another thirteen TSPM seminaries and Bible schools had opened doors to 734 students (Hunter and Chan 1993: 76). Seventeen years later, ten more seminaries opened classrooms as total enrollment increased to 2,000 students (Lambert 2006 [1999]: 48). Today twenty-four TSPM seminaries and Bible schools hold classes nationwide (by comparison the Party closed forty-three operating seminaries in 1950, when the Protestant population was only 2 percent of what it is today) (Bays 2003: 490; Xu 2004: 116).

Although more training facilities have opened, most lack adequate funding because they depend on student tuition and donations to run. Probably one of the poorest TSPM institutions is in Guizhou. The Guizhou Provincial Bible Class can only house twenty-four of its more than seventy students, and these students—all females—crowd twelve to a small room due to a lack of adequate housing. Some students are so poor that they bring food in lieu of tuition (Amity News Service 2001). At the Heilongjiang Provincial Bible School, students' inability to pay RMB 2,500 for tuition leaves an annual shortfall of RMB 100,000. Energy costs (such as for heating, electricity, and water) add another RMB 84,000 to the school's arrears (Heilongjiang TSPM 2003). If TSPM churches in the Northeast send students and cannot cover their tuition, appeals are made to foreign Christian organizations to help cover the shortfall, while intense bargaining by the seminary staff (with local coal suppliers, for example) reduces the operating costs.

The state has greater control over the regional and national seminaries because the State Administration for Religious Affairs disburses state subsidies to them. The national seminary in Nanjing, the premiere TSPM training institution, receives RMB 300,000 to 400,000 yearly while regional seminaries such as Northeastern Seminary in Shenyang receive far less, approximately RMB 150,000 to RMB 200,000 a year (Interviews). By funneling funding from donors abroad to the cash-strapped seminaries, the Religious Affairs Bureau can assert some influence over the instruction of seminary students.[10]

Another way to exert control is to require that seminary applicants be young and therefore more impressionable as students. Of course, given the seminaries' limited funding, spending resources on younger students who are likely to give the longest service is efficient. Yet the average age of Protestants in China is over fifty years old, despite the growing surge of younger members, and older applicants would gladly apply. One man in his thirties in the Northeast told me that the municipal TSPM leader in his hometown had rejected his application because he was too old. National regulations also limit seminary study by age: applicants must be between eighteen and twenty-five years old (though local observation of this restriction varies) (National Religious Affairs Bureau 1999: 59).[11]

State Administration for Religious Affairs funding of TSPM regional and national seminaries provides a lever for the state to influence what is taught, but once students graduate they often receive no salary from the TSPM and rely on funds from their congregations, thereby leaving the state one less source of influence over the pastors. For example, some Nanjing seminary graduates who serve in remote and poor rural areas where average incomes are less than RMB 220 survive on monthly pay of RMB 200 to RMB 300 given directly by believers (Amity Foundation 2004). Even in provincial capitals such as Harbin, graduates earn only RMB 500 per month, far less than urbanites' average monthly wage of RMB 700.[12]

Yet neither age barriers nor the prospect of a life of poverty have reduced a flood of applicants that is far greater than seminaries can enroll. For example, in the early 1990s, eight hundred applicants competed for thirty-five slots at the national seminary. Although competition for admission to regional and provincial seminaries is far less fierce, still many more believers apply than get in: only forty-some students gained admission to Heilongjiang Provincial Bible School out of one hundred twenty applicants in 2002 (Interviews).

The first real limitation that reduces the number of pastors is a lack of funding, because most seminaries do not have the financial resources to accept enough applicants to develop a sizeable corps of pastors. Although state subsidies mean that the national and regional seminaries are better off, the enrollment at these six schools is naturally limited. Half the seminary students in the country attend one of the eighteen provincial Bible schools that receive no subsidy from the state or from the TSPM leadership. Increasing enrollment would be too burdensome for schools in provinces such as Heilongjiang or Guizhou compared with other provincial training institutions, because most of the applicants and their sending churches are poor.

ROLE OF THE RELIGIOUS AFFAIRS BUREAU IN THE APPLICATION PROCESS

With seminaries at all levels financially able to admit only a small portion of applicants, TSPM leaders and Religious Affairs Bureau officials use academic and political tests to narrow the large applicant pool. The seminary staff proctors entrance exams to test basic scriptural, historical, and political knowledge while the Religious Affairs Bureau conducts political background checks (*zhengshen*) to select politically loyal candidates from among the academically successful ones.

The rigorous and lengthy application process begins when students register for the exams with the recommendation of a pastor. Seminary staff members forward the files of the successful examinees to the provincial TSPM/CCC (China Christian Council), which then contacts the Religious Affairs Bureau. The background investigation by the bureau through the local government seeks to ensure that candidates have no record of illegal Christian activity or criminal behavior. Final Religious Affairs Bureau approval is passed on to the provincial TSPM/CCC, which notifies the applicants of successful admission.

The preceding discussion has made it apparent that there is a bottleneck in the application process. Because most of the TSPM churches and seminaries are poor, few applicants can be accepted. The surplus of applicants allows the TSPM seminaries to be very selective in their criteria for admission (dependent upon Religious Affairs Bureau approval). Two criteria are used to cull the applicant pool. Entrance tests of scriptural understanding eliminate some students because of their weak background in religion, while the Religious Affairs Bureau rejects others who have been arrested or linked with unregistered church groups. With limited TSPM finances reducing the number of applicants who are admitted, political considerations enforced by the Religious Affairs Bureau winnowing out some applicants and TSPM educational standards barring others, the full application process reduces the pool of incoming students and hence shrinks the corps of future church leaders.[13] Yet aspiring pastors have no other alternative than to pass through this single pathway to leadership. Without the official imprimatur of seminary certification, no believer may become a pastor.

BARRIERS TO APPOINTMENT FOR SEMINARY GRADUATES

Upon graduation students also face obstacles that can block their paths to appointment in churches and to ordination as pastors. Although seminarians usually receive appointment to a church in their home area, not all graduates can return home. Some may go elsewhere because of problematic relations with the local Religious Affairs Bureau, because a spouse has been assigned to another area, or because a local TSPM leader has moved, severing the personal ties constituting the relationship with the home TSPM church (Interview).

Surprisingly, even with approval by the Religious Affairs Bureau and the TSPM, appointment is not guaranteed for seminary graduates. The receiving church's leadership must also agree to accept graduates. For example, in a county seat in northern Heilongjiang Province, a powerful TSPM leader called Elder Li refused to accept a fresh seminary graduate named Ms. Chen as a TSPM pastor in the early 1980s.[14] Elder Li had been greatly influenced by the late Wang Mingdao, a father of the unregistered church movement who founded an indigenous Protestant sect in the 1930s and chose prison over joining the TSPM in the 1950s.[15] Staunch refusal to accept state-supported liberal theology promoted by the TSPM led Wang Mingdao to reject the TSPM as an illegitimate church. Similarly, Elder Li, inspired by Wang's stance and backed by his congregation, refused the appointment of Ms. Chen. Even though Elder Li agreed to register his church, he rejected TSPM control over personnel (and therefore theological) matters. In this case Elder Li and his congregation preferred no pastor at all to accepting a TSPM graduate (Interview).

Undaunted by this church rejection, Ms. Chen then turned to the Religious Affairs Bureau and found work there. Later, after more than twenty years spent monitoring religious activities, this seminary graduate-turned-bureau official was nearing the mandatory retirement age for state cadres. Ms. Chen decided to return to the TSPM for employment. Provincial TSPM leaders ordained the former Religious Affairs Bureau official and appointed her as a pastor in another church in Elder Li's city (Interview). This transition from seminary graduate to state official and back to church leadership is highly unusual, yet it demonstrates both the TSPM's desperate need for trained leaders regardless of their background and, more significantly, the close working relationship between the TSPM and the Religious Affairs Bureau (Interview).[16]

INTERNAL TSPM POLITICS AS AN OBSTACLE TO ORDINATION

While TSPM congregations may refuse to receive an appointed graduate, as the preceding example in Heilongjiang province illustrates, after appointment a graduate needs the approval of higher-level TSPM leaders to become ordained as a pastor. The typical process begins when a seminary graduate is appointed to serve an apprenticeship lasting from two to five years at a TSPM church. Upon completion of the apprenticeship, he or she then applies for ordination. Next, the local church organization or two pastors recommend the candidate to the provincial TSPM leaders who choose three pastors to examine the candidate, while the Religious Affairs Bureau conducts yet another background check (China Christian Council and Three Self Patriotic Movement 1998). Throughout this process, the Religious Affairs Bureau is closely involved with the ordination and promotion of personnel within the TSPM.

Ordination grants newly minted pastors several benefits. It boosts pastor salaries, ameliorating the low pay of church leaders. More importantly, pastors can usher new members into the TSPM church by performing baptisms (although in areas without pastors, ordained elders may also baptize believers) (China Christian Council and Three Self Patriotic Movement 1998). Enlarging the TSPM membership broadens the financial base of the TSPM churches, increasing the ability of TSPM churches to support students in seminaries. Finally, ordination grants a pastor the power to ordain elders for churches where there are no pastors.

Higher-level TSPM leaders wield considerable influence over when and how these ordinations occur, thereby making the process unpredictable for graduates aspiring to become pastors. Although it might be assumed that higher-level TSPM leaders (whether provincial TSPM leaders responsible for churches outside the capital or city TSPM leaders in charge of the provincial capitals or major cities) would be anxious to ordain these graduates to reduce their own and other pastors' workload, graduates said that TSPM leaders might block ordination because of personality conflicts, mistrust, or greed. In each of the following cases, it is clear that the Religious Affairs Bureau must approve any TSPM ordination.

One TSPM seminary graduate recalled that his ordination had been held up for several years due to conflicts unrelated to him. For reasons unclear to the graduate, conflicts between his ally, the provincial TSPM leader, and his employer, the city TSPM leader, blocked his ordination

(Interview). Another seminary graduate confided that he had applied for ordination three times and been rejected each time; he guessed that his marriage to a foreigner (and suspected connections to foreign Christian organizations) caused his TSPM superiors to view him as untrustworthy (for example, that he might use illegally published materials from abroad, accept foreign financial support, or train unregistered church staff) (Interview). All the recent seminary graduates in a northeastern provincial capital have been prevented from being ordained, probably because the city TSPM leader was "greedy," surmised one pastor, and wanted to use the funds for himself, making him unwilling to grant the graduates the required salary increases (Interview). In that capital, pastors are paid by the city TSPM committee, which collects offerings from all the city's TSPM churches and then disburses payments to TSPM staff while keeping the remaining offerings. The national norm is for individual TSPM churches to pay their leaders directly.

Delaying ordination, however, entails greater consequences than financial dissatisfaction for the unordained church leaders. Without ordination, these frustrated seminary graduates have no more power than other unordained church workers (deacons and preachers) because they all are powerless to baptize new members. Without that power, the seminary graduates are forced to rely on other pastors—including their TSPM superiors—for baptism, putting them in a dependent relationship to these higher leaders for one of their most important responsibilities. While inconveniencing the graduates, delaying ordination is useful for TSPM superiors to keep watch over TSPM seminary graduates as they lead churches underneath them.

Unintended Outcomes of State Efforts to Train Patriotic Pastors

RISE OF SECONDARY LEADERS

Up to this point we have seen that aspiring pastors must overcome high hurdles to get in the door at seminaries, to gain congregational approval for successful appointment, and to satisfy a TSPM superior for ordination. As the rate of membership growth in TSPM churches continues to outstrip the training rate of pastors, congregations in TSPM churches turn to a secondary level of leadership below the pastoral level. With too few pastors completing the lengthy training process, other church staff must fill the shoes of pastors.

Although a pastor usually leads the main TSPM churches in cities, an ordained church worker often leads smaller TSPM churches in urban or rural areas. There are two kinds of ordained workers: assistant pastors (*fumushi*), who are also called teachers (*jiaoshi*), and ordained elders (*anli de zhanglao*). Just like pastors, these ordained church workers are empowered to baptize new members and administer communion. But unordained church workers such as preachers (*chuandao ren*), who may deliver sermons if they have been trained, and deacons (*zhishi*), who are believers responsible for some area of church affairs, are not allowed to baptize new members, according to the Chinese Christian Church Order, which unified the definitions of TSPM church staff positions nationwide (China Christian Council and Three Self Patriotic Movement 1998).

This secondary layer of church staff has come to play an increasingly important leadership role, especially in rural areas where there are no pastors, as well as in urban TSPM churches where pastors serve. An excellent example can be seen in how a set of deacons in a TSPM church overcame Religious Affairs Bureau objections to a highly popular and effective lay worker who sought to apply to seminary.

It began when the city Religious Affairs Bureau refused to allow the applicant to register for the entrance exam, claiming that his excellent foreign language skills made him a risk for emigration after seminary graduation. In fact, he had been a model Youth Communist League member and faced great resistance from league leaders when he became a Christian and cancelled his membership. Perhaps intent on preventing the embarrassment of a former outstanding Youth Communist League member becoming a Protestant pastor, the Religious Affairs Bureau arbitrarily demanded that he find *two* pastors—instead of the usual one pastor—to recommend his application.

The young man located a pastor who agreed to support his application on the condition that he first serve a year in the pastor's church. One year later, that pastor still refused to sign his application; when pressed, he admitted that the Religious Affairs Bureau was pressuring him not to recommend the young man. At this point the deacons of the church affairs organization stepped in. The deacons threatened to sue the government if the pastor didn't keep his word, although the legal basis for a lawsuit was murky because religious affairs are regulated by policies not laws. In order to avoid trouble, however, the pastor suggested that all the deacons of the church recommend him and simply signed, "I agree," under the deacons' signatures. When the Religious Affairs Bureau officials received the letter and saw all the signatures, they feared continued refusal of the application might spark negative publicity from a lawsuit. (The State Administration for Religious Affairs and local Religious Affairs Bureaus are particularly sensitive to their image abroad, especially as the Party is regularly criticized for curtailing religious freedom. Local offices seek to deflect the attention of foreign religious actors from their actions toward the lively religious scene unfolding under their supervision.)[17] In the end, the Religious Affairs Bureau approved the application for examination and the applicant became a TSPM pastor.

In this case, Religious Affairs Bureau officials exerted political pressure through a variety of mechanisms to reject the application of a popular candidate. First, it set an arbitrary requirement that two pastors support the application, though the local Religious Affairs Bureau officials later backed down. Second, the candidate had to serve a year in a TSPM church before applying for the examination. Third, even after the year of service, the Religious Affairs Bureau continued to pressure the pastor not to recommend him until the deacons threatened to expose the irregular maneuverings of the bureau. The deacons, undeterred by the pastor's reluctance and spurred by the inappropriate Religious Affairs Bureau interference, overcame this local state opposition to the candidate.

Although interviews revealed that successful resistance by secondary leaders is unusual because Religious Affairs Bureau disapproval usually carries the day, this case demonstrates that the combination of united lay leadership and the threat of legal action can be sufficient to get the bureau to back down. Lawsuits launched by the TSPM against Religious Affairs Bureaus are rare in China, because such disputes are usually settled out of court, with no publicity.[18] In this case, the specter of public attention on the bureau for its irregular actions was as effective as winning in litigation. After all, the Religious Affairs Bureau might have feared the news would reach overseas Protestant organizations and embarrass the Party by exposing the backroom pressures applied by the bureau on registered churches. For the deacons, their successful confrontation with the local Religious Affairs Bureau reveals that even in the absence of strong TSPM pastoral leadership, a secondary layer of TSPM leadership can prevail against state opposition.

This secondary level of leadership is widespread in TSPM churches because there are so few TSPM pastors. In Jiangsu province, one of the top five provinces in terms of Protestant populations, there were only 98 pastors for nearly a million believers in 1995, as noted above. But there were also 174 ordained staff serving in place of pastors plus 1,050 unordained lay workers who assist the pastors (Zhou 2002: 121, 126). These other church workers (such as elders and ordained elders) provide an intermediate layer of leadership between the members and the TSPM higher-ups, especially in areas where there are no pastors (Bays 2003). In Heilongjiang province, fewer than 35 pastors and 90 seminary graduates and elders minister to 600,000 believers (Heilongjiang TSPM 2003: 1). In Anhui province's 2,000 TSPM churches and meeting points, fewer than 40 TSPM pastors and only 24 elders lead 3 million Protestants; other church workers have to pick up the slack (Lambert 2006 [1999]: 103, 236). The explosive growth of the Chinese Protestant population combined with the Party's religious policies designed to foster a compliant "patriotic" leadership has led to the first unintended outcome: the rising importance of a secondary layer of TSPM leadership—elders, deacons, and others.

NEW LINKS BETWEEN TSPM AND UNREGISTERED CHURCHES

A second unintended outcome of state policy is increasing ties between TSPM pastors and unregistered churches, which is spurred by the departure of TSPM pastors from registered churches to work for unregistered churches. Pastors who leave the TSPM do so for two reasons: financial or theological. Most departing pastors are convinced that state interference in TSPM affairs makes the TSPM churches subordinate to the state and, in their words, no longer a "real" church.

There are a few pastors who simply abandon church work altogether, taking advantage of study abroad to leave the TSPM and the country. The TSPM/CCC representatives left behind by these pastors find it convenient to dismiss the departing pastors as irresponsible or concerned only with bettering their own lives, and ignore the considerable pressures on pastors due to huge congregations, low pay, and round-the-clock work (An 2000). For example, the China Christian Council representative from Heilongjiang province's Qitaihe city complained that the only pastor for 150,000 Protestants stayed in Singapore after her theological study ended "because the living conditions were better [than in China]." Her departure left more than a hundred thousand believers without any pastor (Interview). Rural pastors are typically even busier, with thousands of believers under their care plus additional duties as a representative in the local government. Financial support by rural believers is so meager that many rural pastors do odd jobs or till their fields to make ends meet (An 2000). Outside of congregational offerings, these TSPM pastors and staff receive no financial support. Their departures add to the dearth of pastoral leadership in the TSPM.

Much more common in my research were pastors (and other church staff) who left the TSPM because they perceived a conflict between following TSPM rules and adhering to Biblical authority. Over and over, interviewees said that the TSPM was no longer the "real" church because it adhered to state policies that contradicted the former pastors' understanding of Biblical teachings. One former TSPM pastor in a southern coastal city told me how three short sentences led him to leave his post to work for unregistered churches. He had been working for the TSPM for only two months in 1980 when his TSPM supervisor criticized him by say-ing, "I'm the head of the church. Children eighteen years and younger are not permitted to attend church. And when you preach, I must first approve it." At that time the rules against children in church and against unauthorized preaching had not yet been codified into regulations.[19] But the pastor was so sure that his superior's views reflected the whole TSPM, which he judged was no longer the "authentic" church, that he said, "I left [the TSPM] because all three sentences are against the Bible's teachings" (Interview).

Whether the issue involved regulations promulgated by the central government, rules issued by provincial-level Religious Affairs Bureau offices, or guidelines set by higher-level TSPM leaders, former TSPM pastors decided they all reflected on the TSPM. When state rules over-rode their biblical training, the pastors denounced the TSPM churches as "false." In their view, they agreed with an early critic of the TSPM who said, "the head of the house churches is Christ. . . . The head of the Three Self churches is the government" (Lee 2001: 239).

When TSPM pastors resist these rules and regulations, they do not al-ways choose to leave but may be forced out. This can be seen in the case of an elderly former TSPM pastor working in a large city in Northern China. He had joined the TSPM in the early 1950s and was forced to re-tire by TSPM leaders in the 1990s because he no longer agreed to register new believers with the local government. He complained that while he agreed with the mission of the TSPM in earlier times—to break with a colonial past in the 1950s and to destroy remnant imperialist elements in the 1960s—the Theological Construction Movement in the late 1990s vi-olated his understanding of Christian faith (Interview; Xing 1999: 64ff).

In addition to "diluting" the doctrine of "justification by faith" (see above), TSPM leader and movement founder Bishop Ding Guangxun has supported downplaying distinctions between believers and nonbeliev-ers to avoid harming national unity (Chen and Gu 2002: 65–66). On this issue, Bishop Ding has ridiculed the notion that model Communists, like the soldier Lei Feng, would not go to heaven just because they were not Christians.[20] Destinations of heaven and hell, suggested Ding, should not be linked too closely with whether one believes in Christianity or not (Ding 2001: 289–90). These ideas, said the elderly TSPM pastor, strayed too far from his understanding of biblical teachings (Kindopp 2004: 132).[21]

So when the elderly TSPM pastor was told to follow the rules to reg-ister the baptismal candidates with the local Religious Affairs Bureau, he balked because he understood how such lists had been used in the past to punish believers. His decision to protect the anonymity of the new believers instead of following state rules led the city TSPM to force him to retire. Like others who leave the TSPM, he has lost a public venue from which to teach new believers but gained some latitude to use his theological training as he sees fit. Today, he visits with TSPM and unregistered believers in his home, performs baptisms illegally, and writes what he pleases in pamphlets for the unregistered churches. And because of his advanced age he believes the state would not dare to throw him in jail for his activities (Interview).

HOME MEETINGS, STREAMS OF PROTESTANTISM, AND LEADERSHIP TRAINING

The single channel of TSPM training differs greatly from the multiple pathways of leadership development in the great variety of unregistered churches. To understand leadership training outside state control, we first need to discuss unregistered church structures. Home meetings (called *jiating juhui* by unregistered church leaders and often "meeting points," *juhuidian*, by TSPM leaders) must be distinguished from unregistered churches (called "house churches," *jiating jiaohui*, by both groups) by their different degrees of autonomy. Autonomous unregistered churches are capable of operating alone because they have their own leaders who administer the sacraments (baptism and communion) that form the foundation of a church. Unregistered churches may consist of a single meeting site or many meeting sites, either in a single location or connected in a network across several provinces. By contrast, home meetings, whether unregistered or registered, are generally linked to churches because these meeting leaders are usually dependent upon church leaders higher up, who supervise meetings and preach messages, consult on problems, and administer sacraments during regular visits.

Leadership develops differently in three types of meetings that vary in how resistant their participants are to state linkages through the TSPM. First, approved meetings are formally linked to TSPM churches because TSPM leaders notify the local Religious Affairs Bureau that they are legitimate gatherings. Elderly and sick people who cannot reach TSPM churches usually attend these approved meetings, although young people may also participate if the TSPM churches are too far away. These approved meetings may eventually increase in size until a TSPM church is formed and registered directly with the Religious Affairs Bureau. In other cases, home meetings may grow without TSPM approval (and hence state sanction) and only later register with the bureau, as informants described happening in Jilin and Anhui provinces (Interviews). In this way, home meetings can transform into full-blown churches that must be registered formally with the Religious Affairs Bureau, at which time they may receive appointed leaders.

The second type of meeting is composed of Chinese Protestants who have no links to the TSPM or the state due to ignorance of religious regulations, or because they prefer to maintain informal relations with local cadres without registration (even when the participants are aware of regulations, if their meetings remain small, the danger of being shut down and therefore the incentive to register also remain small). Both TSPM members and unregistered church members may attend these meetings, because it is a pragmatic issue, not a theological or historical one that prevents affiliation with the TSPM. These meetings may constitute an unregistered church if they are of sufficient size and have leaders capable of administering sacraments.

Chinese Protestants who gather in the third type of meeting refuse to register their meetings or churches on principle. Some believers have been jailed for rejecting TSPM membership in the past and continue to be suspicious of any TSPM affiliation. Others refuse to register with the state on theological grounds, because they do not want to come under TSPM control. Scholars disagree as to whether the second or third types of home meetings constitute the majority of Chinese Protestants.[22]

Leaders develop from within the second and third types of meetings (or unregistered churches). For example, a zealous Protestant who first leads a simple Bible study may develop a greater interest in participants' lives as he prays for their problems. Eventually he may find himself acting as a counselor and leader to a growing body of believers. In this way, home meetings can act as miniature greenhouses in which future church leaders sprout and develop, as in Beijing, for example, where a handful of university graduates who met to sing and pray grew to more than fifteen Protestants over several years. The leader added communion to the meeting activities and started to draw up a charter for the meeting-turned-church (Interview).

There are three historical streams of Chinese Protestantism varying by the degree of foreign missionary participation in leadership training that cut across the tripartite typology of meetings and churches (Dunch 2001: 195–216). The first stream of mainline, mission-founded churches became the registered (TSPM) churches, to which the first type of approved meeting is attached and that must follow state regulations curtailing foreign participation. The second, pre-1949 indigenous stream, which formed out of a rejection of exogenous control, comprises unregistered churches whose meetings are mostly of the third type and for whom foreign assistance in training leaders may still be rejected (like the Local Church of Watchman Nee).[23] Some of these indigenous churches folded into the TSPM in the 1950s as registered churches, though many congregations of this stream are well-known for rejecting registration on principle.

Leadership training is shorter and simpler in unregistered churches of the pre-1949 stream that have rejected registration but remain resolutely independent of foreign assistance. An example of unregistered churches of this type is the Local Church, which eschews foreign help of any kind because of its historical antagonism toward foreign control, as a meeting leader from Heilongjiang province made clear (Interview). These often-rural congregations use a basic curriculum that requires few resources because study materials are self-made and based only on the Bible. Training is accelerated by the simple teaching and by the group's anti-education attitude. Their suspicion of education derives from founder Watchman Nee's conviction that public schooling tainted a believer with "worldly" influences. As another informant related, Local Church congregations in rural Anhui province rarely obtain more than a fourth-grade education in part because of this attitude. Such an orientation obviates the need for long years of intense study to become a leader. In the Local Church, membership growth also spurs leadership development because home meetings split as they grow so that meetings are small enough to avoid state attention (see Vala and O'Brien 2007 for how unregistered churches attract new members). New leaders are then chosen from among experienced group members (Interview).

The third stream of Chinese Protestantism comprises churches founded by Chinese in the 1970s as well as churches founded in the 1980s and later by foreign and Chinese Protestants (especially Koreans, Korean Americans, and Taiwanese). Lambert and Zhao and Zhuang describe how Chinese Protestants first formed small gatherings in the early 1970s that grew to unregistered churches in rural and urban areas, including Shanghai (Zhao and Zhuang 1997: 228–35; Lambert 2006 [1999]: 183–87). Some of these churches are radically different from the other streams because they practice a form of Christianity that is focused heavily on direct spiritual experience (as opposed to textual bible study as in the TSPM) and on supernatural healing (examples include the Born Again Sect [*Chongsheng pai*] and Full Scope Church [*Quanfanwei jiaohui*]) (Dunch 2001: 201). Leadership training in these mostly rural sects is less a matter of long hours of textual study and scholastic achievement than a demonstration of "supernatural power" (Balcombe 1997).

The foreign-founded part of the third stream includes urban and rural churches established since the 1980s that have the direct involvement of foreigners in training Chinese church leaders. In the Northeast, one young Chinese woman headed an urban congregation founded by a foreign missionary over a decade ago. Her training consisted of a series of short classes in an "underground" seminary (completely unknown to authorities), preparing her to pastor a 700-member unregistered congregation. In a major North China city, foreign missionaries founded another underground seminary ten years ago to train pastors for unregistered churches nationwide. The first Chinese graduates replaced the foreign teachers and now train subsequent classes of Chinese seminarians, without any ties to the state (Interviews).

Whether the unregistered churches are part of the pre-1949 indigenous stream or the post-1970 indigenous and foreign-founded stream, they have three distinct advantages over the TSPM churches: aspiring church leaders enjoy more training institutions, little state interference, and even the possibility of being trained in TSPM seminaries.

First, far more unregistered than TSPM seminaries and Bible schools operate in China. A former TSPM pastor dismissed for working in unregistered training institutions estimates that there are over one thousand such institutions. These Bible schools use far simpler curricula, have fewer textbooks, employ teachers with lower educational attainment, and offer training that lasts for several months to one year rather than the typical three years in seminaries. They also have the advantage of mobility so they can shut down and relocate quickly if the authorities are close to discovering them (Aikman 2003: 128, 132).

Second, and perhaps most obviously, the Party-state wields less influence in the training institutions of the unregistered churches. As we have seen, the State Administration for Religious Affairs sets political standards to restrict the kinds of students who may attend TSPM seminaries while TSPM politics can prevent seminary graduates from being appointed. The state, by supporting the TSPM's Theological Construction Movement, also attempts to influence what pastors study and teach.[24] Though free of these restrictions, unregistered training institutions are still shaped by the presence of the Party-state in that they have to preserve secrecy, which means class size remains less than thirty students and mobility is a high priority. But the involvement of the Party-state in TSPM affairs also serves as a rallying point for unregistered church leaders, who deride the TSPM as a "false" church for hewing to Party rules and boost congregations' sense of legitimacy as the "real" church.

While many of the unregistered church leaders whom I interviewed vehemently denounced the TSPM as a church, individual leaders still cooperate informally with their counterparts on the other side of state boundaries, especially when there is a mutual perception that they are engaged in the same Protestant endeavor. An older woman who led an unregistered home meeting outside Shanghai said she had been invited to preach monthly sermons in a TSPM church. TSPM pastors seek such cooperation on a one-to-one basis by developing unofficial relationships with un-registered church leaders because they find state regulations too restric-tive but remain convinced they should serve in the registered churches (Interview). However, in this case, when the TSPM leader mentioned that the Religious Affairs Bureau was taking TSPM believers' offerings to help Buddhists build a temple, the outraged unregistered church leader called it a "false" church, ended her preaching arrangement, and expanded her home meeting into an unregistered church (Interview).

In my interviews, I found that there is a new generation of young TSPM pastors who do not share the historical experiences of the older generation of TSPM leaders nor do they accept the Party's requirement to avoid close connections with foreign believers. This new body of TSPM pastors that I met in Guangdong, Heilongjiang, Hunan, Jilin, and Yunnan provinces seeks to welcome unregistered church leaders for joint coop-eration in training and evangelism, though often the TSPM pastors have been frustrated by what they interpret as the unjustified suspicion of these unregistered church leaders against the TSPM. Yet by persistently demon-strating their dedication to Protestant work, these TSPM pastors have fos-tered successful one-on-one relationships (without formal, public coop-eration with the unregistered churches) and trained unregistered church staff members or placed them in TSPM training programs.

A third advantage of unregistered churches and one final pathway for training leadership is the TSPM seminaries. As Jason Kindopp recounts, young TSPM seminary students whom he interviewed said they intended to work in the unregistered churches rather than TSPM ones. Furthermore many more TSPM students, even those who planned to work in the TSPM churches, had at least developed contacts and even participated in training activities set up by unregistered church networks (Kindopp 2004: 135).

LEADERSHIP TRAINING: SINGLE TSPM CHANNEL VS. MULTIPLE UNREGISTERED PATHWAYS

The above examples illustrate that routes to leadership are much more varied in the unregistered churches than in the registered TSPM churches. Whereas TSPM pastors must pass through a single channel under scrutiny by the Religious Affairs Bureau, leaders in the unregistered churches rise up from the ranks of believers and without such attention. Unregistered leaders who seek seminary training have far more options, because while fewer than two dozen TSPM seminaries and Bible schools accept students, as many as five times that number of unregistered training institutions hold classes (Aikman 2003: 132).

Not only are there more training institutions for the unregistered churches, but also the process of becoming a leader is more informal and varied. The rigid TSPM channel from examination to admission, education, appointment, and ordination contrasts with the highly informal process for unregistered church leaders in which they gradually assume more responsibility. Would-be pastors in the TSPM leadership process may run afoul of Religious Affairs Bureau investigations or upset TSPM leaders who are insecure about their popularity, while unregistered leaders can assume church leadership by upgrading and expanding home meetings, planting a church in a new area, or receiving training in an unregistered seminary.

The flexible routes to leadership in the unregistered churches allow nearly anyone to assume a leading role because neither TSPM approval nor Religious Affairs Bureau background checks limit who is authorized to teach Christianity to a gathering of believers. A peasant woman who has so little formal education that she struggles to read the Bible has developed a network of two hundred churches and meetings throughout the Northeast while maintaining a rural training center. She teaches what most Chinese Protestants would agree is orthodox Christianity, yet new believers are attracted by tales of miracles that occur in her gatherings. Peasants can receive basic training to become church leaders in the training center, which is nothing more than a simple farmhouse. Local cadres have commended her for hiring unemployed workers at her dairy farm though they are said to be unaware that it also serves as a training center for church workers (Interview).

Conclusion

This chapter has discussed the principal hurdles that limit the expansion of TSPM church leadership along a single authorized channel. It has highlighted the lack of financial resources as the primary reason, and pointed to political interference at key stages of the process as further reducing the number of effective pastoral candidates. These barriers hinder the development of a large and committed corps of TSPM pastors and reflect both the Party's unease about Christianity's revival and its attempts to shape the future of that revival.[25]

Controlling the flow of pastoral training reaps rewards for a state that has reluctantly accepted the revival of religious practice. When obedient pastors are trained and appointed to TSPM churches, these pastors lead their congregations to heed state instructions, to support the Party's political leadership, and presumably to better contribute to the economic development and social welfare of the country. But the barriers leave a small group of existing TSPM pastors to preside over congregations that are expanding in size and multiplying in numbers.

Without trained leaders, the state has reason to worry about the massive increase in Chinese Protestants, given the historical links between spirituality and religious rebellion in China (Overmyer 1976; Esherick 1987). Emperors were often in danger from self-proclaimed spiritual leaders who claimed a new "mandate of heaven" and organized followers to contest the throne. After reading Protestant tracts, a failed exam candidate launched the Taiping Rebellion in the mid-nineteenth century to restore the "proper worship" of the Christian God, an effort that nearly toppled the Qing dynasty and left as many as twenty million dead (Reilly 2004; Witek 2001: 23–24). The contemporary concerns of the Party are not simply historical legacies, as arrests of unregistered Christian sect leaders in the 1990s make clear (Ownby 2001). In January 2004, central Party leaders called a National Religious Affairs conference to discuss how to handle the rapid rise in the number of Chinese Protestants. Heading the agenda was a documentary on the fervor of Chinese Protestants filmed covertly by a former Tiananmen Square activist now in the United States (Yuan 2003; Kendal 2004).

In response to this growth, the Party has approved the expansion of TSPM seminary enrollment. But, ironically, if educational standards become less restrictive to admit more students, the State Administration for Religious Affairs political standards may become more obvious to applicants. Aspiring applicants who are confident of their test results and sure of pastoral support may come to recognize a rejection as political interference by the Religious Affairs Bureau in the admissions process. So if, as TSPM leaders have announced, the Nanjing seminary starts to admit 500 to 1,000 students instead of its current 170 enrollees, background checks may draw more attention to the influence of the state in TSPM affairs, as in the aforementioned case of Religious Affairs Bureau influence on admissions, and provoke greater disillusionment with TSPM churches (Amity Foundation 2000, 2002, 2004).

Even after graduation, the process of TSPM appointment and ordination presents more hurdles that may lead seminary graduates away from TSPM churches. The corps of TSPM pastors in training will become sparser and the state will further lose power to influence leadership training. The frustrated (and highly trained) pastors who are leaving the TSPM and the growing leadership role of elders and deacons in challenging state control of training reflect an assertiveness that draws on collective resources outside state control to limit the state's power. In the above-described case of the deacons who supported a popular seminary applicant, the deacons drew on their collective unity, conviction that theirs was the right course of action, and confidence that state concerns with its international image would limit its responses. Lay leader Elder Li gained inspiration from the defiance of other unregistered leaders and depended on full support from his congregation to reject the appointment of a pastor by TSPM provincial authorities. Disillusioned TSPM pastors are increasingly drawing on links to unregistered churches to pursue work in a "real" unregistered church as opposed to a "false" TSPM church.

Such resistance makes the training of TSPM pastors a much more ambivalent undertaking for the state, as training pastors increases their authority in the eyes of believers but does not guarantee that the heightened authority will strengthen state power. State policy—including the TSPM training process—designed to bolster state control over Protestantism appears to paradoxically weaken state authority and strengthen lay leadership. It also inadvertently is helping to reestablish linkages between the TSPM and unregistered churches, bridging a divide made concrete through the state's fifty-year support for the TSPM, as church leaders see themselves engaged in a common endeavor as Christians.

Notes

1. New 2005 regulations repeat earlier rules requiring that believers seeking to worship apply to the local government to register as a religious meeting site. Among other stipulations, Protestant leaders must be approved by the TSPM/CCC (Chan and Carlson 2005: 82). Strictly speaking, the Three Self Patriotic Movement is a mass organization, a religious association, and not a church. I use the shorthand "TSPM churches" to denote churches registered by the state with TSPM approval. Using TSPM membership growth figures of 3 million (1982) to 10 million (1995) and 15 million (1999), the national TSPM growth rate is 10 percent. Extending this rate of growth to 2004 produces a figure of 24 million Protestants. Including the unregistered Protestant population, generally acknowledged as larger than registered church membership, doubles this 2004 statistic to 48 million for the entire Chinese Protestant population. An estimate of 40 million to 60 million members therefore is a ballpark, and perhaps conservative, estimate, that agrees with Lambert's assessment (2003).

2. As part of the push to "mutually adapt religion and socialism," Jiang Zemin (2003: 254–55) explained that religious staff and believers are required to be "fervently patriotic" and, as the top teacher at the Central Party school points out, it is the staff who lead these believers to adapt religion to socialism (Gong 2003: 303).

3. A clarification of nomenclature is necessary here. In 1998 the national-level Religious Affairs Bureau, which develops state policy toward religion, was renamed the "State Administration for Religious Affairs." But many local bureaus at the provincial level and below, which implement the policy, have retained the word "bureau" in their names. This chapter observes this distinction; "Religious Affairs Bureau" refers to the state bureaucracy at the provincial level and below.

4. The spectacular growth in Heilongjiang province may be partly due to the

desperate economic situation of the Northeast as well as the presence of many Korean and Korean American missionaries who mix easily among the Korean Chinese population (concentrated in cities in Heilongjiang and rural areas in Jilin and Liaoning) with little fear of discovery.

5. Seen in global perspective, these pastor-believer ratios are somewhat higher than in Protestant churches elsewhere, whether ethnic minority churches in Myanmar (1:380), Lutheran churches in Namibia (1:3,500) or Ghana (1:2,140), or Baptist churches in the Philippines (1:166). From World Council of Churches archive, www.wcc-coe.org/wcc/who/cc2001/cc2001-e.html, accessed July 9, 2007.

6. Such activism was not limited to Fuzhou in the Southeast (Dunch's focus). Chinese Protestants in northeastern Harbin spearheaded the construction of the city's most progressive middle school in the late 1910s (Carter 2002: 51–60).

7. The municipal archives in Harbin, Heilongjiang province, contain records from the Religious Affairs Bureau on accusations penned by TSPM provincial leaders in Cultural Revolution big character posters.

8. Jonathan Chao (Zhao Tian'en) and Zhuang Yuanfang (1997) mention the revival of Protestant meetings in cities such as Xiamen (Fujian province), Wenzhou (Zhejiang), Shantou (Guangdong), and Nanjing (Jiangsu), but especially in rural areas of Henan, Fujian, and Zhejiang provinces.

9. Although the TSPM as an organization accepts when the state identifies a group as a "cult," individual TSPM pastors differentiate between unusual Christian sects that are not harmful and "cults" like Eastern Lightning that use extortion and violence. See Lambert (2006 [1999]: 69–71) on the vagueness of cult definitions.

10. A special foreign donor gives money to support the seminaries. Personal conversation with Professor Kathleen Lodwick, March 6, 2004. Regulations permit direct foreign donations of less than half a million RMB to an individual church but greater sums require approval of the provincial Religious Affairs Bureau (up to RMB 1 million) or national (over RMB 1 million) State Administration for Religious Affairs.

11. Even though Protestants tend to be in their middle ages, young believers constitute a growing percentage of congregations. According to a survey of 12,000 Chinese believers conducted by the Shanghai Academy of Social Sciences, the proportion of believers of all religions under the age of forty nearly doubled from 15 percent in 1980 to 27 percent in 1990 (Li et al. 1999: 205). Shanghai's total Protestant population jumped from 46,000 (1985) to 80,000 (1990) to 120,000 (1993). The changing ratio in Shanghai is not an exception. In addition to Shanghai, the report notes that the proportion of younger believers also increased in Anhui and Henan provinces while Protestants increased greatly in all three areas.

12. See a *Beijing Review* (2004) article citing urban residents' average income of RMB 8,500 while, in 2003, rural residents made RMB 2,622.

13. The Bible schools at the provincial level sometimes set aside their educational criteria because some applicants cannot even read; none of the schools—in my experience—can afford to disregard the political criteria.

14. The story is real but the names are fictitious.

15. For a biography of Wang Mingdao, see Wang (2002).

16. The respondent was a TSPM pastor who commented that the hiring of

Ms. Chen was atypical and reflected the TSPM provincial leader's desire both to help her and to increase the number of trained pastors in the area.

17. The Party-state has made a concerted effort in the last few years to publicize changes in China's religious policies. See, for example, the recent volume by national Religious Affairs Bureau head Ye Xiaowen (1999).

18. A search of TSPM and foreign news sources from 1986 to 2000 in the *China Study Journal* only revealed one lawsuit (over a petty boundary dispute) involving the TSPM. More frequent mention is made of Religious Affairs Bureau intervention on behalf of the TSPM to get local governments to implement church registration according to policy (Yamamori and Chan 2000: 73). Recently, a group of Christian lawyers in Beijing has started to defend unregistered churches nationwide from illegal raids and in registration irregularities. See Carnes (2006).

19. Youth under eighteen years of age are prohibited from participating in religious activities according to Section 4 of *Document 19*. The restriction on preaching appears in provincial regulations issued in 1982 and later.

20. The Party has hailed Lei Feng as a model soldier of the People's Liberation Army whose every thought and act centered on serving the Party. After his death, the Party staged hagiographic exhibitions to exhort the Chinese people to follow his example.

21. According to Jason Kindopp (2004), the movement has had little effect beyond the TSPM/CCC's base of power in Shanghai and Nanjing.

22. Lambert describes the situation of meeting registration as "quite complicated" (2006 [1999]: 56), but never mentions that some Protestants do not register their meetings out of ignorance or to avoid trouble. Leung (1999: 51–52) maintains that most rural churches (which he calls "spontaneous churches") have no objection to the TSPM, although he relies almost entirely on secondary sources. Other recent works make little concrete mention of the position of home meetings vis-à-vis unregistered and TSPM churches. For example, Kindopp distinguishes "house church" Protestants in general from those under TSPM control (2004: 5), though Mickey Spiegel in the same volume mentions the complications of registration (2004: 46–48). Finally, the late Jonathan Chao, an active supporter of the unregistered churches and prominent critic of the TSPM, argued that unregistered churches that rejected registration on principle were the main stream of Chinese Christianity (Zhao and Zhuang 1997: 280).

23. Elder Li's TSPM church in Heilongjiang province is an example of a church of this second pre-1949 stream that accepted registration though not, as was seen, leadership by the TSPM.

24. Since long before the Theological Construction Movement in the 1990s, the state has attempted to shape what TSPM pastors preach, but for Religious Affairs Bureau cadres the movement has clarified what aspects of theology are objectionable and given particular expression to the general pressure they exert on the TSPM.

25. *Document 19* Section 1 states that the Party expects religion will fade away as economic development proceeds. For that reason, the Party does not want more pastors. Yet pastors are the only link connecting the believers in their religious lives to the hierarchy of state. If pastors become disillusioned with state support of the

policy of freedom of religious belief, then many believers may begin to distrust the state and eventually defect to join unregistered churches.

References

Aikman, David. 2003. *Jesus in Beijing: How Christianity Is Transforming China and Changing the Global Balance of Power.* Washington, DC: Regnery.

Amity Foundation. 2000. *Amity Echo.*

————. 2002. *Newsletter.*

————. 2004. *Newsletter.*

Amity News Service. 2001. "A Visit to Guizhou Provincial Bible School in Panxian County, Guizhou." *Amity News Service.*

An, Xiaohui. 2000. "Towards an Understanding of Rural Protestantism—Six Central Notions." *Amity News Service.*

Balcombe, Dennis. 1997. "Revival in China." *Renewal Journal* 1, 9: 22–30.

Bays, Daniel H. 1996. "The Growth of Independent Christianity in China, 1900–1937." In *Christianity in China: From the Eighteenth Century to the Present,* edited by Daniel H. Bays, pp. 307–16. Stanford, CA: Stanford University Press.

————. 2003. "Chinese Protestant Christianity Today." *China Quarterly* 174, 2: 488–504.

————. 2004. "A Tradition of State Dominance." In *God and Caesar in China: Policy Implications of Church-State Tensions,* edited by Jason Kindopp and Carol Lee Hamrin, pp. 25–39. Washington, DC: Brookings Institution.

Beijing Review. 2004. "Rural and Urban China—Worlds Apart." February 26.

Cao Shengjie. 2001. "Zhencheng, jianding, yansu, qiushi—xuexi Ding zhujiao shenxue sikao de jiben taidu" (Sincerely, steadfastly, seriously, seeking truth—the attitudes for studying Bishop Ding's theological reflections). *Tianfeng ganyu, Zhongguo Jidujiao lingxiu Ding Guangxun* (Heavenly wind [and] sweet rain: Chinese Protestant leader Ding Guangxun), edited by H. Liu, pp. 163–169. Nanjing: Nanjing University Press.

Carnes, Tony. 2006. "China's New Legal Eagles." *Christianity Today.* www.christianitytoday.com/ct/2006/september/39.106.html.

Carter, James H. 2002. *Creating a Chinese Harbin: Nationalism in an International City, 1916–1932.* Ithaca, NY: Cornell University Press.

Chan, Kim-kwong, and Eric Carlson. 2005. *Religious Freedom in China: Policy, Administration, and Regulation.* Santa Barbara, CA: Institute for the Study of American Religion.

Chen Mei, and Gu Le. 2002. "'Jiana xuange' weifan shengjing de jiaodao bing tiaozhan xin yu buxin de guanxi" ("Selected songs from Cana" violates the teachings of the Bible and challenges the relationship between belief and unbelief). *Jidujiao dierci shenxue sixiang jianshe yantaohui zhuanji* (Special collection of the second Christian theological thought construction seminar). Shanghai: Shanghai Protestant Lianghui (TSPM/CCC).

China Christian Council and Three Self Patriotic Movement. 1998. "Chinese Christian Church Order." *Chinese Theological Review* 12: 63–79.

Chinai (ed.). 1999. *Dangdai Zhongguo de zongjiao gongzuo* (Religious work in contemporary China). Beijing: Contemporary China Publishing.

Ding Guangxun. 2001. "Danhua yinxin chengyi" (Diluting "justification by faith"). *Tianfeng ganyu, Zhongguo Jidujiao lingxiu Ding Guangxun* (Heavenly wind [and] sweet rain: Chinese Protestant leader Ding Guangxun), edited by H. Liu, pp. 288–91. Nanjing: Nanjing University Press.

Dunch, Ryan. 2001. "Protestant Christianity in China Today: Fragile, Flourishing, Fragmented." In *China and Christianity: Burdened Past, Hopeful Future*, edited by Stephen Uhalley, Jr., and Xiaoxin Wu, pp. 195–216. Armonk, NY: M. E. Sharpe.

Esherick, Joseph. 1987. *Origins of the Boxer Uprising*. Berkeley: University of California Press.

Gong Xuezeng. 2003. *Shehuizhuyi yu zongjiao* (Socialism and religion). Beijing: Religious Cultures Press.

Heilongjiang TSPM. 2003. "Introduction to Heilongjiang Bible School." Harbin: 2.

Hunter, Alan, and Kim-kwong Chan. 1993. *Protestantism in Contemporary China*. New York: Cambridge University Press.

Jiang Zemin. 2003. "Gaodu zhongshi minzu gongzuo he zongjiao gongzuo" (Greatly stress ethnic minority and religious work). In *Xinshiqi zongjiao gongzuo wenxian xuanbian* (Selections of documents from religious work in the new era), edited by Documents Study Office of the Central Party Committee and the Policy and Regulation Office of the State Council State Administration for Religious Affairs. Beijing: Religious Cultures Press.

Kendal, Elizabeth. 2004. "China: Crackdown on House-Churches." Assist News Service.

Kindopp, Jason. 2004. "Fragmented yet Defiant: Protestant Resilience under Chinese Communist Party Rule." In *God and Caesar in China: Policy Implications of Church-State Tensions*, edited by Jason Kindopp and Carol Lee Hamrin, pp. 122–45. Washington, DC: Brookings Institution.

Lambert, Tony. 1994. *The Resurrection of the Chinese Church*. Wheaton, IL: Harold Shaw.

———. 2003. "Counting Christians: A Cautionary Report." *International Bulletin of Missionary Research* 27:1 (January): 6–10.

———. 2006 [1999]. *China's Christian Millions: The Costly Revival*. Grand Rapids, MI: Monarch Books.

Lee, Lydia. 2001. *A Living Sacrifice: The Life Story of Allen Yuan*. Kent, England: Sovereign World.

Leung, Ka-lun. 1999. *Gaige kaifang yilai de Zhongguo nongcun jiaohui* (The rural churches of mainland China since 1978). Hong Kong: Alliance Bible Seminary.

Li Pingye et al. 1999. "Jiushiniandai Zhongguo zongjiao fazhan zhuangkuang baogao" (A report on the development of religion in China in the 1990s). *Jidujiao wenhua xuegan* (Journal for the study of Christian culture). Beijing: People's Daily Press 2: 201–22.

Lutz, Jessie G. 1988. *Chinese Politics and Christian Missions: The Anti-Christian Movements of 1920–1928*. Notre Dame, IN: Cross Cultural Publications.

Meisner, Maurice. 1999. *Mao's China and After*. New York: Free Press.

National Religious Affairs Bureau (Guojia zongjiaoju). 1999. "Ruhe baokao woguo de zongjiao yuanxiao?" (How does one apply to China's religious schools?). *Zhongguo zongjiao* (Religions of China) 17: 59.

Overmyer, Daniel. 1976. *Folk Buddhist Religion: Dissenting Sects in Late Traditional China*. Cambridge, MA: Harvard University Press.

Ownby, David. 2001. "Imperial Fantasies: The Chinese Communists and Peasant Rebellions." *Comparative Studies in Society and History* 43, 1: 65–91.

Reilly, Thomas. 2004. *The Taiping Heavenly Kingdom: Rebellion and the Blasphemy of Empire*. Seattle: University of Washington Press.

Spiegel, Mickey. 2004. "Control and Containment in the Reform Era." In *God and Caesar in China: Policy Implications of Church-State Tensions*, edited by Jason Kindopp and Carol Lee Hamrin, pp. 40–57. Washington, DC: Brookings Institution.

Vala, Carsten T., and Kevin J. O'Brien. 2007. "Attraction without Networks: Recruiting Strangers to Unregistered Protestantism in China." *Mobilization* 12, 1: 79–94.

Wang, Stephen. 2002. *The Long Road to Freedom: The Story of Wang Mingdao*. Kent, England: Sovereign World.

Weng Zhenjin, and Wang Xikui (eds.). 2002. *Dangzheng ganbu minzu zongjiao zhishi duben* (Reader for party and government cadres doing ethnic minority and religious work). Beijing: Religious Cultures Press.

Wang Zuoan. 2002. *Zhongguo de zongjiao wenti he zongjiao zhengce* (China's religious issues and policies). Beijing: Religious Cultures Press.

Wickeri, Philip L. 1988. *Seeking the Common Ground: Protestant Christianity, the Three-Self Movement, and China's United Front*. Maryknoll, NY: Orbis.

Witek, John W. 2001. "Christianity and China: Universal Teaching from the West." In *China and Christianity: Burdened Past, Hopeful Future*, edited by Stephen Uhalley, Jr., and Xiaoxin Wu, pp. 11–27. Armonk, NY: M. E. Sharpe.

Xing, Fuk-tseng. 1999. *Dangdai Zhongguo zheng-jiao guanxi* (Church-state relations in contemporary China). Hong Kong: Alliance Bible Seminary.

Xu, Yihua. 2004. "'Patriotic' Protestants: The Making of an Official Church." In *God and Caesar in China: Policy Implications of Church-State Tensions*, edited by Jason Kindopp and Carol Lee Hamrin, pp. 107–21. Washington, DC: Brookings Institution.

Yamamori, Tetsuo, and Kim-kwong Chan. 2000. *Witnesses to Power: Stories of God's Quiet Work in a Changing China*. Waynesboro, GA: Paternoster.

Ye Xiaowen. 1999. *Ba Zhongguo zongjiao zhenshi de qingkuang gaosu Meiguo renmin* (Tell the American people about the real situation of China's religions). Beijing: Religious Cultures Press.

Yuan, Zhiming. 2003. *The Cross: Jesus in China*. Petaluma, CA: China Soul for Christ Foundation.

Zhao Tianen, and Zhuang Wanfang. 1997. *Dangdai Zhongguo Jidujiao fazhanshi* (A history of Christianity in socialist China, 1949–1997). Taipei: CMI Publishing Company.

Zhou Jiacai. 2002. *Zongjiao gongzuo tansuo* (Exploration of religious work). Beijing: Religious Cultures Press.

CHAPTER 6

Institutionalizing Modern "Religion" in China's Buddhism: Political Phases of a Local Revival

DAVID L. WANK

AFTER THE CULTURAL REVOLUTION China reentered the stream of modernity that takes "religion" as a necessary category of the state.[1] The constitutional right to "freedom of religion" was reemphasized, and a discursive definition of modern "religion" that asserted the basic principles for the existence of religion in a "socialist" order under an "atheist" political authority was issued by the Chinese Communist Party (Party) in 1982. This definition, called *On the Basic Viewpoint and Policy on the Religious Question during Our Country's Socialist Period* (*Document 19*), stipulates the seemingly incongruous principles of freedom of religious belief and religion in service to the state. To reconcile these principles, a categorical distinction is made in *Document 19* between "normal" religious activities, which are legitimated and can be active, from "superstitions," which are not and suppressed. "Normal" religions accept Party leadership, work toward state goals, and are therefore "patriotic.[2] They have the right to "manage" their own religious activities in designated "religious activity sites" (*zongjiao huodong changsuo*) such as temples, churches, and mosques. In this way, the Party's discursive definition of modern "religion" both asserts the authority of the state over religion while signifying that the Chinese state is "modern" because it is a secular one that protects freedom of religion.

This chapter traces the institutionalization of the modern discourse of "religion" in China's Buddhist revival. It starts from the premise that modern discourses have institutional effects that are distinct from what the discourse purports to achieve. For example, as James Ferguson (1990) shows for "development" discourse, even as attempts to enact development failed to achieve their explicit goals, the consequences were a profound rationalization of locales toward central state authority. Similarly, this chapter, looking beyond concerns with the degree of religious freedom and state control in much analysis of religion and state in China, considers the institutional effects of the enactment of the state's discursive definition of "religion."[3] It will trace the effects of enacting "management," "self-sufficiency," and other principles in the state discourse on the expansion of bureaucratic organization and power. In other words the enactment of "modern" religion is consequential not only for the revival of Buddhism but also constitutes modern state formation.

The concept of organizational field focuses this chapter's analysis on the politics of enactment and the institutional outcomes. An organization is a collective actor that has interests, agendas, goals, and resources. A field is "those organizations that, in aggregate, constitute a recognized area of institutional life: key suppliers, resource and product consumers, regulatory agencies, and other organizations that produce similar services or products. It directs attention to the 'totality of relevant actors'" (DiMaggio and Powell 1991 [1983]: 64–65). Organizations in a field all seek to rationalize their activities through a common discourse, such as "religion." Their interactions are political because a discourse contains contradictions and disjunctures that readily enable multiple interpretations to legitimate diverse interests. The actions of organizational actors to organize and represent activities as fitting principles and rules in the discursive institutions define the attributes and interests of organizations and link a local field to national projects and globally authoritative discourses of modernity (Meyer 1987).[4]

A local field of Buddhism traditionally has a large public (*shifangconglin*) temple in terms of size, prestige, wealth with lesser public lineage temples arrayed under it (Gernet 1995 [1956]; Welch 1967).[5] Other more recent actors are Buddhist academies, philanthropic foundations, devotee associations, and overseas Chinese networks. Key state organizations are local Buddhist Association offices and local Religious Affairs Bureaus.[6] These actors draw on various accumulated forms of capital, such as networks, history, property, personnel, and position in the state in the context of the local politics of enacting "religion."

Analysis draws on a total of two years of fieldwork conducted between 1989 and 2003.[7] Data were gathered by intensive interviewing.[8] In Xiamen we interviewed the monks in the six administrative positions in Nanputuo Temple, clergy in all of Xiamen's lesser temples, including lay nun halls (*zhaitang*), the clergy and lay staff of the Xiamen Buddhist Association

(*Xiamen Fojiao xiehui*), and officers and regular members of the Xiamen Buddhist Lodge (*Xiamen Fojiao jushilin*) and dharma chanting groups. We also interviewed staff of county- and city-level Buddhist associations in the Minnan, Putian, and Fuqing regions of Fujian and, at the national level, staff of the Buddhist Association of China, including its vice-head in 1996, and the head of the China Buddhist Academy. As for state officials, we interviewed the head of the Xiamen Religious Affairs Bureau,[9] staff of the Xiamen City United Front Work Department, and staff of the Fujian Religious Affairs Bureau.[10] All interviews were in Mandarin Chinese, which is the main dialect in Nanputuo Temple, as clergy come from all over China. We also used other data. One was our survey of all temples in Xiamen to understand their history and revival since 1979. Documents included drafts of the *Xiamen Annals of Religion* (*Xiamen zongjiaozhi*), publications by Nanputuo Temple and the Xiamen Buddhist Lodge, and state religious policies. Multiple data sources allowed us to crosscheck facts, gauge the accuracy of our understandings, and refine our analysis. The chapter's next section is a sketch of Buddhism in the local field. The third section describes the field's organizational actors. The fourth section describes three political phases of enacting the discursive definition of "religion" in *Document 19* and other state institutions. The conclusion highlights the institutional effects.

The History of Buddhism in Xiamen

The locale is Xiamen city in Fujian, a province known since the Tang dynasty as the "Buddhist Kingdom" (*Foguo*) and famous for its many Buddhist temples. Xiamen is an island just off the southeast coast with one of the best deepwater harbors in China. Upon designation as a treaty port in 1842 it became a thriving node of international trade with a wealthy, cosmopolitan merchant class. In 1980 the city was designated a Special Economic Zone to attract investment and technology from Taiwan and overseas Chinese. By 2000, its population of one and half million people enjoyed one of the highest standards of living in China and had numerous personal and economic links with Southeast Asia, Taiwan, and Hong Kong. There is a lively Buddhist field that contains three dozen temples that bustle with worshippers, tourists, rituals, and teaching.

At the apex of repute, scale, and wealth is Nanputuo Temple. Originally of the Linji sect, it became nondenominational in 1924, and shot to national prominence the following year with its establishment of the Minnan Buddhist Academy. The academy's first head was the famous monk Taixu, a progressive reformer of Buddhism, who advanced the idea of a "human Buddhism" (*renjian Fojiao*), the training of clergy by modern educational principles and techniques, and cultivation of ties with politicians and state officials.[11] Through these activities the temple became an active center of young reformist lay devotees who were concerned about the spread of Christianity in China and sought to reform Buddhism to make it a modern "religion." Additionally, there were several dozen other temples in Xiamen, some having thick connections with Nanputuo Temple while others were lineage and lay nun temples. The peak of this flourishing was the early 1930s when hundreds of clergy resided in Xiamen, including over two hundred at Nanputuo Temple.

Thereafter, Buddhism in Xiamen declined. The outbreak of war with Japan in the late 1930s reduced the wealth of Buddhist patrons and many clergy emigrated to Southeast Asia and then the founding of the People's Republic of China in 1949 drastically reduced the space of religion. Independent associational activities were suppressed and the number of clergy declined as land redistribution eroded the monastic economy and ordinands became fewer. In the mid-1950s military and local government agencies in Xiamen began occupying temples for use as observations posts, factories, schools, and community centers.[12] The remaining clergy were gathered in Nanputuo Temple and then expelled when it, too, was shut down during the Cultural Revolution (1967–77).[13] However, Nanputuo Temple escaped damage by the Red Guards in the destruction of the "Four Olds" (*sijiu*) other than the smashing of a guardian god at the temple gate.[14] Many of Xiamen's other temples were not so lucky and some were totally destroyed during the Cultural Revolution. The Buddhist field in Xiamen was no longer visible.

The state shift to market-driven economic development beginning in 1979 created a new space for religion. The overriding concern of the city government to attract investment from overseas Chinese pushed it to adopt a liberal and tolerant attitude toward religion. Therefore the state policy on religion was implemented quite early and thoroughly relative to other places in China. Temples were rebuilt and became active with clergy and devotees, the Minnan Buddhist Academy reopened, clergy were ordained, ties with overseas Chinese Buddhists were rekindled, lay devotee organizations were revived, a philanthropic foundation was established, and central and local state regulatory agencies and religious associations were reconstituted.[15] By 2001 all of Xiamen's temple sites had been reclaimed by Buddhists and many had been rebuilt on a scale two to three times larger than before. By early 2001 there were over six hundred clergy in residence at Nanputuo Temple with dozens of others in the lesser temples.

Key Organizational Actors

Buddhist temples are under the authority of two organizational actors in the state in accordance with the stipulation of *Document* 19 that "All places of worship are under the administrative leadership of the Religious Affairs Bureau, but the religious organizations and professional religious personnel are responsible for their management" (Chinese Communist Party Central Committee 1987 [1982]: 440). The shared authority of the Buddhist Association of China and State Administration for Religious Affairs, respectively "management" and "administration," requires their ongoing negotiation to establish their jurisdictions vis-à-vis the other. Before describing some contexts of this, let me briefly describe the two organizations.

The Buddhist Association of China was established in 1953 at the urging of prominent disciples of Taixu seeking a place for Buddhism in the Marxist-socialist order. The national association in Beijing consists of prominent monks and lay devotees who consider national policies and their implications for Buddhism and communicate them to Buddhists locally through meetings and publications, mobilize Buddhists to comply with state policies, engage in international Buddhist exchanges, and publish the journal *Chinese Buddhism* (*Zhongguo Fojiao*). Local (provincial, county, city) associations were set up in 1957 for routine temple management by giving salaries to needy clerics, helping temples register property, holding study classes to instill patriotism, mobilizing Buddhists for economic and political campaigns, and starting productive enterprises in temples with clergy labor (Welch 1972). Shut down in 1966, associations were revived in 1979, and the Xiamen Buddhist Association was among the first. It was headed by Miaozhan, an elderly monk who became abbot of Nanputuo Temple. Its executive committee consists of priors of registered temples in Xiamen and prominent devotees and local scholars while the staff has a secretary, vice-secretary, and a dozen clergy and devotees.[16] During the 1980s and 1990s the association staff spent much time negotiating with city government agencies and military units for the return of temple property.[17]

The Religious Affairs Bureau was established in 1954 to educate religious adherents about state ideology and policy, mobilize them to work toward state goals, censor foreign religious publications, monitor foreign religious visitors and give them the good impression that religions are protected and free in China, and nominate all religious personnel for such political bodies as the Chinese People's Political Consultative Conference (Welch 1972: 30–36). Local governments established provincial, county, and municipal offices if there were sufficient religious sites and believers to warrant one. The personnel of these offices were for the most part people with little knowledge of the religions they supervised. During the 1950s many staff members were demobilized People's Liberation Army soldiers, while in the 1980s and 1990s the staff counted numerous personnel with problematic political backgrounds. Abolished during the Cultural Revolution, the national Religious Affairs Bureau (subsequently renamed the State Administration for Religious Administration) was resuscitated in 1979 with roughly the same duties as before under the control of the State Council in the government. The Xiamen Religious Affairs Bureau was also revived that year with a staff of ten officials in three departments.[18]

The two organizations negotiate ceaselessly to establish their jurisdiction over temples, and, more generally, Buddhism. Their perceptions of possible courses of actions and justification of them reflect various principles and stipulations in the state's discursive institutions of "religion." The claim by Buddhists of management authority over temple property and wealth reflects the principle in *Document 19* that religious associations manage "normal" religion, which is freely conducted in designated religious activity sites "without interference by any persons" (Chinese Communist Party Central Committee 1987 [1982]: 440). During an interview, a staff member of the Xiamen Buddhist Association likened the association to a guard inside the temple compound who ensures that it is orderly and well maintained while the Xiamen Religious Affairs Bureau is the policeman who patrols outside the temple to ensure that Buddhism does not escape from the temple compound to be propagated in society.[19] The actions of the Xiamen Religious Affairs Bureau reflect a different view: religion must serve state ends. This is seen in such statements in *Document 19* as: religious followers must accept the "leadership of the party and government" (Chinese Communist Party Central Committee 1987 [1982]: 428), "form a united front [with atheists] in the common effort for socialist modernization" (p. 438), and "center their will and strength . . . on building a powerful, modern socialist state" (p. 436). The actions of the Xiamen Religious Affairs Bureau reflect the view that the tourist potential of temples and appeal to overseas Chinese are related to national state projects of economic development and international relations, thereby justifying the bureau's control through "administrative guidance" of temple property and economic activities.

The negotiation of jurisdictions also reflects the two organizations' competing interpretations of what are the "religious activities" that are subject to "management" or "administration." The actions of the Xiamen Religious Affairs Bureau reflect the definition of religion in the constitution and *Document 19* as "a private matter of religious belief." Perforce it follows that the bureau's control over temple property and economic activities does not violate religious freedom because these are not matters of "individual belief" and therefore do not fall within the jurisdiction of the Buddhist Association of China to "manage religious activities." Instead they lie within the bureau's jurisdiction of the "administration of religion" to support such state and national projects as economic development and overseas Chinese relations. The Buddhist Association of China takes a broader view of the activities of religion. The secretary of the Xiamen Buddhist Association cited relevant parts of *Document 19* in interviews with us: temples are "not only places of worship, but are also cultural facilities of important cultural value" that are maintained, safeguarded, and repaired by the religious associations (Chinese Communist Party Central Committee 1987 [1982]: 440); religious associations should "solve their own problems" and state officials should "not monopolize or do things that these organizations should do themselves" (p. 441); religions should be economically "self-sufficient" (p. 441), and clergy should be economically "productive" (p. 438).[20] These various principles can buttress the claims of Buddhists for greater "self-management" authority.

Negotiations between the two organizations occur within the state's dual structure of Party and government (*zhengfu*). The Party is in charge of ideology and policy making while the government is in charge of policy implementation and enforcement; furthermore the authority of the former trumps that of the latter at the same level of the state. However, the situation can be ambiguous, as is the case in Xiamen. The Buddhist Association of China is a "mass association" (*chunzhong tuanti*) under the authority of the United Front Work Department, the branch of the Party that has supervised non-Party mass social groups since the 1950s. Local Religious Affairs Bureaus can be an agency within the local government, as in Xiamen. Therefore, the situation in Xiamen is ambiguous because a government agency—the Xiamen Religious Affairs Bureau—"leads" an agency under Party control, namely the Xiamen Buddhist Association. Buddhists use this ambiguity to appeal to the Party for support.

In their negotiations, the two organizations seek recognition of their claims and positions from other organizations by using their distinctive forms of capital. One form is the symbolic capital stemming from the positions of their leaders. It is important to note here that neither religious associations nor Religious Affairs Bureaus are structurally part of any national ministerial system of personnel appointments (*xitong*). Instead local offices are established by local governments and Party branches if there is sufficient local religious activity. Yet their respective staffs possess very different positional capital in local negotiations. The head of a local Religious Affairs Bureau is only the head of that agency. The head can garner support from other government agencies in the locale because the agencies might want to present a united face toward non-state actors (*guanguan xianghu*).[21] In contrast, a leading cleric can hold multiple positions in the local field and within the state hierarchy. For example, Miaozhan, who became abbot of Nanputuo Temple, was also: in Xiamen, head of the Minnan Buddhist Academy, the Xiamen Buddhist Association, and the Nanputuo Temple Philanthropy Foundation; in Fujian province, abbot of Gushan Temple (*Gushansi*) and Yongle Temple (*Yonglesi*), head of the Fujian Buddhist Academy, and head of the Fujian Buddhist Association; at the national level, vice-chair of the Buddhist Association of China. Such multiple positions, which mimic the strategies of state officials to accumulate power, can enhance Buddhists' prestige and flexibility in dealing with local governments. At the local level the multiple positions of Buddhist leaders enable them to negotiate with local government by making multiple claims from different the organizations that they lead. Positional appointments at higher levels of the state can help them to invoke state authority to support their claims and help resolve local disputes.

Additionally, the staffs of the two organizations have different social capital. The personnel of local Religious Affairs Bureaus are natives of the locale. They have their personal connections in other agencies and can speak the local patois, which can create some feelings of intimacy and closeness. In contrast, the Buddhists who took the lead in local revivals from the late 1970s were often elderly monks who had been ordained before 1949 and were clerics during the first decade and a half of the People's Republic of China.[22] Therefore, they were likely to have a personal relationship with leaders of the Buddhist Association of China, such as Zhao Puchu, the elderly devotee who had been secretary of the pre-1949 Chinese Buddhist Association and head of the Buddhist Association of China established after 1949 until his death in 2000. This kind of personal relationship greatly enhances rapid communication between local Buddhist fields and central authority. In sum, the ambiguous structural relation of the two organizations and their respective social capital are contexts for the implementation of "religion."

Political Phases of the Reviving Buddhist Field

The change in state policy created a discursive space for religion that then gradually filled up with rituals, beliefs, teachings, networks, organizations, and resources. This process can be traced in Xiamen by the interaction of the two aforementioned organizations, as well as temples, devotees and believers' associations, overseas Chinese networks, and other state agencies. There are three phases of interaction from the late 1970s to the early 2000s, each characterized by a distinct politics of resources allocations and power relations. The first, from 1979 to 1989, consisted of cooperation among actors to revive the moribund field by restoring Nanputuo Temple as its center. The second, from 1989 to 1995, saw increasing conflict among the actors in the context of the flourishing field, leading to the direct intervention of the central authorities. The third, from 1995 until approximately 2001, was marked by a shift in orientation of Nanputuo Temple toward the central state and the realignment of the other actors in the local field.

RECONSTRUCTING THE CENTER, 1979–1989

The first task was to revive the field's center, Nanputuo Temple. Over the decade it changed from an abandoned and decaying compound to an active and wealthy temple. From the beginning an elderly monk called Miaozhan (1910–95) took the lead. Born in Liaoning province, he had been an elementary school principal before renouncing lay life in 1939. He was a disciple of Tanxu (1875–1963) and served in administrative capacities in several well-known temples before coming to Nanputuo Temple in 1957.[23] The following year he was appointed prior of the temple. When the temple was shuttered during the Cultural Revolution he lived in a small shack next to the temple. His devotion to Nanputuo Temple and determination to restore it after 1979 gave him enormous respect and goodwill among Buddhists locally, nationally, and overseas. He immediately began to revive the networks of devotees in Xiamen and clergy overseas who had left Xiamen before 1949 and worked with the Xiamen Religious Affairs Bureau to restore the temple compound. He was very successful in garnering overseas Chinese financial support, especially donations from monks and devotees in Southeast Asia, that quickly exceeded the state funds for restoration.

New organizations were created to support the revival. As noted above, the Xiamen Buddhist Association was revived in 1979 and Miaozhan was appointed as its head. Also, an entity called the Nanputuo Temple Administration Commission (*Nanputuosi guanli weiyuanhui*) was established inside the temple by the Xiamen Religious Affairs Bureau to support the monks in managing the temple. Its head was Miaozhan but the rest of the membership was decided by the bureau, which staffed it with recently retired bureau officials. Also during this time, in a reflection of Miaozhan's prestige, he was appointed head of the Fujian Buddhist Association and a member of the executive committee of the Buddhist Association of China in Beijing (Nanputuo Temple 1997: 97–98).

Under Miaozhan's leadership the reconstruction of Nanputuo Temple proceeded apace. Land occupied during the Cultural Revolution was reclaimed and the temple compound was restored. Abundant donations from overseas Chinese financed this expansion as well as the reconstruction of Xiamen's other temples. By the late 1980s Nanputuo Temple's original compound had been restored and an ambitious project was underway to expand the Minnan Buddhist Academy, and build a new mediation hall, library, abbot's residence, and guest facilities. This expansion of Nanputuo was also made possible by the temple's creation of its own financial resources. In keeping with *Document 19* that religions should be self-supporting, several profit-making activities were established in the temple. An enterprise (*qiye*) was set up that consisted of a vegetarian restaurant, photo booths, and souvenir shops that generated an income, in 1988, of RMB 240,000. The enterprise was administered by the Nanputuo Temple Administration Commission, and its accountant, a former Xiamen Religious Affairs Bureau official who was not a Buddhist, controlled its income and made decisions about its daily operations and long-term plans. The temple facilities (*shiye*) also generated other income that, in 1988, totaled RMB 1,400,000 from gate receipts (RMB 100,000), sales of texts and scriptures (RMB 20,000), the donation box (RMB 500,000), and ritual fees and donations directly to the abbot (RMB 780,000). This income was controlled by the clergy. The distinction between enterprise and facilities followed the wording in *Document 19* that clergy could receive donations and run stores that sold religious paraphernalia. But as no mention was made of tourist facilities and sales of non-Buddhist materials, the Nanputuo Temple Administration Commission could justify separating the enterprise from the clergy's control.

The performance of rituals also started up when the temple opened. Routine rituals performed in Nanputuo Temple are about the same as at any other temple in the region: daily morning and evening chanting, a service for lay persons on the fifteenth of each lunar month, and a Thousand Buddha rituals (*baiqianfo*) three times a year. Others, such as funerary (*chaodu*) and ghost feeding (*fangyankou*) rituals, are performed when commissioned by laypersons, producing a rich stream of income directly to the monks. Such special rituals as abbot's ascension, ordination (*shengzuo*), plenary mass (*shuilu*), and ghost feeding that are not regularly performed were being reorganized in the 1980s. Few clergy knew how to perform them and so several elderly clerics in the countryside were invited to perform the more elaborate ones while younger monks went to Hong Kong and Singapore to learn them. The Xiamen Buddhist Association is important for legitimating rituals because some, such as Guanyin's Birthday and ghost feeding, could be readily seen as fitting state policy definitions of superstition. So the Xiamen Buddhist Association prohibits the more blatantly superstitious aspects of these rituals such as the burning of paper money from being conducted inside the temple compound. This satisfies the Xiamen Religious Affairs Bureau without significantly changing the rituals' significance to their participants.

The temple's establishment for the training and education of monks was also revived. This was crucial because the temple was facing an extreme shortage of clergy. Ordinations had started up in Fujian province in 1982. Many ordinands in the first classes were elderly, mostly illiterate monks who had been forced to return to lay life during the Cultural Revolution and, upon reordination, returned to their rural temples. A main concern for Nanputuo Temple, therefore, was to train a corps of young, energetic, well-educated clerics for its teaching, ritual, and administrative staff. A preparatory class was opened in 1982 and the Minnan Buddhist Academy was reopened in 1985. In keeping with the tradition of Taixu, its curriculum offered both religious and secular instruction. Religious instruction includes sutras, Zen practice and philosophy, Buddhist art, basic rituals, monastic regulations, and the history of Chinese Buddhism. Secular courses include politics (modern Chinese history, basic legal knowledge, social science), Chinese literature (high school and college level), Chinese philosophy, Chinese religious policy and related law, accounting, mathematics, foreign languages (Japanese and English), etiquette, acupuncture, and Chinese herbal medicine. The teachers are monks and nuns, Xiamen University professors of history, literature, philosophy, and religious studies, and intellectual devotees hired through connections with the abbot and the Xiamen Buddhist Association. The only restriction is that a Buddhist teaches Buddhism courses.

Also, during this period, the other temples in Xiamen started to be reclaimed from the state and their restoration got underway. Many had been taken over as factories or recreation halls by district governments, street and neighborhood committees, and collective enterprises. Some of the best known temples, such as Hongshan Temple and Bailudong Temple, were strategically located on hills overlooking Nationalist-held islands off the coast and had been occupied by the military since the 1950s. The Xiamen Religious Affairs Bureau and Xiamen Buddhist Association worked together to negotiate with the military units and government agencies occupying these sites to smooth their transfer to Buddhists. The Xiamen Buddhist Association received funds from Buddhists to pay compensation to the state units and fund their restorations. Much of the money was donated by master monks overseas who had personal ties with specific temples (Ashiwa and Wank 2006). The devotees of the Buddhist Lodge also obtained a site, the Yangzhenggong Temple, a former Daoist temple in downtown Xiamen, and began organizing members throughout the city.

INTENSIFYING CONFLICT BETWEEN
LOCAL ACTORS, 1989–1995

The second phase, from roughly 1989 to 1995, was characterized by conflict between the Xiamen Religious Affairs Bureau and an increasingly confident and capable Buddhist clergy. Several events signified the start of this phase. One was the official ascension in 1990 of Miaozhan as the first abbot of Nanputuo Temple since the Cultural Revolution. This position strengthened his authority as the leader of Buddhists in Xiamen, increased his stature nationally, and enhanced the profile of Nanputuo Temple as a rapidly reviving temple. Another event was the graduation in 1989 of the first class of clergy of the revived Minnan Buddhist Academy. The brightest were appointed to positions in the new temple administration that Miaozhan established in Nanputuo, which consisted of six departments (*jianyuan*): precentor, business office, sacristan, rituals, enterprise, and education. The Xiamen Buddhist Association also acquired valuable personnel resources, including a former official of the Xiamen Religious Affairs Bureau who had served on the Nanputuo Temple Administration Commission. This individual had come to sympathize with the monks while working on the commission, and after retiring in 1989 became the full-time secretary of the Xiamen Buddhist Association. Although a Party member, he respected Miaozhan and gave him very useful advice on dealing with the government.

The association's new personnel was skilled at positioning Buddhist activities with reference to the state's discourse of "religion" while at the same time making this palatable to the clergy. For example, immediately after the 1989 student movement, the state ordered Buddhists to increase political study to promote "patriotic religion" (*aiguo aijiao,* literally "love the state, love religion")—loyalty to the Party and government above all else—because Buddhist monks had participated in demonstrations in Beijing. The Xiamen Buddhist Association was put in charge of this and its new secretary decided to teach a course a course on Chinese history rather then one on Marxism. This satisfied the Xiamen Religious Affairs Bureau that "patriotic religion" was being taught, while the clergy did not find the content objectionable (Ashiwa and Wank 2006: 352).

However, this heightened capacity of the Buddhists in Xiamen fueled tension between the clergy and the Xiamen Religious Affairs Bureau. Whereas the clergy had once welcomed the support of the Nanputuo Temple Administration Commission, the rapid increase in the number of young monks and nuns who were capable of handling temple administration now led the clergy to see the commission as interfering in Nanputuo Temple's internal affairs. Commission control of the enterprise especially annoyed the monks. The enterprise employees were the offspring and kin of Xiamen Religious Affairs Bureau officials and much of its income went toward paying their salaries and bonuses. The commission accountant invested the rest of the profits in enhancing the temple's tourist appeal. He built a luxury three-story restaurant in a side compound that catered to overseas Chinese tourists and visiting dignitaries. He justified this action by claiming that it supported the city government's overriding goal of developing the Xiamen Special Economic Zone. This further angered the monks, who wanted to use the money to expand temple facilities for religious cultivation and study by clergy and devotees.

Over the next few years saw escalating conflict between the Nanputuo Temple clergy and the Xiamen Religious Affairs Bureau. The monk appointed by Miaozhan to supervise the enterprise as part of the new temple administration was not recognized by the Nanputuo Temple Administration Commission. The commission said that Buddhist precepts forbade monks from engaging in business. So Miaozhan then appealed to Zhao Puchu, head of the Buddhist Association of China in Beijing, who dispatched an investigation team to Xiamen. The team affirmed the clergy's ownership of the enterprise while also recommending that it be leased out to its lay manager. The investigation team also concluded that the Nanputuo Temple Administration Commission was usurping activities that the clergy were now capable of doing, in contravention of *Document 19*. It recommended curtailing the commission's authority and changing its name to Nanputuo Temple Firm (*Nanputuosi shiwusuo*) to indicate that it was no longer an administrative entity. Thus, while the clergy won in principle, control of the enterprise remained unchanged due to its continued operation by its lay manager, the former Xiamen Religious Affairs Bureau official.

Conflict intensified when the monks discovered that the lay manager had, unbeknownst to them, registered himself as the enterprise's legal representative (*faren daibiao*) with the Industrial and Commercial Bureau, which issues business licenses. The Xiamen Buddhist Association protested to the Xiamen Religious Affairs Bureau that this violated the recently agreed upon principle of temple ownership of the enterprise but the bureau did not concede. So again Miaozhan appealed to Zhao Puchu in the Buddhist Association of China in Beijing. When the Xiamen Religious Affairs Bureau cadres heard of this they summoned Miaozhan to their office and tried to intimidate him. In a manner reminiscent of the previous political era, they forced him to write a self-criticism statement that he was stubborn and disobeying bureau orders. This intimidation was also reported to the Buddhist Association of China in Beijing and the Xiamen Religious Affairs Bureau was reprimanded.

Things became violent when the enterprise manager discovered a plan written by monks on how they would manage the enterprise when they controlled it. Thereupon the manager obtained a letter from the city government that acknowledged the temple's ownership of the enterprise but prohibited monks from managing it. In obtaining it, the manager played on the concern of the city government for the safety of the numerous national and foreign dignitaries who dined at the restaurant when visiting Xiamen by arguing that their security should not be entrusted to the monks. The Xiamen Religious Affairs Bureau followed this up by convening a meeting in the vegetarian restaurant to announce a new "three party management" (*sanfang guanli*) arrangement for the enterprise that involved the Xiamen Religious Affairs Bureau, Public Security Bureau, and clergy. The monks were incensed, especially the young monks studying in the Minnan Buddhist Academy. They locked the officials from the Public Security Bureau and Xiamen Religious Affairs Bureau in the restaurant and hung banners outside the temple listing their grievances over the enterprise. The officials remained locked up overnight until Public Security Bureau forces stormed the temple in the morning to release them. Afterwards the local government wanted to treat the matter as a political one by labeling the monks' actions as "counter-revolutionary." So once again Zhao Puchu and the Buddhist Association of China sent down an investigation team. Upon examining the banners that had hung outside the temple, it concluded that the monks had not criticized the government but only complained of their lack of control over the enterprise. The matter was dismissed.

During the conflict the Xiamen Religious Affairs Bureau retaliated by obstructing and harassing the clergy. It blocked the monks' plans to expand the temple's religious facilities. For example, Miaozhan wanted to build a large meditation hall for monks and devotees. However, the Xiamen Religious Affairs Bureau criticized the plan as wasteful, claiming that lazy monks did not need a new place to sleep during the day. It also noted that the architect and donor had Taiwan connections, raising the specter of Taiwan spies. Next the Xiamen Religious Affairs Bureau opposed the abbot's plan to build two towers in front of the temple on the grounds that they would destroy the frontal view of the temple for tourists.

Miaozhan's greatest achievement during this second phase was the creation of the Nanputuo Temple Philanthropy Foundation (*Nanputuo cishan jijinhui*) in 1994, China's first Buddhist philanthropy. It was registered with the Ministry of Civil Affairs as a philanthropic foundation. Is membership was open to all and it provided social services in the temple through a well staffed medical clinic, and made large donations for social welfare and disaster relief throughout China. Because it was a philan-thropic rather than religious organization, there was no opening for the Xiamen Religious Affairs Bureau to control it. But the foundation was clearly part of Nanputuo Temple as it was located on the premises and staffed by monks and nuns. It used the characters for "Nanputuo Temple" in its name and charity was disbursed by the abbot in publicized trips to disaster regions and poor areas. One of the foundation's first major acts was to aid victims in a rural area of Yunnan province that had been dev-astated by a large earthquake. It sent its personnel to assess the victims' needs, donated cash and clothing, and established a free primary school in one village. In this way the monks expanded their potential to reach the masses of people.

The end of this second phase of Nanputuo Temple's development was marked by Miaozhan's death in 1996 and a final confrontation with the Xiamen Religious Affairs Bureau. Nanputuo monks wanted to cremate his body on the hill behind the temple in accordance with the practice for deceased abbots. But the Xiamen Religious Affairs Bureau, citing safety reasons, ordered the corpse to be cremated in a distant rural temple with cremation facilities. It also ordered the funeral procession to depart from the temple at midnight and pass through Xiamen's streets during the darkness. But the monks held back until early morning and the procession traveled in daylight for fifty miles along roads lined with kneeling people who had been waiting all night. They knew of Miaozhan's sufferings dur-ing the Cultural Revolution and his contributions to revive Nanputuo and Buddhism in Xiamen and elsewhere. Coincidently, a hill behind the city government caught fire the next day and all the trees were burned down. Buddhists saw this as sign of Miaozhan's anger at the city government.

BIFURCATION OF THE LOCAL FIELD, 1995–2001

The death of Miaozhan in 1995 marked the beginning of a third phase. A characteristic of this phase was the Xiamen Buddhist Association's greater distance from Nanputuo Temple. The Xiamen Religious Affairs Bureau had already taken steps to reduce the capacity of the Xiamen Buddhist Association to support Nanputuo even before Miaozhan's death. According to regulations, civil associations such as the Xiamen Buddhist Association can elect their own leadership. However, the Xiamen Religious Affairs Bureau claimed sole authority to nominate the candi-dates who stood for election. It then presented a slate of officers that did not contain the capable personnel who had helped the temple challenge the Xiamen Religious Affairs Bureau. The adoption of this slate removed key personnel who were most familiar with the state procedures and knew how to position the clergy's claims in terms of *Document 19* and other state discursive institutions. Miaozhan's death also weakened the attachment of many of the young capable monks who had been motivated by his self-less dedication to restore Nanputuo Temple and further Buddhism. These monks, many of whom had occupied administrative posts in the temple, now began to drift away, putting the temple at a further disadvantage.

After Miaozhan's death, the Xiamen Religious Affairs Bureau further increased the distance of the Xiamen Buddhist Association from the Nanputuo Temple clergy, thereby affecting the leadership of the Xiamen Buddhist Association. From 1979 until his death, Miaozhan had been the leader of the association. But now the Xiamen Religious Affairs Bureau insisted that Miaozhan's successor as Nanputuo abbot (see below) could not concurrently serve as head of the Xiamen Buddhist Association. This new arrangement reduced the possibilities for local positional power by Xiamen's leading cleric, and also ended the tradition in Xiamen stretching back before 1949 of the Nanputuo abbot representing all the clergy in Xiamen.

Thereupon the Xiamen Religious Affairs Office sought to inaugurate a more compliant leadership. It did so by manipulating regional differences among the clergy. Let me note that there are factions in many organizations in China based on dialect and native place or origin. In Nanputuo there is tension between so-called northern and Fujian monks. The northern monks come from Manchuria (Miaozhan was from Liaoning province), Zhejiang, and other places outside of Fujian and are more likely to be from urban areas, better educated, and considered more pious by devotees. They dominated the Nanputuo leadership and administration. Fujian monks, many of whom came from poorer areas on the fringes of the Minnan region and from the Putian region directly adjacent to Minnan, were less educated, from rural backgrounds, and considered more pragmatic. The Xiamen Religious Affairs Bureau nominated Putian monks to be the head and vice-head of the Xiamen Buddhist Association. These monks were much less likely to challenge the Xiamen Religious Affairs Bureau and more willing to enter into relations based on exchange of favors.[24]

The new leadership of the Xiamen Buddhist Association moved to distance itself from Nanputuo Temple. Whereas the previous association leadership had welcomed Nanputuo Temple's financial support, the new chair and secretary saw this as a dependency that undermined the association's authority by making it appear as an office of the temple. This greater distance was signified by the move of the Xiamen Buddhist Association office from a prominent position near the temple's main gate to a side compound. No longer was the signpost of the Xiamen Buddhist Association the first thing that a visitor would see upon entering the temple compound; the association became invisible in the temple.

Greater distance was also signified by the attempt of the Xiamen

Buddhist Association to diversify its income away from heavy reliance on the temple. To do so, it turned to Xiamen's other temples, which were registered as religious activity sites and were thriving through donations and ritual performances commissioned by overseas Chinese and the rising local business class, and operating their own vegetarian restaurants and other for-profit tourist businesses. The Xiamen Buddhist Association demanded that all temples pay it 15 percent of their annual income and pay fees for permission to perform rituals. The Xiamen Religious Affairs Bureau reinforced this demand by decreeing that all new construction in temples required the permission of both the Xiamen Buddhist Association and Xiamen Religious Affairs Bureau. The implication was clear: temples that did not share revenue with the Xiamen Buddhist Association could be denied this permission, putting a brake on their development. Furthermore, the two organizations even tried to become partners in developing the real estate potential of some temples. The Xiamen Buddhist Association agreed to let the Xiamen Religious Affairs Bureau construct a commercial building and hotel on an old temple site in the city's center. The Xiamen Religious Affairs Bureau would run it for a profit, thereby increasing its income. It would also give the Xiamen Buddhist Association office space to let it move away from Nanputuo temple. However, this plan ran afoul of Xiamen's master urban development plan and did not start up.

As the Xiamen Buddhist Association shifted away from Nanputuo Temple toward cooperating with the Xiamen Religious Affairs Bureau and focusing on the supervision of Xiamen's secondary temple, Nanputuo became more institutionalized as a prominent national temple with ties to the state. This stemmed from the selection of a new abbot. The death of Miaozhan created a vacuum in temple leadership. As residents of a non-denominational temple, the Nanputuo monks could elect their own abbot. For two years the temple's clergy sought in vain for a successor. Miaozhan had died at the height of the conflict between Nanputuo and the Xiamen Religious Affairs Bureau. One likely successor was so frightened by the conflict that he withdrew his name from contention. Other monks were considered too young and lacking in stature and experience to lead the temple. Thereupon, the Buddhist Association of China in Beijing intervened. It was also seeking prominent positions for graduates of the China Buddhist Academy and nominated as abbot a member of its first graduating class, a monk called Shenghui. He was formally ensconced as abbot in an ascension ceremony in 1997.

Shenghui was in his mid-forties and considered a future leader of Buddhism in China. He was also seen as an expert in temple management, having written his master's thesis on temple management according to Buddhist doctrines. His prestige and power were, like those of Miaozhan, seen in his multiple positions. In Xiamen he was appointed abbot of Nanputuo Temple, and head of the Minnan Buddhist Academy and Nanputuo Temple Philanthropy Foundation. In his home province of Hunan he was abbot of Mt. Guli Temple (*Gulishansi*) and head of the provincial Hunan Buddhist Association. He was also vice principal in charge of education at the China Buddhist Academy and the Mt. Jiuhua Buddhist Academy (*Jiuhuashan Foxueyuan*). Yet despite his prestige, Shenghui projected an entirely different image from that of Miaozhan. While the latter was widely viewed with affection as a fatherly pioneer in reviving Buddhism in Xiamen, Shenghui projected the imperious air of a cadre, and was, therefore, both respected and feared. He had been born after 1949 and raised entirely in the People's Republic of China, was skilled in bureaucratic maneuvering and knew how to project authority in dealing with Party and government officials, and was concerned with national and international Buddhism and politics. Within a few years after coming to Nanputuo Temple, he would go on to participate in the People's Political Consultative Conference, lead the Chinese delegation to the China-Japan-Korea Buddhist Friendship Exchange Conference (*Zhong-Ri-Han Fojiao youhao jiaoliu huiyi*), and testify as a Chinese representative before the United Nations Human Rights Commission in Geneva.

As Nanputuo's abbot he enforced discipline in the temple, insisting that clerics be on time for meals and not loiter in the courtyard. He also dealt firmly with the Xiamen Religious Affairs Bureau. He notified the enterprise lay manager that he might shut down the enterprise, forcing the manager to become more accountable to the monks. Shenghui also required all nun novices applying to the Minnan Buddhist Academy to have shaved heads. By conforming to the orthodox idea of a nun, he ended the practice established by Miaozhan of accommodating the southern Fujian lay nun (*zhaigu*) tradition. Under his reign Nanputuo Temple sidelined some claims of the Xiamen Religious Affairs Bureau and became more established as a national temple with a comprehensive administrative bureaucracy, a major Buddhist academy, and center of Buddhist philanthropy.

This brings the narrative up to 2001. Over the two decades of the revival documented in this chapter, various organizations and persons have interacted to revive Buddhism in Xiamen. This revival started with a focus on Nanputuo, Xiamen's major temple. Along with its revival, it has become increasingly identified with the central state and detached from the local organizational field. We have described how Nanputuo Temple became disengaged from local politics even as the Xiamen Religious Affairs Bureau and Xiamen Buddhist Association shifted their focus to the other temples in Xiamen. This detachment can be seen not only as a separation between central and local political orientations but also between Mandarin- and Minnan-speaking peoples. Nanputuo Temple is dominated by persons from outside the Minnan region, and its administrative language and language of communication with believers and other groups is not the Minnan dialect but Mandarin, whereas most of Xiamen's other temples are entrenched in the Minnan-speaking community. Many of the clergy heading the secondary temples are, with the exception of the few appointed by the Nanputuo abbot, Minnan speakers who interact in dialect with the Minnan-speaking Xiamen Religious Affairs Bureau personnel and local followers. Also, a dharma chanting society of middle-aged and retired women that had formed around the few Minnan-speaking monks at Nanputuo Temple and held their activities in one of the temple side-compounds decided in the late 1990s to build a new temple in the suburbs to house their activities. Finally, the southern Fujian lay nuns unable to enroll in the Minnan Buddhist Academy turned their attention to developing their own temples. This further indicates the distancing of Nanputuo Temple from the concerns of the local field and the reorientation and diversification of the temples and devotees.

This detachment can also be seen as a reflection of the history of the local field. Nanputuo is well known as a modern reform temple with an illustrious history linked to Taixu, who is revered by many Buddhists and recognized by the state for modernizing Buddhism. Therefore, the rising prominence of Nanputuo Temple was supported by both the clergy and the central state for their respective interests and purposes. The clergy had expectations that the temple's rising prominence would better enable the temple to develop Buddhism and become disentangled from the structures and stratagems of local politics. The central state had expectations of Nanputuo Temple contributing to the local economy (through tourism) and furthering its relations with overseas Chinese and other Buddhist countries. Thus, the detachment of Nanputuo temple from the local field also reflected a shifting alignment of interests between the state and the temple.

Conclusion

The change of national religious policy in the late 1970s reestablished institutions that acknowledged the existence of "religion." This opened up a discursive space for its existence by asserting such principles as "self-management," "religious activity sites," and "self-sufficiency," and identifying the key organizational actors to implement them. Although we have described only a small portion of its complexity, it is evident how the change in state policy created a discursive space for religion that then gradually filled up with rituals, teachings, networks, organizations, and interests. We have traced this process as the politics of a reviving local field where actors strive to legitimate their actions in accordance with the state discourse of "religion." Nanputuo Temple was the first Buddhist temple to recover after the Cultural Revolution and provided much support for the revival of other temples in the local field. In Nanputuo Temple we can see the politics among Nanputuo Temple, the Xiamen Buddhist Association, and the Xiamen Religious Bureau and the intersection of this politics of the local field with central state power and overseas Chinese networks.

Tracing two decades of the reemergence of Xiamen's Buddhist revival shows several dynamics of institutionalization. Actors are constantly organizing themselves. In this process they are defining themselves and the attributes of the field. Key to this organizing is the state's discourse of "religion." Actors' interpretations and enactments of its principles shape their organizational characteristics and relations in the field. Multiple interpretations of principles among actors that are expressed in specific situations cause tensions as well as opportunities. The consequences of this are reallocations of power and resources. A good example is the competition between the Xiamen Religious Affairs Bureau and Nanputuo Temple to control the vegetarian restaurant. This conflict produced three things. First, it redefined the power of Nanputuo Temple and the Xiamen Religious Affairs Bureau. Second, it ended an existing organization, the Nanputuo Temple Administration Commission, and created a new one, the Nanputuo Temple Firm. Third, it invited the intrusion of central state power, which became an active element in the field.

Roles and relations among organizations are constantly shifting and even producing innovative configurations as, through their interactions, organizations change their characters and interests. This can be seen in the initial local orientation of the Nanputuo Temple clergy to work closely with the Xiamen Buddhist Association and Xiamen Religious Affairs Bureau and then attempt to transcend the local field to become closer to the central state as its resources and interests changed. This can also be seen in the dramatic shift in the position of the Xiamen Buddhist Association. It used to be close to Nanputuo Temple as if it were the abbot's secretariat and was hostile to the Xiamen Religious Affairs Bureau but subsequently became an ally of the bureau. None of this stems directly from the content of the state religious policy or from any inherent characteristics of religious communities or the state administration. Rather it reflects the attempts of the various organizations to position themselves in the best possible light in the context of the state's religious policies to pursue not only issues directly related to the practice of religion but also to control economic resources, personnel appointments, and lines of communication to the center.

Also, actors can maintain flexibility in legitimating their actions by spanning several spaces that are defined by the state. The Nanputuo Temple Philanthropy Foundation is an especially interesting case in point. It is licensed by the Ministry of Civil Affairs as a "philanthropic" rather than a "religious" organization and, therefore, is not under the authority of the State Administration for Religious Affairs and its local bureaus. It enables Buddhists to participate in the field of philanthropy populated by such organizations as the China Charity Federation (*Zhonghua cishan hui*) and the Red Cross to engage in activities as Buddhists that are not considered religious. Yet everyone knows that the philanthropy foundation is Buddhist and part of Nanputuo Temple. People donate to the philanthropy foundation precisely for this reason and its activities are even promoted in the state media as an example of how Buddhists are actively engaged in national projects of disaster management and social welfare. Therefore, the philanthropy foundation enables Buddhism to move out of the delimitations that it faces as "religion."

Furthermore, central actions not only rationalized the local field in accordance with its religion policies but with other institutions as well. For example, competition over the temple enterprise invoked legal property rights, a major concern of the central state in promoting the market economy, through questions of ownership and control over productive assets. Central state judgments on the issue of "self-management" in the religion policy also clarified the allocation of temple assets in terms of legally defined property rights. Another example is the central state action regarding the problem of leadership succession in Nanputuo Temple after Miaozhan's death. The Buddhist Association of China in Beijing took this opportunity to appoint a new abbot who reinforced administrative discipline and regularization, a national priority in the 1990s. These examples show that the institutionalization of religion not only reshapes organizational boundaries and authority relations within the field but also positions it with regard to such other state institutions as property rights and administrative reform.

Here it is important to note that this chapter's account of the institutionalization of "religion" in Buddhism explains only those aspects of Buddhism that are consciously enacted as modern "religion." Of course, there also exist many popular beliefs that not oriented by toward the state's modern definition of "religion" but rather are enacted as part of people's daily lives. Examples can be seen in this chapter, such as the circumstances of Miaozhan's funeral. The reverence of the mourners who lined his funeral route and their belief that the burning trees expressed his wrath toward the city government are not positioned by people in the state's modernist framing of "religion." Also, in decreeing the time and place of the abbot's cremation, the Xiamen city government expressed its concern with state control and popular mobilization rather than Buddhism's "modernity" per se. An analysis of these beliefs and concerns in relation to the state's discourse of modern "religion" is, however, outside of the scope of this chapter (but see the chapters by Ashiwa and Dean in this volume).

In sum, this chapter has sought to describe the institutionalization of "religion" in Buddhism since the late 1970s as China entered a new phase of modern state building. It has done so through an institutional approach that conceives of Buddhism as a field of organizational actors whose activities are positioned within the state's discursive space of "religion." Within this field it has traced the revival of Buddhism in terms of a politics of organizational formation and strategic interaction to control the discourses of modern "religion" that reflects the Party's interpretation of the modern value of secularism. The institutionalization of "religion" proceeds through the organizational bureaucratization of multiple actors who are enacting it. These actors come to constitute religious fields within modern "state" formation," which, as Max Weber has argued, is an intriguing character of "religion" in modernity.

Notes

1. Since the early twentieth century Chinese elites have seen the modern category of "religion" imported from the West as a necessary category of the modern state that they have been building (Ashiwa, this volume). The right to freedom of religion has been included in all four of the constitutions of the People's Republic of China. However, during the Cultural Revolution (1966–76) the right was not observed because all religion was considered to be "superstition," eliminating the space of "religion."

2. See Vala (this volume) for "patriotic religion."

3. For a discussion of tendencies in extant analyses on China's state and religion, see the literature review by Ashiwa and Wank in this volume's "Introduction."

4. See Chau (this volume) for a compatible analysis in regard to popular religion.

5. In a lineage temple, the abbots and priors are dharma descendents of a founding monk, while leadership in a public temple is more open. Large public temples tend to be ecumenical (*shifangconglin*) and open to clergy of all denominations.

6. The state bureaucracy of religious management was called the Religious Affairs Office from 1951 to 1954 and the Bureau of Religious Affairs from 1954 until 1998. The current name—State Administration for Religious Affairs—was adopted in 1998. This chapter uses the current name to refer to the post-1949 bureaucracy at the national level. Local offices of religious administration at the provincial level and below often use the word "bureau" in their name; therefore the term "Religious Affairs Bureau" refers to local levels.

7. The fieldwork was conducted together with Yoshiko Ashiwa in 1989–90 with

shorter periods in 1995, 1998, 1999, 2000, and 2002–3. In addition to Xiamen, we conducted fieldwork elsewhere in Fujian province, most notably in the Putian and Fuqing regions and the cities of Fuzhou, Zhangzhou, and Quanzhou. Outside of Fujian we visited temples in Guangzhou and Beijing and followed Nanputuo Temple's transnational connections in field research conducted over ten years from 1993 in the United States (Boston, Los Angeles, New York, San Francisco, Seattle), Singapore, and the Philippines. We interviewed clergy whom we had originally met in Nanputuo Temple, as well as devotees and other clergy with ties to Xiamen and its temples.

8. The research was supported by grants from the Japan Ministry of Education Scientific Research for documentary research, and the John D. and Catherine T. MacArthur Foundation Program on Peace and International Cooperation Research and Writing Grant for fieldwork in 1998–2000. Additionally, Wank conducted documentary research and fieldwork while a Kukin Fellow at the Harvard Academy for International and Area Studies in 1992–94, and Ashiwa was supported in China by a grant from Kobe Yamate Women's College in 1989–90.

9. The official name of the bureau is the Bureau of Ethnic and Religious Affairs of Xiamen (*Xiamen shi minzu yu zongjiao shiwu ju*). In this chapter it is shortened to Xiamen Religious Affairs Bureau. For a discussion of one bureau managing both ethnic and religious affairs, see Ashiwa and Wank (2006: 344n12)

10. We also interviewed current and former staff members of some of these organizations who had emigrated to or were traveling in Southeast Asia and the United States.

11. On Taixu, see Welch (1968), Pittman (2001).

12. During the 1950s Buddhism was used for the state's foreign diplomacy toward Buddhist countries (for example, Japan, Sri Lanka) and large public temples were maintained through state subsidies as showcases of religion under socialism to impress foreign visitors. But the innumerable secondary temples in locales ceased operating while many were taken over and used by local governments.

13. We learned in interviews that the remaining clergy returned to their home villages and became farmers.

14. The Four Olds were old customs, old culture, old habits, and old ideas. During the Cultural Revolution, Red Guards destroyed anything they considered the Four Olds, including Buddhist temples. Nanputuo Temple was spared, supposedly as part of Prime Minister Zhou Enlai's directive to protect cultural sites of national significance (*zhongdian*) from Red Guards. The destruction of the Four Olds in Xiamen can be glimpsed in the account of the Cultural Revolution in Xiamen by a local Red Guard leader (Ling 1972).

15. Through conversations with overseas Chinese who frequently visit Xiamen we learned that even in the early 1980s tens of thousands of worshippers crowded Nanputuo Temple on Guanyin's Birthday. For an account of the history of the connection of Buddhism in Xiamen with overseas Chinese communities and the resources they have provided for its revival, see Ashiwa and Wank (2005).

16. Only "regularized" temples with a head monk, accountant, cashier, and administrative framework that is verified in annual inspections can be represented. According to the Xiamen Religious Affairs Office, by the year 2000, there were sixteen fully "regularized" temples, about half the total number of temples in Xiamen.

"Local scholars" are persons with extensive knowledge of local history and customs who have had long careers in secondary school administration and teaching, and in state cultural and propaganda bureaus. During the 1980s and 1990s, they served as consultants to local governments, universities, and associations on the revival of revival of religion and popular practice. (See Chau, this volume.)

17. At monthly association meetings temples report on their situations and the Xiamen Religious Affairs Bureau announces new policies and regulations.

18. The Xiamen Religious Affairs Bureau has three departments: Department One for Buddhism and folk beliefs; Department Two for Islam, Protestantism, and Catholicism; Department Three for national minorities. For a Religious Affairs Bureau also to handle minority affairs was quite common in the 1980s and 1990s. This appears to have grown out of an attempt to consolidate administrative activities. The same personnel dealt with both religious and minority affairs (Sueki and Cao 1996: 77).

19. The claim that the association's jurisdiction was over all activities in the temple compound is only possible in the context of wealthy temples, such as those in Xiamen. Revenue flows in through their gates in the form of donations, tourism, and commissions on rituals performed within their compounds. However, temples in poorer areas could not make such a claim because their clergy would have to travel outside of the temple compound to perform rituals in the houses of devotees and worshippers in order to earn money. I am grateful to Kenneth Dean for pointing this out.

20. To help Buddhists in these negotiations, the Buddhist Association of China disseminates knowledge about the policy to local Buddhist Association offices. Its flagship publication, *China Buddhism*, contains sections on new religious policies and laws and reports on their implications. It also publishes handbooks with such titles as *Questions and Answers on Religious Policy and Legal Knowledge* (*Zongjiao zhengce falü zhishi dawen*) that contain indexed questions about religion that are answered with quotations from relevant sections of *Document 19* and other state policy documents. The Xiamen Buddhist Association secretary told us that these various documents are very useful to support claims when negotiating with city government agencies.

21. Working in a local Religious Affairs Bureau office is not a desirable career because of the political sensitivity of religion and paucity of gain-seeking opportunities (for example, bribes, special fees, etc.). In a conversation with us, a scholar who has visited many local Religious Affairs Bureau offices called them a "dumping ground" for problematic personnel. However the situation is changing through efforts to heighten knowledge of religions by bureau staff in intensive courses in religion (Stockwell 1993: 45), while younger staff members are more likely to have college degrees in history and philosophy and even graduate degrees in religious studies (Chan and Carlson 2005: 7–8).

22. Some members of the association staff, especially the lay devotees, are also locals.

23. Tanxu was renowned for his seminaries for clergy education.

24. Welch (1967: 405) notes that temples in southern Jiangsu province were dominated by clergy from the poorer northern part of the province who spoke a different dialect.

References

Ashiwa, Yoshiko, and David L. Wank. 2005. "The Globalization of Chinese Buddhism: Clergy and Devotee Networks in the Twentieth Century." *International Journal of Asian Studies* 2, 2: 217–37.

————. 2006. "State, Association, and Religion in Southeast China: The Politics of a Reviving Buddhist Temple." *Journal of Asian Studies* 65, 2: 337–59.

Chan, Kim-kwong, and Eric R. Carlson. 2005. *Religious Freedom in China: Policy, Administration and Regulation; a Research Handbook.* Santa Barbara, CA, and Hong Kong: Institute for the Study of American Religion and Hong Kong Institute for Culture, Commerce and Religion.

Chinese Communist Party Central Committee (Zhonggong zhongyang). 1987 [1982]. "Guanyu woguo shehuizhuyi shiqi zongjiao wentide jiben guandian he jiben zhengce" (Regarding the basic viewpoint and policy on the religious question during our country's socialist period). In *Shiyijie sanzhong quanhui yilai zhongyao wenxian xuandu* (Collection of important documents since the third plenum of the Eleventh Party Congress), v. 1, pp. 428–48. Beijing: Renmin chubanshe.

DiMaggio, Paul J., and Walter W. Powell. 1991 [1983]. "The Iron Cage Revisited: Institutional Isomorphism and Collective Rationality in Organizational Fields." In *The New Institutionalism in Organizational Analysis,* edited by Walter W. Powell and Paul J. DiMaggio, pp. 63–82. Chicago: University of Chicago Press.

Ferguson, James. 1990. *The Anti-Politics Machine: "Development," Depoliticization, and Bureaucratic Power in Lesotho.* Cambridge, UK: Cambridge University Press.

Gernet, Jacques. 1995 [1956]. *Buddhism in Chinese Society: An Economic History from the Fifth to the Tenth Centuries.* Translated by Franciscus Verellen. New York: Columbia University Press.

Ling, Ken. 1972. *The Revenge of Heaven: From School Boy to Little General in Mao's Army.* Translated by Miriam London and Lee Ta-ling. New York: Putnam.

Meyer, John. W. 1987. "The World Polity and the Authority of the Nation-State." In *Institutional Structure: Constituting State, Society, and Individual,* edited by G. M. Thomas et al. Beverly Hills, CA: Sage

Nanputuo Temple. 1997. *Miaozhan heshang ji'nianji* (A commemorative collection for venerable Miaozhan). Xiamen: Nanputuo Temple

Pittman, Don A. 2001. *Toward a Modern Chinese Buddhism: Taixu's Reforms.* Honolulu: University of Hawai'i Press.

Stockwell, Foster. 1993. *Religion in China Today.* Beijing: New World Press.

Sueki Fumihiko, and Cao Zhangqi. 1996. *Gendai Chūgoku no Bukkyō* (Buddhism in contemporary China). Tokyo: Hirakawa shuppansha.

Welch, Holmes. 1967. *The Practice of Chinese Buddhism, 1900–1950.* Cambridge, MA: Harvard University Press.

————. 1968. *The Buddhist Revival in China.* Cambridge, MA: Harvard University Press.

————. 1972. *Buddhism under Mao.* Cambridge, MA: Harvard University Press.

CHAPTER 7

Islam in China: State Policing and Identity Politics

DRU C. GLADNEY

THE COMPLEX NATURE of institutional linkages between religion and ethnicity in China is dramatically illustrated by contrasting responses to Chinese rule by its diverse Muslim communities. China has attempted to "manage Islam" through a nationality policy that recognizes certain Muslim communities as official minority nationalities. The institutional links between the state and the policing of religion and Muslim identity politics in the People's Republic since September 11, 2001, have become even more apparent as China attempts to limit the spread of radical Islam, prevent separatism among Muslims on its northwestern frontier, and successfully integrate its 21 million Muslims into the broader Chinese mainstream. How have China's Muslims accommodated themselves to Chinese rule? Have Chinese institutions succeeded in integrating its Muslims? Is the Uyghur resistance in Xinjiang a viable threat to Chinese rule in Xinjiang? What about Muslim diversity in China? What are some of the institutions engaged in taxonomizing, monitoring, and actually identifying China's Muslims as "safe" or threats to state security? China's Muslims are now facing their second millennium under Chinese rule. Many of the challenges they confront remain the same as they have for the last 1,300 years of continuous interaction with Chinese society, but many others are new as a result of China's transformed and increasingly globalized society, and especially the watershed events of the September 11th terrorist attacks with the subsequent "war on terrorism." Muslims in China live as minority communities amid a sea of people who, in their view, are largely pork-eating, polytheist, secularist, and "heathen" (*kafir*). Nevertheless, many of their small and isolated communities have survived in rather inhospitable circumstances for over a millennium. This chapter seeks to map, through heuristic interpretive schemes, the integration and nonintegration of Muslim groups and organizations in China today, charting the background of recent expressions of violence among some Muslim groups.

Though small in population percentage (about 2 percent in China, 1 percent in Japan, and less than 1 percent in Korea), the Muslim populations of East Asia are nevertheless large in comparison with those of other Muslim states. In fact, there are more Muslims living in China today than there are in Malaysia, and more than in every Middle Eastern Muslim nation except Iran, Turkey, and Egypt (and about the same number as in Iraq). As Lipman (1997: 2) insightfully noted, these long-term Muslim communities have often been the "familiar strangers" found in small enclaves throughout Asia. And if Kosovo and Bosnia are to serve as lessons, failure to accommodate Muslim minorities can lead to national dismemberment and international intervention. Indeed, China's primary objection to NATO involvement in Kosovo centered on its fear that this might encourage the aiding and abetting of separatists, a potential problem in light of the fact that independence groups in Xinjiang, Tibet, and even Taiwan, remain a major Chinese concern.

This chapter will examine state institutions and Muslim identity politics in China, not only because it is where this author has conducted most of his research, but also because as the largest Muslim minority in East Asia, China's Muslims are clearly the most threatened in terms of self-preservation and Islamic identity. Most relevant to this is the thesis put forth that successful Muslim accommodation to minority status in China can be seen to be a measure of the extent to which Muslim groups allow the reconciliation of the dictates of Islam to the contexts of their particular socio-historical setting. This goes against the opposite view that can be found in the writings of some analysts of Islam in China, such as Raphael Israeli and Michael Dillon, who have consistently argued that Islam in the region is almost unavoidably rebellious and that Muslims in general are inherently problematic to a non-Muslim state (Israeli 1981, 2002; Dillon 1997, 2004). Many of these analyses posit an antagonistic relationship between Islam and the state in China, failing to see not only a wide spectrum of accommodation among various Muslim communities, but also ignoring the important institutionalized relationship between ethnicity and religion for China's Muslim nationalities.

Islam in China

According to the reasonably accurate 2000 national census of China, the total Muslim population is 20.3 million, including: Hui (9,816,805); Uyghur (8,399,393); Kazakh (1,250,458); Dongxiang (513,805); Kyrgyz (160,823); Salar (104,503); Tajik (41,028); Uzbek (14,502); Bonan (16,505); Tatar (4,890).[1] This represents about a 40 percent population increase over 1990 census figures. The Hui speak mainly Sino-Tibetan languages; Turkic-language speakers include the Uyghur, Kazakh, Kyrgyz, Uzbek, Salar and Tatar; combined Turkic-Mongolian speakers include the Dongxiang and Bonan, concentrated in Gansu's mountainous Hexi corridor; and the Tajik speak a variety of Indo-Persian dialects. It is critical for this chapter, however, to point out that in China, religious membership for Muslims is measured by membership in their ethnic nationality community. In other words, the Chinese census registers people by nationality, not religious affiliation, so the actual number of Muslims is still unknown, and all population figures are clearly influenced by politics in their use and interpretation.

While there may be individuals belonging to the Hui, Uyghur, or Kazakh nationalities that no longer profess belief in Islam (be they Chinese Communist Party [Party] members, secularists, or converts to other religions, such as Christianity), their numbers do not show up in the census, which like the United States census, does not count religious membership. In addition, nonminority converts to Islam are also not measured. Nevertheless, there are few Han converts to Islam, and perhaps even fewer members of the ten nationalities listed above who would dare to say they are not Muslim, at least in front of their parents. As I have argued earlier (Gladney 1996: 4–21), Muslim identity in China can best be described as ethnoreligious in that history, ethnicity, and state nationality policy have left an indelible mark on contemporary Muslim identity and it is almost impossible to discuss Islam without reference to ethnic and national identity. Here the institutionalized link between China's nationality policy and religion is critical to understanding contemporary Muslim identity in China.

Archaeological discoveries of large collections of Islamic artifacts and epigraphy on the southeast coast suggest that the earliest Muslim communities in China were descended from Arab, Persian, Central Asian, and Mongolian Muslim merchants, militia, and officials who settled first along China's southeast coast from the seventh through the tenth centuries. Later, larger migrations to the North from Central Asia under the Mongol Yuan dynasty in the thirteenth and fourteenth centuries added to these Muslim populations by gradually intermarrying with the local

Chinese populations, and raising their children as Muslims. Practicing Sunni, *Hanafi* Islam, and residing in independent small communities clustered around a central mosque, these communities were characterized by relatively isolated, independent Islamic villages and urban enclaves, who related with each other via trading networks. However, these scattered Islamic settlements shared a common feeling of belonging to the wider Islamic community (*umma*) that was validated by origin myths and folktales, and continually reinforced by traveling Muslim teachers known locally as *ahung*.[2]

Hui Muslims and Islamic Accommodation to Chinese Society

Islam in China has primarily been propagated over the last 1,300 years among the people now known as *Hui*, but many of the issues confronting them are relevant to the Turkic and Indo-European Muslims on China's Inner Asian frontier. Though Hui speak a number of non-Chinese languages, most Hui are closer to Han Chinese than other Muslim nationalities in terms of demographic proximity and cultural accommodation. The attempt to adapt many of their Muslim practices to the Han way of life has led to criticisms amongst some Muslim reformers. In the wake of modern Islamic reform movements that have swept across China, a wide spectrum of Islamic belief and practice can now be found among those Muslims in China referred to as the Hui.

The Hui have been labeled the "Chinese-speaking Muslims," "Chinese Muslims," and most recently, as "Sino-Muslims."[3] However, this terminology is misleading since by law all Muslims living in China are "Chinese" by citizenship, and there are large Hui communities who speak primarily the non-Chinese languages dominant in the areas where they live. To paraphrase Aihwa Ong, in this case, citizenship, like religious membership, is rather inflexible in China.[4] This is the case, for example, with the Tibetan, Mongolian, Thai (*Daizu*), and Hainan Muslims of China, who are also classified by the state as Hui. These "Hui" Muslims, speak Tibetan, Mongolian, and Thai as their first-languages, with Han Chinese the national language that they learn in school, along with the Arabic and Persian that some of them also learn at the mosque. Interestingly, since Tajik is not an official language in China, for the Tajik of Xinjiang (who speak a Darian branch language, distantly related to old Persian, and quite different from the Tajik languages spoken in Tajikistan) their children attend schools where the language of instruction is either Turkic Uyghur or Han Chinese.[5]

Nevertheless, it is true that compared to the other Muslim nationalities in China, most Hui are closer to the Han Chinese in terms of demographic proximity and cultural accommodation, adapting many of their Islamic practices to Han ways of life. However, this type of cultural accommodation can also become the target of sharp criticism from some Muslim reformists. In the past, this was not as great a problem for the Turkic, Mongolian, and Tajik groups, as they were traditionally more isolated from the Han and their identities not as threatened, though this has begun to change in the last forty years. As a result of the state-sponsored nationality identification campaigns launched in the 1950s, these groups began to think of themselves more as ethnic nationalities, as something more than just "Muslims." The Hui are unique among the fifty-six identified nationalities in China in that they are the only nationality for whom a religion (Islam) is the only unifying category of identity, even though many members of the Hui nationality may not actively practice Islam. Indeed, in Yang Shengmin's (Yang and Ding 2002: 35) ethnography of China, the Hui are included with the Han in the section dedicated to "Han language nationalities" (*hanyu minzu*). In addition, there are nearly a million "unidentified" (*moshibie minzu*) nationalities, listed in Yang's (Yang and Ding 2002: 435–38) section, including such transnational groups as the Sherpa, Khmer, Deng, and Baima peoples (the last two already belonging to the Tibetan nationality but continue to seek separate nationality status).[6]

The Nationalist Party's "nationality" policy identified five peoples of China, dominated by the Han. They included Uyghurs under the general rubric of "Hui Muslims," which referred to all Muslim groups in China at that time. The Communists continued this policy and eventually recognized fifty-six nationalities. Uyghurs and eight other Muslim groups were split out from the general category "Hui" (which henceforth was used only with reference to Muslims who primarily spoke Chinese or did not have a separate language of their own). As a policy of ethnic control, this owed much to practices that the Soviet state had applied earlier to Central Asia. It proved to be an effective means by which the Chinese Communists could integrate the western regions into China.

The state institution most responsible for delineating the official nationalities and overseeing the establishment of the autonomous region system is the State Ethnic Affairs Commission (*Guojia minzu shiwu weiyuanhui*). Set up by the Organic Law of February 22, 1952, and with roots in the Qing dynasty's Bureau of Mongol and Manchu Affairs, the State Ethnic Affairs Commission continues to wield enormous power and influence in the border autonomous regions.[7] Indeed, the entire evolution of the officially recognized ethnic groups as *minzu* (the Chinese term that can be translated "nationality," "ethnicity," "nation," "people," etc.) has been a subject of great debate within and without China, with most experts agreeing that it refers only to those fifty-six enumerated ethnic groups that receive special state recognition under the auspices of the State Ethnic Affairs Commission.[8]

Since the extension of Chinese administration and control over the region of Xinjiang is profoundly influenced by China's overall policy on nationalities, it is critical to understand the origins of that policy in the years prior to 1949. The Communist Party formulated the nationality policy of the future People's Republic of China during the 1930s for the strategic purpose of enlisting the support of peoples disgruntled both with Qing rule and with Chiang Kai-shek's nationality policy, which deemphasized ethnic difference in favor of the unity of all peoples as members of the Chinese race. This policy took shape during the Long March from the Southwest to the Northwest, an arduous trek that led the Communists through the most concentrated minority areas. It was then that the Chinese Communist leaders became acutely aware of the vibrant ethnic identities of the Muslims and other peoples they encountered. The fathers of the yet to be born Chinese Communist nation were faced with a stark choice between their own extermination or promising the minorities—specifically the Miao, Yi (Lolo), Tibetans, and Hui—that they would receive special treatment. The Communists set up the first Hui Muslim autonomous county in the 1936 in Tongxin, southern Ningxia, as a demonstration of their goodwill toward the Muslim Hui.

Mao vehemently lectured troops of the Eighth Route Army to respect Hui customs, lest the soldiers offend the Hui and provoke conflicts. Mao (1936: 1–3) appealed to the Northwest Hui to support the Communists' cause, even exhorting China's Muslims to learn from and emulate the renaissance of Turkey that occurred under Ataturk's rule. Snow noted a slogan (1938: 320) posted by Hui soldiers training under the Communist 15th Army Corps, which read: "Build our own anti-Japanese Mohammedan Red Army." Later Party documents (*dangshi wenshi ziliao*) that have come to light from the Long March reveal that up to 1937 Chairman Mao explicitly promised "self-determination" to the minorities. Not only did he offer them privileges, but also the right to secede from the Communist state, as Stalin had provided to Soviet minorities in his constitution of 1937. However, this right was withdrawn by 1940 and replaced with guarantees only of a limited regional "autonomy." The transition in Chinese terminology from "self-determination" (*zizhu*) to "autonomy" (*zizhi*) may not seem great, but for the minorities themselves it represented a major shift in policy. Even though the right of secession was written into the constitution of the Soviet Union, the Soviet state never hesitated to use force against groups that actually sought to exercise it. In China no such right exists, and any individuals or groups aspiring to secede are regarded simply as criminal. This, along with the "anti-ethnic strife" law (Sautman

1999), provides the legal basis for Beijing to consider all Xinjiang activist groups pushing for independence as separatists and to execute their members. As Walker Connor (1984: 89) observed, "a request that prerevolutionary promises be honored became counterrevolutionary and reactionary."

Though the Party promised autonomy, it quashed any illusions of separatism in the hope that by this means it would preserve "national unity." The contradiction between policies that promote ethnic autonomy and policies that promote ethnic assimilation continues to vex China's nationality policy. As June Dreyer (1976: 17) has observed: "The Communist government of China may be said to have inherited a policy of trying to facilitate the demise of nationality identities through granting self-government to minorities. It has in fact been struggling with the consequences to this day."

Thus, the Communists assigned a high priority to the integration of Muslims into the system of Chinese socialist control long before they moved into Xinjiang. Even before they gained control there, they had charted out the pattern for ethnic control that was to have a dramatic impact on the Uyghurs and other ethnic groups in the region. That Xinjiang came to figure so prominently in the history and evolution of early Communist policy toward Muslims and nationality identification may have been strongly influenced by the fact that Chairman Mao's brother had been killed in Xinjiang in 1942, in the midst of struggles fed by interethnic and intra-Muslim factionalism (Forbes 1986: 157–59).

Another institution responsible for monitoring Muslim activities in China is the China Islamic Affairs Association (*Zhongguo Yisilanjiao xie-hui*). This association, founded in 1956 at the same time China formed the "Three Self Patriotic Movement," which is responsible for monitoring all Protestant activities, makes the final recommendations to the government regarding the establishment of new mosques, formation of Islamic schools, and general policy regarding the legality of certain Islamic practices (such as outlawing headscarves in public schools), and plays an increasingly important role in China's Middle Eastern international affairs (see below).

In the Northwest, in addition to allowing from two to four students (*halifat*) to train privately in each mosque, the government approved and funded several Islamic schools (*yixueyuan*) throughout the region. In 1988 the state provided funding to establish a large Islamic seminary and mosque complex outside the West Gate of Yinchuan near Luo Village. Similarly, in Urumqi the Islamic College was established in 1985 and other regional and provincial government's have followed suit. This indicates a "regionalization" of state-sponsored Islamic education, which until the 1980s had been officially concentrated at the China Islamic Affairs Commission in

Beijing, located near the Oxen Street Mosque in the Xuanwu district in southwest Beijing.

The increased promotion of exchange with foreign Muslim countries is exposing more urban Hui to international aspects of their religious heritage. Though in the past media coverage of the Palestinian-Israeli conflict was rather minimal, increased coverage of the first Gulf War raised Muslim awareness of political and religious conflicts in the region. Widespread coverage of the war in Iraq has exposed Muslims in China like never before to the many tensions in the Middle East. Among urban Hui, Islamic knowledge tends to be higher than in rural areas, perhaps because of increased educational levels and more media exposure. Unlike the vast majority of Hui in rural areas, many urban Hui interviewed keep up on international affairs, and they often read the magazine published by the China Islamic Affairs Association, *Zhongguo Musilin* (China's Muslims). Few were aware of and interested in the sectarian disputes in the Iran/Iraq conflict, but most knew of Shi'ism.

Institutions engaged in managing China's Muslims, and the Muslims themselves, have all been strongly affected by Middle Eastern affairs over the last two decades. The People's Republic of China, as one of five permanent voting members of the United Nations Security Council, and as a significant exporter of military hardware to the Middle East, has become a recognized player in Middle Eastern affairs. With a temporary but precipitous decline in trade with many Western nations after the Tiananmen massacre in June 1989, the importance of China's Middle Eastern trading partners (most of them Muslim, since China did not recognize Israel until 1992), rose considerably. This may account for the fact that China established diplomatic relations with Saudi Arabia on July 21, 1990, with the first direct Sino-Saudi exchanges taking place since 1949 (Saudi Arabia canceled its long-standing diplomatic relationship with Taiwan and withdrew its ambassador, despite a lucrative trade history). In the face of a long-term friendship with Iraq, China went along with most of the United Nations resolutions in the war against Iraq. Although it abstained from Resolution 678 on supporting the ground war, and did not endorse the United States–led coalition war against Saddam Hussein in 2003, China continues to enjoy a fairly "teflon" reputation in the Middle East as an untarnished source of low-grade weaponry and cheap reliable labor (see Harris 1993; Shichor 1984). In the words of the late Hajji Shi Kunbing, former lead imam of the famous Oxen Street Mosque in Beijing, whom I interviewed during Ramadan in 1985: "With so much now at stake in the Middle East, the government cannot risk antagonizing its Muslim minorities." At the same time, China maintains good relations with Israel, having established formal diplomatic relations on January 24, 1992.

Interestingly, although China's government did not endorse the United States–led coalition war against Iraq, and only voiced "strong concern" about the possible collateral injury of civilians, urging a peaceful resolution, its Muslim population was ahead of the government in publicly condemning the United States–led war. In a statement issued on March 23, 2003, by Chen Guangyan, vice president of the China Islamic Association, he said the following:

We strongly condemn the United States and its allies for attacking Iraq and not turning to diplomacy to resolve this conflict. . . . We side with the war protesters in the US and elsewhere around the world. We strongly urge the US to stop its campaign and to return to the negotiating tables to resolve this issue. War is wrong. (Cited in Cheng 2003)

The next day, Hajji Muhammad Nusr Ma Liangji, lead imam of the Great Mosque in Xi'an, which boasts 70,000 members, made the following statement: "Though we don't go to the Middle East that often, we are all part of the same brotherhood. . . . Mr. Bush's invasion of Iraq is an incursion of Iraq's sovereignty. Islam is a religion of peace and the US shouldn't do this. No one in the world agrees with this and we in the Muslim community in China absolutely object to this" (cited in Cheng 2003). I was able to visit the headquarters of the China Islamic Association in the Niujie district of Beijing shortly after these statements were made, and Hajji Yu Zhengui, president of the China Islamic Association, confirmed that Muslims across China were deeply angered by the United States–led war, and had been asking the government for permission to engage in public street protest. As of late March 2003, permission had not been granted by the government for the Muslims to protest, though there were rumors of small Muslim protests in Changzhi (Shanxi), Tianjin, Nanjing, Beijing, and Shandong. The Chinese did give permission for some limited protests by foreigners and students in late March and early April, but perhaps out of fear that a Muslim protest might get out of hand, possibly disturbing social stability, or even worse, disrupting improving China–United States relations, the Muslims were never allowed to protest the war in Iraq. These examples illustrate the increasing international role of institutions and individual Muslim leaders engaged by the state in helping to manage (and in some cases, police) China's Muslims.

Managing Islamic Diversity in China

The state has had to address a host of issues related to the various schools of Islam that have spread gradually throughout China over the course of the last 1,300 years. Following the general spread of traditional Islam,

Sufism began to make a substantial impact in China proper in the late seventeenth century, arriving mainly along the Central Asian trade routes with saintly shaykhs, both Chinese and foreign, who brought new teachings from the pilgrimage cities. These charismatic teachers and tradesmen established widespread networks and brotherhood associations, including most prominently the Naqshbandiyya, Qadariyya, and Kubrawiyya. Unlike Middle Eastern or Central Asian Sufi orders, where one might belong to two or even three brotherhoods at once, the Hui belong to only one. Among the Hui, one is generally born into one's Islamic order (*menhuan*), or converts dramatically to another. In fact, this is the only kind of conversion I encountered among my sojourn among the Hui. I never met a Han who had converted to Islam in China without having been married to a Hui or adopted into a Hui family, though I heard of a few isolated instances. Fletcher records the conversion to Islam of twenty-eight Tibetan tribes as well as their "Living Buddha" by Ma Laichi in Xunhua, Qinghai, in the mid-eighteenth century (Trippner 1961: 154–55). After the 1784 Ma Mingxin uprising, the Qing government forbade non-Muslims from converting to Islam, which may have had some influence on the subsequent rarity of recorded Han conversions. This goes against the common assumption that Islam in China was spread through proselytization and conversion. Islamic preachers in China, including Ma Laichi, Ma Mingxin, Qi Jingyi, and Ma Qixi, spent most of their time trying to convert other Muslims. Islam in China for the most part has grown biologically through birth and intermarriage.

The tensions and conflicts that led to the rise and divisions between various Islamic orders (*menhuan*) in China, and subsequent non-Sufi reforms, are impossible to enumerate in their complexity. An overview of major developments can, however, give evidence of the ongoing struggles that continue to make Islam meaningful to Hui Muslims. These tensions between Islamic ideals and social realities are often left unresolved. Their very dynamism derives from the questions they raise and the doubts they engender among people struggling with traditional meanings in the midst of changing social contexts. Questions of purity and legitimacy become paramount when the Hui are faced with radical internal socioeconomic and political change, and exposed to different interpretations of Islam from the outside Muslim world. These conflicts and reforms reflect an ongoing debate in China over Islamic orthodoxy, revealing an important disjunction between "scripturalist" and "mystical" interpretations.

In a similar fashion, the study of Southeast Asian Islam has often centered on the contradiction and compromise between the native culture of the indigenous Muslims and the shari'a of orthodox Islam, the mystical and scriptural, the real and the ideal.[9] The supposed accommodation of orthodox Islamic tenets to local cultural practices has led scholars to dismiss or explain such compromise as syncretism, assimilation, and "sinification," as has been described among the Hui. This fails to note the wide variety of accommodation of China's Muslims to the Chinese cultural terrain as well as the Chinese state. An alternative approach, and one perhaps more in tune with the interests of Hui themselves, sees this incongruence as the basis for ongoing dialectical tensions that have often led to reform movements and conflicts within Muslim communities (Eickelman 1976: 10–13). Following Max Weber (1978), one can see the wide variety of Islamic expression as reflecting processes of local world construction and programs for social conduct whereby a major religious tradition becomes meaningful to an indigenous society.

In the competition for scarce resources, these conflicts are also prompted by and expressed in economic concerns. For example, Fletcher notes that one of the criticisms of the Khufiyya order in China was that their recitation of an Islamic religious text entitled the *Ming Sha Le* took less time than the normal Quranic *suras* as read by non-Sufi clergy and, therefore, their imams were cheaper to hire at ritual ceremonies. Fletcher suggests that this assisted their rise in popularity and contributed to the criticism they received from traditional religious leaders (Fletcher 1996: 21). In a similar manner, the Chinese Muslim reformists referred to as the *Yihewani* criticized both traditional Muslims and Sufis for only performing rituals in believers' homes for profit, and condemned the practice altogether. They summarized their position on such matters in the oft-repeated axiom, "If you recite, do not eat; if you eat, do not recite" (*nian jing bu chi, chi bu nian jing*).

Tendencies toward Acculturation and Purification

The tensions arising from the conflict of Chinese cultural practices and Islamic ideals have led to the rise and powerful appeal of Islamic movements among Hui Muslims that have a direct effect on Muslims' relation with the state. In China there have been many attempts to reconcile Chinese culture with Islam, leading to a range of alternative practices. At one extreme there are those who reject any integration of Islam with Chinese culture, advocating instead a return to an Arabicized "pure" Islam, often moving against or away from the state. Conversely, at the other extreme, there are those traditionalist Chinese Muslim leaders who accepted greater degrees of integration with traditional Chinese society. Likewise, Ma Qixi's Xi Dao Tang stressed the complete compatibility of Chinese and Islamic culture, the importance of Chinese Islamic Confucian texts, the harmony of the two systems, and the reading of the Quran in Chinese.

In between, one finds various attempts at changing Chinese society to "fit" a Muslim world, through transformationist or militant Islam, as illustrated by the largely Naqshbandiyya-led nineteenth-century Hui uprisings. The Jahriyya order sought to implement an alternative vision of the world in their society, and this posed a threat to the Qing as well as to other Hui Muslims, earning them the label of "heterodox" (*xie jiao*) and persecution by the Chinese state. By contrast, other Hui reformers have attempted throughout history to make Islam "fit" Chinese society, such as Liu Zhi's monumental effort to demonstrate the Confucian morality of Islam. The alternative advocated by the Qadariyya order in China represents resolution of this tension through ascetic withdrawal from the world. A shaykh of this order, Qi Jingyi, advocated an inner mystical journey where the dualism of Islam and the Chinese world is resolved through grasping the oneness of Allah found inside every believer. These various approaches in Chinese Islam represent sociohistorical attempts to deal with the relationship of relating the world religion of Islam to local Chinese culture.

The hierarchical organization of these Sufi networks helped in the mobilization of large numbers of Hui during economic and political crises of the seventeenth through the nineteenth centuries, assisting widespread Muslim-led rebellions and resistance movements against late Ming and Qing imperial rule in Yunnan, Shaanxi, Gansu, and Xinjiang. In the late nineteenth and early twentieth centuries, Wahhabi-inspired reform movements, known as the *Yihewani*, rose to popularity under Nationalist and warlord sponsorship, and were noted for their critical stance toward traditionalist Islam, which they viewed as being overly acculturated to non-Muslim Chinese practices, and to forms of popular Sufism such as saint and tomb veneration.

Beyond such internal Muslim critiques, the Chinese state has also launched its own criticisms of certain Islamic orders among the Hui. The stakes in such debates have often been economic, as well as ideological. For example, during the Land Reform campaigns of the 1950s, the state appropriated mosque and *waqf* (Islamic endowment) holdings from traditional Muslim religious institutions. These measures met with great resistance from the Sufi *menhuan* that had accumulated a great deal due to their hierarchical centralized leadership.

Islam and Chinese Nationalism

In the twentieth century, many Muslims supported the earliest Communist call for economic equality, autonomy, freedom of religion, and recognized nationality status, and were active in the early establishment of the

People's Republic of China. However, many of them later became disenchanted by growing critiques of religious practice during several periods in the People's Republic of China beginning in 1957. During the Cultural Revolution (1966–76), Muslims became the focus for both anti-religious and anti-ethnic nationalist critiques, leading to widespread persecutions, mosque closings, and at least one large massacre of one thousand Hui following a 1975 uprising in Yunnan province. Since Deng Xiaoping's post-1978 reforms, Muslims have sought to take advantage of liberalized economic and religious policies, while keeping a watchful eye on the ever-swinging pendulum of Chinese radical politics. There are now more mosques open in China than there were prior to 1949, and Muslims are allowed to go on the hajj to Mecca as well as engage in cross-border trade with coreligionists in Central Asia, the Middle East, and increasingly, Southeast Asia.

With the dramatic increase in the number of Muslims traveling back and forth to the Middle East came new waves of Islamic reformist thought, including criticism of local Muslim practices in China. Through similar channels, other Chinese Muslims have also been exposed to various types of new, often politically radical, Islamic ideologies. These developments have fueled Islamic factional struggles that have continued to exacerbate China's Muslims' internal divisions. For example, in February 1994, four Naqshbandi Sufi leaders were sentenced to long-term imprisonment for their support of internal factional disputes in the southern Ningxia region that had led to at least sixty deaths on both sides and People's Liberation Army intervention.

Increasing Muslim political activism on a national scale and rapid state responses to such developments indicate the growing importance that Beijing attaches to Muslim-related issues. In 1986, Uyghurs in Xinjiang marched through the streets of Urumqi protesting against a wide range of issues, including the environmental degradation of the Zungharian plain, nuclear testing in the Taklamakan district, increased Han immigration to Xinjiang, and ethnic insults at Xinjiang University. Muslims throughout China protested the publication of a Chinese book, *Sexual Customs*, in May 1989, and a children's book in October 1993, that portrayed Muslims, particularly their restriction against pork, in a derogatory fashion. In each case, the government responded quickly through the Chinese Islamic Association and the State Ethnic Affairs Commission, meeting most of the Muslims' demands, condemning the publications and arresting the authors, and closing down the printing houses.

These developments have influenced all Muslim nationalities in China today. However, they have found their most overtly political expressions among those Hui who are most directly faced with the task of accommodating new Islamic movements within Chinese culture. By comparison, among the Uyghur, a more recent integration into Chinese society as a result of Mongolian and Manchu expansion into Central Asian has forced them to reach different degrees of social and political accommodations that have challenged their identity. In terms of integration, the Uyghur as a people are perhaps the least integrated into Chinese society, while the Hui are, due to several historical and social factors, at the other end of the spectrum.

One way to examine this range of alternatives is to generalize about the Muslim nationalities themselves. In this scheme, the Uyghur can be seen to be much more resistant to accepting integration into Chinese society than other Muslims groups, in that they are the only Muslim minority in China expressing strong desires for a separate state, which they may sometimes refer to as Uyghuristan, or more often as East Turkistan. However, it is by no means clear that all Uyghur desire such independence. At the other extreme, it could be argued that the Hui are the most integrated of all the Muslim minorities into Chinese society and culture. This is both an advantage and a disadvantage in that they often have greater access to power and resources within the Chinese state, but at the same time risk either the loss of their identity or the rejection of other Muslim groups in China as being too assimilated into Chinese society, to the detriment of Islam. In between there is a range of Muslim nationalities who are closer to the Uyghur in resisting Chinese culture and maintaining a distinct language and identity (Uzbeks, Kazakhs, Kyrgyz, and Tajiks), and those who are much closer to the Hui in accommodation to Chinese culture (Dongxiang, Bonan). Much of this difference is due to historical interaction and locale, and can also serve as a heuristic way of examining the challenges faced by each Muslim minority in their daily expression of identity and Islam in Chinese society. It must be clearly noted, however, that there are many exceptions to this overly generalized pattern. For example there are some Uyghur, such as Party officials and secularists, who are quite integrated into Chinese society, while at the same time there are also some Hui, including some religious leaders and rebellious youths, who live their lives in strident resistance to Chinese rule.

Increased Muslim activism in China might be thought of as "nationalistic," but it is also a nationalism that may often transcend the boundaries of the contemporary nation-state, via mass communications, increased travel, and the internet. Earlier Islamic movements in China were precipitated by China's opening to the outside world. No matter what conservative leaders in the government might wish, China's Muslims' politics have reached a new stage of openness. If China wants to participate in an international political sphere of nation-states, this is unavoidable. With the

opening to the West in recent years, travel to and from the Islamic heart-
lands has dramatically increased in China. In 1984, over 1,400 Muslims left
China to go on the hajj to Mecca. This number increased to over 2,000 in
1987, representing a return to pre-1949 levels, and in the late 1990s, official hajj numbers regularly surpassed 6,000, with many others traveling in
private capacities through third countries. Several Hui students are pres-
ently enrolled in Islamic and Arabic studies at the Al-Azhar University in
Egypt, with many others seeking Islamic training abroad.

Encouraged by the Chinese state, relations between Muslims in China
and their co-religionists in the Middle East are becoming stronger and
more frequent. This appears to be motivated partly out of a desire to establish trading partners for arms, commodities, and currency exchanges, and
partly by China's traditional view of itself as a leader of the Third World.
Delegations of foreign Muslims regularly travel to prominent Islamic sites
in China, in a kind of state-sponsored religious tourism, and donations are
encouraged. While the state hopes that private Islamic investment will assist economic development, the vast majority of grants by visiting foreign
Muslims have been donated to the rebuilding of Islamic mosques, schools,
and hospitals.

Uyghurs, Muslims, and Chinese Citizenship

The links between Islam, ethnicity, and the state in China are nowhere
more apparent than in Xinjiang, where China faces the so-called Uyghur
problem. As part of China's continuing efforts to maintain national unity
and police separatist movements at home and abroad, on December 14,
2003, for the first time in its history, China's Ministry of Public Security
released a list of four organizations and eleven individuals that they
deemed to be terrorists. This list included the East Turkistan Islamic
Movement (ETIM), which was identified as an international terrorist
organization by the United Nations in 2002 after Chinese and United
States prompting (see below), as well as the East Turkistan Liberation
Organization (ETLO), the World Uyghur Youth Congress (WUYC)
and the East Turkistan Information Center (ETIC). The eleven identified
"East Turkistan" terrorists were: Hasan Mahsum, Muhanmetemin Hazret,
Dolqun Isa, Abudujelili Kalakash, Abudukadir Yapuquan, Abudumijit
Abduhammatkelim, Abudula Kariaji, Abulimit Turxun, Huadaberdi
Haxerbik, Yasen Muhammat, and Atahan Abuduhani ("China Releases"
2003). Interestingly, included in the list was a Mr. Hasan Mahsum, the re-
puted leader of East Turkistan Islamic Movement, who had been reportedly
previously killed in a Pakistani raid on an al-Qaida camp in Waziristan
on October 2, 2003 (Radio Free Asia 2003). On November 10, 2003, I

had actually met Mr. Dolqun Isa, a young Uyghur living in Munich, who was also included on the list as one of eleven identified international terrorists, and the elected president of the World Uyghur Youth Congress (also listed as one of four terrorist organizations). During that meeting he claimed that he had nothing to do with terrorism, that such violence was contrary to his devout faith in Islam, and handed me a printed anti-terrorism brochure of the East Turkistan (Uyghuristan) National Congress that was entitled: "Help the Uyghurs to Fight Terrorism" (East Turkistan [Uyghuristan] National Congress 2003).

In 1997, bombs exploded in a city park in Beijing on May 13 (killing one person) and on two buses on March 7 (killing two persons), as well as on February 25 in the northwestern border city of Urumqi, the capital of Xinjiang Uyghur Autonomous Region (killing nine persons). Though sporadically reported since the early 1980s, such incidents have been increasingly common since 1997 and are documented in a recent scathing report on Chinese government policy in the region by Amnesty International (1999). A report in the *Wall Street Journal* of August 11, 1999 (Johnson 1999), on the arrest on of a well-known Uyghur business woman named Rebiya Kadir during a visit by the United States Congressional Research Service delegation to the region, indicated China's early concern with the Uyghur separatism issue and relative unconcern about Western criticism of such measures. Despite Rebiya Kadir's release and exile to the United States in March 2006, China continues to arrest members of her family and any other Uyghur deemed to be a threat to the state. While religious practice is allowed in Xinjiang, and the mosques are increasingly filled with young Uyghur men, any political activism is not tolerated. Here the state seeks to drive a strong wedge between ethnic activism that might claim independence and sovereignty, and religious practice.

As we consider the interaction of Uyghur Muslims with Chinese society, we must examine three interrelated aspects of regional history, economy, and politics. First, Chinese histories notwithstanding, most Uyghur firmly believe that their ancestors were the indigenous people of the Tarim basin, which did not become officially known in Chinese as "Xinjiang" ("new borderland") until 1884. Nevertheless, I have argued elsewhere the constructed "ethnogenesis" of the Uyghur, in which the current understanding of the indigeneity of the present people classified as Uyghur by the Chinese state is a rather recent phenomenon related to Great Game rivalries, Sino-Soviet geopolitical maneuverings, and Chinese nation-building (Gladney 1990: 3). While a collection of nomadic steppe peoples known as the "Uyghur" has existed since before the eighth century, this identity was lost from the fifteenth through the twentieth centuries. In the historical record we find the beginnings of the Uyghur empire following the fall of the Turkish khanate (552–744 C.E.) when Chinese historians first mention a people called the *Hui-he* or *Hui-hu*. At that time the Uyghur were but a collection of nine nomadic tribes, who initially, in confederation with other Basmil and Karlukh nomads, defeated the Second Turkish Khanate and then dominated the federation under the leadership of Koli Beile in 742.

Gradual sedentarization of the Uyghur, and their defeat of the Turkish khanate, occurred precisely as trade with the unified Tang state (618–907) was becoming especially lucrative. During that time sedentarization and interaction with the Chinese state was accompanied by socioreligious change: the traditional shamanistic Turkic-speaking Uyghur came increasingly under the influence of Persian Manichaeanism, Buddhism, and eventually, even Nestorian Christianity. Extensive trade and military alliances along the old Silk Road with the Chinese state developed to the extent that the Uyghur gradually adopted many cultural, and even agricultural, practices of the Chinese. Conquest of the Uyghur capital of Karabalghasun in Mongolia by the nomadic Kyrgyz in 840 led to further sedentarization and crystallization of Uyghur identity. One group of Uyghur moved out to what is now Turpan. There they took advantage of the unique socioecology of the glacier-fed oases surrounding the Taklamakan to preserve their merchant and limited agrarian practices, gradually establishing Khocho or Gaochang, the great Uyghur city-state that lasted for four centuries (850–1250).

From that time on, the people of Turpan-centered "Uyghuristan" who resisted Islamic conversion until the seventeenth century were the last to be known as "Uyghur." Uyghurs who converted to Islam or settled in the region were no longer known as "Uyghurs," but were referred to either by the name of their local oasis settlement or by the generic term of "Turki." Thus, with the further spread of Islam in the region, the ethnonym "Uyghur" faded from the historical record. It was not until 1760 that the Manchu Qing dynasty exerted full and formal control over the region, establishing it as their "new borderland" (Xinjiang). This administration lasted for a century before it fell to the Yakub Beg rebellion (1864–77) and expanding Russian influence (see Kim 2003). With the resumption of Manchu Qing rule in the region, the area became known for the first time as Xinjiang, the "new borderland," in 1884. The end of the Qing dynasty in 1911 and the rise of Great Game rivalries between China, Russia, and Britain saw the region torn by competing loyalties and marked by two short-lived and drastically different attempts at independence: the establishment of an "East Turkistan Republic" in Kashgar in 1933, and another in Yining in 1944 (Benson 1990). As Andrew Forbes has noted, these rebellions and attempts at self-rule did little to bridge competing political, religious, and regional differences among the Turkic people who had only became known as the Uyghur in 1921 under the Nationalist Party governor, Sheng Shicai, who was catering to Soviet nationality "divide-and-rule" strategies of recognizing groups such as Uyghur, Uzbek, and Kazakh as separate Turkic nationalities (Forbes 1986: 29). Furthermore, Justin Rudelson's (1997) research suggests that there remains persistent regional diversity along three, and perhaps four macroregions of Uyghuristan: the northwestern Zungaria plateau, the southern Tarim basin, the southwest Pamir region, and the eastern Kumul-Turpan-Hami corridor.

Uyghur Indigeneity and the Challenge to Chinese Sovereignty

The *minzu* policy under the Chinese Nationalists identified five peoples of China, with the Han in the majority. The recognition of the Uyghur as an official Chinese "nationality" (*minzu*) under a Soviet-influenced policy of nationality recognition contributed to a widespread acceptance today of the idea of a continuity with the ancient Uyghur kingdom and their eventual "ethnogenesis" of the concept of "Uyghur" as a bona fide nationality. This policy was continued under the Communists, who eventually recognized fifty-six nationalities, with the Han occupying a 91 percent majority in 1990. The "peaceful liberation" of Xinjiang by the Chinese Communists in 1949, and its subsequent establishment as the Xinjiang Uyghur Autonomous Region on October 1, 1955, perpetuated the Nationalist Party policy of recognizing the Uyghur as a minority nationality under Chinese rule (Shahidi 1984). However the designation of the Uyghur as a "nationality" masks tremendous regional and linguistic diversity. For it also includes groups such as the Loplyk and Dolans that have very little in common with the oasis-based Turkic Muslims that had come to be known as the Uyghur. At the same time, contemporary Uyghur separatists look back to the brief periods of independent self-rule under Yakub Beg and the East Turkistan Republics, in addition to the earlier glories of the Uyghur kingdoms in Turpan and Karabalghasun, as evidence of their rightful claims to the region.

Today a number of Uyghur separatist organizations exist, based mainly in foreign cities such as Istanbul, Ankara, Almaty, Munich, Amsterdam, Melbourne, and Washington, DC, and, while they may differ on their political goals and strategies for the region they all share a common vision of a unilinear Uyghur claim on the region that has been disrupted by Chinese and Soviet intervention. The independence of the former Soviet Central Asian republics in 1991 has done much to encourage these Uyghur organizations in their hopes for an independent "Turkistan," despite the

fact the new, mainly Muslim Central Asian governments all signed protocols with China in the spring of 1996 that they would not harbor or support separatists groups.

Within the region, though many portray the Uyghur as united around
separatist or Islamist causes, Uyghur continue to be divided from within
by religious conflicts, in this case competing Sufi and non-Sufi factions,
territorial loyalties (whether they be oases or places of origin), linguistic
discrepancies, commoner–elite alienation, and competing political loyalties. These divided loyalties were evidenced by the attack in May 1996 on
the imam of the Idgah Mosque in Kashgar by other Uyghurs, as well as
the assassination of at least six Uyghur officials in September 2001.

It is also important to note that Islam was only one of several unifying
markers for Uyghur identity, depending on those with whom they were
in cooperation at the time. For example, to the Hui Muslim Chinese, the
Uyghur distinguish themselves as the legitimate autochthonous minority, since both share a belief in Sunni Islam. In contrast to the nomadic
Muslim peoples (Kazakh or Kyrgyz), Uyghur might stress their attachment to the land and oases of origin. In opposition to the Han Chinese,
the Uyghur will generally emphasize their long history in the region.
It is this contested understanding of history that continues to influence
much of the current debate over separatist and Chinese claims to the region. The multiple emphases in defining their identity have also served
to mitigate the appeal of Islamic fundamentalist groups (often glossed as
"Wahhabiyya" in the region), such as the Taliban in Afghanistan, among
the Uyghur.

Alleged incursions of Taliban fighters through the Wakhan corridor
into China where Xinjiang shares a narrow border with Afghanistan led
to the area being swamped with Chinese security forces and large military exercises, beginning at least one month prior to the September 11
attack. These military exercises suggested growing government concern
about these border areas much earlier than 9/11. Under United States and
Chinese pressure, Pakistan returned one Uyghur activist to China, appre-
hended among hundreds of Taliban detainees, which follows a pattern of
repatriations of suspected Uyghur separatists in Kazakhstan, Kyrgyzstan,
and Uzbekistan. During the war in Afghanistan, United States forces arrested as many as twenty-two Uyghurs fighting with the Taliban, who
were incarcerated in Guantanamo Bay, Cuba. Amnesty International has
claimed that Chinese government roundups of so-called terrorists and
separatists have led to hurried public trials and immediate, summary ex-
ecutions of possibly thousands of locals. Troop movements to the area, related to the nationwide Strike Hard campaign against crime launched in
1998 that includes the call to erect a "great wall of steel" against separatists

in Xinjiang, were reportedly the biggest since the suppression of the large Akto insurrection in April 1990.[10]

International campaigns for Uyghur rights and possible independence have become increasingly vocal and well organized, especially on the internet. Repeated public appeals have been made to Abdulahat Abdurixit, the Uyghur People's Government chairman of Xinjiang in Urumqi. Notably, the former chair of the Unrepresented Nations and People's Organization (UNPO) based in the Hague was the Uyghur Erkin Alptekin, son of the separatist leader Isa Yusuf Alptekin, who is buried in Istanbul, where there is a park dedicated to his memory. In spring 2004, Erkin Alptekin was elected by several international Uyghur organizations as the head of a newly formed World Uyghur Congress. In 2007, he was replaced by Rebiya Kadir as the elected leader of the World Uyghur Congress. The growing influence of "cyber-separatism" and international popularization of the Uyghur cause concerns Chinese authorities, who hope to convince the world that the Uyghurs do pose a real domestic and international terrorist threat.

While further restricting Islamic freedoms in the border regions, at the same time the Chinese state has become more keenly aware of the importance that foreign Muslim governments place on China's treatment of its Muslim minorities as a factor in China's lucrative trade and military agreements. The establishment of full diplomatic ties with Saudi Arabia in 1991 and increasing military and technical trade with Middle Eastern Muslim states enhances the economic and political salience of China's treatment of its internal Muslim minority population. The official protocols signed with China's Central Asian border nations beginning in 1996 with the group known as the "Shanghai 5" (China, Russia, Kazakhstan, Kyrgyzstan, Tajikistan) and expanded in 2001 to include Uzbekistan, underlines China's growing role in the region and concerns over transnational trade and security. The increased transnationalism of China's Muslims will be an important factor in their ethnic expression as well as practiced accommodation to Chinese culture and state authority. Here we see a direct institutional link between Islam and the state in China in that one of the main goals of the Shanghai Cooperative Organization that was proposed by China and is now based in Beijing is to fight Islamic separatism in China as well as in Central Asia.

With respect to its "autonomous" status, Xinjiang falls under the same laws as other autonomous regions, prefectures, counties, and villages. Nevertheless, domestic and international factors strongly influence how these laws are applied. Thus, the International Campaign for Tibetan Independence and the Dalai Lama's government in exile shape how China's law on autonomy is applied in Tibet. In the same way, Xinjiang's proximity to the dissolving Soviet Union during 1991, the increasing importance of its oil reserves, and its 2001 war on terrorism, influence the implementation of laws on autonomy in Xinjiang.

Financial support for these Islamic organizations and websites come mostly from private individuals, foundations, and subscriptions (though these are rare). While it has been reported that wealthy Uyghur patrons in Saudi Arabia and Turkey, who became successful running businesses after migrating to these countries in the 1940s, have strongly supported these organizations financially in the past, there is no publicly available information on these sources. Many Uyghur who migrated to Saudi Arabia and Turkey in the 1930s and 1940s became successful in the construction and restaurant sector, and were thus in a much better position to support Uyghur causes than more recent Uyghur émigrés. Uyghurs in Central Asia and in the West who have been able to migrate from Xinjiang in increasing numbers in the last twenty years or so have generally been much poorer than the earlier émigrés to the Middle East. This is starting to change, however, as they and their children become better established in the United States, Canada, Europe, and Australia.

As noted above, the East Turkistan Islamic Movement was recognized by the United States and the United Nations in October 2002 as an international terrorist organization responsible for domestic and international terrorist acts, which China claimed included a bombing of the Chinese consulate in Istanbul, and assassinations of Chinese officials in Bishkek and Uyghur officials in Kashgar who were suspected of collaborating with Chinese officialdom. This designation, however, created a controversy in that China and the United States presented little public evidence to positively link the East Turkistan Islamic Movement with the specific incidents described (*People's Daily* 2001; Eckholm 2002; Hutzler 2002). In 2001, the United States Department of State released a report that documented several separatist and terrorist groups operating inside the region and abroad, agitating for an independent Xinjiang (McNeal 2001).[11] Clearly, the Chinese state is getting some international support in its move to institutionally limit Islamic radicalism in China through encouraging and supporting efforts to list terrorist organizations.

The real issue for this chapter, however, is that despite the designation of the East Turkistan Islamic Movement as an international terrorist organization, there are active Uyghur-related activist groups that can be said to support terrorism, but have never been proved to be directly implicated in any specific incident. State institutions such as the Islamic Affairs Association, the State Ethnic Affairs Commission, and state security forces routinely monitor and support crackdowns on anyone suspected of supporting or being affiliated with these organizations.

Chinese authorities are clearly concerned that increasing international attention to the treatment of its minority and dissident peoples has put pressure on the region, with the United States and many other Western governments continuing to criticize China for not adhering to its commitments to signed international agreements and human rights. In 2003, China ratified the International Covenant on Economic, Social, and Cultural Rights. Article One of the covenant says: "All peoples have the right of self-determination. By virtue of that right they freely determine their political status and freely pursue their economic, social and cultural development." Article 2 reads: "All peoples may, for their own ends, freely dispose of their natural wealth and resources without prejudice to any obligations arising out of international economic cooperation, based upon the principle of mutual benefit, and international law. In no case may a people be deprived of its own means of subsistence." Although China continues to quibble with the definition of "people," it is clear that the agreements are pressuring China to answer criticisms by Mary Robinson and other high-ranking human rights advocates about its treatment of minority peoples. Clearly, with Xinjiang representing the last Muslim region under communism, large trade contracts with Middle Eastern Muslim nations, and five Muslim nations on its western borders, Chinese authorities have more to be concerned about than just international support for human rights. China has thus institutionally sought to address Islamic issues through agreeing to these protocols, but it has not yet followed through on them.

China's Uyghur separatists are small in number, poorly equipped, loosely linked, and vastly out-gunned by the People's Liberation Army and People's Police. It should also be noted that that China's nine other official Muslim minorities do not in general support Uyghur separatism, although they are sometimes disgruntled about other rights' and mistreatment issues. There is continued enmity between Uyghur and Hui (Tungan) in the region. Few Hui support an independent Xinjiang, and one million Kazakh in Xinjiang would have very little say in an independent "Uyghuristan." Local support for separatist activities, particularly in Xinjiang and other border regions, is ambivalent and ambiguous at best, given the economic disparity between these regions and their foreign neighbors, including Tajikistan, Kyrgyzstan, Pakistan, and especially Afghanistan. Memories in the region are strong of mass starvation and widespread destruction during the Sino-Japanese and civil war in the first half of the twentieth century, including intra-Muslim and Muslim-Chinese bloody conflicts, not to mention the chaotic horrors of the Cultural Revolution. Many local activists are not calling for complete separatism or real independence, but generally express concerns over environmental degradation, nuclear testing, restrictions on religious freedom, over-taxation, and recently imposed limits on childbearing. Many ethnic leaders are simply calling for "real" autonomy according to Chinese law for the five Autonomous Regions that are each led by first Party secretaries who are all Han Chinese controlled by Beijing. Freedom of religion, protected by China's constitution, does not seem to be a key issue, as mosques in the region are full and pilgrimages to Mecca are often allowed for Uyghur and other Muslims (though some visitors to the region report an increase in restrictions against mosque attendance by youth, students, and government officials). In addition, Islamic extremism does not as yet appear to have widespread appeal, especially among urban, educated Uyghur. However, the government has consistently rounded up any Uyghur suspected of being "too" religious, especially those identified as Sufis or the so-called Wahabbis (a euphemism in the region for strict Muslim, not an organized Islamic school). These periodic roundups, detentions, and public condemnations of terrorism and separatism have not erased the problem, but have forced it underground, or at least out of the public's eye, and increased the possibility of alienating Uyghur Muslims even further from mainstream Chinese society. During the 2001 Asia-Pacific Economic Cooperation (APEC) meetings in Beijing, it was widely reported that Uyghur travelers were not allowed to stay in hotels in the city and often prevented from boarding public buses due to fear of terrorism.

The history of Chinese-Muslim relations in Xinjiang has been one of relative peace and quiet, broken by enormous social and political disruptions, sparked by both internal and external crises. The relative quiet of the last few years does not indicate that the ongoing problems of the region have been resolved or opposition dissolved. Interestingly, a recent *neibu* (internal circulation only) collection of articles discussing the "Xinjiang problem" and the challenges of separatism and terrorism (with the terms often conflated), recognizes that there have been no incidents since the year 2000, and blames the tensions between Han and Uyghur in the region on the "internationalization" (*guojihua*) of the issue (see Ma 2003: 128).[12]

The opposition to Chinese rule in Xinjiang has not reached the level of Chechnya or the Intifada, but similar to the Basque separatists of the ETA in Spain, or former IRA in Ireland and England, it is one that may erupt in limited, violent moments of terror and resistance. And just as these oppositional movements have not been resolved in Europe, the Uyghur problem in Xinjiang does not appear to be one that will readily go away. The admitted problem of Uyghur terrorism and dissent, even in the diaspora, is thus problematic for a government that wants to encourage integration and development in a region where the majority population are not only ethnically different, but also devoutly Muslim. How does a government integrate a strongly religious minority (be it Muslim, Christian, or Buddhist) into a Marxist-capitalist system? China's policy of intolerance toward dissent and economic stimulus has not seemed to resolve this issue.

Conclusion

This chapter has argued for a wide variety of Muslim responses to Chinese rule and a spectrum of adaptation, both between the official Muslim nationalities, and within their various religious and political groups. Clearly, the configuration of Islamic communities has been directly influenced by the state's ethnic and religious policies. Due to China's *minzu* policy, it is nearly impossible to distinguish ethnic from religious identities among China's Muslim minorities, and elsewhere I have argued it is best to describe these as "ethnoreligious" identities.[13] Hui, Uyghur, and other minority groups in China are fully aware of the use the state is making of their identities in both international relations and the construction of national identity, which allows for the justification of internal control over not only individual politics, but cultural and religious difference as well. Through several protests—I witnessed a Uyghur march against a Han exhibition of "minority art" at the Overseas Hotel in Urumqi in fall 1987 that the Uyghur found to be denigrating and degrading—Uyghur have often attempted to object to their *National Geographic*–like portrayals as "happy, sensual natives." It is doubtful that today, despite widespread civil protests throughout China, Uyghurs in Xinjiang would be allowed to engage in such a public protest. Clearly, state recognition of the "East Turkistan separatists" and the "Xinjiang problem" have indicated a willingness to recognize the ongoing tensions in the region that fifty years of minority special treatment, economic development programs (such as the Great West Development Program), and harsh crackdowns (such as the four-year Strike Hard campaign), have yet to resolve.

At the same time, Uyghur and other minorities are taking advantage of their official minority status and objectified identities, ill-fitting or not, to promote their own religious, political, and personal interests. Opportunities to study and travel abroad are hard to come by, even for Han, and the Uyghur are eager to take advantage of every little crack in the Chinese system. When the state allows those cracks to appear, albeit for very specific foreign policy and economic goals, it may not be able to anticipate the many unintended results—results that might include a strengthened transnational Uyghur identity, both Turkish and Muslim.

China is not immune to the new tide of religious nationalism and "primordial politics" sweeping Europe, Africa, and Asia in the post–Cold War and post-9/11 periods. Much of it is clearly due to a response to globalization in terms of localization: increasing nationalism arising from the organization of the world into nation-states. No longer content to sit on the sidelines, the nations within these states are playing a greater role in the public sphere (Habermas 1989). In most of these nationalist movements, religion, culture, and racialization play a privileged role in defining the boundaries of the nation. In China, as elsewhere, Islam will continue to play an important role in defining the nation, especially when nationality is defined by a mix of religion and ethnicity.

Notes

Portions of this chapter were previously published in the article "Islam in China: Accommodation or Separatism," in *Religion in China Today*, edited by Daniel L. Overmyer (Cambridge: Cambridge University Press, 2003) (*China Quarterly* special issue, n.s., no. 3).

1. For an analysis of the 2000 population statistics, see Yang and Ding (2002).

2. For a study of Muslim origin myths and their relevance for contemporary identity politics, see Gladney (2004: 99–115).

3. For the debate over the definition of Hui and reference to them as "Sino-Muslims," see Lipman (1997: xxiv), and Gladney (1996: 21–35).

4. See Ong (1999: 23). Uyghurs waiting for an independent Uyghuristan find Chinese citizenship the least flexible, especially when threatened with extradition while in the diaspora, while Hui have rarely challenged Chinese citizenship. Similarly, membership in the Muslim community in China is legislated by birth, in the sense that once born a Hui, always a Hui, regardless of belief or even membership in the Party.

5. Tajiks are the only official nationality still lacking a script, and must learn in either Uyghur or Han Chinese in their own Tajik Autonomous Country of Tashkurgan (Tashkurgan county chairman interview, August 25, 2001). Yang Shengmin has indicated that Uyghur cadres opposed granting a separate written language to the Tajiks (personal communication December 4, 2003); however, political concerns over links to Iran and Tajikistan through the promulgation of a Persian script are clearly an important factor.

6. Interestingly, although the Deng and Baima regard themselves as separate nationalities, and they have minority status under the Tibetan nationality, it is Tibetan cadres who do not wish them to be separately recognized, so as not to diminish total Tibetan population numbers (Yang Shengmin, personal communication). The State Ethnic Affairs Commission in 1994 ruled out the possibility of recognizing additional nationalities, some believe, in order to avoid having to recognize too many new nationalities, including the Chinese Jews, which might alienate Middle East trading partners (see Gladney 2004: 103, 168).

7. For more information on the State Ethnic Affairs Commission, see Gladney

(1996: 261–88), Dreyer (1976: 95–96), and Sautman (1999: 53–55). In the late 1990s, the State Ethnic Affairs Commission changed the English translation of its name from "State Commission for Nationality Affairs" to the "State Ethnic Affairs Commission," reflecting evolving debates in China about the translation of the term *minzu* into English and state policy toward minorities. See Gladney (1996: 84–87).

8. The debate over the translation and meaning of *minzu* has become an intellectual industry in and of itself. See Duara (1995), Dikötter (1992), and Gladney (1996: 6–20).

9. This distinction was most fully articulated by Roff (1985).

10. This was the first major uprising in Xinjiang that took place in the Southern Tarim region near Baren township, which initiated a series of unrelated and sporadic protests.

11. See also Scott Fogden's (2002) excellent Msc. Econ thesis.

12. "Since the first half of the year 2000, the situation in Xinjiang has been peaceful (*pingjing*), despite my earlier description of the seriousness of this issue, and should be accurately described as dramatically changed since the internationalization of the Xinjiang problem (*Xinjiang wenti guojihua*)" (Ma 2003: 128).

13. On "ethnoreligious" identity in China, see Gladney (1996: 112–18).

References

Amnesty International. 1999. *Peoples Republic of China: Gross Violations of Human Rights in the Xinjiang Uighur Autonomous Region.* London (April 21).

Benson, Linda. 1990. *The Ili Rebellion: The Moslem Challenge to Chinese Authority in Xinjiang, 1944–1949.* Armonk, NY: M. E. Sharpe.

Cheng, Allen T. 2003. "A Surprise Move by the Mainland's Islamic Community." *South China Morning Post* (March 25).

"China Releases List of International Terrorists." 2003. *Xinhua* received by NewsEDGE/LAN: 14-12-03 19:10.

Connor, Walker. 1984. *The National Question in Marxist-Leninist Theory and Strategy.* Princeton, NJ: Princeton University Press.

Dikötter, Frank. 1992. *The Discourse of Race in Modern China.* Stanford, CA: Stanford University Press.

Dillon, Michael. 1997. *Hui Muslims in China.* London: Curzon
———. 2004. *Xinjiang: China's Muslim Far Northwest.* London: Routledge/Curzon.

Dreyer, June. 1976. *China's Forty Million: Minority Nationalities and National Integration in the People's Republic of China.* Cambridge, MA: Harvard University Press.

Duara, Prasenjit. 1995. *Rescuing History from the Nation.* Chicago: University of Chicago Press.

East Turkistan (Uyghuristan) National Congress. 2003. "Help the Uyghurs to Fight Terrorism." Munich. Collected November 11, 2003.

Eckholm, Erik. 2002. "U.S. Labeling of Group in China as Terrorist Is Criticized." *New York Times* (September 13).

Eickelman, Dale F. 1976. *Moroccan Islam: Tradition and Society in a Pilgrimage Center.* Austin: University of Texas Press.

Fletcher, Joseph. 1996. *Studies on Chinese and Islamic Inner Asia*, edited by Beatrice Manz. London: Variorum.

Fogden, Scott. 2002. "Writing Insecurity: The PRC's Push to Modernize China and the Politics of Uighur Identity." Msc. Econ thesis. Aberystwyth: University of Wales.

Forbes, Andrew D. W. 1986. *Warlords and Muslims in Chinese Central Asia*. Cambridge, UK: Cambridge University Press.

Gladney, Dru C. 1990. "The Ethnogenesis of the Uighur." *Central Asian Survey* 9, 1: 1–28.

———. 1996 [first ed., 1991]. *Muslim Chinese: Ethnic Nationalism in the People's Republic*. Cambridge, MA: Harvard University Press, Council on East Asian Studies.

———. 2004. *Dislocating China: Muslims, Minorities, and Other Subaltern Subjects*. Chicago: Chicago University Press.

Habermas, Jürgen. 1989. *The Structural Transformation of the Public Sphere*, translated by Thomas Burger and Frederick Lawrence. Cambridge, MA: MIT Press.

Harris, Lillian. 1993. *China Considers the Middle East*. London: I. B. Tauris.

Hutzler, Charles. 2002. "U.S. Gesture to China Raises Crackdown Fears." *Wall Street Journal* (September 13).

Israeli, Raphael. 1981. *Muslims in China: A Study in Cultural Confrontation*. Scandinavia Monographs in East Asian Studies 29. New York: Prometheus Books.

———. 2002. *Islam in China: Religion, Ethnicity, Culture and Politics*. Lanham, MD: Rowman and Littlefield.

Johnson, Ian. 1999. "China Arrests Noted Businesswoman in Crackdown in Muslim Region." *Wall Street Journal* (August 18).

Kim, Hodong. 2003. *Holy War in China: The Muslim Rebellion and State in Chinese Central Asia, 1866–1877*. Stanford, CA: Stanford University Press.

Lipman, Jonathan. 1997. *Familiar Strangers: A History of Muslims in Northwest China*. Seattle: University of Washington Press.

Ma Dazheng. 2003. *Guojia liyi gaoyu yiqie: Xinjiang wending wenti de guancha yu sikao* (The state takes precedence: research and analysis on the Xinjiang stability problem). Urumqi: Xinjiang renmin chubanshe.

Mao Zedong. 1936. "Appeal of the Central Government to the Muslims." *Tou-cheng* 105 (July) 12: 1–3.

McNeal, Dewardic L. 2001. "China's Relations with Central Asian States and Problems with Terrorism." *U.S. Department of State, Congressional Research Service Report*.

Ong, Aihwa. 1999. *Flexible Citizenship: The Cultural Logic of Transnationality*. Durham, NC: Duke University Press.

People's Daily. 2001. "China Also Harmed by Separatist-Minded Eastern Turkestan Terrorists." (October 10).

Radio Free Asia. 2003. Uyghur service, "Separatist Leader Killed in Waziristan," December 15, 2003. www.rfa.org/service/index.html?service=uyg.

Roff, William. 1985. "Islam Obscured? Some Reflections on Studies of Islam and Society in Asia." *L'Islam en Indonesie* 1, 29: 8–10

Rudelson, Justin Jon. 1997. *Oasis Identities: Uyghur Nationalism along China's Silk Road*. New York: Columbia University Press.

Sautman, Barry. 1999. "Legal Reform and Minority Rights in China." In *Handbook of Global Legal Policy*, edited by Stuart Nagel, pp. 49–80. New York: Marcel Dekker.

Shahidi, Burhan. 1984. *Xinjiang wushi nian* (Xinjiang: fifty years). Beijing: Wenshi ziliao chubanshe.

Shichor, Yitzhak. 1984. "The Role of Islam in China's Middle-Eastern Policy." In *Islam in Asia,* vol. 2, edited by Raphael Israeli and Anthony H. Johns. Boulder, CO: Westview.

Snow, Edgar. 1938. *Red Star Over China*. New York: Grove.

Trippner, Joseph. 1961. "Islamische Gruppe und Graberkult in Nordwest China." *Die Welt des Islams* 7.

Yang Shengmin, and Ding Hong (eds.). 2002. *Zhongguo minzu zhi* (An ethnography of China). Beijing: Central Nationalities Publishing House.

Weber, Max. 1978. *Economy and Society.* 2 vols. Berkeley: University of California Press.

CHAPTER 8

Further Partings of the Way: The Chinese State and Daoist Ritual Traditions in Contemporary China

KENNETH DEAN

HOLMES WELCH'S *Parting of the Way: Lao Tzu and the Taoist Movement*, written in 1957, outlined what the author saw as a sharp divide between the mystical Daoist philosophy of the classical period and the debased religious Daoism of later dynasties. This vision of the decline of Daoism has now been overturned by several decades of scholarship on the Daoist religion (see Seidel 1990; Schipper and Verellen 2005).[1] Most scholars now date the institutionalization of the Daoist religion to the second century AD and the founding of the Zhengyi Tianshi Dao (Orthodox Unity Celestial Master) movement in Sichuan by Zhang Daoling and Zhang Lu. A second major parting of the way is often drawn between the Orthodox Unity movement and the Quanzhen (Complete Perfection) school of monastic Daoism, founded by Wang Zhe (1113–70) in the Song dynasty. The Complete Perfection school borrowed heavily from monastic Buddhism, while the various branches of the Orthodox Unity school for the most part maintained a hereditary ritual tradition with close ties to local communal religion.[2] New revelations and new ritual traditions were a regular feature of Daoism. Continuous partings were an intrinsic aspect of the Way, despite state and clerical efforts at systematization and appropriation.[3] Recent fieldwork has shown that in addition to the two main currents of Daoism mentioned above, a wide range of localized Daoist ritual traditions are currently practiced across China, including the Lüshan rites practiced throughout a wide stretch of southern China, the Duangong ritual and theatrical traditions of Sichuan, and the Thunder rites of Hunan, amongst others.[4]

Given the preliminary state of research on the vast range of different forms of local communal religion in China, not to mention the paucity of research into the ritual activities of both Zhengyi ritual masters and Quanzhen monks and nuns in relation to their multiple local contexts, it is extremely difficult to broach an institutional analysis of Daoism.[5] Due to the complex, intricate ties between Daoist ritual traditions and local communal religion, one could argue that it is impossible to clearly distinguish the space of Daoist ritual from the constantly changing informal rules of local level Chinese society concerning religious, or should we say communal ritual activity. In fact, it is misleading to separate out a specifically "religious" space from other aspects of communal life at this level. Such analytic distinctions may themselves be seen as part of the project of modernity.[6]

Talal Asad (2003: 13) defines the project of modernity as "a project—or rather, a series of interlinked projects—that certain people in power seek to achieve." While discounting the universalist claims of modernization theory, he notes that the teleologically charged project of modernity has had real impacts on everyday life and experience around the globe. The Chinese state could certainly be said to have been engaged in such a project for over a century, vigorously attempting to impose formal rules and definitions of religion over a complex web of local, informal rules governing social ritual practices. In combination with the impact of capitalist forces, the Marxist and Maoist attacks on temples, Daoist ritual masters, and structures of everyday ritual life in China have had a devastating impact. A vast number of temples have been destroyed and countless lives have been ruined. The long-term combined impact of these forces can be seen in the institutionalization of principles such as consumerism, freedom of the market, and secularism, which are especially evident in China's cities, where an earlier dense network of neighborhood and ward temples, most celebrating Daoist rites, has been largely destroyed. But an examination of Daoism solely from the point of view of its response to state legislation or the forces of modernization would be to tell only one side of a complex, multifaceted story. For over the past twenty-five years, in the villages and temples of rural China, especially in the south, temples have been restored and Daoist rituals are again being celebrated at key points in the lives of individuals, families, and communities.

Asad (1993: chs. 1, 2) also provided a genealogical analysis of the concepts of religion and ritual. He argues that the very concept of religion as an abstract system of beliefs is marked by its development out of Western Christian theology, and that there is no possible transhistorical, universal definition of religion. This suggests that there are no pure natural pools of religiosity beyond the reach of the state or clerical or other cultural institutions. Asad calls instead for the study of different historically constituted modes of practical knowledge, of disciplinary practices rather than representational practices. He sees ritual as a range of modes of disciplining bodies within specific regimes of knowledge, power, and discourse. This approach calls our attention to the years of training in ritual performance, dance, gesture, meditation, and visualization techniques involved in becoming a Daoist ritual master. The performative dimension of Daoist ritual, and the vital relationship between Daoist rites and larger communal festivals, is also central to this approach.

Asad (1993: ch. 6) furthermore questions mainstream practices of "cultural translation" within anthropology, arguing that the inequality of languages in the current world order and the implicit model of psychoanalytic interpretation of the "other" transform cultural translation into an act of appropriation. He argues instead for a mode of translation related to Walter Benjamin's call for an effort to create within one's own language the troubling effects of difference and otherness. With this call in mind, an effort is made in the concluding section of this chapter to "translate" the ritual view of the role of *cosmo-political forces* within contemporary Daoist and communal ritual events.[7]

Close Links between Daoism and Local Communal Religion

Two recently discovered sources help illustrate the links between Daoism and local communal religion. The first is a stone inscription I located in Leshan ward of Hui'an city in Fujian, carved in 1909, and entitled "Stele Displaying an [Official] Prohibition in Leshan Ward."[8] This inscription records the Hui'an district magistrate's decision in favor of a group of gentry who had defied a local Daoist ritual master named Zhang Fu, who maintained that he had hereditary rights as the local *shizhu* (master of dispensations) to perform rituals in all the temples and homes of the Leshan ward. The gentry had raised funds and hired an outside Daoist to perform the rites, after heeding complaints that Zhang Fu was arrogant and charged too much. That a district magistrate would find it necessary to carve an inscription and erect a stele in the ward denying the Daoist's claims to the territory gives an indication of the power of local Daoist ritual masters in this region.

The second source is a manuscript recopied in the late 1980s by a local Daoist ritual master in the Fengting region of Xianyou county, just north of Hui'an county. This manuscript lists the birthdays of the gods of the most important temples in the area. Arranged chronologically, it covers over 200 gods celebrated in over 150 temples, all within 100 square kilometers. These were the dates of Daoist rituals of celebration to which the Daoist ritual master and his fathers before him had been invited for generations. The Daoist ritual master told me that almost one hundred of these temples had been restored over the past twenty years, and that as a result, he was very busy performing rituals.

Several scholars have demonstrated the key role of local temples in both village and urban life in late imperial and Republican China (Schipper 1993; Duara 1988; Naquin 2000; Goossaert 2007). A number of scholars have also emphasized the key role of Daoist ritual within the ritual events of local communal religion (Schipper 1993; Lagerwey 1987; Dean 1993). Regardless of whether one argues that: (1) the Daoists were promoting a hierarchical relationship with the gods with themselves as the necessary mediators (Hymes 2002); (2) their participation was a process of the universalization of local cults through the *writing* of the local cult into liturgy and scripture and an identification of the local gods as transformations of higher Daoist deities in their ritual performances (Dean 1993); or even (3) Daoist ritual was one key node (center of attraction and emergent organization) within the multi-centered, complex ritual events of Chinese local religion (Dean and Lamarre 2003), the close link between Daoist ritual specialists and local cults and village temples cannot be denied. Thus any attack on the role of the local temples of local communal religion would inevitably constitute an attack on the basis of the way of life of the Daoist ritual masters.

As mentioned above, Daoist ritual masters can be divided into Quanzhen Complete Perfection monks based in monasteries or nunneries, or a variety of locally based, hereditary ritual masters loosely derived from the Zhengyi Tianshi Orthodox Unity Celestial Master movement. Over the Yuan, Ming, and Qing dynasties, Quanzhen orders spread from North China across the empire, to Sichuan (*Qingchengshan*), Hunan, and Guangzhou (*Luofushan*), and more recently to Hong Kong (*Qingsongshan*).[9] Quanzhen and Zhengyi Daoism were unlikely to both be strong in the same areas. However, in recent years, temples with a mixed population of Quanzhen and Zhengyi Daoists (such as the Baiyunguan in Shanghai in the early 1980s) have struggled to work together. In this context, it is important to note that despite their different institutional settings, both Quanzhen and Zhengyi ritual masters perform variations of what is in fact a common core of Zhengyi Lingbao (Spiritual Treasure) Daoist ritual for their clients. It is interesting to note that in the Qing, even Quanzhen monks and nuns were seldom concentrated exclusively in large monastic centers; instead, they were often widely dispersed in smaller monasteries, nunneries, and temples in close proximity to local society.[10] In addition to performing rituals in their monasteries, they would on occasion travel to participate in rituals held in temples that sponsored major regional temple fairs.

Whereas Quanzhen monks and nuns live and practice within Daoist monasteries, specifically Zhengyi Daoist temples are far more difficult to single out from the mass of temples dedicated to popular deities across China, especially in the south. Most cities and major towns prior to the Republican reforms or the establishment of a state by the Chinese Communist Party (Party) had City God temples in which either Quanzhen or Zhengyi Daoist ritual masters were often based. These City God temples functioned as a kind of hinge between the official sacrificial system and the local hierarchy of the cults of the gods (Taylor 1990). Many cities and towns also had Daoist *guan* (temples, or belvederes) with Zhengyi or Quanzhen ritual masters in residence. Most cities or towns also had a temple to the Eastern Peak in which could be found Daoists specializing in funerals, requiems, and guided spirit medium encounters with the dead. These three or four ubiquitous kinds of temples had a stronger Daoist presence than the host of other temples dedicated to local gods. Some of these temples have been restored, such as the Beijing Dongyuemiao and the Shanghai City God temple, but most are not fully under the control of Daoist ritual specialists any longer. Many have instead been turned into tourist attractions or museums.

In contrast to the Quanzhen monks and nuns, the Zhengyi Orthodox Unity Celestial Master tradition, and that of the multiple alternative Daoist ritual traditions mentioned above, generally take the form of Daoist ritual specialists who work out of their homes, where they maintain altars dedicated to Lord Lao(zi) (or another deity associated with their particular ritual tradition), and usually claim some allegiance to Zhang Daoling, founder of the Daoist religion. The practitioners of the primarily southern tradition of Zhengyi and that of other local Daoist traditions are often referred to as *huoju* (hearth dwelling) or *sanju* (dispersed dwellers) Daoists. They have had a much more contentious relationship with the Religious Affairs Bureau in the People's Republic of China.

This is primarily because there is no single institutional framework for these ritual specialists. These Daoist ritual masters transmit their liturgical texts and practices to their sons and disciples in discrete, local lines of transmission. Such transmissions culminate in ordinations, now presided over by collections of local Daoist ritual masters, although some ordination certificates still make reference to Longhushan, the hereditary center of the Zhengyi Tianshi Celestial Masters. Many such local Daoist ritual masters maintain troupes of acolytes who perform rituals as a team. They may also have long-standing connections with sets of local musicians. It is also common for the Daoists to play a variety of instruments, particularly the drum, which sets the rhythm for the entire oratorio-like liturgy. They are also expected to sing, chant, and dance, and to write in a range of calligraphic styles, including talismanic writing.

As shown above, long-established relations between such localized Daoists and nearby temples sometimes solidify into proprietarial claims over elements or levels of the local ritual marketplace. A local hierarchy of Daoist ritual troupes tends to develop over time in each locale, serving different classes of clients. Depending on their particular liturgical tradition and the cultural area in which they operate, the ritual services of local Daoists include the observances of communal sacrifices (*jiao*) at local temples dedicated to the gods of the local pantheon, funerals and requiem services for individual families, and minor rites for individuals and families (blessing of marriage, exorcism of demonic disease vectors, improvement of fate, healing rituals, etc.). The elite Daoist ritual master was considered a member of elite circles, whereas the less well trained and less proficient Daoists served a less well off clientele. Daoists rites could be performed in highly extended, complex forms over several days, or in dramatically simplified form, in a single afternoon, depending on the needs of the sponsors. In addition to Daoist ritual specialists, temples, families, and individuals could also turn to Buddhist monks and other local ritual specialists (such as spirit mediums or the Three in One Scripture Masters in the Xinghua region). Marionettists, puppeteers, and carpenters also performed rituals, and ritual was required to consecrate the stage prior to operatic performances as well. Most major communal ritual events involved the simultaneous performance of many such groups of ritual performers.

Clearly, further research is needed on the history of the forms of local organization, management, and mobilization within village organizations (including lineage formations and temple networks) that developed over time and in different parts of China. In a provisional description of the state of current religico-social activities in coastal Fujian, I characterized the networks of local temple systems and village lineages active in this region as "China's second government," in that they have over the past several hundred years provided a growing range of social and cultural services and infrastructural improvements at the local level whenever and wherever central government control or intervention declined (Dean 2001). These organizations sponsor Daoist rites as part of their celebrations of local communal rites. In recent years, people living in some of these areas could attend ritual performances (including opera) 250 days out of the year. At this level, communal ritual events are simply an intensification of the ritual core of everyday life. Each household is mobilized to participate in village ritual events, but this is based on the fact that each household is already a ritual unit, with its own altar dedicated to ancestors and gods, and its daily, monthly, seasonal, and annual rites. Social and gender relations are highly ritualized as well. These rites and ritualized relations are intensified in communal observances.

However, other regions of China present a very different picture. In a recent (2004) trip to Shanxi, I met with local Quanzhen Daoists in Linfen county who explained that the restoration of popular temples and the holding of temple fairs with Daoist rituals had just begun in parts of that province, twenty years after similar processes began in Fujian. It remains to be seen whether this long gap in ritual practice will prove insurmountable for the transmission of earlier ritual traditions.

The role of Daoism in relation to local communal ritual activity in China has to be seen in historical perspective. In general, what one can see developing in many regions of China from at least the mid-Ming onwards are new modes of subjectivation within emerging forms of local power.[11] Some of the institutional arenas for the capture of the forces of these new forms of local power in this process were the varieties of lineage formations, the expanding temple networks, and the sectarian movements. Official elite models such as community compacts, model neo-Confucian lineages, or local academies or poetry associations were often absorbed and adapted to local needs by emerging social groups. Most of these models were centered on ritual performance. Some of these rituals involved Daoist ritual specialists. Others involved primarily local *lisheng* (masters of ceremony). Ritual forms and specializations were invented or modified in an effort to channel and contain emergent social and cosmo-political powers. This entire process could be characterized as the rise of a new form of power, parallel but distinct from what Michel Foucault described as "pastoral power" in Western Europe.[12] Perhaps one could refer to this new form of power in increasingly autonomous local networks as "ritual power."

These local organizations and their new modes of power and discourse responded very creatively to state initiatives in the realms of taxation, household registration, and ritual ordering. But local society did more than just adapt to state institutional pressures and cultural hegemonic initiatives. Changes to what I have termed the "syncretic field" of Chinese ritual experience were also initiated at the local level, based on emerging social needs and social forces, and justified by the notion that *li yi yi qi* (ritual arises from the meaning of the participant's intentions). Local society was a hotbed of creative cultural involution, generating worlds of difference within local communal ritual events (see Conclusion). It is also important to consider that along with the changing consistency of the syncretic field and its local social elements, the nature of the state also shifted dramatically over time, especially from the viewpoint of the local communities.[13]

Brief Overview of State Attitudes toward Daoism

During the Ming dynasty (1368–1644), the court maintained close ties with the Longhushan Tianshifu (Headquarters of the Celestial Masters), and several descendants of the Zhang Daoling lineage and their associates held important positions of power at court. The Ming court also patronized the Daoist temples of Wudangshan and promoted the cult of Xuantian shangdi. The founder of the Ming, Zhu Yuanzhang (Ming Taizu) established the Daolusi (Bureau of Daoist Registration) within the Ministry of Rites in 1371. At the provincial level, he set up Daozhengsi (Bureaus of Political [Supervision] of Daoists), and the Daohuisi (Bureaus of Daoist Assemblies) at the district level. Some 96,000 Daoists were listed in 1373. Ming Taizu also set up and staffed with Daoists the Shenyueguan (Temple of Divine Music) in 1379, an independent office responsible for court ritual music. This office supplied Daoist ritual specialists to Ming noble households across the empire, perhaps contributing to the Daoist conversion of certain minorities such as the Yao in South China. He furthermore instituted the *Zhouzhice* (All-knowing register) to list the Daoists in monasteries across China and to keep track of their movements (de Bruyn 2000).

While Zhu Yuanzhang supported Daoism at one level, at another level he was deeply concerned about its links to local communal organization and potential rebellious movements. He banned certain popular Daoist festivals in 1372, instituted an empire-wide cult of Confucius, and established a consciously archaic system of altars to the soil and the harvest throughout the empire to promote Confucian values such as loyalty. Many local cults were forbidden, and they were excised from the imperial Register of Sacrifices. The system of official altars at the sub-canton level soon mutated into new forms of hybrid popular temples and localized ritual networks (Dean 1998b). Despite this tendency, zealous, if not fanatical neo-Confucian local administrators periodically attempted to eradicate local cults they deemed licentious or unorthodox. This tendency would increase during the Qing dynasty.

Several Ming emperors were ardent practitioners of Daoist self-cultivation techniques and promoted Daoist rituals at court. Some Ming emperors took on Daoist titles, and welcomed successive Celestial Masters to court, where they were honored with high rank and entitled Zhenren (Perfected Being). The Ming Yongle emperor (r. 1403–24) sponsored the compilation of the Ming *Daoist Canon* under the supervision of the forty-second Celestial Master, Zhang Yuqing.[14] Cracks in imperial support began in 1568, when the Celestial Master was un-inivited to court, and suffered demotion in rank. But this policy was partially reversed under Shenzong (r. 1572–1619), who sponsored the publication of the *Xu Daozang* (Supplement to the Daoist canon). At the popular level, the annual festival of Yanjiujie in Beijing was celebrated in the first lunar month by Daoist rites featuring over 40,000 Daoist ritual masters. The festival of the Temple of the Eastern Peak on the twenty-eighth of the third lunar month, and the pilgrimage to Miaofengshan in the fourth lunar month were all major festivals with considerable Daoist ritual participation.

The Qing dynasty (1644–1911) seems to have been highly suspicious of popular level Daoism. The *Qing shigao* (Draft history of the Qing) includes a 1673 decree stating that "shamans, Daoist ritual masters, and spirit mediums who exorcise ghosts and drive away demons in order to delude the hearts of the people should be put to death, and those who invite spirit mediums should also be charged with a crime" (juan 117, zhi 90). In 1676, it was decreed that the Bureaus of Buddhist and Daoist Registration throughout the empire should enforce this law (cited in Schipper 2002: 148).

Despite court suspicions, in the first half of the Qing dynasty representatives of the Celestial Masters were still allowed to set up regular ordination platforms in certain areas of China, where they would stamp ordination certificates and collect fees.[15] One such ordination certificate issued by the Longhushan Celestial Masters in 1704 has recently been found in the possession of a Daoist ritual master in a remote region at the Jiangxi-Hunan border (Liu 2000: 263). The right to confer ordinations in this way was ultimately suspended by the Qianlong emperor in 1739 (*Xu wenxian tongkao*, juan 99, quoted in Schipper 2002: 148; Goossaert 2000). In 1740, Mei Gucheng (d. 1763), an imperial censor, memorialized that "Daoists are mean people, and it is not appropriate that they besmirch court audiences," whereupon the fifty-seventh Celestial Master was prevented from attending court (*Qing shigao*, juan 115, zhi 90, quoted in Schipper 2002: 149). In 1742, the Qianlong emperor had Confucian ritualists replace Daoists as Music Masters in the Court of Imperial Sacrifices, where they had served since the Ming dynasty. And in 1752, the Qianlong emperor demoted the Celestial Masters from Rank 3 to Rank 5. They were not allowed into court audiences and could not request titles. Nor were they any longer considered the general administrators of Daoism.

Although later Celestial Masters were occasionally welcomed back to court by his successors, the prestige of Daoism continued to decline, until in the Daoguang period (1821–50) the relationship between the court and the Celestial Masters appears to have come to an end, when the Jiajing emperor terminated the quintennual visits to court (Esposito 2000; Xun

2004: 98). Court support for Quanzhen Daoist monasteries in the capital came from local officials and court eunuchs, and later from Dowager Empress Ci Xi (Xun 2004). Many of the Daohuisi (Offices of Daoist Associations), which had since the Ming dynasty maintained self-regulation of Daoist activities at the local level, with a renowned local Daoist made responsible for the activities of other Daoists in his district, appear to have been disbanded by the late Qing dynasty. In general, the ability of Daoism to provide a key liturgical framework to Chinese popular religion was enough to arouse the suspicions of the Chinese state, especially after the rise of religious rebellions in the late eighteenth century. Paradoxically enough, the Tianshifu of the Celestial Masters, which had been restored at Qing imperial behest in 1731, would be burned by the Taiping rebels.

Nineteenth and Early Twentieth Century Challenges

This long historical process of the emergence of a variety of forms of relative local autonomy, featuring increasing self-regulation, self-governance, and cultural self-definition, and the important role within this historical process of Daoism, forms the essential backdrop to an understanding of the last 150 years of attacks on Daoism (and Chinese clericism in general) and on local communal religion. One of the most striking early manifestations of this attack took the form of the Taiping Rebellion, which took aim at local cults, temples, and ritual networks, smashing god statues and razing temples across a wide area of South China. The Tianshifu of the Celestial Masters was just one of thousands of temple complexes destroyed by the Taiping armies. Philip Kuhn has demonstrated that the Taiping administration developed a much stronger hierarchy linking the Taiping court to local administration in areas under its control than had existed under the Qing administrative order. The Taipings' revised order of governance grew out of their profound awareness of the key role of the cults and local temples in local self-governance.

Although the Qing court recognized and rewarded through canonization a great many local gods of those that had supported the court against the Taiping rebels and many other localized rebellions (Dean 1993), other forces continued to undermine the role of local communal religion. In a series of judgments from 1861 to 1872, the Zongli Yamen supported the Catholic minority in villages in Shanxi in their demand to be exempted from village temple fees, the principle form of funding for local communal organization required of all village residents. The Zongli Yamen's decisions in favor of Catholic communities in North China effected a modernist divide between "culture," now isolated as a sphere of aesthetic activity, and "religion," now defined as a set of actions and institutions defined by specific beliefs (Litzinger 1996; Thompson 1996). This division profoundly challenged the communal nature of local religion.

In even more striking ways, conditions of extraterritoriality in Shanghai and other treaty ports presented a new model of modern nation-state–society relations. New understandings of state-society relations, and the right of the extraterritorial state to regulate society, led in Shanghai in the mid-nineteenth century to the registration of hundreds of hitherto informal local-level social organizations (as shown in Brook 1997). By asserting the power of the state to regulate local cultural institutions, the autonomy of local life, and the ability of local ritual events to generate worlds of difference, were fundamentally compromised.

Anti-religious discourse went through several transformations in the late Qing. In 1898 Kang Youwei attacked Daoism, Buddhism, and local communal religion, proposing instead a cult of state Confucianism that would be based in Confucian academies in converted temples. This can be seen as one of several experiments in designing a modern nation-state, with ideological institutions all the way down to the village level. Traditional fundamentalist Confucian anti-clericism aimed at Buddhists, Daoists, and the spirit-mediums of local communal religion here began to combine with modern nation-state cultural nationalism. When Liang Qichao introduced the terms and discursive field of a Western conception of religion as an area distinct from other aspects of culture and society in 1901, the discourse changed from narrowly anti-clerical to broadly anti-religious, and the target broadened from the priesthood and the spirit mediums to the basic structures of local communal organization, the temple networks. The collapse of the Boxer Rebellion exacerbated the critique of local communal religion and local forms of self-organization. By 1904, the turning point in the movement against the temples of Chinese local communal religion had been reached when the Ministry of Rites refused to canonize any more local gods.

The anti-religion, anti-superstition campaigns of the early Republican period have been studied by Duara (1995), Goossaert (2001), and Nedostup (2001). The degree of success of or resistance to these campaigns varied greatly. But changes at the local level may have been even more significant than government reform campaigns. Transformations in the form, structure, and nature of local chambers of commerce and the establishment of local parliaments provided new areas of activity and new discourses of capitalism and modern nation-state building for the educated elite. Temple committees fought back, but these new discourses and new institutions were too powerful in most areas. After a series of laws calling for the confiscation of temples and their transformation into schools (or police stations) by the late Qing and Republican governments, by 1937 it has been estimated that half of the temples in China had been destroyed (Goossaert 2003a), although the extent of the destruction varied regionally.

The People's Republic and Daoism

The rise of Marxist critiques of Chinese class society added the patriarchal lineage and the religious monastery to the list of targets, attacking the major forms and resources of local self-governance in Chinese society. The complex interlinking of lineage, monastery (or network of ritual specialists), and local cults in the many different regions of China is too complex to summarize here. Suffice it to say that throughout the Anti-Japanese War and the civil war that followed, the Party developed a comprehensive critique of the lineage along with Buddhist and Daoist monasteries, and the temples of local religion. Central to their critique was a Western (Marxist) conception of religion.

Article 36 of the Chinese constitution states that "citizens of the People's Republic of China enjoy freedom of religious belief. . . . The state protects normal religious activities" (Potter 2003: 19). Implied in this statement is a denunciation of "unacceptable religious activities." These are listed in one 1986 news report: "indiscriminate building of temples . . . invoking immortals to exorcise evil spirits, praying for rain, divining by the eight trigrams, telling fortunes . . . practicing physiognomy and geomancy are feudal superstitious activities which should be resolutely banned . . . resolutely suppressed" (Dean 1993: 174).[16]

Unfortunately, all these activities are integral aspects of local communal religion, and all have intimate connections with the ritual practices of Daoism. Daoism has been officially recognized as one of the five religions of China, even though it is difficult to characterize it according to the definition of religion espoused by the state. According to that definition, a religion should have a doctrine, an organization and leadership, rules of conduct, and rituals expressing its beliefs (Dean 1993: 173–76). However, despite the efforts of the court and the Longhushan Celestial Master organization, Daoist ritual traditions were dispersed across China without a unified organization or religious leader. Daoist ritual provided one of many central liturgical frameworks for local communal rituals dedicated to local gods, but doctrinal elements are not emphasized, and thus no clear set of beliefs need be articulated. Although one can extract a cosmological model out of Daoist ritual, this is not presented as a rationale behind a set of rites representing the beliefs of the participants at the rite. Rather, the Daoist ritual masters preserve the details of their own ritual visualizations, and present only the outer aspect of their liturgy to the participants at local communal rituals, many of whom are drawn into the ritual performance in some capacity. In requiem services and exorcistic rites as well, the performative element prevails over the expression of specific beliefs. There is no exposition of the meaning of scriptures, or interpretation to the public of the features of liturgy. All this is even truer of most forms of local communal ritual practice.

Thus the imposition of conceptions of religion rooted in Western historical experience intensified the process of the destruction of local communal religion by adding an ill-fitting conceptual framework, one that encouraged misunderstanding by state authorities and led to wanton destructiveness. Vincent Goossaert (2003a) suggests that half of all China's local temples had been destroyed by the end of the Republican period. Tens of thousands of the remaining temples were destroyed over the second half of the twentieth century, particularly during the Cultural Revolution. A full account of the destruction of temples, the physical attacks on Daoist ritual masters and other ritual specialists, the burning of scriptures and the smashing of icons, etc., in each region of China would fill many volumes. Nonetheless, the resilience of local communal religion in China is extraordinary, and the restoration, reinvention, and recycling of ritual traditions in the context of local communal ritual practice has been documented by several scholars in different parts of China (Siu 1989; Dean 1993, 1998a, 2003; Feuchtwang 2001; Chau 2006).

Daoism and the Chinese State after 1979

The National Daoist Association was originally established in 1911. A number of its branches and local leaders are described in the *Huabei zongjiao nianjian* (Yearbook of North Chinese religion) published by the Japanese Xinya Religious Association in the early 1940s. It was reestablished in 1957. After a period of savage repression of Daoism during the Cultural Revolution, the Daoist Association was reestablished for a third time in 1979. By 1999 the Daoist Association claimed to have formed 133 branch organizations across China to supervise the restoration of temples, the ordination of Daoist ritual masters, and the ritual activities of the latter.[17] A series of specific laws of the Chinese state touch on aspects of the freedom of religion, such as Article 77 of the Civil Law of 1986, which calls for the protection of the property of religious organizations. The National Daoist Association, which is made up of Daoist ritual specialists, only has authority under the auspices of the Religious Affairs Bureau. In this capacity, it has also issued regulations. The principal regulations affecting Daoism include two issued in 1992, namely "Methods for Administering Daoist Temples" and "Tentative Methods Related to the Administration of Daoist Ritual Masters Who Live at Home." Two more regulations were issued in 1994: "Rules about the Transmission of Precepts for the Quanzhen Order" and "Rules Related to Conferring Registers of Ordination for the Zhengyi Ritual Masters" (Lai 2003: 111; see the texts of these regulations in Li 2000: 107–12).

The Religious Affairs Bureau of each province and major city is empowered to issue local regulations on the control of religion. These provide provisions for state supervision over religious affairs, registration and supervision of religious organizations, personnel, places of worship, and religious activities, education, and property (Potter 2003: 17). Thus most temples in Fujian now display a certificate of authorization as a place of religious practice (*zongjiao shiyong changsuo*), often alongside a set of regulations banning foreign intervention and control of religious activities and organizations. Televised broadcasts in early 2002 showed members of the Fujian Bureau of Religious Affairs working on regulations for the fiscal regulation of local temples. This has become a major issue in Fujian, with the investment of considerable sums for the restoration and development of key temples. This is true elsewhere in China as well. Lai (2003) notes that the Maoshan Yuanfu Wanninggong Daoist temple receives over 650,000 pilgrims and tourists each year, and makes over RMB 6.5 million a year.

Parallels with the history of the growing regulation of religion in Taiwan under the Nationalist Party after 1945 may be instructive. The Nationalist Party government found itself at odds with Taiwanese popular religion, and initially attempted to restrict and limit religious ritual, especially that of the seventh lunar month Pudu Universal Deliverance (of the Hungry Ghosts) festival. However, Chiang Ching-kuo and other Nationalist Party leaders gradually realized the importance of popular religion and temple networks within Taiwanese society for local organization as well as for vote purchasing. Over several decades, a set of regulations was developed for the official registration, financial oversight, and supervision of the activities of the popular temples. The *Zongjiao lisu faling huibian* (Collected statutes on religions rites and practices), published by the Taiwanshengzhengfu minzhengting in Taipei in 1984, gathers 145 regulations together, along with official commentaries. Some relate to the official cult (of Chinese cultural nationalism), such as the rites of Confucian temples, date back to the 1930s, and are still maintained at official temples to Confucius in Tainan and Taipei. Some regulations outline the invented rituals of modern nation-states (i.e., new forms of medals, awards, and honors for service to the state). Others show an increasing acceptance of the need for fiscal oversight and legal property rights for popular temples and local cults. This process of increasing legalization and regulation of local communal religion and related Daoist ritual appears to be underway in China in the early twenty-first century.

A recent overview article by Lai Chi-Tim (2003) notes that significant numbers of Daoist temples have been restored since the Cultural Revolution. Twenty-one temples were restored in 1982, 400 were officially opened by 1992, 1,200 in 1995, and 1,600 by 1998. A total of 1,722 Daoist temples were declared to have been opened by 1996 by Li Yangzhen, associate director of the National Daoist College, in his *Zhongguo Dangdai Daojiao* (Contemporary Chinese Daoism), published in 1997. Several major temples have been visited by outside scholars and described in a range of publications (Japanese accounts include Hachiya Kunio's 1995 two-volume reports on several renowned Daoist temples; see also the newsletters of the Hong Kong Daoist Studies Association, and the web announcements of the Save Daoist Sites organization). According to Li Yangzheng, in 1996 there were 7,135 Daoist ritual masters resident in Daoist temples at that time, with 4,139 Quanzhen monks, 2,311 Quanzhen nuns, and 685 Zhengyi ritual masters. Li further claimed that there were approximately 20,000 Zhengyi Daoist ritual masters "living at home" across southern China and in Sichuan. Lai Chi-Tim (2003) notes that several provincial Daoist associations provide other figures: over 4,000 in Quanzhou, Putian, and Jinjiang in 1989, 1,000 in Shanghai (1990), 1,605 in Wenzhou (1992), 1,200 in Gansu (1993), over 4,000 in Jiangsu (2000). These regional figures suggest that the overall figure of 20,000 is far too small for China as a whole. Whether the numbers have attained the level of 200,000 at the end of the Qing is, however, doubtful.

Lai (2003) points out that Quanzhen Daoist ordinations were begun anew in at the Beijing Baiyunguan in 1989 for 45 monks and 30 nuns. A second Quanzhen ordination was held in 1995 at Qingchengshan for 400 monks and nuns. The Quanzhen tradition has accommodated fairly readily to supervision through the Daoist Association of the Religious Affairs Bureau since 1949. Several major Quanzhen monasteries have been restored, and Daoist Academies have been established in Beijing's Baiyunguan and in Shanghai's Daoist School.[18]

As mentioned above, the right to confer Zhengyi Daoist ordinations was held for many centuries by the Celestial Master Zhang lineage based in Longhushan in Jiangxi. More recently, the sixty-third Celestial Master, Zhang En-pu (1904–69), fled to Taiwan. According to Ding Huang (2000), a grandson of the Zhang lineage was trained at the Beijing Baiyunguan in the 1980s, but later was asked to resign. No successor to the line of Celestial Masters has been recognized by the state. Only in 1995, for the first time in over a hundred years, did the National Daoist Association itself stage ordination ceremonies in the newly restored Celestial Master

Headquarters on Longhushan for 200 Daoist ritual specialists, in a modernized version of the *shoulu* (transmission of the register) ceremony (see Lai 2003: 116 for details). Thus while some ordinations have resumed, the politics of legitimation of contemporary Daoism are complicated by the refusal of the state to allow any restoration of the independent position of the Celestial Master.

Yang Der-Ruey (2003) has recently written a dissertation on the Shanghai Daoist School and the gradual reabsorption of its graduates back into what he characterizes as a traditional ritual marketplace composed of "freelance" Daoists, trained as apprentices in the outlying regions around Shanghai by a surviving older generation of Daoist ritual masters. Whereas the Daoist School graduates were placed in government jobs in Daoist temples within Shanghai, most of the over 600 freelance Daoists operating in the greater Shanghai area either performed rituals illegally in private homes or in outlying temples dedicated to local gods. As government subsidies diminished, the Shanghai Daoist temples had to raise more and more of their own funds through payments for rituals performed in their temples. Yang notes the frustration of the young seminarians with their mode of training, which gave them theoretical knowledge of a homogenized Daoist theology, along with Party political education, but little practical ritual performance skills. Only occasionally in music class did they feel themselves entering the field of Daoist ritual experience, with its unique modes of wordless transmission and its alternative "animistic" temporalities. Younger ritual masters started working with middlemen to join troupes of Daoists performing at temples and in homes. Enterprising temple directors rented out their compounds to free-lance troupes. Yang points out that the drive to modernize under Maoism "rarely signifie[d] freedom and pluralism but often connote[d] uniformity and State control." By contrast, "the retreat of the State and the penetration of various types of foreign economic forces during the past two decades has resulted in a more active folk society, which has already and will continue to articulate its autonomy through certain archaic forms such as lavish ritual expenditure." This statement could be said to apply to many forms of local religious activity in contemporary China (Yang 2003: 233).

The Revitalization of Daoist Ritual Traditions across Contemporary China

Daoist ritual specialists in many parts of China have struggled to rebuild fragmented ritual traditions (see Dean 1993, 1998a for this process in Fujian). However, Yang's analysis suggests a sharp divide between "tradition" and "modernity," albeit with a certain powerful return of the repressed. I would prefer to frame the role of Daoist ritual in contemporary China within a broader historical process of the establishment of (temporary) zones of autonomy in an ongoing negotiation with the forces of the state and capital. As suggested above, this history can be traced back to the mid-Ming, if not before. This has clearly not been a continuous process or an uninterrupted curve, rather, the intensity of state control has shifted dramatically at different times, and the admixture of modern nation-state institutions and discourses of modernization has fundamentally altered the relationship of state and society. Thus any consideration of contemporary Daoist ritual cannot ignore the gap between, on the one hand, the cosmological discourses and sporadic, if sometimes savage, campaigns of destruction of "licentious cults" in the late imperial times, and on the other hand, the enlightenment discourse of the destruction of superstition alongside far more comprehensive institutional mechanisms for the destruction of temples, including the imprisonment and "reeducation" of Daoist ritual specialists, temple leaders, and spirit-mediums in post-1949 China. The entire syncretic field of Chinese religion has been shifted and deeply affected by the rise of this modernist field of discourse and the imposition of these modes of state control.

Nonetheless, continued further cross-fertilization and invention of ritual traditions (both from within China and from overseas) is always possible in contemporary Daoism. In recent years, informal visits from groups of Taiwanese Daoist ritual specialists have begun in Fujian. Troupes of Daoists have been invited to Singapore from both the Baiyunguan in Beijing and from Taiwan. Unlike the situation in Taiwan, which officially registers all temples that are not specifically Buddhist as being Daoist, Singapore religious policy does not recognize Daoism as an official religion. However, there is an active Daoist ritual scene in Singapore, with performances by Hokkien, Guangdong, Hakka, and Hainan Daoists for their respective communities. The leaders of this scene have staged elaborate international Daoist ritual events and conferences of Daoist scholars to highlight the inequities they are forced to live with as a result of these official classifications. Most serious of these is their inability to bid for the spaces set aside for religious property in the "model cities" being built across Singapore. Daoists across Asia are beginning to become aware of each other's political situations and limitations.

Other smaller sub-ethnic communities, such as the Xinghua immigrants of Singapore, who celebrate a decennial Pudu (Rite of Universal Deliverance) in commemoration of the defeat of the Japanese army, have also invited Daoist and Buddhist ritual masters and opera performers from Putian to conduct the ceremonies and to perform the *Mulian Saves His Mother* mystery opera/ritual at the fifth decennial celebration in 1994. The problem was that these plays had been outlawed in China since 1949, and thus the Chinese actors had to base their performance on the Singapore script and local amateur performance tradition. When the troupe returned to China, they were nonetheless received as the embodiment of an ancient performance tradition, newly authenticated by their successful foreign tour. They began to perform the Mulian plays at large religious festivals in the Putian area. Similarly, the Singapore temples have also been very active in reintroducing to Putian a tradition of collective training of male spirit mediums and their altar assistants, complete with Daoist diplomas and Daoist rites of predeath attainment of immortality—a local tradition that they claim was transmitted to Singapore from Putian in the 1920s (see Dean and Zheng 1993a for a detailed account of these rituals in Jiangkou township of Putian county in Fujian; see Dean 2003 for an account of the process of infinite mirroring and reinvention of "ritual tradition" under conditions of transnational diaspora). Such transnational flows of ritual tradition and reinvented local communal religious traditions demonstrate the limits of state control over Daoism and local culture.

One of the temples that held a Mulian opera in the Xinghua region in 1995 was the Linshan Temple in Fengting, which represents a ritual alliance of thirty-eight villages. Across from the temple on a nearby hill called Tadoushan (Stuppa Mountain) stands a 20-foot-high square stone stuppa built a thousand years ago in the Song dynasty, with carved Buddhist images on each side. The Linshan temple committee leaders began in 2003 to plan to build a Yuhuang Jade Emperor Temple under this Song stuppa to rival another major mountaintop temple in the region, the Lingfeng dian, which draws pilgrims from throughout the Xinghua region. In order to get permission to proceed with this project, the temple committee formed a Fengting Local Historical Association, under the auspices of the local government.

The temple committee absorbed local, district, and city government levels of support and brought in local entrepreneurs, who paid tens of thousands of yuan to become deputy directors of the association. These entrepreneurs note that the new temple will bring in more than its construction costs in no time if it proves efficacious. But these same entrepreneurs are also involved in many other local development projects, including the building of docks on the coast and a new industrial park being developed across from the site of the new dock. They are also thinking about the new railroad station planned at the base of Mt. Tadou, and the major natural gas works planned for further up the Meizhou Bay.

At the meeting held in the late summer of 2004 in the local government office building to announce the formation of the local historical association, the position paper of the leader of the association (and a major figure in the local temple alliances) described the need to protect local cultural artifacts. His paper also described the need for self-awareness in the face of modernization. He stated that the local leaders of the temples need to feel responsibility for their heritage. He further claimed that this sense of responsibility arises from the realization that the temple committee plays a vital role in the transmission of the past. His comments showed an aware-ness of the role of the temples in the negotiation of the forces of moder-nity. He also adroitly mentioned cultural tourism and financial returns for cultural investment. This provided, obviously, an alternative modernity discourse for the local government representatives to expound upon.

Local government representatives demanded the development of one or two "cultural icons" for the Fengting area along the lines of the Eiffel Tower, Niagara Falls, or the Egyptian Pyramids (behind them was a logo bearing an image of the Song stuppa). They pointed out that this was the first local historical association of its kind established in Putian, and com-pared Fengting's lack of cultural development with nearby Quanzhou's lucrative claims to be part of the "silk road of the sea," and immediately complained about the lack of economic development of Fengting as com-pared to Quanzhou. This lament became a leitmotif, as they reiterated over and over on the need to cash in on "local culture," going so far as to claim that it is culture itself that is holding back development. In the most extreme self-contradictory statement by a local government official, "culture" was portrayed as inherently backwards and in need either of complete transformation into a cash cow, or elimination, as if that were possible. Such officials want to profit from "local culture," which they view as a potential source of development and as yet at the same time the source of current underdevelopment. Until "culture" is commercialized, they consider it backward.

Despite the disparity between the views of the government officials and those of the temple leaders, one senses that it is the former who are out of step with events, and especially with the forces of self-organization of the community. Even though the local Party secretary shouted himself hoarse at the meeting, and the city level officials still command the respect of the authority of the Party, the entire event seemed to swallow them up in a prearranged ritual of government authorization of a preexisting sociocul-tural force. One is reminded of the series of "conferences of the gods" that were held in the Minnan and Xinghua area through the 1980s and early 1990s (Dean 1998a). These were sponsored by temple committees, backed by overseas Chinese funding, and attended by local scholars and govern-ment officials. The latter harangued about the dangers of falling back into feudal superstition, and cautioned the scholars to restrict their comments to the historical facts concerning the deities in question. But the fact that the conferences were held at all was a testimony to the growing strength of the temple networks. The main difference with the Fengting Historical Association was that now the temple association had in a way joined the government, and had a foot in the door. This quasi-official status would facilitate continued control over the development of the temple site by the temple committee.

At the meeting the entire paper trail of the establishment of the association with government permission, including petitions, documents granting permission, and the constitution and rules of the association, along with the entire membership of the board of management and the consultant specialists were read out loud, and rapid votes by hand were held to present a image of democratic process to a prearranged decision. Letters of congratulations from every level of local government, academics, and media demonstrated the range of forces the temples were able to mobilize.

During the speeches by the Party and government officials, local artists collectively painted a mural-sized traditional Chinese painting of pine trees and plum flowers for the new association office. Gifts of calligraphy and couplets were presented to the leaders of the association by local artists, playwrights, and calligraphers. The association paid for the luncheon held after the meeting, in which several hundred were fed.

By contrast with the growing strength of the temple associations, the overextension of the township level government—which is vastly in debt and in many areas does not pay out salaries for months at a time—is increasingly evident. The costs of various jobs (township and district leader, etc.) are coldly analyzed in terms of the bribes necessary to attain the position, and the bribes needed to be collected from the people in order to recover the personal investment. The reduction of the local government to a tax collecting and policing organization is noted. Also noted is the propensity to sell off public assets such as land, water (for electricity), etc., to cover the lack of local finances and to obtain personal profits from positions of authority. Tax collection quotas are set at the district level with little regard for the ability of specific regions to pay. Local officials are forced to resort to extortion to meet the limits and ensure their careers. Fewer and fewer officials are invited to the endless round of meals and drinks associated with the collective joint-investment nature of local business. At the village level, local leaders are increasingly unwilling to serve as selected/elected representatives. By contrast, membership in the temple committees is a mark of prestige in the community. Temple committees in this area now include many retired district mayors and vice mayors, as well as Party commissars. Wealthy entrepreneurs pay significant sums to win acceptance into these committees. All this is indicative of the trend to growing local autonomy of the temple networks and the commercial networks as they build into a kind of second level of local government (see Dean 2001).

In early 2004, the Temple of the Jade Emperor was opened with a Daoist ritual featuring a large troupe of Daoist priests from throughout the area, as well as performances of marionettes, opera, and communal worship. A new node in the local network of temples had been established, and legitimized through the performance of Daoist rituals as much as by the granting of government permits.

Theoretical Explorations: The Generation of Worlds of Difference in Daoist Ritual Events

This final section provides a brief response to Talal Asad's call for *cultural translation* mentioned above—"an effort to create within one's own language the troubling effects of difference and otherness" when thinking through the ritual experiences of other cultures. This section explores the role of *cosmo-political forces* within contemporary Daoist and communal ritual events.[19] I will argue that ritual events generate distinct worlds with alternative spatial and temporal parameters of experience. Extraordinarily, these seemingly impossible worlds coexist with the worlds of increasing capitalism and modernization, at least as long as ritual retains a certain autonomy. Consider this a thought experiment.

The post-1979 softening of the pejorative official attitude toward "religion" indicates only a partial reconsideration of the state's modernization paradigm. In some sectors, there is a growing awareness of the possibility of some kind of role for religion as a marker of Chinese culture in a narrative of potential Chinese "alternative modernity" (Yang 2004). Such a vision of alternative modernity would reclaim Daoist ritual and the temples of local communal religion as elements in a selective reworking of tradition, one that would complicate and multiply the origins of modernity but that would nonetheless ultimately converge with other capitalist modernities in a totalistic social formation containing all the essential elements of the modern.[20] In such analyses, there is a tendency to return to concepts such as civil society and the public sphere. Only in place of a dissident intelligentsia (who failed to appear as predicted by more politically inflected post-1989 versions of the civil society theory), the sphere of local communal religion is instead put forth as the potential seedbed of modernization and democracy. The evidence from Southeast China however, raises serious doubts as to the applicability of modernization theory or alternative modernity theory to this aspect of Chinese experience (Dean 1997). What other perspectives are then available?

It is undeniable that the modern gaze (both that of ethnographers/

social scientists and the modern state) frames ritual practices and intro-duces epistemological divides and domains that have an impact on the practices themselves (Fabian 1983). In areas where ritual life is active, how-ever, the temple leaders seem adept at deflecting or refracting that gaze, with various practices of recording, observing, and incorporating outside observers (state observers, heritage tourists, and Chinese and Western eth-nographers), folding them into the ritual process.[21]

There is a continuing tension in the intersection of the forces of the communist state and global movements of capital within ritual practices. It is an uneasy encounter in which ritual practices seem ever in danger of being captured, being caught between the state apparatus and global capital. For example, one could point to a number of temples in various parts of China, especially in urban centers, which have been reduced to a mummified, museum-like existence, selling tickets to tourists, with little open interaction with the surrounding community or any active internal ritual or contemplative life. The mutual capture of ritual by state and capi-tal would frame ritual practices in such contexts, once and for all, as some-thing like heritage, local color, or traditions. This process is underway in many locations in contemporary China.

Alternatively, in areas of China with vibrant local communal ritual events, one sees that by acknowledging and re-inscribing these frames (of state and capital), the temple leaders have successfully broken the fram-ing that strives to contain ritual forces. In other words, temple leaders are working with something like alternative modernity (as in the discussion of the Fengting Local Historical Association above) perhaps only in or-der to allow ritual activities to produce their own, singular, effects. In this view, temple leaders are not simply restoring or preserving ritual activities as traditions but giving ritual forces time and space to operate—in order to produce something else, something incommensurable with the mod-ern. Temple leaders know that ritual practices strive to produce another world, a world of difference.

Daoist and communal ritual events produce what we could call a "ritual view." This ritual view reveals that local powers are differentiated expres-sions of immanent cosmological forces. Temple leaders and ritual masters are acting together (but differently) on a set of cosmo-political relations.

In order to take the logic of this field of ritual practice seriously, we need to come to terms with its own, unique, forms of temporality. Daoist rituals and the local communal rites in which they are embedded pro-vide an occasion to think in terms of "a-modern" temporalities.[22] Daoist rituals include both the *reversal of time* in a return to the undifferentiated Dao in the meditative visions of the ritual master, as well as an *acceleration of cosmic cycles* in the revelation of scriptures and the placing of talismans.

Through the overcoding of the altar and the visualizations of the ritual masters, the space of the ritual is charged with cosmological powers and transformed. The celebration of Daoist rites on the birthdates of the local gods simultaneously reinterprets these deities as avatars of higher emanations of the Dao, and at the same time unleashes the unstable forces of the local pantheon by sending these gods into motion through and around the community, often leading to spirit possession of mediums by these gods. The spatio-temporal parameters of spirit medium possession open up additional worlds.

One of the most extraordinary features of these ritual events is the taboo on doctrinal contradiction, which allows for the simultaneous manifestation and worship of different versions of the same deity, or multiple deities, as well as the parallel performance of very similar rites addressed to different deities within the same overall ritual event. Such ritual events can be characterized as the workings of a *positive* collective unconscious, which is also seen in the mobilization of the entire population of the locale during the ritual event.

Within these ritual events there is one center (the temple with its gods), but this center is at the same time intrinsically multiple. Not only can there be more than one deity, but also each resident deity is multivalent, embodying and emanating different qualities, which shift over time. These deities are at heart unstable, or, more precisely, they are metastable.[23] As a consequence, moving a deity from its perch in a temple is a powerful act, one that potentially alters an entire field of forces. Summoning a deity opens its fundamental asymmetry or instability. The question then is, what happens to this cosmological difference? How does it work in ritual? Is the goal of ritual ultimately to contain cosmological difference, to assure that, in the end, everything returns to what it was? Can one even return to a metastable state? Or do rituals unleash and attempt to channel cosmo-political forces to generate simultaneous but different worlds within/alongside the worlds of capitalism and nationalist modernity?

After extensive preparations, the ritual event begins with the Daoist ritual specialists setting up portable altars in the temple and in the temple courtyard in order to generate spaces heavily overcoded with symbolism—the altars are arranged in accordance with ritual patterns, and the ritual specialists dance and run between and around the altars in various cosmological configurations. This is the prelude to summoning forth the deities from within the temple—a shift in their situation that serves to transform their "instability" into a force. The carefully coded space is designed to prevent a chaotic, undirected release of that force.

The movement of the deities inscribes a loop (in and out of the temple, around the village, around the courtyard, and so forth), generating *nodes* that spin minor resonant loops—some planned, others spontaneous—that become minor worlds in the sense that they are performative sites with coherent viewing positions (the points of view of individual worshippers, of the temple committee, of crowds moving as one, groups watching opera, shifting centers of attraction and attention within the unfolding ritual event, even the pantheon of the gods overseeing the event from above). The multiplicity of these nodes of perception and affect reveals the immanence of ritual power, underlying all aspects of the event and mobilizing all involved through their range of participatory roles and particular points of view.

Because it is the immanent unity of a multiplicity of points of view, the ritual event is open to all kinds of temporal difference. For each node (or point of view) has great potential for autonomy in relation to other nodes and the deities. This is precisely why ritual activities in Fujian province are able to serve as conduits for, and refractors of, state capital, global capital, and local economies.

Local, state, or global formations will continue to attempt to exploit the autonomies of the ritual event in order to frame and flatten the multiple temporalities of these events. The best one could hope for under those circumstances would be a form of alternative modernity. This is because the power of capital also lies in its immanence, its ability to increasingly infiltrate and subsume social relations. The movement of capital tends to generate contradictions in the ritual space of noncontradictions, which then usually demand resolution in the form of local or national identity. For example, in some areas of western and southwestern China, entire monastic complexes have been contracted out to business entrepreneurs, responsible for the hawking of incense and religious paraphernalia and tourist trinkets, leading to conflicts between ritual communities that formerly shared the site without contradictions. In other areas, temples dedicated to transnational cults such as Mazu's cult are exploited for nationalistic purposes. Command ritual performances are sometimes performed for tourists in Han Chinese temples or in temples of "minority" peoples. Clumsy attempts to capitalize on ethnic exoticism have alienated worshippers at many contested temple sites in regions where local ritual practices have not succeeded in generating a degree of local autonomy.

Capitalism operates as a powerful expanding immanent logic within the realm of everyday life in contemporary China, as in many other parts of the world, but the immanence of local, Daoist ritual need not necessarily give way to the immanence of capital. This is not to position ritual events nostalgically or romantically as acting in opposition or resisting the logic of capitalism. For the ritual event is not simply an obstacle to the movement of capital or a contradiction within it. It is a different kind of movement altogether. This *multilectical* movement is a kind of fabulation or creative involution, leading to the generation of worlds of difference.[24] Ritual events are the site of an ongoing negotiation of the forces of modernity.

Conclusion

The current relationship between the Chinese state (at both national and local levels) and Daoism is thus immensely complex and locally differentiated. In those regions where Daoist ritual is continuing to provide one key node (a minor world or performative site with a coherent viewing position) within the ritual events of evolving local communal religion, one can speak of the continued contribution of Daoism to the creation of worlds of differences marked by alternative temporalities and spatialities. A full-scale analysis of the ritual practices of even one local tradition such as the Minnan Daoist ritual tradition is unfortunately beyond the scope of this chapter. Each of these nodes or openings (of distinct local Daoist ritual traditions) would have to be analyzed *in situ*, and understood in relation to its local or regional historical trajectories. This would require a careful historical survey of the relationships between coexisting ritual traditions (Daoist, Buddhist, sectarian, spirit-possession, sacrificial, etc.) in any given area, and between these ritual traditions and their local communities, as well as with the state and its agencies. In many areas Daoist rites have already been absorbed into public spectacles in mass-mediated events suffused with flows of capital. In even more places, Daoist ritual practices have collapsed almost entirely, and only the barest rudiments of collective ritual life live on. Yet the Way continues to part—and the pathways continue to trace their way into multiple worlds of local difference.

Notes

Portions of this chapter are based on "Ritual Matters," by Kenneth Dean and Thomas Lamarre, in *Impacts of Modernity*, edited by T. Lamarre and Kang Nae-Hui (Hong Kong: Hong Kong University Press, 2003), pp. 257–84.

1. In this chapter, the term "Daoist" refers to a ritual specialist initiated into a Daoist ritual tradition. Daoists in their own self-definition drew no such distinction between *Daojia* (Daoist philosophic texts) and *Daojiao* (Daoist religion), as is evident from the incorporation of Daoist and other philosophic works into the *Daoist Canon*, and from the important role of passages and concepts from these texts within Daoist individual cultivation texts, scriptures, and liturgy.

2. It is important to recall, however, that other monastic forms of Daoism preceded the Song. See Kohn (2003).

3. The Zhengyi tradition had by the Tang incorporated early Celestial Master

texts and ritual practices with the Shangqing and Lingbao revelations of the fourth and fifth centuries into a multileveled hierarchy of grades of initiation, with different scriptures, registers of gods, and ritual texts. Later revelations in the Song led to new ritual traditions such as the Tianxin zhengfa, Jingming xiaodao, Shenxiao, Leifa, and Qingwei schools. Each of these was absorbed into Zhengyi Daoism, as led since the Song by the putative descendants of Zhang Daoling, the Celestial Masters, based in Longhushan in Jiangxi. This Daoist center also recognized and granted ordinations to a wide range of practitioners of local Daoist ritual traditions (including Lüshan rites), all the while encouraging Daoist masters from these traditions to practice more orthodox forms of Daoist ritual.

4. For materials on Lüshan ritual traditions, see Berthier (1988) and Ye Mingshen (1999). For Duangong traditions, see Lagerwey (2002a and 2002b). For Hunan Thunder rites, see Fava (2006).

5. See Goossaert (2007) for a detailed and stimulating study of Daoist masters and institutions in the "sacred city" of Beijing.

6. Critics of "comparative religion" such as Fitzgerald (2000) have built on the work of Asad to raise serious concerns about the very applicability of the notion of "religion" to non-Western cultural contexts. Others, including the editors of this volume (see Ashiwa and Wank, and Ashiwa), argue that it is nonetheless important to examine the contesting definitions of religion applied by different groups in modern China, along with the institutions they attempt to create, control, or struggle to maintain within the constraints imposed by these new discourses and related discourses of nationalism and modernity. By using the term "local communal religion" to raise the issue of the enormous number of local organizations (temple committees, regional ritual alliances, lineage associations, spirit-medium cults, etc.) that mobilize entire village and regional communities across rural China, with numbers far in excess of any count of the adherents of the five "official religions" of China, I hope to show that these questions have only just begun to be examined in the Chinese context.

7. The concept of cosmo-political forces in this chapter draws on the works of philosopher and historian of science Isabelle Stengers in her *Cosmopolitiques*, 7 vols. (Paris: La Decouverte, 1997, 2003), where she defines cosmo-politics as a political struggle between different cosmologies, replete with suprahuman and nonhuman entities and forces, and based in different understandings of the nature-culture continuum quite distinct from the "mono-naturalism" of the Western sciences.

8. Dean and Zheng (2003: vol. 2, Inscription No. 781, p. 784).

9. Based on 1736–39 census data from the Qianlong Ministry of Rites, Goossaert (2000) estimates that there were over 45,000 Daoist ritual masters listed in China at that time. Through comparison with a 1930s survey of Buddhist clergy, he suggests the Qianlong figures should be doubled to over 90,000. Half of the Daoist clergy were Quanzhen monks and nuns, and half were Qingwei Lingbao (apparently registered or based in monasteries) or *huoju* (hearth-dwelling) Daoists. In a more recent estimate, Goossaert (2007) suggests a figure of 200,000 Zhengyi Daoists active at the end of the Qing, but goes on to say that this figure does not include a much larger number of local ritual masters and spirit mediums, some of whom were linked to local Daoist ritual traditions. Goossaert also notes that there were also large numbers

of Buddhist monks and nuns, as well as a smaller number Confucian ritual special-ists (*lisheng*) drawn from the ranks of the 5 million or so students and graduates of the civil service examination system. All these religious practitioners interacted in complex ways within the multiple, different local cultures of China.

10. During the late Qing, the Quanzhen tradition maintained some twenty or-dination centers (Goossaert, 2003b, quoting Yoshioka Yoshitoyo, *Dōkyō no kenkyū* [Kyoto: Hozokan, 1952: 221]). Yoshioka noted that thirty-one ordinations had been held at the Beijing Baiyunguan from 1808 to 1927 for 5,469 Daoists. An additional 1,740 Daoists were ordained between 1823 and 1909 at the Tiqinggong in Shenyang. Another important Quanzhen center in Beijing was the Dongyuemiao (Temple of the Eastern Peak). Although Quanzhen monks were found in all provinces covered by the survey, their numbers were greater than those of Zhengyi and other Daoists only in Shandong and Hunan, and by a slim margin in the greater Beijing area.

11. "Subjectivation" is a term used by Michel Foucault (1980) to describe the creation of a historically bounded form of subjectivity through the operations of particular relations of power.

12. Michel Foucault succinctly outlines the workings of "pastoral power" in his essay "Omnes et Singulatim: Towards a Critique of Political Reason," *Tanner Lectures on Human Values*, vol. 2, ed. by S. M. McMurrin (Cambridge, UK: Cambridge Uni-versity Press, 1981).

13. For a brief statement on the "syncretic field" of Chinese religion, see Dean (1998); for further discussion, see Davis (2001). The concept of cultural involution is drawn from Deleuze and Guattari (1987). It should be noted that this interpreta-tion of the rise of locally differentiated *ritual power* from the mid-Ming onwards is in contrast to much recent scholarship on the hegemonic effects of imperial cultural policy.

14. Most local Daoist ritual specialists are unaware of the existence of a printed *Daoist Canon*. They work instead with liturgical manuscripts and scriptures handed down and recopied within lines of hereditary transmission.

15. The Qing Manchu court tended to patronize the reconstructed Quanzhen tradition based in the Baiyunguan (White Cloud Monastery) in Beijing, and gradu-ally demoted the Celestial Master tradition (see Xun 2004; Goossaert 2007).

16. In March 2005 the Chinese government issued a set of forty-five new regu-lations governing religious activity. For the most part, these regulations continue earlier approaches, but include greater supervision of the financial, educational, and ritual activities of religious organizations. It is too soon to tell how they will be implemented.

17. The sixth congress of the National Daoist Association was held in 1998. Ming Zhiting was elected chairman, and nine others were elected vice-chairmen.

18. Yoshioka (1979) wrote a study of the Quanzhen Baiyunguan in Beijing, and more recently other Japanese scholars have discussed this temple. This is a highly significant tradition within Daoism that is only recently receiving scholarly attention (Kohn 2000, 2003; Goossaert and Katz 2001; Goossaert 2007).

19. For the concept of cosmo-politics see Stengers (1997–2003).

20. Theories of "alternative modernity" are discussed and critiqued by Stuart Hall (1995) and Thomas Lamarre (2003, introduction).

21. See Dean and Lamarre (2003) for further elaboration of these arguments.

22. The concept of the "a-modern" is raised here as a means to think different historical trajectories and different modes of spatiality/temporality. This concept draws upon theories of "a-modality" in recent neuroscientific research on sensation, perception, and synaethesia.

23. A physical system is said to be in metastable equilibrium (or false equilibrium) when the least modification serves to break the equilibrium. Any system in a metastable state harbors potentials that are incompatible insofar as they belong to heterogeneous dimensions. This is why systems in a metastable state can only perpetuate themselves by dephasing, that is, by a change in the state of the system. On metastablity see Muriel Combes, *Simondon. Individu et collectivité* (Presses Universitaires de France 2000), pp. 10–12. On dephasing (change of state) see Ian Stewart, *Nature's Numbers: The Unreal Reality of Mathematics* (Basic Books, 1995).

24. A multilectical movement is one that does not polarize into a dialectic, or fall prey to the immanence of capital or to reappropriation by the state. Its very multiplicity is its strength. Such movements can be described as forms of collective invention and experimentation, or fabulation. The entire process of the increasing complexification of local culture through the performance of ritual events can be described as a process of creative cultural involution.

References

Asad, Talal. 1993. *Genealogies of Religion: Discipline and Reasons of Power in Christianity and Islam*. Baltimore: Johns Hopkins Press.

———. 2003. *Formations of the Secular: Christianity, Islam, Modernity*. Stanford, CA: Stanford University Press.

Berthier, Brigitte. 1988. *La Dame-du-bord-de-l'eau*. Nanterre: Société d'Ethnologie.

Brook, Timothy. 1997. "Auto-organization in Chinese Society." In *Civil Society in China*, edited by Timothy Brook and Michael Frolic, pp. 19–45. Armonk, NY: M. E. Sharpe.

Chau, Adam Yuet. 2006. *Miraculous Response: Doing Popular Religion in Contemporary China*. Stanford, CA: Stanford University Press.

Da Ming shilu. 1961–66 (Historical records of the Great Ming dynasty). Nangang: Shiyusuo.

Davis, Edward. 2001. *Society and the Supernatural in the Song*. Honolulu: University of Hawai'i Press.

Dean, Kenneth. 1993. *Taoist Ritual and Popular Cults of Southeast China*. Princeton, NJ: Princeton University Press.

———. 1997. "Popular Religion or Civil Society: Disruptive Communities and Alternative Conceptions." In *Civil Society in China*, edited by Timothy Brook and Bernard Frolic, pp. 172–95. Armonk, NY: M. E. Sharpe.

———. 1998a. *Lord of the Three in One: The Spread of a Cult in Southeast China*. Princeton, NJ: Princeton University Press.

———. 1998b. "The Transformation of State Sacrifice at the She Altar in the Late Ming and Qing in the Xinghua Region." *Cahiers d'Extrême-Asie* 10: 19–75.

———. 2001. "China's Second Government: Regional Ritual Systems in Southeast

China." In *Shehui, minzu yu wenhua zhanyan guoji yantaohui lunwenji* (Collected papers from the international conference on social, ethnic and cultural transformation), pp. 77–109. Taipei: Center for Chinese Studies.

———. 2003. "Local Communal Religion in Contemporary Southeast China." In *Religion in China Today*, China Quarterly Special Issues New Series 3, edited by Daniel L. Overmyer, pp. 122–44. Cambridge, UK: Cambridge University Press.

Dean, Kenneth, and Thomas Lamarre. 2003. "Ritual Matters." In *Impacts of Modernity*, edited by T. Lamarre and Kang Nae-Hui, pp. 257–84. Hong Kong: Hong Kong University Press.

———. 2007. "Microsociology and the Ritual Event." In *Deleuzean Encounters: Studies in Contemporary Social Issues*, edited by Anna Hickey-Moody and Peta Malins, pp. 181–96. Hampshire: Palgrave Macmillan.

Dean, Kenneth, and Zheng Zhenman. 1993a. "Group Initiation and Exorcistic Dance in the Xinghua Region." *Min-su ch'u-i* 85: 105–95.

———. 1993b. "Min Tai Daojiao yu minjian zhushen chongbai chukao" (A preliminary study of Fujianese and Taiwanese Taoism in relation to popular religious worship). *Bulletin of the Institute of Ethnology, Academia Sinica* 73: 33–52.

———. 1995. *Fujian zongjiao beiming huibian: Xinghuafu fence* (Epigraphical materials on the history of religion in Fujian: the Xinghua region). Fuzhou: Fujian renmin chubanshe.

———. 2003. *Fujian zongjiao beiming huibian: Quanzhoufu fence* (Epigraphical materials on the history of religion in Fujian: the Quanzhou region). 3 vols. Fuzhou: Fujian renmin chubanshe.

De Bruyn, Pierre-Henry. 2000. "Daoism in the Ming (1368–1644)." In *Daoism Handbook*, edited by Livia Kohn, pp. 594–622. Leiden: Brill.

Deleuze, Gilles, and Felix Guattari. 1987. *Thousand Plateaus*, B. Massumi trans. Minneapolis: University of Minnesota Press.

Ding, Huang. 2000. "The Study of Daoism in China Today." In *Daoism Handbook*, edited by Livia Kohn, pp. 765–69. Leiden: Brill.

Duara, Prasenjit. 1988. *Culture, Power, and the State: Rural North China 1900–1942*. Stanford, CA: Stanford University Press.

———. 1995. *Rescuing History from the Nation: Questioning Narratives of Modern China*. Chicago: University of Chicago Press.

Esposito, Monica. 2000. "Daoism in the Qing (1644–1911)." In *Daoism Handbook*, edited by Livia Kohn, pp. 623–58. Leiden: Brill.

Fabian, Johannes. 1983. *Time and the Other: How Anthropology Makes Its Object*. New York: Columbia University Press.

Fava, Patrice. 2006. *Han Xin's Revenge: A Daoist Mystery*. DVD. Paris: CNRS productions, EFEO.

Feuchtwang, Stephan. 2001. *Popular Religion in China: The Imperial Metaphor*. Richmond, Surrey: Curzon.

Fitzgerald, Timothy. 2000. *The Ideology of Religious Studies*. New York: Oxford University Press.

Foucault, Michel. 1980. *History of Sexuality, Vol. 1: An Introduction*, translated by R. Hurley. New York: Vintage.

Goossaert, Vincent. 2000. "Counting the Monks: The 1736–1739 Census of the Chinese Clergy." *Late Imperial China* 21: 40–85.

———. 2001. "The Invention of an Order: Collective Identity in Thirteenth Century Quanzhen Taoism." *Journal of Chinese Religions* 29: 111–89.

———. 2003a. "Le destin de la religion chinoise au 20ème siècle." *Social Compass* 50, 4: 429–40.

———. 2003b. "The Quanzhen Clergy, 1700–1950." In *Religion and Chinese Society: The Transformation of a Field*, edited by J. Lagerwey, pp. 699–771. Hong Kong: Ecole Française d'Extrême-Orient and Chinese University of Hong Kong Press.

———. 2007. *The Taoists of Peking, 1800–1949: A Social History of Urban Clerics*. Cambridge, MA: Harvard University Press.

Goossaert, Vincent, and Paul Katz (eds.). 2001. "New Perspectives on Quanzhen Taoism: The Formation of a Religious Identity." *Journal of Chinese Religions* 29.

Hachiya Kunio. 1995. *Chūgoku no Dōkyō: sono katsudō to dōkan no genjō*. Tokyo: Tōkyō daigaku tōyō bunka kenkyūjo.

Hall, Stuart et al. 1995. *Modernity: An Introduction to Modern Societies*. Cambridge, UK: Polity Press.

Hymes, Robert P. 2002. *Way and Byway: Taoism, Local Religion, and Models of Divinity in Sung and Modern China*. Berkeley: University of California Press.

Ishida Kenji. 1992. "Mindai Dōkyō shijō no Zenshin to Seii" (The Quanzhen and Zhengyi orders in Daoist history during the Ming dynasty). In *Taiwan no shūkyō to Chūgoku bunka* (Religion in Taiwan and Chinese culture), edited by Sakai Tadao, pp. 145–95. Tokyo: Fukyosha.

Kohn, Livia. 2003. *Monastic Life in Medieval Daoism: A Cross-cultural Perspective*. Honolulu: University of Hawai'i Press.

———, (ed.). 2000. *Daoism Handbook*. Leiden: Brill.

Lagerwey, John. 1987. *Taoist Ritual in Chinese Society and History*. New York: Macmillan.

———. 2002a. "The Altar of Celebration Ritual in Lushan County, Sichuan." In *Ethnography in China Today: A Critical Assessment of Methods and Results*, edited by Daniel Overmyer, pp. 75–79. Taipei: Yuan-liou.

———. 2002b. "Duangong Ritual and Ritual Theatre in the Chongqing Area: A Survey of the Work of Hu Tiancheng." In *Ethnography in China Today: A Critical Assessment of Methods and Result*, edited by Daniel Overmyer, pp. 85–107. Taipei: Yuan-liou.

Lai Chi-Tim. 2003. "Daoism in China Today, 1980–2002." In *Religion in China Today*, China Quarterly Special Issues New Series No. 3, edited by Daniel Overmyer, pp. 107–21. Cambridge, UK: Cambridge University Press.

Lamarre, Thomas. 2003. "Introduction: Impacts of Modernities." In *Traces 3: Impacts of Modernities*, edited by T. Lamarre and Kang Nae-hui, pp. 3–35. Hong Kong: University of Hong Kong Press.

Li Yangzheng. 2000. *Dangdai Zhongguo Daojiao* (Daoism in modern China). Beijing: Dongfang chubanshe.

Litzinger, Charles. 1996. "Rural Religion and Village Organization in North China: The Catholic Challenge in the Late Nineteenth Century." In *Christian-*

ity in China: From the Eighteenth Century to the Present, edited by Daniel H. Bays, pp. 41–52. Stanford, CA: Stanford University Press.

Liu Jinfeng. 2000. *Gannan zongjiao shehui yu Daojiao wenhua yanjiu* (Research on the Daoist culture of Gannan religion and society). Hong Kong: International Hakka Studies Association, Ecole Française d'Extrême-Orient, Overseas Chinese Archives.

Maruyama Hiroshi. 1995. "The Historical Traditions of Contemporary Taoist Ritual." *Acta Asiatica* 68: 84–104.

Ming huidian. 1989 (1587). Beijing: Zhonghua.

Naquin, Susan. 2000. *Peking: Temples and City Life, 1400–1900*. Princeton, NJ: Princeton University Press.

Nedostup, Rebecca Allyn. 2001. "Religion, Superstition, and Governing Society in Nationalist China." Ph.D. dissertation, Columbia University.

Overmyer, Daniel (ed.). 2000. *Ethnography in China Today: A Critical Assessment of Methods and Results*. Taipei: Yuan-liou.

Potter, Pitman. 2003. "Belief in Control: Regulation of Religion in China." In *Religion in China Today*, China Quarterly Special Issues New Series No. 3, edited by Daniel Overmyer, pp. 11–32. Cambridge, UK: Cambridge University Press.

Schipper, Kristopher. 1993. *The Taoist Body*, Karen Duval, trans. Berkeley: University of California Press.

———. 2002. "Daojiao zai jindai Zhongguo zhi bianqian" (Daoism in the transformations of modern Chinese history). In *Zhongguo wenhua jiyinku* (The database of Chinese culture), *Beida xueshu jiangyan congshu* 17, pp. 146–62. Beijing: Beijing daxue chubanshe.

Schipper, Kristopher, and Franciscus Verellen. 2005. *Handbook of the Taoist Canon*. 3 vols. Chicago: University of Chicago Press.

Seidel, Anna. 1990. "Chronicle of Taoist Studies in the West 1950–1990." *Cahiers d'Extrême-Asie* 5: 223–347.

Siu, Helen. 1989. "Recycling Rituals: Politics and Popular Culture in Contemporary Rural China." In *Unofficial China: Popular Culture and Thought in the People's Republic of China*, edited by Perry Link, Richard Madsen, and Paul Pickowicz, pp. 121–37. Boulder, CO: Westview.

Stengers, Isabelle. 1997–2003. *Cosmopolitiques*, 7 vols. Paris: La Decouverte.

Taylor, Romeyn. 1990. "Official and Popular Religion and the Political Organization of Chinese Society in the Ming." In *Orthodoxy in Late Imperial China*, edited by Liu Kwang-Ching, pp. 126–57. Berkeley: University of California Press.

Thompson, Roger R. 1996. "Twilight of the Gods in the Chinese Countryside: Christians, Confucians, and the Modernizing State, 1861–1911." In *Christianity in China: From the Eighteenth Century to the Present*, edited by Daniel H. Bays, pp. 53–73. Stanford, CA: Stanford University Press.

Wang Qi. 1994 [1586]. *Xu wenxian tongkao*. Shitong ed. Taipei.

Welch, Holmes. 1957. *Parting of the Way: Lao Tzu and the Taoist Movement*. London: Metheun.

Xun, Liu. 2004. "Visualizing Perfection: Daoist Paintings of Our Lady, Court Patronage, and Elite Female Piety in the Late Qing." *Harvard Journal of Asiatic Studies* 64, 1: 57–115.

Yang, Der-Ruey. 2003. "The Education of Taoist Priests in Contemporary Shanghai, China." Ph.D. dissertation, London School of Economics and Political Science.

Yang, Mayfair. 2004. "Spatial Struggles: State Disenchantment and Popular Re-Appropriation of Space in Rural Southeast China." *Journal of Asian Studies* 63, 3: 719–56.

Ye Mingsheng. 1999. *Fujiansheng Longyanshi Dongxiaozheng Lushanjiao guangjitan keyiben* (The ritual texts of the Guangji Altar of the Lushan sect in Dongxiao town, Longyan municipality, Fujian). Taipei: Hsin-wen-feng.

Yoshioka Yoshitoyo. 1979. "The Taoist Monastic Life." In *Facets of Taoism*, edited by Holmes Welch and Anna Seidel. New Haven, CT: Yale University Press.

Zhao Erxun. 1986–87 [1927]. *Qing shigao*. Beijing: Zhonghua shuju.

Zongjiao lisu faling huibian (Collected statutes on religions rites and practices). 1984. Taipei: Taiwanshengzhengfu minzhengting.

CHAPTER 9

Expanding the Space of Popular Religion: Local Temple Activism and the Politics of Legitimation in Contemporary Rural China

ADAM YUET CHAU

THE SPACE OF RELIGION in China today is in a crucial way a byproduct of the Chinese state to construct a modern image for the nation and for the political regime (see Ashiwa and Wank, this volume). Caught between two conflicting criteria to appear modern, i.e., being rational and scientific on the one hand and being respectful of the freedom of and right to personal belief on the other, the modern Chinese state in the twentieth century (regardless of political leaning) constructed a space *for* religion and thus the space *of* religion. Yet constructing the space of religion is as much a process of inclusion as a process of exclusion. The religious policies of the People's Republic of China grant freedom of religious belief as long as one belongs to one of the five officially recognized religions (Buddhism, Daoism, Catholicism, Protestantism, and Islam). On the other hand, these policies consign a wide range of popular religious practices to the category of feudal superstitions (*fengjian mixin*), which the state prohibits (see Anagnost 1987). In other words, these so-called superstitions do not belong to the space of religion proper. Yet ironically, during the reform era the state's control over the five recognized religions remains firm, whereas its grip on popular religion is relatively loose.[1] The result has been that popular religious practices have enjoyed considerable revival and growth from the early 1980s onward. A "space of popular religion" exists in contemporary China and is rapidly expanding.

Popular religion has enjoyed a momentous revival in China, especially in many parts of the countryside. New temples have been built and old temples restored; local opera troupes crisscross the countryside performing traditionally themed opera pieces for deities and worshippers at temple festivals (*miaohui*); fengshui masters (geomancers) are busy siting graves and houses and calculating auspicious dates for weddings and funerals; spirit mediums, Daoist priests, gods, and goddesses are bombarded with requests to treat illnesses, exorcise evil spirits, guarantee business success, and retrieve lost motorcycles; before anti-Falungong suppressions began in 1998, qigong sects of all manners competed for followers not only in the cities but in rural areas as well.

This chapter examines how popular religious temples in contemporary rural China engage in various strategies to expand the space of popular religion and to ensure legitimacy for temple activities. It is based on a case study of the Black Dragon King Temple in Shaanbei (northern Shaanxi Province) in northcentral China.[2] It looks at the zone of interaction between the temple and outside social actors, especially various local state agencies, to show how reviving village temples and expanding the scope of temple activities serve as a locus of local elite and communal activism, and it explores the sociopolitical implications of this activism. It focuses especially on how nonreligious activities provide heightened legitimacy for the temple.

Despite the problematic and simplistic binary opposition between "high" and "low," scholars have traditionally understood Chinese religion (excluding Christianity and Islam) as consisting of two levels: the first of elite practices, such as sutra translation, scripture commentaries, and meditation; and the second of popular practices, such as beseeching deities for divine assistance or sponsoring a spirit medium séance. By and large, popular religious practices put emphasis on the efficacy (*ling* or *lingying*) of divine assistance in solving practical problems. In late imperial times, not only the Confucian scholar-officials but also the elite Buddhist and Daoist establishments regularly condemned and attempted to eradicate or reform religious practices at the popular level. The majority of local temples were built without the state's approval and enshrined deities or spirits that were not part of the imperially approved pantheon. However, so-called licentious worship (*yinsi*) thrived despite official sanction. In other words, many popular religious practices had struggled with issues of legitimacy for centuries before the modernist regimes (Republican, the Communist on the mainland, or the Nationalist on Taiwan) began *their* efforts to suppress them. By legitimacy (*zhengdangxing*) I mean primarily acceptability in the eyes of the ruling elite or political regime, often in terms of legality (*hefaxing*, e.g., in the form of registration with the authorities). In the eyes of the authorities, degrees of legitimacy constitute a sliding scale, ranging from the very illegitimate (e.g., antiregime sectarian movements), to the tolerably illegitimate (e.g., many popular practices such as fortune-telling and temple festivals), to the legitimate (e.g., worship in registered temples). Of course the criteria for distinguishing the legitimate from the illegitimate vary across regimes and often across time within each regime. For example, during the radical leftist years of the Cultural Revolution all religious activities became illegitimate and faced suppression.

Because legitimacy has long been a problem popular religion has to grapple with, one might understand popular religion as consisting of two broad categories of religious practices depending on their degree of acceptability to the authorities. And I will limit my discussion to the situation in the People's Republic of China. The first category of practices can be called "intolerable superstitions." These are activities that the state is unlikely to ever accept as legitimate. Examples in this category include fortune-telling, spirit mediumism, exorcism, fengshui siting, and sectarian proselytizing. Yet these activities are being conducted widely, and not always clandestinely, and will not be easily eradicated. The second category of popular religious practices can be called "tolerable superstitions." These are activities that the state might accept as legitimate and decide to register and regulate rather than to eradicate. In other words, once deemed tolerable, superstition can pass as religion;[3] a portion of the space of popular religion has been allowed entrance into the space of religion. Many rural, local temples and their accompanying activities such as temple festivals have fallen under the "tolerable superstition" rubric in the reform era, largely through a process of collusion of interests between the temples and the local authorities. Seeking protection under the law as legitimate (i.e., officially recognized) religious institutions, local temples apply to the Religious Affairs Bureau (*Zongjiaoju*) to be affiliated with either the Buddhist Association or the Daoist Association. At the same time, they also resort to many other strategies to heighten their legitimacy (i.e., acceptability) in order to win the approval of the authorities, or at least their acquiescence.[4] For example, in their self-representation to the authorities, local temples downplay practices that are clearly objectionable (e.g., animal sacrifice, divination, magical curing, spirit possession) and highlight socially beneficial activities funded by temple income (e.g., the building of roads and schools, charitable work, providing periodic entertainment to the masses). From the perspective of local state agencies (i.e., the authorities) that come into interaction with local temples, the revival of popular religion presents many benefits such as increased revenue for the agencies' coffers (e.g., through charging taxes and fees on businesses at temple festivals) and the voluntary improvement of local infrastructure by temple funds. In other words, the local state justifies its acceptance of popular religious activities by their functional utility understood in secular terms. The local state therefore permits or even actively encourages local temple activities as long as doing so does not appear to higher authorities to be encouraging superstition (hence all the more incentive for the local state to "upgrade" local temples from the category of superstition to the category of religion).

In this chapter I introduce two related conceptual frameworks to examine the dynamic interactions between local temples and the outside world: "local temple activism" and "the politics of legitimation." By local temple activism I mean the various religious and nonreligious activities that local temples are engaged in, thus making temples a motor of social mobilization. Temples and other traditional social institutions (e.g., lineages, crop-watching societies) were important elements of the "cultural nexus of power" in late imperial China, only to be challenged and suppressed by the modern state in the twentieth century (Duara 1988). During the post-Mao years some of these traditional social institutions have been revived to form the basis of local social mobilization. Temple-based social activism exemplifies what Mary Rankin has called the "outward thrust of locally based social initiative" (Rankin 1986: viii), which contrasts sharply with the downward thrust of Party-state initiative typical during the Maoist era. That popular religious temples can serve as such intense nodal points of social mobilization indicates that the contours of the agrarian social landscape have changed in fundamental ways in the reform era.

The activists in our story are not the Maoist activists who expressed their ideological enthusiasm in political campaigns, often sacrificing local interests in blind pursuit of central state directives; rather, they are communal activists whose social influence derives from their staunch localist orientation through the idiom of local temple activism.[5] Some scholars have called temple-based popular religion "local communal religion" (Dean 2003) or "local temple religion" (Weller 1999), both emphasizing the "local" and the "communal" focus of popular religion, and both highlighting the capacity of local temples to harness social energy. Kenneth Dean has suggested that the range and intensity of social activities organized by and around local temples make the temples and temple networks a "second tier of local government" (Dean 2003: 338). Robert Weller has documented the role local temples play in locale-specific protest movements against the encroachment of environmentally harmful industries (Weller 1999: 116–17). Jun Jing has shown how the revival of a lineage temple in rural Gansu provided the impetus for not only a flurry of lineage-based activities (e.g., the rebuilding of a destroyed lineage hall, the reconstruction of the village genealogy, the remembering and restaging of rituals) but also the basis for social protest to redress past and current injustices perpetrated against the village community (Jing 1996, 2000). Stephan Feuchtwang and Wang Mingming have examined the crucial role of local charismatic leaders in building and reviving temples and forging a moral community around these folk institutions (Feuchtwang and Wang 2001). Lily Tsai has shown how temples and lineage halls are effective idioms through which funds are raised for village public service projects such as road-paving (Tsai 2002). All of these studies demonstrate the political potential of local temples and how local leaders engage in social activism based on their role as popular religious leaders. Yet one needs to distinguish temple-based social activism from ideologically driven political activism familiar to scholars of social movements; though socially expansive, local temple activism will remain locale-specific in the current political climate in China.[6]

The expansiveness of local activists' imagination and activism extends the Black Dragon King Temple's functions beyond the ostensibly religious (i.e., those depending on the Black Dragon King's divine efficacy) into nonreligious realms that are important to the local communities: agriculture, commerce, education, entertainment, and reforestation. The temple's functional expansiveness and concerns of legitimacy necessarily draw in social forces beyond the village. These translocal maneuvers include forming inter-village alliances, securing support and protection from local state agencies, attracting media attention, and engaging with cosmopolitan and even foreign non-governmental organizations. These translocal maneuvers are an important component of the politics of legitimation, as they all contribute to bolstering the temple's legitimacy and assisting the temple activists to negotiate local power struggles. By focusing on local temple activism and the politics of legitimation, we learn more not only about the dynamism of Chinese popular religion in the modern era but also the shifting state-society relationships in rural China today.

The chapter is divided into several sections. The first briefly describes the popular religious landscape in Shaanbei. Then attention turns to the problem of temple registration in light of the incongruence between religious practices on the ground and religious policies. The next section introduces the Black Dragon King Temple by tracing the story of its revival in the reform period and explicating its organizational structure. I use local temple activism as a conceptual framework to understand the social expansiveness of the temple (i.e., the expansion of temple activities within the efficacy-related religious domain as well as from the religious domain to various nonreligious domains). This framework for studying state-religion interactions complements the analytical move that begins with examining state religious policies. The chapter then looks at the key episodes in the temple's expanding social activism. It examines in particular how over time frequent interactions and a web of mutually dependent relationships developed between the temple and various local state agencies.

This chapter will show that even though local temple activism is, by definition, based on the local temple, a popular religious institution, the contents of this activism need not be related to religion (even though the operations of these nonreligious activities are funded by the temple's incense donation money that the deity's reputation for divine efficacy attracts). In fact, these kinds of temple-based nonreligious activities often serve as a legitimating shield against a possible government crackdown on religious activities, because the core, religious activities are likely to be always categorized as illegal superstitions according to official religious policy. Furthermore, even though the activities center on the temple that is by definition rooted in a particular locale, the locus of this activism need not be confined to the locale. For the Black Dragon King Temple and many other temples, translocal processes have become an intrinsic part of their existence.

The Revival of Popular Religion in Shaanbei

Amongst the broad range of disparate phenomena under the umbrella term "popular religion," temple-based religious activities are the most exciting and most enjoyed in Shaanbei. Shaanbei people build temples for their gods and goddesses because they think the deities deserve a beautiful abode and out of communal pride. A beautiful and well-maintained temple and "red and fiery" (*honghuo*) temple festivals reflect the strength and state of blessedness of the community. A government agency in Shaanbei's Yulin Prefecture estimated that by the mid-1990s there were well over ten thousand temples in the prefecture alone (Fan 1997: 98). Most of them are village-level temples with very local appeal, though some enjoy regional fame.[7]

The most common religious activities at local temples are divination and magical curing (through magical talismanic medicine or a spirit medium's exorcistic ritual). Temple festivals on the other hand comprise a wide range of activities, including performances by folk dance troupes (*yangge*) and musical bands and storytellers, folk opera, "offering presentation" processions, animal sacrifices, agricultural fairs, various types of amusements, and so forth. Because of Shaanbei's increasing prosperity, temples and temple festivals in the region today are often many times larger than they were in the past. All temple operations are funded by incense donation money (*bushi*) from the worshippers. Worshippers visit the temples with their problems and promise the deities that they will donate a certain amount of money if the problems are eventually solved with the divine assistance of the deities. The worshippers typically come to bring the donation money during the temple festivals. This monetary promise and its repayment are called *xuyuan* (making a promise) and *huanyuan* (repaying on the promise).

A Shaanbei saying goes: Wherever there are temples there are temple festivals (*you miao jiu you hui*). This saying also implies that the physical structure of a temple is a necessary precondition for the staging of temple festivals. Temple festivals by definition always take place on temple grounds, as the opera performances are in principle for the deities to enjoy and the most important activity for people is "paying respect to the deities" (*jingshen*). Temple festivals are occasions not only for worshippers to give thanks to the deity, to watch opera performances, and to participate in the production of fun and excitement (*honghuo*), but also for merchants, peddlers, traders, and all kinds of professional entertainers to conduct business. In other words, the temple grounds and the annual fixed dates of the temple festivals provide the spatial as well as temporal parameters for staging temple festivals, the most exciting and vibrant folk event productions in today's rural landscape in Shaanbei.

The form (organizational framework) of temple-based popular religion is relatively simple: there are no elaborate and symbolically complicated rituals; there are no intricate theological maneuvers; there is typically no priesthood. One can even characterize popular religious temples as *minimalist religion*. However, even though the form is simple, the contents need not be. Under unfavorable conditions, popular religion survives in its minimalist, barebones state, almost hibernating. Elaborate temples and statues are replaced by secret home altars and small, carved statuettes; long chants accompanied by bells and drums are replaced by a few muffled murmurs. Under favorable conditions, however, popular religion expands, elaborates, and no degree of exuberance is unimaginable. Many of Taiwan's temples and their festivals attest to popular religion's expansiveness. Temples, temple oracles, temple associations, temple festivals, opera troupes, and worship and pilgrimage all go together to form a cluster of mutually constituting and reinforcing popular religious cultural idioms or elements. Because of this close interconnectedness, the revival of one cultural idiom necessarily sparks off a chain-reaction of the revival of the other cultural idioms. Throughout Chinese history, popular religion has waned and waxed, minimalized and elaborated, and thus what we have witnessed over the past half century is simply one cycle in the long course of its changing fortunes.

The temple festivals and other temple activities are organized by temple associations, which comprise a small group of responsible and generally respectable adult men (called *huizhang*, literally, association heads) whose leadership roles are based on communal acceptance and approved by the deity by divination. Each temple association customarily has a leader (*da-huizhang*, literally, big association head)—that is, the temple boss—who is usually the person who is most capable, as well as most respected by members of his community. Most temples are managed by ordinary villagers and do not have any resident clergy. Some temples have affiliated spirit mediums, though most of these work out of their own homes. Unlike popular religious temples in southeastern China (see Dean 1993, 1998), local temples in Shaanbei do not hire Daoist priests or other religious specialists to conduct elaborate rituals at temple festivals.

The rebuilding of temples and the staging of temple festivals and other popular religious activities constitute the most basic forms of local temple activism because these activities are products of a kind of systematic social mobilization that was strictly forbidden and unthinkable during the Maoist high-socialist era (roughly between the period of the Socialist Education Movement in 1964 and the end of the Cultural Revolution in 1976). This activism is a synergy between the popular religiosity of the village masses, the leadership and ingenuity of the temple organizers, i.e. the members of the temple associations, as well as the generally liberalized economic sphere that has allowed the manufacture of religious paraphernalia (e.g., incense, spirit money) and all kinds of commercial activities. It is no exaggeration to characterize temples as the motor of popular religious revival and a major locus of peasant cultural productions, and the temple association as the most significant institutional player in Shaanbei's peasant cultural revival.

Popular Religion and Temple Registration

Freedom of religious worship is protected by the constitution of the People's Republic of China, but superstition is not. It is up to the state to categorize one activity as proper religion (*zhengdang zongjiao huodong*) and another as feudal superstition (*fengjian mixin*). Much of Shaanbei popular religion hovers in the huge gray area between legitimate religion and illegitimate (thus illegal) superstition. After the founding of the People's Republic of China in 1949, the Yulin and Yan'an Prefecture Civil Affairs Bureaus (*Minzhengju*), which have branches in the county governments, were responsible for overseeing religious affairs in Shaanbei. Recently, a separate Religious Affairs Bureau has been established in reaction to the growing prominence of religion in Shaanbei society.[8] Theoretically, it is the officials of the local Religious Affairs Bureau who make the distinctions between legitimate religion and illegitimate superstition, following directives and religious policies set by their superiors (in the Religious

Affairs Bureau offices at the provincial and central levels) and by the central government. The same bureau is responsible for supporting proper religion by registering and supervising religious institutions and personnel, leaving it to the local police to crack down (*daji*) on superstition. However, in specific instances on the local level, the decisions distinguishing proper religion from superstition are not easily made, nor do such distinctions easily translate into government action. To my knowledge, there has been no effort targeting superstitious activities in Shaanbei since the 1980s—a laxity that partly accounts for the vibrant popular religious life there— even though much of Shaanbei popular religious life (divination, mediumism, rain prayers, symbolism of hell and divine retribution, etc.) would qualify as superstition according to criteria of the Maoist era.[9]

The criteria used to distinguish superstitions from "proper religion" are still the same, but the behavior of the local state has changed. Nowadays the relevant agents of the local state (e.g., officials of the Religious Affairs Bureau and the Public Security Bureau) are not interested in taking action against superstition, because they derive no benefit from doing so. Unlike during the Maoist era, being fervent (*jiji*) in stamping out superstition is no longer a sign of political rectitude and good political performance (*zhengzhi biaoxian*). In fact, a fervent anti-superstition attitude is so connected in people's minds with the ultraleftism of the Cultural Revolution era (which has been officially declared as aberrant and wrong) that it earns its holder a bad political reputation. And it is quite plain to everyone in the local state that to crack down on popular religion, no matter how superstitious in appearance, will meet with popular disapproval and even resistance; it "will not win people's hearts" (*bude renxin*).

The shift away from radical antitraditionalism to regulatory paternalism is best demonstrated by the registration of temples by the prefectural Religious Affairs Bureau. In theory, only temples that are legitimately Daoist or Buddhist can become institutional members of the official national Daoist Association or Buddhist Association. However, in practice it is extremely difficult to ascertain the Daoist or Buddhist qualities of different temples. The overwhelming majority of Shaanbei temples do not have clergy or an easily identified set of doctrines. And the range of religious activities at any one temple can be quite wide and confusing to anyone who is looking for some pure Daoist or Buddhist characteristics. Even historically Daoist or Buddhist temples have accommodated elements that are "impure." In a word, most Shaanbei temples are what scholars of Chinese religions have called folk or popular religious temples, exhibiting a hodgepodge of different practices that have their origins in different traditions.

Adding to the problem of apparently indiscriminate Daoist and

Buddhist syncretism is the presence at many temples of clearly "superstitious" activities such as spirit mediumism, which is condemned by not only the Religious Affairs Bureau but also the official Daoist and Buddhist associations. Despite these apparent difficulties, the process of temple registration was in full swing in the 1990s, probably to catch up with more than a decade of their mushrooming growth. The Religious Affairs Bureau was also supposed to carry out the state's religious policies (*guanche zongjiao zhengce*). In 1999, an official of the Yulin Prefecture Religious Affairs Bureau was named a province-level model worker for his outstanding work in the effort—a far cry from the high socialist era, when a cadre would have been praised for smashing a lot of temples, not for registering them.[10] As I spoke to temple officers of different temples that were applying for registration, I found that this process always took some time and a lot of effort. Typically, a temple association has to treat the official representatives of the local state—from the Religious Affairs Bureau and other related bureaus and offices—as guests of honor at temple festivals, at banquets, and on other occasions. The local state and the temples have thus developed a patron-client relationship: officials support temples that pay them respect and tribute.

Jean Oi (1999), studying the political economy of reform-era rural China, has highlighted the active role of the local state in enabling local economic growth. She calls this phenomenon local state corporatism. I suggest that the behavior of the Shaanbei local state toward the temples can be interpreted similarly: temples are like enterprises that generate prosperity for the local economy (especially if they are regional pilgrimage centers) and income for the local state. It is thus in the interest of the local state to protect local temples as it would local enterprises. The local state's new, regulatory relationship with local society is characterized by practical mutual dependence. Registering temples and thereby making "superstitious" local cult centers into respectable, official Buddhist or Daoist "venues for religious activities" (*zongjiao huodong changsuo*) is an act of indulgence, granting these local temples protection against any possible future anti-superstition campaign coming from the central government.[11]

The Black Dragon King Temple (Heilongdawang ci), the Dragon King Valley Complex (Longwanggou), and Local Temple Activism

Shaanbei people resort to many deities for divine assistance when they have the need. However, the dragon king (*longwang*) is the agrarian deity par excellence, especially in drought-prone north China. He is the provider of the most important agricultural resource, water (in the form of rainfall). There are many dragon kings in Shaanbei, each with a different origin story and separate turf. Heilongdawang (the Black Dragon King) has been a local rain god administering the Zhenchuan township vicinity.[12] Compared to the throng of village dragon kings, Heilongdawang is considered a much more powerful god because he has an imperially conferred official title, the Marquis of Efficacious Response (*Lingyinghou*).[13] In the past, peasants in nearby areas who had failed to obtain rain from the lesser dragon kings came to Heilongdawang for help. In the past as well as today, believers come to Heilongdawang to pray for divine assistance not only for rain but also for all kinds of other problems. In the past decade or so, however, more and more people ask Heilongdawang to help them with their businesses, to bless them so they will get rich.

Torn down completely by the villagers themselves during the Cultural Revolution and rebuilt from scratch in 1982, the temple has been expanding in grandeur ever since.[14] Its fame really took off in the mid- and late-1980s, when stories of Heilongdawang's efficacy spread widely in Shaanbei, and when the Heilongdawang Temple began to host by far the longest, the most diverse, the best, and the most expensive opera performances in Shaanbei. The temple coffers swelled as its fame grew phenomenally. It is now the richest nongovernment-managed temple in Shaanbei, receiving a few million RMB in donations from worshippers each year.[15] Though the temple is hidden away in a long, narrow valley, its recently constructed carved-stone grandiose main entrance gate (*pailou*) stands right on the east-side curb of Shaanbei's only north–south thoroughfare that connects Baotou in Inner Mongolia and Xi'an, the provincial capital of Shaanxi.

The new Heilongdawang Temple perches majestically on the edge of a cliff on one side of Longwanggou (Dragon King Valley). Similar in setup to most Chinese temples, the temple main hall houses a statue of Heilongdawang and those of his attendants, divination instruments, a donation box, incense pots, an exquisitely carved mural lauding the deity's divine power, a stele recounting the legend of the deity and the rebuilding of the temple in the reform era, and numerous plaques and banners donated by worshippers praising Heilongdawang's efficacy. Next to the temple is a natural spring in which the dragon king is supposed to dwell. The spring is believed to have magical curing power and is sought after by many visitors. Like most village-level temples in Shaanbei, the Heilongdawang Temple is a popular religious temple run by ordinary villagers and does not have any professional clergy or elaborate ritual repertoire. Even though the temple was granted Daoist status by the Yulin Prefectural Religious Affairs Bureau in 1998, this change was only in name and the temple did not change its popular religious makeup in its management personnel and modes of operation (more on this below).

Local temple activism in the reform era typically follows two stages, as the revival of the Heilongdawang Temple illustrates. The first stage is the building or rebuilding of the temple structure and its grounds (often including an opera stage, temple offices, etc.). Depending on the political climate, sometimes the rebuilt temples began as very modest and makeshift structures but later expanded to become larger and permanent. The second stage is the resumption of temple activities including those that are ostensibly religious (efficacy related) and some that are nonreligious.

As mentioned earlier, temples are the foundation of temple-based popular religious activities. Temples are cultural monuments around which social labor and meanings coalesce (Gates 2000: 316; see also Goossaert 2000; Yang 2004). At the most fundamental level, it takes considerable activism to build or rebuild the physical structure of a temple. Traditionally the process of building a temple follows a definitive pattern. A deity appears to a villager either in a dream or through a medium asking the villagers to build a temple for him (or her), or a villager feels grateful for the help given by a particular deity and decides to build the deity a temple in his own village, or a deity decides to make a villager his spirit medium by possessing the latter. Whether or not a temple will be built depends on whether or not other villagers are convinced of the importance of the task and the availability of resources. The maintenance and expansion of the temple would then depend on how efficacious the deity proves himself to be in responding to the villagers' requests. If the deity becomes less efficacious over time, his following and temple donations will dwindle, and eventually the temple will fall into disrepair and the cult will disappear. The same cult can revive, however, after years of relapse, if another villager makes a convincing case for the deity.

More often than not, the initiation of the rebuilding of the temples in the reform era has depended on a miraculous (re)appearance of the deity to the villagers. In the case of the Heilongdawang Temple, in 1980 a villager dreamt that Heilongdawang wished to come back to dwell in Longwanggou, and a small group of elderly men began the planning of rebuilding the temple. Once the idea of rebuilding the temple took shape, an unstoppable cascade of activities followed. A temple association was formed and leadership elected; funds were raised from each village household; construction plans were drawn; building materials were secured; tools and equipment were bought; different portions of the construction were contracted out to different labor gangs; artisans and craftsmen were sought and hired; volunteer helpers were mobilized and coordinated. In the short span of a few years, the original site of the Heilongdawang

Temple, which was little more than complete ruins, metamorphosed into a beautiful temple complex that includes the temple main hall, an opera stage, a grand audience stand conforming to the contour of the hillside, one large stone gate at the mouth of the valley and another even bigger one at midsection between the temple and the first gate, an additional hall dedicated to Heilongdawang's four dragon king brothers and their mother (a fertility goddess), a three-story dormitory building, a primary school (first housed in the temple dormitory and later having its own building separate from the temple site), and a reforestation and botanical project called the Longwanggou Hilly Land Arboretum that encompasses more than 1,200 *mu* of hilly land surrounding the temple with hundreds of species of trees and other plants.[16] Construction never seems to stop at the temple; each year some new features were added to further embellish the temple site. I call this entire amalgam of physical features the Longwanggou Complex or simply Longwanggou. All the operations of this complex are funded by the incense money donations to the temple by worshippers.

Shaanbei people's enthusiasm for reviving popular religion is most evident in their willingness to contribute money and volunteer labor to help rebuild temples. Most village temples are modest in size and are relatively uncomplicated to build. They typically comprise one hall, a few simple statues, a couple of simple murals, an incense pot, a donation box, a divination set, and a small courtyard. However, a certain number of temples that were of some stature in the past all aspired to resume if not surpass their former grandeur. The Heilongdawang Temple is a prime example of this expansionary vision; the number of its component parts as well as their size far exceeds those of an average village temple and those of its previous incarnation before the Cultural Revolution.

What I have just described are only the physical infrastructural features of the Heilongdawang Temple. Many social activities transpire on or off the temple grounds that are direct products of expansive temple activism, the most obvious of which are the exuberant temple festivals. Just as other popular religious temples in Shaanbei, Longwanggou stages temple festivals twice a year, one during the Lunar New Year (on the fifteenth of the first lunar month) and the other for Heilongdawang's birthday (for six days culminating on the thirteenth of the sixth month).[17]

The recognition of temples as economic institutions in addition to being religious institutions is important to our understanding of their mode of operation, as all temple projects involve monetary expenses. In principle, the incense money donated to a temple is for the general upkeep of the temple and the temple festivals. Worshippers who donate a sizable amount might say that the donation is for "writing" (i.e., contracting, purchasing) a piece of opera performance for the deity, which is why sometimes the donation is also called "money for writing operas" (*xie-xiqian*), underscoring the direct relationship between donating incense money and the temple festival. Traditionally temple festivals are occasions when all the donation money would have been spent. However, a temple such as the Heilongdawang Temple receives much more in donations than it could possibly spend on hosting festivals. The surplus has to be spent in ways that are acceptable to the worshippers and the villagers, and look legitimate to the authorities (more on this below). At Longwanggou, this large donation surplus has been one of the most important driving forces behind the temple's branching out into nonreligious domains of social activism. This nonreligious social activism includes most notably the Longwanggou Primary School and the Longwanggou Hilly Land Arboretum, but the temple has also initiated irrigation, road building, water control, and other projects, and sponsored local folklore research, sports events, and social welfare.

The motivations for popular religious temples such as Heilongdawang Temple to expand their functions beyond the purely religious realm are multifold. This functional expansiveness is a product of both traditional idioms of grassroots level self-organization and self-help and conscious concerns over legitimacy. For example, temple-funded schools are established partly in reaction to the state's lack of financial support for village schools. On the other hand, the channeling of incense donation money to legitimate causes such as education, reforestation, irrigation, road building, and welfare lends legitimacy to the religious activities that can still be construed as superstitious (e.g., divination, magical curing, etc.). This instrumentalist reading of the temple association's maneuvers should not of course distract us from the fact that the villagers also genuinely wished to have a better school or a reforestation project for their own sake. And equally important, temple associations want to make sure that they spend and reinvest all the incense donation money rather than having a sizable surplus lying idle, which might invite unwanted predatory attention from the local state (even though various local state agencies pay predatory attention anyway).

Temple Organization at Longwanggou

Traditionally the Heilongdawang Temple was run by three adjacent villages: Chenjiapo, Hongliutan, and Batawan. Chenjiapo was the richest and biggest village and dominated temple affairs before Liberation. Chenjiapo thus was the "First Association" (*yihui*) and Hongliutan and Batawan together formed the "Second Association" (*erhui*). The two associations alternated yearly responsibilities for the temple and its festivals. After the Chenjiapo landlords were eliminated during the Land Reform, the management of temple affairs became more equalized among the three villages. During the Smash the Four Olds Movement in 1966, all three production teams (corresponding to the three villages) shared the task of tearing down different parts of the temple, following instructions from the commune government. But because the temple now sits on hilly land that belongs to Hongliutan, Hongliutan villagers have become the major players in the temple's revival since 1980. Hongliutan in principle owns the temple. This shift in temple ownership and leadership is partly a historical accident, because the land where the temple sits on used to belong to Chenjiapo but was given to Hongliutan by the commune in the 1960s to apportion the size of land according to the population of the production teams. Some Chenjiapo villagers resent the fact that Hongliutan "stole" their temple, but there is nothing they can do to reclaim it. But as the original villages that have historical ties to the temple, both Chenjiapo and Batawan are strong supporters of the temple's revival.

At the very beginning of the revival of the temple in the early 1980s, six more villages were added to the temple association: Liuwan, Gaoliang, Zhuzhai, Heshang, Yangzhuang, and Huaqu. The nine villages altogether used to belong to one brigade (*shengchan dadui*) during the commune era and now constitute an administrative sub-district, the "southern spread" (*nanpian*), of the Zhenchuan Township. Adding the other six villages was a strategic move on the part of the then temple association leaders in a time of dire need for labor and monetary resources for rebuilding and of great vulnerability in the face of uncertain official attitudes.[18] However, representatives from the original three villages, especially Hongliutan, still form the core of the temple association, and now only one formal association runs the temple, with no more rotation of responsibilities between different associations/villages as in the past.

The larger temple association (*dahui*) is comprised of a core managing committee and three representatives (usually the village Party secretary, village head, and accountant) from each of the nine participating villages. All members of this larger association meet only a few times a year for elections and other extremely important matters. Otherwise, the core members of the managing committee take care of all temple operations. Members of the core managing committee include temple boss Lao Wang and six other temple officers, who were all experienced men in their forties or fifties during my fieldwork in 1997–98.[19] These seven men constituted the brain of Longwanggou and they were always seen together, engaged in heated discussions over temple matters or just idle bantering. It is worth noting that even though the idiom of the temple association is traditional, the organizational structure and the officer positions of the managing committee are clearly influenced by the management structure of the production teams of the commune era and that of the village committee in today's rural China and bear little resemblance to the informal structure of temple associations of traditional times.

Besides the managing committee members, there are almost two dozen people who are regular employees of the temple. These include the main temple hall caretaker; the divine message interpreter; the caretaker of the new temple halls in the back of the main hall; the forestry technician who manages the Longwanggou Hilly Land Arboretum; the arboretum watchman who watches against thieves (there are many fruit trees in the arboretum) and chases away the occasional hunters of small game; the general laborer for doing all kinds of chores; the gardener; two cooks; the ten teachers of the Longwanggou Primary School. On top of this long list of people who are regular, paid employees—Lao Wang is the only person in Longwanggou who does not receive any salary, which is his choice— a number of other people are hired whenever the need arises: a computer operator, a bulldozer operator, an artistic director and "court literatus," an auditor, an opera contractor, not to mention a small army of day laborers, craftsmen, and volunteers when there are large temple building projects.

In about two decades, Longwanggou evolved from a village temple to become a large and complex corporate body with multiple functions and the ability to mobilize diverse resources. Even though religious activities are still at the core of the temple's identity, it is the other, major nonreligious undertakings such as the primary school and the arboretum that have emerged as indispensable components of the temple.

Local Temple Activism Meets the Local State's Regulatory Paternalism

Now I turn to an analysis of the role local state agencies and agents play in the revival of popular religion in Shaanbei. While the reform era (beginning in the early 1980s) has unleashed social energy in local society in the form of local temple activism, among other things, it has also provided opportunities for local state agencies to act more independently of central state policies and to interact with local society in a more accommodating manner. Some central policies, e.g., birth control policies, are not flexible and local state agencies must carry them out seriously. Some other policies are more flexible and allow considerable room at the local level for negotiation and mutual accommodation between policy and local desires. The treatment of popular religion is a prominent example of such accommodation.

The local state, in contrast to the central or the provincial state, refers to the government of the prefectural, county, and township levels. Each local state is composed of several dozen local state agencies, though the organizational complexity of local states varies across China. In Shaanbei, for example, each county government normally consists of about three or four dozens different bureaus (*ju*) and offices (*bangongshi*).[20] As the economic reform deepens, the local state at different levels in rural China becomes increasingly unwilling as well as unable to fulfill its fiscal obligations to its subsidiary agencies. This results in the widespread phenomenon in Shaanbei of backed-up salaries in most local state agencies.[21] Sometimes the salaries are four or five months overdue, causing massive dissatisfaction among local state employees (especially school teachers, factory workers, staff at peripheral bureaus). And many local state-owned enterprises have had to close down as they could not turn a profit and subsidies eventually dried up. As the local state takes care of its agencies less and less, the latter in response become less and less politically and fiscally accountable to the local state. This has resulted in the disintegration of the previously unitary local state through a process of compartmentalization: different local state agencies have become more autonomous from one another and from the local state's leadership.

In this context of local state financial atrophy, each local state agency has subsequently begun to treat its own jurisdiction as "backyard profit centers" for rent seeking (Lin and Zhang 1999). Many agencies set up for-profit enterprises that can benefit from the special resources and power of the parent agencies, e.g., through commodifying agency-owned properties, expertise, networks, and agency personnel. These enterprises include construction and real estate companies, hotels, restaurants, karaoke bars and dance halls, retail stores, factories, entertainment troupes, and so on. The profit they gain or income they extract from these backyard profit centers contribute to these individual agencies' slush fund to pay for salaries, bonuses, or other benefits such as housing, banquets, vacation trips, and the like. Of course some local state agencies are better situated than others in terms of possible sources of backyard revenue. Those better situated are in taxation, commerce, trade, education, banking, the postal service, telecommunications, transportation, construction, the police, the traffic police, etc. Inevitably, the revival of popular religion has created a new space in which local communities interact with agents of the local state. The reemergence of temples and temple festivals has presented some local state agencies with new opportunities to intervene, regulate, squeeze, co-opt, and even cooperate.

As many local temples expand their sphere of activities beyond the divine efficacy-related religious realm, the interactions they have with the local state also become more complicated. Local state agencies have been involved with aspects of the popular religious revival from the very beginning. The first local state agency the temple associations had to deal with was the local Public Security Bureau (*Gonganju*). According to the law, the police are supposed to crack down on superstitious activities (i.e., any religious activities not registered with and approved by the Religious Affairs Bureau), yet except in the very beginning of the temple revivals in the early 1980s where there were some sporadic crackdowns and arrests, the police quickly worked out a way to benefit from the temple activities.[22] Or rather, the threat that the police could crack down on temple activities gave them the leverage to extort contributions from the temples under their jurisdiction. The typical way to do this is to make sure that during temple festivals the police are invited to maintain order and be thanked for their "hard work" with gifts, free food, drinks, cigarettes, and "subsidies." On the other hand, temple festivals do benefit, perhaps minimally, from the presence of the police to ward off potential troublemakers.[23] And the temple associations can rest assured that the police will not intentionally meddle with their festivals. At the annual Longwanggou temple festival the temple association has to invite the police from not only the Zhenchuan Public Security Post (*Paichusuo*) but also the Yulin county and Mizhi county Public Security Bureaus, as the latter two also want a piece of the pie. To ensure an amicable relationship with the local police force, Longwanggou has also sponsored the Zhenchuan Public Security Post to purchase electric batons, uniforms, motorcycles, and a police car.

   To divert official attention from religious activities (incense-burning, beseeching the deity for divine assistance, divination, magical curing, animal sacrifice, offering processions, exorcism, etc.), the Longwanggou temple festival at first took place under the guise of an agricultural fair (*luoma dahui*, literally "ass and horse big congregation"), in which thousands of horses, cattle, pigs, and goats changed hands. As an economic activity, the fair attracted the intervention of the Zhenchuan Town Industry and Commerce Bureau (*Gongshangju*) and Taxation Bureau (*Shuiwuju*). As the scale of the festival expanded over the years to include hundreds of small temporary stalls selling all kinds of goods and a dozen or so performance and exhibition tents (song and dance troupes and even freak shows), the revenue for these bureaus increased exponentially. Cadres from these bureaus came to the festival and levied fees and taxes upon all the businesses, including the old ladies walking around with their baskets selling incense and spirit money. Traditionally, commerce had always been an important part of temple festivals, even though the temple association's choice of labeling the festival initially as an agricultural fair indicated a deliberate attempt to highlight its socially and politically acceptable aspects. Later on, as the temple festival became clearly acceptable to the authorities, the label changed to the straightforward "temple festival" (*miaohui*), though often modified by the words "old" (*gu*) or "traditional" (*chuantong*) to mark it as harmlessly folkloric. The agricultural fair aspect of the festival is still kept today, even though the religious festival aspect (e.g., processions, divination, exorcism) has become far more prominent and explicit.

Let me briefly describe the presence of different local state agencies at a typical Longwanggou annual temple festival. At the mouth of the valley, members of the Yulin County Traffic Police Brigade (*Jiaojing dadui*) help direct the heavy and chaotic festival traffic. Members of both the Zhenchuan and Mizhi Public Security Bureaus are stationed at strategic nodal points on the festival grounds to help ensure law and order.[24] Members of the Zhenchuan Industry and Commerce Bureau and Taxation Bureau mill among the stalls with their folders and forms, registering them and exacting fees and taxes. All stall owners complain about how voracious these *Gongshang shuiwu* officials are. To avoid paying high fees and taxes they have to bribe the officials and feed them or let them sample their merchandise for free. At the temple association headquarters a few members of the Zhenchuan and Yulin Cultural Station (*Wenhuazhan*) help with writing the opera performance advertisements to be posted in nearby towns.[25] Clerks from the Mizhi Town Credit Union (*xinyongshe*) come daily to accompany designated temple association officers bringing the large amount of donation money to be deposited at the bank. The presence of local state agencies at the temple festival is so strong primarily because it is during this time that the temple and its activities are the most "squeezable" (because they had an abundance of cash).

Legitimation through Many Channels: Temple–Local State Interactions

Even though popular enthusiasm from villagers and worshippers was an important source of legitimacy for the temple, it was not enough to ensure that the temple could survive another anti-superstition campaign, such as those during the Maoist era. Official endorsement from the government was a must for such an assurance. So temple boss Lao Wang and his associates at Longwanggou endeavored to secure official institutional status for the temple from the very beginning of the temple's revival to legitimize the whole enterprise. These endeavors required that the temple officers go beyond their home turf and interact with local state agents at the county and prefectural levels and other social actors from even farther afield. Alongside their application to the Religious Affairs Bureau to be recognized as a Daoist temple (the only reasonable religious affiliation the temple could aspire to), the temple associations engaged in various significant nonreligious institution building around the temple. Arising partly out of real need and partly out of concern about the temple's legitimacy, these nonreligious activities brought the temple proper recognition from various local state agencies, media attention, and symbolic capital (in terms of status). From the perspective of the temple, there was nothing unnatural or contradictory in expanding the influence of the temple to these diverse nonreligious realms such as irrigation, education, and reforestation; from the perspective of the local state, these community efforts to improve local infrastructure were to be applauded and encouraged, a model of turning something undesirable (i.e., superstition) into something desirable (i.e., communal benefits). Below I chronicle the various phases of Longwanggou's initiatives and the major official statuses that it has accrued over the years to show how its legitimacy got consolidated over time.

In 1982, the recently rebuilt temple was blessed by the Cultural Relic Management Committee (*Wenwu guanli weiyuanhui*) of Yulin County with the designation of a county-level cultural relic (*xianji wenwu*). The Longwanggou Cultural Relic Management Office (*Longwanggou wenwu guanlisuo*) was established as a result. The temple could garner this "cultural relic" (*wenwu*) status not because of the newly constructed temple site, despite its magnificence, but because of the beautiful Republican-era stone temple gate that was spared destruction during the Cultural Revolution. This was the temple's attempt to protect the temple by claiming its cultural-historical and artifactual value. Even though strictly speaking this status only protected the stone gate, not the entire temple, at least the temple now had an officially sanctioned status.

In 1988, with help from government forestry bureaus, the temple initiated a reforestation project as a strategy to lend additional legitimacy to the temple's activities: the incense donation money is used to plant trees, an obviously meritorious act. The Yulin Prefecture Forestry Bureau (*Linyeju*) subsequently granted the project an official name: the Longwanggou Hilly Land Arboretum (*Longwanggou shandi shumuyuan*). The significance of this project has to be seen in the larger context of rising national environmental concerns in the reform era and Shaanbei's harsh environmental setting. Yulin County and many other of Shaanbei's northern counties, being part of the Maowusu Desert of Inner Mongolia that extends southward into Shaanbei, face the constant threat of desertification and dust storms, and because of its long history of human settlement and dry climate Shaanbei has a severe tree shortage. As a result reforestation has always been a high-profile issue in Shaanbei. The Longwanggou reforestation project capitalized on the moral virtue of environmentalism and quickly gained regional, national, and even international attention as the first civic (non-governmental) hilly land arboretum in China. Newspapers reported on the arboretum; officials and foreign dignitaries visited it; botanists, forestry specialists, and other scientists came to bestow their approval and marvel at this folk initiative; environmentalist groups from Beijing and NGO groups from Japan came to plant trees. One cannot overestimate the aesthetic and emotional appeal of the green hills around the temple set against the often parched landscape of the Shaanbei loess plateau. Because the reforestation project would not be possible without the money from donations to the temple, the arboretum justified the superstitious activities of the Heilongdawang Temple. The success of the arboretum was a huge boost to the official status and image of the temple, and the temple had been riding on this success ever since. In the 1990s a few other Shaanbei temples had followed suit in using temple funds to initiate reforestation projects.

In 1996 the temple association, working with the Hongliutan village committee, founded the Longwanggou Primary School (funded by temple incense money) to replace the original Hongliutan village school (funded by village fees). Neighboring Batawan village was only happy to close down their small and dilapidated village school and send all their children to the new Longwanggou Primary School. The classrooms and teachers' offices of the new school were housed on the third floor of the new and spacious three-story temple dormitory building, and the children used the large temple courtyard as a playground. The temple is situated midway between the two villages so the children had to walk a little more than they had to before, but that was a small price to pay for a much better school. Founding the school involved getting approval from the Yulin County Education Bureau (*Jiaoyuju*). All school expenses were covered by temple funds. Except for two teachers who were on government payroll (*guan-pai*), all the rest of the dozen teachers were so-called people-run (*minban*) teachers on the temple's payroll. The parents of the school children needed only to pay a minimal fee for tuition and books. Because of the better and well-funded conditions at the Longwanggou Primary School compared to other local schools, it quickly became the best primary school in the entire Zhenchuan township in academic achievement, even outdoing the long-established and well-equipped government schools in Zhenchuan town. (The school instituted cash prizes for teachers and students as rewards for high achievement.) The Longwanggou Primary School is a nongovernment operated (*minban*) school. As China's reform-era educational policies allowed increasingly more "societal forces" (*shehui liliang*) to support education, the founding of the school was capitalizing on a national trend. The school's accomplishments would not have been possible without temple funds.[26] As a result, the school provided ample justification for the temple activities, despite the apparent incongruence between secular education—the students are taught to look down on superstition—and folk religious tradition.

Though important in the legitimation of the Heilongdawang Temple, the above-mentioned official endorsements of the temple had been indirect. None was really granted to the temple per se. However, in 1998 a long-awaited blessing finally came: the Yulin Prefectural Religious Affairs Bureau granted Longwanggou the official status of the "Longwanggou Daoist Shrine Management Committee" (*Longwanggou daoguan guanli weiyuanhui*). In other words, the Heilongdawang Temple was now officially a Daoist temple and Heilongdawang a Daoist deity. From then on the temple itself was finally legitimate and enjoyed the legal protection of the constitution of the People's Republic of China. As popular religious deities, dragon kings have traditionally hovered at the edge of official Daoism and were not quite members of the Daoist pantheon. But these were just minor details that both the temple association and the Religious Affairs Bureau officials were willing to ignore. To turn messy reality (i.e., popular religious practices on the ground) into a few simpler categories (i.e., Daoism or Buddhism) is a process James Scott has called "seeing like a state" (Scott 1998). The "Dao-ification" of the Heilongdawang Temple and other similar popular religious temples in a way made these temples "legible" to the state even if it involved a willful misreading.

Conclusion

Obtaining the above-mentioned official statuses and endorsements was the Longwanggou temple association's cunning dissimulation strategy to protect the temple by highlighting its cultural-artifactual, environmentalist, educational, and official-religious aspects. In other words, these officially sanctioned statuses were a clever cover for temple activities that would otherwise be condemned as superstitious (e.g., provisioning divine spring water and divination, two of the temple's key appeals). Anthropologists studying popular religion in Taiwan have noted Taiwanese people's ingenuity in cleverly disguising their rituals to make them more palatable to the authorities that intended to repress or reform them (Ahern 1981, Weller 1987). Similar techniques have also been at work in China, where some compromise was struck between complete submission to Party-state ideological control (presumably atheism) and total assertion of popular religious autonomy. The temple officers willingly subjected the temple to state regulation only so as to be able to do what they liked. The local state agents, on the other hand, permitted what was permissible and turned a blind eye to what was not. Both parties came out of the transaction happy. In this way local state agencies and temples entered into a mutually dependent, symbiotic patron-client relationship (see Wank 1999).

I have hoped to show in this chapter the amount of social labor involved in the revival of popular religion in contemporary rural China. This labor is not only expressed in the construction of temples and the production of temple festivals but also in the forging of multivillage alliances, the expansion of temple functions into nonreligious realms, the dealing with local state agencies, and the capturing of useful social forces from far beyond the locale (e.g., media attention, cosmopolitan and foreign NGOs, etc.). I have called this multifaceted labor local temple activism.

Yet I have also attempted to show that local temple activism is not a sign of complete local communal autonomy from the state. Local state agencies have quickly responded to local temple activism and the temple's expansion into diverse realms such as infrastructural development (e.g., building roads and irrigation networks), commerce, cultural production, education, forestry, and tourism. The local state's regulatory paternalism is a form of local state activism, whereby local state agents also actively seek ways to expand their resource and profit base. For example, the establishment of the Longwanggou Hilly Land Arboretum exemplifies the negotiation, mutual co-optation, and cooperation between Longwanggou and local state agencies in the forestry sector.

The Longwanggou case study shows that even though the temple is theoretically a "religious" institution, its actual activities have gone far beyond those that relate directly to divine efficacy. Therefore it is not adequate to consider only the state's religious policies and examine how local temples react to these policies. Instead, we also need to look at what local temples and local state agencies do. The Heilongdawang Temple's various religious and nonreligious domains of activities have all induced the various branches of the local state to descend upon Longwanggou. Of course Longwanggou often invited the presence of these local state agencies out of a concern for legality and legitimacy. Elsewhere I have called this dense web of interaction between popular religious temples and local state agencies the "channeling zone" (Chau 2005). Other scholars have argued that this kind of "state embeddedness" is not necessarily bad or unproductive for social organizations (see Chamberlain 1993; Saich 2000; Weller 1999). As these vertical ties between different local state agencies and popular religious temples multiply and thicken, the legitimacy of the temples increases, as no single local state agency alone (not even the Religious Affairs Bureau) can determine the fate of these temples. This functional expansiveness of popular religious temples demonstrates that the emerging space of religion in today's China is often shot through with institutional arrangements and practices that are non-religious, and often these non-religious aspects play the role of legitimating the religious aspects of the temples. This is particularly true in the case of popular religion as compared to the officially recognized five religions because of the status of the former as theoretically illegal feudal superstition. With the registration of thousands of popular religious temples in China, the space of popular religion is rapidly expanding into the space of religion. Will this development spur changes in the state's understanding and legislation of "religion"?

Notes

This chapter is based on materials collected during eighteen months of ethnographic fieldwork in Shaanbei between 1995 and 1998. I gratefully acknowledge the following agencies and organizations for funding my field research in Shaanbei and its write-up: the Mellon Foundation, Stanford's Center for East Asian Studies, the Wenner-Gren Foundation for Anthropological Research, the Committee on Scholarly Communications with China, and the China Times Cultural Foundation. I am most grateful to my dissertation committee members for guidance and help: Arthur P. Wolf, Hill Gates, and Andrew G. Walder. Many ideas in this chapter emerged from numerous discussions with Luo Hongguang, of the Institute of Sociology, Chinese Academy of Social Sciences, who pioneered the anthropological study of Shaanbei. I also thank the organizers of and participants in the Politics of Religion in Contemporary China Conference held at Stanford University in spring 2004, especially Yoshiko Ashiwa, David Wank, and my discussant Richard Madsen. The detailed comments on an earlier draft by David Wank and Yoshiko Ashiwa were crucial for improving the clarity of the chapter. I also received input from Liu Tiksang, Hideko Mitsui, Elizabeth Perry, and Robert Weller. Finally, I thank the many wonderful Shaanbei people, especially temple boss Lao Wang of the Black Dragon King Temple. The reader is directed to an article of mine that appeared in the journal *Modern China* in 2005 entitled "The Politics of Legitimation and the Revival of Popular Religion in Shaanbei, North-central China," of which this chapter is a companion piece. A number of passages in this chapter are drawn from the *Modern China* piece.

1. That the recognized religions are organized and institutionalized makes it easier for the state to exert control and supervision, whereas most popular religious activities are dispersed and thus less amenable to state control. In other words, the effort to make a particular religion (e.g., Daoism, Buddhism) become recognized, and thus protected, by the state also makes it vulnerable to state control.

2. Administratively, Shaanbei comprises Yan'an and Yulin prefectures. My principal fieldsite was in Yulin County, one of the twelve counties of Yulin Prefecture. Yulin City is the seat of both the Yulin county and prefecture governments. The loess plateau and cave dwellings of Shaanbei were made famous when the Central Red Army, led by Mao Zedong, made Yan'an the capital of their revolutionary base

area from 1935 until 1945 (my fieldsite in Yulin was under Nationalist rule during that period). Even though my research focused on the Heilongdawang Temple, I visited dozens more temples and their festivals and spoke to Shaanbei people from all walks of life on diverse occasions. Because I engaged informants in casual conversations rather than formal interviews, I have not provided citations to the interviews. I conducted the fieldwork without being accompanied by officials. In addition, participant observation was important for data collection. For a fuller view of the characteristics of Shaanbei popular religion, see Chau (2003, 2004, 2006).

3. In fact, given the Communist Party-state's atheist ideology, all religions, including the five recognized religions, are really tolerable superstitions. The criteria for what counts as religion are based on a modernist epistemology that originated in the Western experience and are quite arbitrary and ill-fitting to Chinese religious practices on the ground, which are products of an entirely different historical trajectory (see Asad 1983). The current religious policy presents the curious situation where "feeding hungry ghosts" (a standard Buddhist ritual) is considered proper religious activity as long as it is conducted within the confines of Buddhist temples while beseeching a fertility goddess for a son is considered superstition; yet both activities operate upon comparable "unmodern" and "unscientific" assumptions.

4. Many temple association officers in Shaanbei are clear about their temples' vulnerability as unregistered temples. They are also aware that some temples in other provinces had been torn down, as these incidents were sporadically reported in the newspapers and on television and the radio. The sporadic official anti-superstition actions are what Ann Anagnost calls the state's "fetishized demonstrations of political efficacy" (1994: 244).

5. The politics of legitimation refers not only to the efforts of popular religious temples to gain the recognition of and protection from the state but also the efforts of local temple activists to gain acceptance and support from their communities. The political aspect of popular religion has long been noted by scholars (e.g., Duara 1988; Rohsenow 1973; Seaman 1978). In reform-era rural China, however, we witness the reemergence of a site of local political contest and negotiation that had been completely suppressed during the Maoist era. The political possibilities promised by the realm of popular religion may have motivated local activists like temple boss Lao Wang (head of the Black Dragon King temple association) to revive and enlarge this realm and to compete for the tangible and intangible benefits that it yields. Yet the growth of this realm also brings about contestations over resources and power struggles. Hence the abundance of what F. G. Bailey has called the "small politics of reputation" (quoted in Strand 1990: 230). For a more detailed analysis of power struggles surrounding the Heilongdawang Temple, see Chau (2005). This chapter focuses, however, on the interactions between the temple and local state agencies.

6. Regarding the locale-specific characteristics of ritual networks in Fujian, Kenneth Dean has written, "Local geographic features frame most ritual networks. An ecology of local power holds ritual networks back from direct confrontation with the state. Instead, the networks expand and become more complex within effective, appropriate levels and niches in the continually evolving, agonistic relation with state power" (2003: 357). This locale-specific tendency contrasts sharply with the

alocal and translocal characteristics of qigong sects, whose networks float independently of local topographies and communities.

7. Of these temples, 300 to 500 (i.e., less than 5 percent) had supralocal or supracounty influence, about 1,000 (about 10 percent) were at the township or rural district level, and the rest (85 percent) were village-level temples (Fan 1997: 98).

8. In Shaanbei, the Religious Affairs Bureau has no county-level offices and operates only at the prefectural level.

9. The nationwide campaign against Falungong beginning in 1998 targeted only translocal qigong sects but left alone popular religious expressions such as the temple activities mentioned in this chapter.

10. Much like the current practice in the People's Republic of China, all popular religious temples in Taiwan that are not obviously Christian, Muslim, or Buddhist are identified and registered as Daoist by the government (Jordan and Overmyer 1986: 243).

11. While the imperial government attempted religious control by frequently granting majestic-sounding titles to individual deities (e.g., Mazu, Guandi; see Watson 1985), the same strategy is not available to the secular state today. But in registering the temples in order to regulate them if necessary, the modern state is employing a control strategy long used by the late imperial state.

12. Zhenchuan is the township at the southern end of Yulin County, bordering Mizhi County to the south. Zhenchuan is a town of major commercial significance in Yulin Prefecture, second only to Suide, 50 kilometers to the south. Nicknamed the "little Hong Kong of Shaanbei" (*Shaanbei xiao Xianggang*), Zhenchuan is about three *li* to the north of the Black Dragon King Temple. The fate of the Black Dragon King Temple has been intricately tied to Zhenchuan's commercial strength. Many of the petty capitalist entrepreneurs who donate large sums of money to the temple today have extensive business dealings in Zhenchuan.

13. I have not been able to verify the historical authenticity of this title. Genuine or spurious, the title is used in the cultural construction of Heilongdawang's divine power and legitimacy. Temple records trace the origin of the Heilongdawang Temple to the Zhengde reign (1506–21) of the Ming dynasty.

14. Many temples were torn down by the villagers following directives from the communes, which allowed the reuse of many of the building materials such as timber and bricks.

15. The Daoist White Cloud Mountain (*Baiyunshan*) in a nearby county remains the most famous and most visited religious site in Shaanbei, but is completely under the county government's control.

16. The temple dormitory can house up to 600 people during the temple festival, including members of four or five opera troupes, local officials and visiting dignitaries, Public Security Bureau officers, temple association officers, and volunteer helpers. It also includes a large kitchen capable of feeding thousands of visitors daily during the temple festival. An average village temple typically has a few rooms attached to the temple for temporary housing during the festival, and one or two makeshift stoves that would be constructed for cooking. Opera troupe members and other visitors would be housed in villagers' homes.

17. For a description and analysis of the temple festival as a folk event production, see Chau (2004).

18. These other six villages all had their own temples in the past but they were also destroyed during the Cultural Revolution. Their initial willingness to join forces with the three Longwanggou villages to rebuild the Heilongdawang Temple was primarily a gesture of submission to the power of Heilongdawang because in the past they had begged for rain at the Heilongdawang Temple. All six villages subsequently rebuilt their village temples as well with some financial subsidy from Longwanggou.

19. These six officers included an accountant, a treasurer, an electrician, a custodian, a purchasing agent, and a driver.

20. To give the reader a sense of the structure of the local state, I list below the names of the bureaus in a typical county government: county general affairs, civic affairs, labor and personnel, cadre affairs, county gazetteer, county archive, jurisprudence, public security (police), planning, statistics, finance, grain, industry, commerce, provisions, construction, economics, transportation, science, education, sports and cultural affairs, hygiene and health care, family planning, broadcasting, agriculture, irrigation and water conservancy, forestry, animal husbandry and herding, village and township enterprises, land administration, public morality advocacy, tobacco sales, environmental protection, mining, foreign trade, structural reform, etc. See Shue (1995) on the phenomenon of "state sprawl" in post-Mao China. See also Blecher and Shue (1996) for a description and analysis of the expansion of a county-level local state in Hebei Province.

21. Shaanbei is not unique in this aspect. Most rural areas have the same problem.

22. See Dean (1993: 103–14) for a detailed account of how the local religious community clashed with the local police at a temple festival in southern Fujian in the early 1980s. The police do not need to work with the Religious Affairs Bureau to crack down on superstitious activities because all religious activities taking place outside of approved venues for religious activities (*zongjiao huodong changsuo*) are in theory illegal.

23. Fights occur frequently at temple festivals due to excessive drinking, the chance meeting of enemies, and disagreements over purchases.

24. The temple has many volunteers who serve as security guards and control traffic and parking. They have red armbands with the word "order-keeping" (*zhian*). Interestingly, the temple purposefully hires a few half-wit young men as security guards because their fierce and crazy demeanor frightens people into listening to them.

25. One local official cultural worker is Mr. Ren, the temple's official literatus consultant for many years. He is well educated and the same age as temple boss Lao Wang (mid-fifties in 1998), and they were primary school classmates. He works for the Zhenchuan Town Cultural Station, collecting folklore and writing articles and plays. Because of their old school ties, Mr. Ren agreed to help Lao Wang with temple affairs whenever his literary and performing arts talents were needed. Mr. Ren's contributions include writing the text of the temple reconstruction commemorative stele and choreographing the Longwanggou Primary School *yangge*

dance troupe, which performs at all Longwanggou temple festivals. His involvement with the temple is an excellent example of a government cultural worker and official socialist propagandist defecting to folk cultural production. During the Maoist era the government subjected these grassroots cultural elites to socialist cultural propaganda while mobilizing them to transform peasant customary traditions. Surprisingly, however, many were also the first to revive local traditions as soon as their role as symbolic-ideological missionaries was temporarily forsaken.

26.   Funding village schools is a priority for many villages that derive sufficient income from either village enterprises (Ruf 1998: 140) or temples.

References

Ahern, Emily Martin. 1981. "The Thai Ti Kong Festival." In *The Anthropology of Taiwanese Society*, edited by Emily Martin Ahern and Hill Gates, pp. 397–425. Stanford, CA: Stanford University Press.

Anagnost, Ann S. 1987. "Politics and Magic in Contemporary China." *Modern China* 13, 1: 40–61.

———. 1994. "The Politics of Ritual Displacement." In *Asian Visions of Authority: Religion and the Modern States of East and Southeast Asia*, edited by Charles F. Keyes, Laurel Kendall, and Helen Hardacre, pp. 221–54. Honolulu: University of Hawai'i Press.

Asad, Talal. 1983. "Anthropological Conceptions of Religion: Reflections on Geertz." *Man* (n.s.) 18, 2: 237–59.

Blecher, Marc, and Vivienne Shue. 1996. *Tethered Deer: Government and Economy in a Chinese County*. Stanford, CA: Stanford University Press.

Chamberlain, Heath B. 1993. "On the Search for Civil Society in China." *Modern China* 19, 2: 199–215.

Chau, Adam Yuet. 2003. "Popular Religion in Shaanbei, North-Central China." *Journal of Chinese Religions*. 31: 39–79.

———. 2004. "Hosting Funerals and Temple Festivals: Folk Event Productions in Contemporary Rural China." *Asian Anthropology* 3: 39–70.

———. 2005. "The Politics of Legitimation in the Revival of Popular Religion in Contemporary Rural China." *Modern China* 31, 2: 236–78.

———. 2006. *Miraculous Response: Doing Popular Religion in Contemporary China*. Stanford, CA: Stanford University Press.

Dean, Kenneth. 1993. *Taoist Ritual and Popular Cults of Southeast China*. Princeton, NJ: Princeton University Press.

———. 1998. *Lord of the Three in One: The Spread of a Cult in Southeast China*. Princeton, NJ: Princeton University Press.

———. 2003. "Local Communal Religion in Contemporary South-east China." *China Quarterly* 174 (Special Issue: Religion in China Today): 338–58.

Duara, Prasenjit. 1988. *Culture, Power, and the State: Rural North China, 1900–1942*. Stanford, CA: Stanford University Press.

Fan Guangchun. 1997. "Dangdai Shaanbei miaohui kaocha yu toushi" (An investigation of contemporary Shaanbei temple fairs). *Yan'an daxue xuebao shehui kexue ban* (Journal of Yan'an University, Social science edition) 1, 19: 97–100.

Feuchtwang, Stephan, and Wang Mingming. 2001. *Grassroots Charisma: Four Local Leaders in China*. London: Routledge.

Gates, Hill. 2000. "Religious Real Estate as Indigenous Civil Space." *Bulletin of the Institute of Ethnology, Academia Sinica*. Special Issue in Honor of Professor Li Yih-yuan's Retirement (I): 313–33.

Goossaert, Vincent. 2000. *Dans les Temples de la Chine: Histoire des Cultes, Vies des Communautés*. Paris: Albin Michel.

Jing, Jun. 1996. *The Temple of Memories: History, Power, and Morality in a Chinese Village*. Stanford, CA: Stanford University Press.

———. 2000 "Environmental Protests in Rural China." In *Chinese Society: Change, Conflict and Resistance*, edited by Elizabeth J. Perry and Mark Selden, pp. 143–60. London: Routledge.

Jordan, David K., and Daniel L. Overmyer. 1986. *The Flying Phoenix: Aspects of Chinese Sectarianism in Taiwan*. Princeton, NJ: Princeton University Press.

Lin, Yi-Min, and Zhanxin Zhang. 1999. "Backyard Profit Centers: The Private Assets of Public Agencies." In *Property Rights and Economic Reform in China*, edited by Jean C. Oi and Andrew G. Walder, pp. 203–25. Stanford, CA: Stanford University Press.

Oi, Jean C. 1999. *Rural China Takes Off: Institutional Foundations of Economic Reform*. Berkeley: University of California Press.

Rankin, Mary Backus. 1986. *Elite Activism and Political Transformation in China: Zhejiang Province, 1865–1911*. Stanford, CA: Stanford University Press.

Rohsenow, Hill Gates. 1973. "Prosperity Settlement: The Politics of Pai-pai in Taipei, Taiwan." Ph.D. dissertation, Department of Anthropology, University of Michigan.

Ruf, Gregory A. 1998. *Cadres and Kin: Making a Socialist Village in West China, 1921–1991*. Stanford, CA: Stanford University Press.

Saich, Anthony. 2000. "Negotiating the State: The Development of Social Organizations in China." *China Quarterly* 161: 124–41.

Scott, James L. 1998. *Seeing Like a State: How Certain Schemes to Improve the Human Condition Have Failed*. New Haven, CT: Yale University Press.

Seaman, Gary. 1978. *Temple Organization in a Chinese Village*. Asian Folklore and Social Life Monographs, vol. 101. Taipei: Orient Cultural Service.

Shue, Vivienne. 1995. "State Sprawl: The Regulatory State and Social Life in a Small Chinese City." In *Urban Spaces in Contemporary China: The Potential for Autonomy and Community in Post-Mao China*, edited by Deborah S. Davis et al., pp. 90–112. Cambridge, UK: Woodrow Wilson Center Press / Cambridge University Press.

Strand, David. 1990. "Mediation, Representation, and Repression: Local Elites in 1920s Beijing." In *Chinese Local Elites and Patterns of Dominance*, edited by Joseph W. Esherick and Mary Backus Rankin, pp. 216–35. Berkeley: University of California Press.

Tsai, Lily Lee. 2002. "Cadres, Temples and Lineage Institutions, and Governance in Rural China." *China Journal* 48: 1–27.

Wank, David L. 1999. *Commodifying Communism: Business, Trust, and Politics in a Chinese City*. New York: Cambridge University Press.

Watson, James L. 1985 "Standardizing the Gods: The Promotion of T'ien Hou ('Empress of Heaven') along the South China Coast, 960–1960." In *Popular Culture in Late Imperial China*, edited by David Johnson, pp. 292–324. Berkeley: University of California Press.

Weller, Robert P. 1987. "The Politics of Ritual Disguise: Repression and Response in Taiwanese Popular Religion." *Modern China* 13, 1: 17–39.

———. 1999. *Alternate Civilities: Democracy and Culture in China and Taiwan*. Boulder, CO: Westview.

Yang, Mayfair Mei-hui. 2004. "Spatial Struggles: Postcolonial Complex, State Disenchantment, and Popular Reappropriation of Space in Rural Southeast China." *Journal of Asian Studies* 63, 3: 719–55.

CHAPTER 10

The Creation and Reemergence
of Qigong in China

UTIRARUTO OTEHODE

THE REEMERGENCE OF QIGONG since the 1980s is viewed by scholars as an important social phenomenon in China's economic reform and social liberalization. There are two competing interpretations of its reemergence among scholars in China. One, by historians of qigong who consider it a Chinese traditional medical treatment or a traditional culture, sees its reemergence as reflecting widespread popular interest in pursuing good health and well-being after the exhaustion of the Cultural Revolution (Ma 1983; Zhao 1987). The other interpretation claims that the term *qigong* is being used as a cover of respectability for superstitious (*mixin*) and antiscientific (*weikexue*) activities (Zhang 1996; Yu 2000). This interpretation became the state's position in 1999 with the crackdown on Falungong as both a qigong group and a cult (*xiejiao*).[1] Among scholars in Japan and North America there is convergence on the view that qigong's reemergence reflects changes in Chinese society since the late 1970s. Hishida Masaharu (2000) sees it as part of the broader emergence of new religions as communist ideology weakens and the value system diversifies. For Nancy Chen (1995) and Jian Xu (1999), qigong's reemergence signifies the appearance of private space in urban China, and the declining power of politics and growth of individual power.

The views of both Chinese and non-Chinese scholars are based on highly selective and partial observations that fail to grasp qigong's reemergence in broader context. The view of qigong as an historical phenomenon reflecting the retreat of the state from society ignores how its initial formation and shifting position have been intertwined with the state from the founding of the People's Republic of China. The interpretations of qigong and its position in the 1950s are quite different from those since the 1980s. To understand this, it is necessary to locate qigong within both the overarching modernization policies of the state and Chinese Communist Party (Party) and the specific political, ideological, and social contexts of each period.

This chapter eschews categorical definitions and characterizations of qigong as these are variable and have been moving between the dichotomies of science/religion, modernity/tradition, and materialism/idealism in the different contexts over the past fifty years. Instead, it illuminates these shifts by examining the dynamic institutionalization of qigong in two periods: in the 1950s during the first decade of the People's Republic of China and during the introduction of a market economy and social liberalization since the late 1970s. The analysis pays special attention to the roles of high-level officials and qigong-related organizations that operate behind the scenes and are crucial to the way that qigong has developed and relates to religion in each period.

The first part focuses on institutionalization in the 1950s. It describes how qigong therapy (qigong liaofa) emerged from traditional body cultivation practices to become known as a national medical heritage (zuguo yixue yichan), and analyzes the modernization of qigong by tracing its history and positioning vis-à-vis modern science. The second part looks at the period from the late 1970s to the 1990s when qigong was legitimated anew, grew into a broad social movement, and most recently has returned to its original Buddhist and Daoist sources. The conclusion summarizes the understandings that can be gleaned from the different interpretations of qigong and its institutionalization over the second half of the twentieth century.

The data mostly come from qigong literature collected in China in 2002. Several key journals are: New Chinese Medicine (Xin zhongyiyao) (1950–58), one of the most important academic journals of traditional Chinese medicine;[2] Qigong and Science (Qigong yu kexue) (1982–93), sponsored by the Guangzhou City Qigong and Science Research Association (Guangzhoushi qigong kexue yanjiu xiehui), the best-known qigong journal in the early 1980s; Chinese Qigong Science (Zhongguo qigong kexue) (1994–2000), a national journal with comprehensive coverage of qigong research and news; Chinese Somatic Science (Zhongguo renti kexue) (1990–97), a major academic journal of the science of the human body sponsored by the Chinese Academic Association of the Science of the Human Body (Zhongguo renti kexue xuehui) and Shanghai Jiaotong University. A large number of other sources dating from 1914 to 2004 are also referenced on the topics of Buddhist and Daoist body cultivation, Chinese traditional medicines, and qigong.

Emergence and Institutionalization of Qigong Therapy in the 1950s

QIGONG'S CHANGING STATUS: FROM BODY CULTIVATION METHOD TO NATIONAL MEDICAL HERITAGE

The pursuit of modernity in China began in earnest in the early twentieth century as many traditional values were revisited and restructured. Old bodily practice methods, such as *zuochan*, *liandan*, *shoushen*, *fuqi*, and *neigong* that originated from Buddhism, Daoism, Confucianism, medicine, and martial arts were labeled as cultivation methods (*xiulianfa*) and practiced as religious activities, for medical treatment, and as bodily training. Despite different definitions due to their various origins and techniques, they all fell broadly within the value systems of Buddhism, Daoism, or Chinese traditional medicine. With the increasing influence of such modern concepts as science and religion in the early twentieth century, these largely religious practices faced an imperative to redefine themselves.

Well-known examples of this redefinition are *Meditation* (*Jingzuofa*) by Jiang Weiqiao (1873–1958) and Chen Yingning's *Study of Unworldliness* (*Xianxue*). Jiang was active from 1901 in the Society of Chinese Education (*Zhongguo jiaoyuhui*) in promoting modern education in China. In 1912, he became chief secretary of education in the Provisional Government of the Republic of China (*Zhonghua minguo linshi zhengfu*). He understood Japanese, and visited Japan several times to study Japan's modern educational system (Chen 1986). Influenced by a popular body cultivation practice in Japan called *Seizahō* developed by Okada Torajiro, Jiang wrote *Yinshizi's Meditation Method* (*Yinshizi jingzuofa*) to record his experience of Buddhist body cultivation. His book was very popular and was reprinted twenty-one times between 1914 and 1927. Chen Yingning (1880–1969) was a famous Daoist thinker. In the Republic of China (1912–), he developed *xianxue*, which focused on body cultivation and he was active reforming Daoism and establishing organizations to propagate it.

Intellectuals, especially in Shanghai, were greatly interested in these books that used popular language and scientific interpretations to describe old practice methods from Buddhism and Daoism. Most of these books were translations of publications from Japan, itself a model of modernity for China. For instance, books describing Okada Torajirō and Fujita Reisai's *Meditation* (*Jingzuofa*), very popular in Japan from the late

Meiji period, were translated into Chinese and read extensively in China.[3] Jiang's *Yinshizi's Meditation* was one of many books styled after Okada's book *Seizahō* and was widely appreciated for its vernacular text, modern appeal, and production in China. Through the huge reception of his book, Jiang transformed the body cultivation practice originating from Buddhism into *jingzuofa* (meditation) by stressing its "scientific nature" (*kexuexing*). A similar work was Chen Yingning's *Xianxue* (The study of unworldiness), which evolved from Daoist body cultivation to position itself as a special science (*teshu de kexue*) (Yin 1917; Yao 1990).

Jiang and Chen were both keenly aware of the relationship between body cultivation practice and modern science. Jiang was impressed by the scientific quality of Okada-style *Seizahō* and reinterpreted Buddhist body cultivation using scientific terms and sought to prove its value through modern scientific approaches. As for Chen, his endeavor to save Daoism from decay led him to redevelop Daoist body cultivation as a "special science" that was equivalent to modern science. This shows how indigenous body cultivation practices were restructured by both accepting the authority of modern science and seeking to cast their values and institutions as equivalent to modern science.

Attempts to relate traditional body cultivation practice and modern science continued in the People's Republic after 1949. The names and interpretations of indigenous body cultivation practice were reformed and legitimized as methods of medical treatment and physical training. Such newly invented terms as deep breathing therapy (*shenhuxi liaofa*), breathing massage (*huxi anmo yundong*), breathing therapy (*huxi yangshengfa*), meditation therapy (*jingzuo liaofa*), and qigong therapy (*qigong liaofa*) were introduced as medical gymnastics (*yiliao tiyu*) and preventive medicine (*yufang yiliao*) in *New Chinese Medicine* and other journals. Among them, "qigong therapy" as a technical term was retained and its methods were extensively developed and integrated into the state's medical system. Ma Jiren (1983) has pointed out that the terms "qigong" and "qigong therapy" were rare but could be found in the records of Daoism and martial arts, as well as Republican-era medical books.[4]

However, the term "qigong therapy" that appeared in the 1950s and was institutionalized within the state's medical system had no connection with its previous usage and contexts. Previously qigong had been used mainly in martial arts and was called both *yangqi* and *lianqi*. The former referred to a Daoist training method and the latter a martial arts training method (Ma 1983). In the 1950s the term *qigong* acquired a completely different interpretation and positioning through the restructuring of body cultivation practice into a medical treatment. An individual called Liu Guizhen and his personal experience of coping with illness greatly influenced the new state's medical and modernization policies.

Liu played an important role in introducing qigong as a body cultivation practice popular among the common people to state organizations. Liu was a local government official in Nangong county of Hebei province. In 1948, he was diagnosed with gastric ulcer, pulmonary tuberculosis, and neurasthenia. Despite receiving various medical treatments he did not recover. He finally went back to his rural hometown hoping to recuperate and there he happened to hear from an old villager of a body cultivation practice called *neiyanggong*. After only three months of practice he was completely cured of all his illnesses. The following year, he was assigned to be secretary of a local cadre sanitarium and began teaching body cultivation to the cadre patients. Their rapid recoveries confirmed its high therapeutic effectiveness and attracted the attention of other officials and the local health office.

With this new support, Liu started to conduct research on *neiyanggong* and other methods of body cultivation in order to document them as medical treatments. He referenced numerous old body cultivation practices and incorporated knowledge of Chinese traditional medicine (*zhongyi*) and Western medicine (*xiyi*) to document the specific methods of cultivation and give them names. An example is "health maintenance training method" (*baojiangong*). Liu drew on the indigenous cultivation methods of *neigong*, *daoyinfa*, and *shier duanjin* to compile a qigong practice method consisting of eighteen movements. This qigong practice method was subsequently endorsed by a Soviet professor of sports medicine at Beijing Medical University (*Beijing yixueyuan*) as according with the structure of the human body. The professor added three movements and thereafter this practice method with twenty-one movements became known as *baojiangong* (Liu 1957). Liu ascribed the term "qigong therapy" to this traditional body cultivation practice because he considered it to be a medical treatment. It was this *baojiangong* that was later compiled and recorded in the *Outline of Chinese Traditional Medicine* (*Zhongyixue gailun*) as a qigong therapy with "a long history" (Nanjing zhongyi xueyuan 1959).

Liu claimed that numerous methods of body cultivation popular among the people were prototypes of qigong, and he sought to remove their "superstitious and bad elements" (*mixin zaopo*) by analyzing them from a medical perspective and calling them qigong therapies to signify their applicability as medical treatments (Liu 1957). He removed the superstitious and bad elements through a series of reforms that included: replacing the spells and words derived from Buddhism and Daoism with modern terms and Chinese traditional medicine terminology; permitting body cultivation to be taught to women; and shifting the teaching of body cultivation from an oral tradition and apprenticeship system to printed materials and modern educational methods. Specifically, Liu removed religious terminology and Buddhist and Daoist rituals and interpretations, leaving only the instructions for body cultivation that he then explained in medical terms. These changes successfully integrated qigong with the state's key policy agenda to "study and develop the national medical heritage" (*jicheng he fayang zuguo yixue yichan*) by transforming it into a legitimate "national medical heritage" and establishing body cultivation as a form of medical treatment. This policy agenda promoted a practical role for Chinese traditional medicine in the national public health sector and the scientization of medical theories and the modernization of medical institutions. It especially encouraged efforts to study and develop traditional medical knowledge while raising the status of the practitioners of Chinese traditional medicine and their organizations. These national policies exerted a strong influence on Liu Guizhen's qigong therapy.

Liu was a pioneer in institutionalizing qigong in the national medical system. His research work and medical activities on qigong from 1949 gradually gained recognition and garnered praise from officials in local government health offices and other agencies. With the support of the Tangshan city government and health office, Liu rented a place in a city-run worker's sanitarium (*Tangshanshi gongren liaoyangyuan*) and founded the Tangshan City Qigong Sanitarium (*Tangshanshi qigong liaoyangsuo*). Operating under the auspices of the Tangshan City Health Office (*Tangshanshi weishengju*), the sanitarium was the first qigong organization in China. It was not only a clinic for patients seeking qigong therapy, but also a key site for communicating knowledge of qigong. It activities expanded as patients started coming from Beijing, Tianjin, and other big cities and the range of illnesses treated by qigong therapy increased. Twice a year Liu was dispatched to Beijing by the city health office to give a report on the qigong sanitarium to the Ministry of Health, in order to highlight its contribution to the development of the national medical heritage.

Various outreach activities further disseminated knowledge of qigong. In September 1954 the health office, in accordance with the new national policy of "Western medicine studying Chinese medicine" (*xiyi xuexi zhongyi*), invited many doctors of Western medicine to study qigong therapies at the Tangshan Qigong Sanitarium. A similar activity in May 1955 brought doctors of Western medicine from many sanitariums to the Tangshan Qigong Sanitarium for three months' training in qigong therapies. These doctors went on to introduce qigong therapies to their own sanitariums and soon sanitariums all over China started to use qigong, including such prestigious ones as the Haibin Central Government's Sanitarium (*Haibin zhonggong zhongyang zhishu xiuyangsuo*), and Beijing 124 Sanitarium (*Beijing yaoersi liaoyangyuan*). In this way the Tangshan Qigong Sanitarium and its qigong activities became nationally renowned.

In 1950 the first National Conference on Public Health established the basic principle that traditional medicine and modern Western medicine should be harmonized.[5] In 1954, Mao Zedong and other national leaders praised the contributions of traditional medicine to public health and ordered the development of the national medical heritage. This led to, among other things, increased status and pay for doctors of traditional Chinese medicine and their increasing employment in hospitals, the expanded use and development of Chinese herb medicine, the documentation of Chinese traditional medicines, and the establishment of many research institutes on Chinese traditional medicine.

In December 1955, the Tangshan Qigong Sanitarium received an award at the founding ceremony of the China Academy of Traditional Chinese Medicine (*Zhongyi yanjiuyuan*), the top research institute of traditional medicine and directly under the Department of Health. The award cited the sanitarium's qigong activities as an "important contribution to research on the national medical heritage." The ceremony itself was a large affair, attended by four hundred people, including high-level officials, intellectuals, medical technicians, and medical professionals from the Soviet Union and Vietnam (Hua 1995). This state recognition not only furthered research on qigong but also the dissemination of knowledge about it. From 1956, papers on qigong therapy were regularly published in national and local journals of Chinese traditional medicine, such as *New Chinese Medicine* (*Xin zhongyiyao*) and *Shanghai Chinese Medicine* (*Shanghai zhongyiyao*). The national Ministry of Health and local health offices organized qigong seminars throughout the country. The following year the national Ministry of Health mandated the establishment of the Shanghai Qigong Sanitarium (*Shanghai qigong liaoyangsuo*), which provided systematic training to become a qigong master.[6] Trainees, who came from all over the country, were mostly doctors of traditional medicine but some doctors of Western medicine attended as well. After training they returned to their own hospitals and clinics to practice qigong therapy. All of this dramatically deepened the institutionalization of qigong.

Thus far, I have described how the indigenous body cultivation techniques practiced by a common villager were communicated to a local official who reformulated them as qigong therapy, which became institutionalized in the state's national medical system. Key to this institutionalization was the legitimation of qigong theory through its transformation into a "national medical heritage," which enabled it to obtain recognition from the state's modern medical system, thereby creating a space for it to be active.

REVISION OF QIGONG'S "HISTORY" AND ELABORATION
OF QIGONG'S "THEORETIC PROOF"

To be institutionalized in the modern state's medical system, qigong had to conform to two expectations. First, it needed a proper history as a "national medical heritage." Second it needed theoretic proof of its efficacy. The revision of qigong history and its theoretical elaboration started in the 1950s along with the development of the Party's view of history and its modernization policy. Qigong quickly conformed to the state maxim that "the great Chinese people are creators of history and therefore the main actors on the historical stage." To achieve this conformity it was necessary to sever the links to Buddhist and Daoist body cultivation practices.[7] The connection with Buddhism and Daoism was problematic because the state linked religion to superstition and idealism and labeled it a product of the "feudal class." Thus doctors of Chinese traditional medicine promoted new views of qigong therapy that denied the link to religion. One view located it in the working class by maintaining that "qigong therapy was born from the knowledge of the great working people but, unfortunately, was exploited by Buddhism and Daoism and cloaked in superstition and mystery" (Xu 1954: 26). Another simply covered the religious connection by noting that "qigong's origin is no longer verifiable" (Zeng 1954: 23). In this way, qigong therapy was recognized by the state as part of the Chinese traditional medicine establishment.

During the process of institutionalization, qigong's origins were integrated with that of traditional medicine in order to give it a history appropriate for a national medical heritage. The state's policy to develop a national medical heritage in the 1950s focused mainly on traditional medicine. The state emphasized that local health offices should "sift the national medical heritage" (zhengli zuoguo yixue yichan) to discern and classify secret formulas popular among the people. Viable ones were identified and entered into the Encyclopedia of Chinese Medicine (Zhongyao yaodian). During this process, qigong therapy together with secret formulas (mifang) of producing medicines were recognized and tagged by local health offices as "national medical heritages." Qigong therapy was further categorized as a component of Chinese traditional medicine and its "history," it was claimed, was documented in Huangdi neijing, the earliest classic of Chinese traditional medicine, and all subsequent famous works of traditional medicine.[8] Thus, the medical treatment named "qigong" by Liu Guizhen acquired a long literary record of more than two thousand years, the same time span as that of traditional medicine.

At the same time qigong therapy also acquired a theoretical basis that was "appropriate" for a modern state's medical system and that reflected the state's approach to modernizing traditional medicine. Pavlov's theory (*Bafuluofu xueshuo*) was invoked to provide a modern and scientific theory basis for qigong. This stemmed, in part, from the national movement underway in the 1950s to "learn from the Soviet Union" (*xuexi Sulian*), which involved, among other things, the extensive study and wide application of theories of Russian scientists in the medical field. For example, the Ministry of Health (*Zhongyang weishengbu*) and the Chinese Academy of Sciences (*Zhongguo kexueyuan*) sponsored a 35-day Pavlovian theory study workshop (Ministry of Health, Pavlov Theory Study Association) in Beijing in fall 1953 for twenty-two professors, researchers, and doctors of physiology, psychology, and clinical medicine. It proclaimed Pavlovian theory to be a "great and materialist physiology and the only right theory leading the development of medical science in the New China" (Ministry of Health 1954).

Another reason for the use of Pavlov's theory is that the mechanism of qigong therapy could be "properly" explained by the Pavlovian theories of conditioned response (*tiaojian fanshe xueshuo*) and hypnosis (*cuimian xueshuo*). The effectiveness of qigong for treating neurasthenia was attributed to the stimulation and restraining of the cerebral cortex through the therapy's breathing and exercise techniques. Also, just as Pavlov's hypnosis theory claimed that doctors' words stimulated the cerebral cortex of patients, so it was claimed that movements caused by qigong in the respiratory system and internal organs stimulated the cerebral cortex (Chen 1958). Thus, Pavlov's theories provided scientific "proof" for qigong therapy, further sweeping away all possible connections with Buddhism and Daoism (Chen 1958). So it was that qigong therapy acquired a scientific explanation as part of the state's huge modernization project, thereby further institutionalizing it in the state's medical establishment.

The process begun in the 1950s by Liu Guizhen of the Tangshan Qigong Sanitarium, Chen Tao and Jiang Weiqiao of Shanghai Qigong Sanitarium, and others to furnish qigong with a "correct" history and "appropriate" theory also reflects how China re-created itself as a modern state. Phenomena that embody the attributes of "national" and "Chinese" on the one hand, and "scientific" and "modern" on the other hand, are an ideal of modern China envisioned by the Party. Within this framework, qigong was reborn, drawing on traditional Chinese medicine's history for the former and Pavlov's theories for the latter. Furthermore, in order for qigong to retain its uniqueness and be differentiated from such modern sports as radio gymnastics, its advocates had to constantly revisit qigong's Buddhist and Daoist sources and revise its practices, as the next section discusses.

Revival of Qigong in China from the Late 1970s

During the Cultural Revolution radicals criticized qigong therapy as feu-
dalistic and superstitious (*fengjian mixin*) and suppressed it. Those who had
propounded qigong therapy were thrown into prison and qigong-related
organizations were either shut down or merged with other organizations.
The initiator of qigong therapy, Liu Guizhen, was called the "creator of
the 'poisonous' qigong" (*qigong daducao chuangshiren*) and his book criticized as "a tool for publicizing bourgeois obscenity" (*xuanchuan zichanjieji yinhui sixiang de daducao*). Liu himself was expelled from the Party and
sent to a reform-through-labor (*laodong gaizao*) camp while the Tangshan
Qigong Sanitarium was closed (Liu 1984; She 1999).

Despite this, qigong swiftly revived after the Cultural Revolution both
in the state and in society. Liu Guizhen and other qigong practitioners
who had been persecuted during the Cultural Revolution were rehabilitated and they once again began their qigong activities. Qigong's health
and therapeutic effects caught the public's attention and people started
practicing qigong in parks and other public places. Meanwhile, a heated
debate broke out among high-level officials in the central state on the importance of qigong research with the revival of qigong-related organizations forcefully advocated by a group of influential Party members. In this
new phase of its development, the institutionalization of qigong therapy
proceeded not only within the state and but also increasingly began to
involve more organizations and individuals in society. New connections
brought private qigong organizations under direct state supervision and
private groups that had thus far been outside of qigong fields came to be
part of its development. Qigong thus entered a dynamic period of institutionalization characterized by organizations and activities in both the
state and society, and dissemination throughout the country, leading to its
full-scale revival in the early 1990s, when it was claimed there were 100
million qigong practitioners. This section will introduce qigong's legitimatization process in the state realm, its institutionalization and popularization in societal and private areas, and its return to Buddhist and Daoist
sources.

LEGITIMATIZATION OF QIGONG'S STATUS
IN THE REALM OF THE STATE

The biggest challenge for the state following the Cultural Revolution
has been to address the kind of modernization that it should pursue and
the priorities and emphases in its modernization agenda. Qigong was located in these debates through the issues of the modernization (*xiandaihua*)
of Chinese traditional medicine and the government's position on the research of supernatural power (*teyi gongneng*).

As mentioned above, modernizing Chinese traditional medicine through the application of science and technology was state policy in the 1950s and remained so all through the Cultural Revolution. After the Cultural Revolution, the question of how to achieve the modernization of traditional medicine came to be openly discussed among doctors of traditional medicine. The national policy of "integrating Chinese and Western medicine" (*zhong xi yi jiehe*) that was formulated in the 1950s was now challenged as possibly leading to the "Westernizing" (*xiyihua*) of traditional medicine, a fate depicted as tantamount to its demise. A search began for a Chinese style of "modernization" or "scientification" without influence from the West. Important in this quest was Lü Binkui, a famous practitioner of traditional medical and director of the State Administration of Chinese Medicine and Pharmacology (*Guojia zhongyiyao guanliju*), the highest government authority of traditional medicine and directly under the State Council. Lü proposed the introduction of the latest concepts from modern science and technology, including physics, chemistry, and biology to modernize Chinese traditional medicine and legitimize a "Chinese-style modernization" (*Zhongguoshi de xiandaihua*) (Lü 1980). His goal was to build a new theoretical system to replace traditional medicine's indigenous theories of dialectical dualism (*yinyang*) and the five elements (*wuxing*)—metal, wood, water, fire, and earth.

Lü attached much value to an experiment in 1979 by a physics researcher from Shanghai that confirmed that the *qi* emitted in qigong therapy is an actual substance. For Lü this experiment embodied the sort of progressive steps needed to document the scientific nature of traditional medicine in terms of physics and biology. He lobbied leading officials of the State Council, Ministry of Health, and Chinese Academy of Sciences on the importance of qigong research and proposed the establishment of qigong research institutes in the national medical system and science research institutes. While his efforts did not lead to the revision of the national policy of integrating Chinese and Western medicine, they did establish a link between qigong research and the modernization of traditional medicine and led to the state attaching importance to qigong research. In 1980, the Ministry of Health took the lead in setting up qigong institutes. The central state approved detailed proposals to establish qigong research offices and laboratories inside various state organs and to set up national qigong academic bodies. Accordingly, the first national qigong academic body, the All-China Association for Chinese Medicine Qigong Science Research Institute (*Zhonghua quanguo zhongyi xuehui qigong kexue yanjiuhui*), was founded the next year with Lü as its head.

Another context in which qigong emerged on the agenda of the central state was a debate over supernatural power (*teyi gongneng*). The debate began in 1979 and involved many journalists, intellectuals, high officials, and such important state organs as *People's Daily* (*Renmin ribao*), the Ministry of Propaganda (*Xuanchuanbu*), and the State Council. It centered on whether or not clairvoyance—specifically the capacity of ears to recognize written characters—existed. At stake were two key issues. One was whether research on supernatural power should be considered idealistic or materialistic. This debate reflected the fundamental issue of the extent to which materialism could be adhered to as the basic ideology of the communist state. The other debate was whether research on supernatural power should be conducted inside national scientific research organizations and whether the research activities and results should be publicized in the mass media. This latter debate transformed into questions over the extent of scientists' freedom of research and freedom of the press. Heated debates continued for four years until the Ministry of Propaganda approved guidelines that stipulated "no promoting," "no criticizing" and "no encouraging" research on supernatural power (Ministry of Propaganda 1982). Commonly referred to as the "Three No's Policy" (*sanbu zhengce*), the guidelines were seen as a compromise between the two opposing views of supernatural power (Shen 2001).

With this compromise in place, supporters of supernatural-power research, including such high-ranking officials as the celebrated military scientist Qian Xuesen and the famous general Zhang Zhenhuan, appealed to the head of the Ministry of Propaganda and the general secretary of the Party for the removal of all restrictions on research on supernatural power.[9] Permission was granted to some researchers for small-scale activities. The Ministry of Propaganda also permitted the findings from this supernatural-power research to be disseminated among interested scientists and researchers for review and discussion. However, other rules and regulations against such research remained in place and so supernatural-power research, while tolerated, still lacked legal protection and clear policy support.

To enhance the status of the research as legitimate Qian sought to reinforce the links between supernatural power and qigong and Chinese traditional medicine. First, he advanced a new definition of qigong that maintained that it not only was efficacious in curing diseases and managing health but also gave people supernatural power. He broadly grouped qigong into two categories. One is extrasensory perception (ESP) as in the "ability to recognize words by ear" (*erduo renzi*). The other category, psychokinesis, involves, for example, the "ability to overcome the barrier of space" (*tupo kongjian zhang'ai*). With a connection between qigong and supernatural power established by this new definition, Qian created a new category of science called human body science (*renti kexue*) that integrated the three research fields—research on "supernatural power," research on qigong, and research on Chinese traditional medicine (Qian 1988). Around 1985, an expert Committee on Science of the Human Body (*Renti kexue zhuanjia xiaozu*) was set up under the direct control of the State Council, and subsequently two organizations were established: the China Academic Association on Science of the Human Body (*Zhongguo renti kexue xuehui*), under the supervision of the Commission of Science Technology and Industry for National Defense (*Guofang kexue jishu gongye weiyuanhui*); and the China Qigong Science Association (*Zhongguo qigong kexue yanjiuhui*), under the National Economic Restructure and Reform Commission (*Guojia jingji tizhi gaige weiyuanhui*).

Two aspects of the above description of the institutionalization of qigong in the realm of the state need to be emphasized. First, the creation of a human body science dissolved structural conflicts between supernatural-power research and the state's fundamental principle of materialism, thereby further legitimizing research on supernatural power within state organizations. Second, by bringing together qigong, Chinese traditional medicine, and supernatural-power research, human body science moved close to the space of popular culture by bringing myths of immortality and eternal soul widespread among the people into this new category of science. These myths then became part of the redefinition and reinterpretation of qigong.

THE INSTITUTIONALIZATION OF QIGONG IN SOCIETY

Qigong's institutionalization proceeded in both the state and society after 1979 when qigong research was first proposed to the central state authorities. Within the state, institutionalization proceeded in the traditional medical establishment through the creation of qigong research institutions, qigong clinics, and courses added to the curriculum of Chinese traditional medicine. However, due to its origins in body cultivation practices, qigong was constrained by a paucity of intellectual and human resources and its institutionalization in the state was limited. Although new links developed between qigong activities in the state's medical system and groups in society, these links were weak and so qigong's institutionalization in the state has few implications for the growth of qigong as a popular movement.

The institutionalization of qigong in society developed in qigong practitioner groups and academic organizations. An example of the former is Guolin New Qigong (*Guolin xinqigong*), a practitioner group enjoying much national popularity in the early 1980s. Guolin New Qigong was formed by a professional artist, Guo Lin (1909–84), and got its start in

Beijing in the 1970s. Guo Lin was diagnosed with uterine cancer and operated on several times. In the 1960s she started to seriously practice the
body cultivation she had learned as a child from her grandfather, a Daoist
priest (*chujia daoshi*). Based on this knowledge and her own practice, she
formed the movements of her Guolin New Qigong and in 1970 began to
teach it in Beijing's Dongdan and Ditan parks to people suffering from
various ailments (Guo 1980). Many were cured and they began to teach
Guolin New Qigong to colleagues and relatives in their offices and hometowns. The number of practitioners rose sharply and they spontaneously
began to set up training classes and study groups in the public parks of
many cities.

These training classes and study groups were the prototype of the
qigong practitioner groups that emerged in the early 1980s. Organizers of
those groups often were once very ill and then had been cured by qigong
practice. Such groups have neither legal status nor official registration.
Although groups appear regularly for qigong practice in specific parks,
they are characterized by rapid membership turnover. In this way, qigong
practice groups organize and develop swiftly, facilitating extensive connections among enthusiastic practitioners of various professions—Party members, bureaucrats, soldiers, workers, and others. These practitioners and the
groups they formed played a key role in disseminating qigong among private individuals. An account of this found in Guo Lin's essay (1983) "A
Collection of Examples of New Qigong Therapy Cures" (*Xin qigong liaofa
zhiliao bingli xuanjie*) is the case of an engineer called Huang Huaizhang
from Xi'an who was diagnosed with breast cancer on a business trip to
Beijing in 1975. After failing to recover following Western medical treatment, she began to learn qigong practice directly from Guo Lin. Her illness soon stabilized and she returned to work in Xi'an in 1980 where the
story of her recovery from cancer was published in the *Xi'an Evening News*
(*Xi'an wanbao*). Many cancer patients began to beseech her to teach them
Guolin New Qigong. She was permitted to organize Guolin New Qigong
training classes in her factory and was assigned as the trainer. Over the next
three years more than 1,500 people participated in a dozen training classes.
Another example is Wan Niwen, a junior high school teacher in Chengdu,
who was diagnosed with breast cancer. She started to practice Guolin New
Qigong in 1979 and then returned to Chengdu to start a training class with
the approval of Guo Lin. Over the next two years she trained more than
seven hundred people. She then established a Guolin New Qigong study
group (*Chengdu xinqigong yanjiuzu*) composed of practitioners with the approval of the Chengdu Institute of Chinese Traditional Medicine (*Chengdu
zhongyi xuehui*), and with the cooperation of the Chengdu College of
Traditional Medicine (*Chengdu zhongyi xueyuan*) and Sichuan Medical

College (*Sichuan yixueyuan*). This study group supported research on the use of qigong to treat gastritis and cancer.

Shortly thereafter, qigong researchers from universities and research institutes also quickly began to establish academic associations. Key were the Beijing Qigong Institute and the All-China Association of Chinese Medicine Qigong Science Research Institutes. These associations connected doctors of traditional medicine, qigong practitioners, university researchers of qigong, and government officials in nationwide networks. The members who are researchers conduct their qigong research in the organizations that employ them, including universities and research institutes, thereby expanding sites of qigong research within the state's educational and research sectors. These associations developed rich links with high officials that gave qigong access to state resources to disseminate qigong in society. The composition of the second-term board members of the All-China Association of Chinese Medicine Qigong Research Institutes indicates these high level links: it included the former ministers of Public Security and Public Health, the director of the Institute of Research on Religion of the Chinese Academy of Social Sciences, the vice president of the National Navy Hospital, the vice-director of the National Sports Committee, and other high officials, as well as well-known scholars from the Party, government, and army. In addition to these high level links, associations also developed links with the aforementioned study groups and their qigong masters who became important collaborators in qigong research and were invited to universities and research institutes to participate in experiments. This greatly enhanced the social position and reputation of the qigong masters and gave them access to new resources in the state to propagate their qigong far and wide in society.

The career of one local qigong master, Yan Xin (b. 1950) from Sichuan province, illustrates the link between local practitioner groups and the associations in the dissemination of qigong in society. Yan studied Chinese traditional medicine at the Chengdu College of Traditional Medicine from 1973 to 1977 and started to work at the Chongqing Research Institute of Traditional Medicine (*Chongqing zhongyi yanjiusuo*) in 1981. He started using qigong therapy in his clinical practice and developed a reputation in the area as a qigong master. His reports on his activities in 1985 in the journal *Qigong and Science* (*Qigong yu kexue*) brought him to the attention of qigong researchers in Qinghua University (*Qinghua daxue*) who invited him to participate in experiments there. The results of the experiments were subsequently reported at length in the leading newspaper *Guangming Daily* (*Guangming ribao*). Yan became famous overnight. He was then encouraged by General Zhang Zhenhuan, chairman of the China Qigong Science Association, to travel around the country giving speeches on his qigong practice in large stadiums and auditoriums and even to speak in Japan and the United States. This significantly enhanced his visibility and reputation and aided the rapid dissemination of his publications on his qigong training methods among the people.

These associations were very active and successful in promoting these new methods of qigong practice by documenting the training techniques of masters and then establishing practitioners' groups to spread them. A closer look at the Beijing Qigong Institute (*Beijing qigong yanjiuhui*) illustrates this. It was set up jointly in 1979 by the Beijing Municipal Trade Union (*Beijingshi zonggonghui*) and Beijing Science and Technology Association (*Beijingshi kexue jishu xiehui*). In the following ten years, it started fifty-six qigong practitioner groups as its sub-branches all over the country and trained more than 10,000 qigong masters in China's twenty-eight provinces, autonomous regions, and centrally administered municipalities (*Zhongguo qigong kexue* 1994, 12: 2). In December 1980 it also organized the first national qigong training class (*diyici quanguo qigong fudaozhan peixunban*) in which 144 participants from all over China received training in the qigong technique of *yiquan zhanzhuang gong* at the Beijing Workers Stadium (*Beijing gongren tiyuchang*) (*Zhongguo qigong kexue* 1994, 12: 3). This training class also reveals an interest convergence at work among the various organizations and officials. The class was actually commissioned by the All-China Trade Union (*Zhonghua quanguo zonggonghui*), whose officials were on the board of the Beijing Qigong Institute. This enabled the Beijing Qigong Institute to have access to this public resource while the trade union received some of the profits taken in as management fees.[10] In this manner, such qigong academic organizations as the Beijing Qigong Institute constituted a system that was highly organized and wide in scope and that used the media and training classes to disseminate qigong training methods nationally.

The associations also further rationalized qigong training methods. The qigong training methods that originated from Buddhism and Daoism were registered as the Qigong Research Team (*Gongfa yanjiuzu*) in the Beijing Qigong Institute. This Qigong Research Team contained such practitioners' groups as the Daoist group (*dayan qigong*), the Buddhist group (*huiliangong*), and Tibetan cabalistic group (*mixiugong*). Those qigong practitioners' groups and their masters taught qigong to people from all walks of life in parks, squares, private residential areas, and school sports grounds. Some practitioners' groups even established offices and built comprehensive organizational structures to quickly convey new methods of qigong practices to a wide range of people. The well-known Falungong group, with its extensive organizational structure, is one of the most prominent examples of this trend. Falungong was registered with the China Qigong

Science Association in 1992 and then developed into a huge qigong organization that claimed hundreds of millions of practitioners.

The crucial point in the foregoing discussion is that it was the qigong academic associations that provided administrative legitimacy for the activities of the qigong practitioners' groups. That this was possible stemmed from policies adopted in the 1970s that enabled private associations and organizations to emerge. Thanks to this policy, their scale and numbers increased dramatically in the 1980s. This, in turn, created an increasingly pressing policy issue for the state of how to position and regulate private groups and associations. However, until the 1998 "Regulatory Measure on Social Groups" (*Shehui tuanti guanli tiaoli*), the registration and supervision of private groups and associations was unclear and involved many different government agencies—the Ministry of Civil Affairs (*Minzhengbu*), the Party's Central Committee (*Dang zhongyang weiyuanhui*), various ministries and offices of the State Council, and the National Economic Restructure and Reform Commission. Furthermore, private groups and associations with good connections to a state agency could register with that agency and be supervised by the agency as an agency branch. Examples of this arrangement are the Beijing Qigong Institute and China Qigong Science Association. Their members are mostly state officials who retired from ministries that managed the qigong organizations, with many having been responsible for managing them. In their efforts to spread qigong more rapidly these qigong associations created sub-branches that were registered with the parent organization, thereby offering them administrative legitimacy as well as some management expertise and access to various resources. Thus, even without explicit permission from the state, the registration of a qigong practitioners' group with a qigong association was tantamount to a license to operate the group. This simple registration procedure enabled the wide spread of countless qigong practitioners' groups throughout the country.

QIGONG'S RETURN TO ORIGINAL SOURCES

One of the most important characteristics of the qigong reemergence in the 1980s is its return to its Buddhist and Daoist origins. This has occurred through two trends. One is the reorientation of the government's religion policy from suppression to recognizing aspects of qigong as an expression of a country with an emerging market economy. The other trend is the shift in the development and documentation of new methods of qigong practices from a state monopoly to societal organizations. Although qigong's newly acknowledged link to religion is explicitly recognized by both state and societal organizations, there are big differences in their interpretations.

The first trend is seen in a new interpretation that religion is an important component of qigong. The state's shifting religion policy from suppression to accommodation has been accompanied by a reevaluation of the history of religion. For example, the scholar Zhang Honglin of the Qigong Research Division of the Academy of Chinese Traditional Medicine (*Zhongyi yanjiuyuan qigong yanjiushi*) writes, "Qigong is an important part of China's traditional medicine" and has a close historical relationship with Confucianism, Daoism, Buddhism, and martial arts (Zhang 1996: 1). He also writes, "to be objective, parts of Buddhist doctrines and practice have had a profound influence on the development of qigong" (Zhang 1996: 214). This trend can also be seen in *Qigong Study in Chinese Traditional Medicine* (*Zhongyi qigongxue*), a textbook used in traditional medicine schools that categorizes qigong into six groups: medical qigong (*yijia qigong*), Confucianist qigong (*rujia qigong*), Daoist qigong (*Daojiao qigong*), Buddhist qigong (*Fojia qigong*), qigong martial arts (*wushu qigong*), and popular qigong (*minjian qigong*) (Song 1994). It is clear that historical religious influences are now fully recognized in the state's qigong research sector and also considered part of the explanation of qigong in educational materials. In other words, the state now acknowledges religion as a critical element of qigong's historical development and considers classic Buddhist and Daoist texts as part of its historical documentation.

The second trend is intertwined with the first but differs by not involving formal documents and classic texts but rather forms of practice that are more approachable to common people as so-called folk belief (*minjian xinyang*). As we have seen, the efforts to promote qigong practice methods and document them as "modern" and "scientific" shifted from the state in the 1950s to societal organizations in the 1980s. Qigong academic organizations and members of qigong practice groups took part in state-sponsored qigong research activities in furthering its development. To prove qigong's scientific character and popularize it, experienced qigong masters were needed. However, by the 1980s the masters who had been trained in the state qigong organs in the 1950s had either passed away or were frail and elderly. Therefore, the researchers turned to masters who were members of qigong practitioner groups and active in qigong academic organizations. Many of them had begun practicing body cultivation techniques on their own through Daoist and Buddhist training methods in the 1950s and even earlier. Unlike the professionally trained qigong masters active in the 1950s, these practitioners had not been visible either on the public stage or in the state medical establishment. Being outside the professional qigong organizations enabled them to escape the persecution experienced by the recognized qigong masters during the Sweeping-out Superstition movement in the early 1950s and the subsequent Crashingdown on Religion movement during the Cultural Revolution and to simply carry on in secret with their training. In the 1980s they participated in qigong practitioner groups where, due to their advanced techniques, they were recognized as qigong masters by many qigong research organizations and qigong academic associations and became very active in promoting qigong to the population at large. Examples of such masters are Tian Ruisheng, founder of *xianggong*, and Yan Xin, initiator of *Yanxin qigong*. They were the best-known qigong masters in the 1980s and regarded as indispensable talents of the China Qigong Science Association. Their qigong practice methods became increasingly popular.

In this manner, in the 1980s practitioners of Buddhist and Daoist training methods gradually attracted attention and came to be acknowledged as qigong masters. None of them had received any professional qigong training nor were they disciples of Buddhism or Daoism or members of groups affiliated with these religions. Instead they presented their own idiosyncratic methods and emphasized their efficaciousness. These new qigong masters did not seek to clarify the complex philosophic doctrines of Buddhism and Daoism but rather made highly original and colorful stories based on their own experiences of qigong practice to explain the origins of their methods. Some older masters represented themselves as successors of training methods long popular among the people. For example, Ma Litang, the initiator of *Ma Litang yangqigong,* learned *liuzijue yangshengfa*, a training method, from Puzhao Laoren of the Beijing Confucian Group (*Beijing kongjiaohui*). After decades of practice, Ma developed a new method, called *yangqigong*, which was very popular in the 1980s (Ma 1985). The stories of these masters on the origins and development of their qigong training methods can be traced historically to some extent since they include actual historical figures, events, and records.

Other, mostly younger masters who had learned qigong in the early 1980s represented themselves as the founders of new qigong methods. After several years of practice, they declared themselves the founder of one or another qigong training method and created many stories about it to embellish its "greatness" and "long history." Such stories are often impossible to document historically. A prominent example is Li Hongzhi, a qigong master and leader of the Falungong qigong group. He regards his practice method as reflecting the core of Buddhism and Daoism and the true nature of human beings. In order to return to an original pure state, one needs to apply the key principles of Falungong—truth (*zheng*), thoughtfulness (*shan*), and tolerance (*ren*)—in one's daily life (Li 1994). It is easy to see the links between this story and philosophy and many characteristics of folk belief—the idea of the unity of the three religions (*sanjiao heyi*), the connection of Buddhist and Daoist practices with daily life, and the brevity of doctrines and rich use of popular imagery.[11] In this manner, the qigong that came to be practiced widely in society recaptured a "religious" character that is very close to people's daily life.

Conclusion

This chapter has discussed how qigong, generally considered part of Chinese "traditional medicine" or part of its "traditional culture," was actually a new concept that was created in the 1950s, and has been given different interpretations that have become institutionalized. In this process, the state has managed to impose it's dominating ideology. The various key actors promoting qigong in different periods have had to reconcile it with such principles and doctrines held by the Party and Chinese state as materialism, scientism, and socialism. Therefore qigong, variously recognized by its promoters as a religious way of practice and as a supernatural power, had to be legitimized and justified with regard to the various state policies of each period, such as "sustain and modernize Chinese traditional medicine through scientific approaches," "learn from the Soviet Union," and "promote Chinese style modernization," so as to create a space for itself in the state as well as in society. The focus on the two different periods of the 1950s and after 1980s has illuminated the degree to which the above-mentioned national policies have changed or not since the market reform and social opening up since the late 1970s, and how they have influenced the interpretation of qigong and its institutionalization.

The chapter's intent has been to present a more complete picture of qigong in the state realm and popular society. In the realm of the state, qigong was institutionalized inside the national medical system from the 1950s as a "national medical heritage" and "a component of Chinese traditional medicine." This process emphasized searches among historical records and grounding in scientific interpretations to fit the state's modernization policy. Both the policies of learning from the "Soviet model of modernization" in the 1950s and pursuing "Chinese style modernization" in the 1980s have exerted important influences over scientific interpretations of qigong in each period. Furthermore, qigong's institutionalization came to be firmly positioned in the national medical system as a component of Chinese traditional medicine and has been reproduced in the national medical education system. Since the 1980s, graduate programs in qigong leading to the master's degree have been started in universities, further reproducing it in the state's medical system.

It is also clear that institutionalization since the early 1980s has diversified qigong due to its popularization in society. For comprehending qigong, people are more concerned with qigong's "effectiveness" rather than its "scientific credibility." In order words, the common people demand neither the "scientific proof" nor the "modern" nature of qigong that the state does. Instead, they value qigong as an intuitively appealing experience that brings them health and happiness. They accept qigong masters' religious interpretations of qigong that are excluded from the state realm but that broaden the societal base of qigong supporters. Additionally, with the indirect management by qigong academic associations from the early 1980s private qigong practice groups have enjoyed increased autonomy in their activities. However, as this autonomy was only guaranteed by particularistic administrative understandings with specific agencies, it lacked a legal basis. Consequently, qigong groups were easily targeted for suppression and dismantling when the regulatory framework for societal groups was tightened in the late 1990s.

Finally, it must be emphasized that qigong's reemergence since the early 1980s is not a transient phenomenon. On one hand, the state has continuously suppressed and reformed qigong groups since 1996 while, on the other hand, it has gradually strengthening its legal and administrative supervision of qigong activities in society. This helps legitimize qigong activities, enriching the soil for the growth of qigong groups all over the country that are acceptable to the state and the rejuvenation of qigong activities among common people. Now in the new qigong practice methods and therapies that have recently been approved by the Qigong Division of the National Ministry of Sports (*Guojia tiyu zongju*) qigong is defined as a "sport": it is easy to see qigong as playing an important role in promoting the new state slogan of "healthy and wholesome." Thus, more scholarly attention should be paid to the space being developed and secured by qigong with a strong religious element in the context of this new slogan and the state's stance in coping with this development.

Notes

1. Exposing the cult-like nature of Falungong became both the main concern of academic research, especially in the social sciences, and an important aspect of the state's suppression of Falungong.

2. Its launch date of March 17 commemorated a 1929 protest in Shanghai by doctors of Chinese traditional medicine against the policy to abolish Chinese traditional medicine in the Republic of China.

3. Two examples of translations of Okada Torajirō's meditation are *Meditation for Three Years* (*Jingzuo sannian*) translated by Hua Wenqi in 1916 and *Okada-Style Meditation Psychology* (*Gangtianshi jingzuo xinli*) translated by Lei Tongqun in 1920. *Harmonization of Body and Mind* (*Shenxin tiaohefa*), translated by Liu Renhang in 1916, is a translation that introduced Fujita Reisai's meditation method. Jiang Weiqiao wrote the prefaces to all three books.

4. Attempts to relate bodily cultivation practice and modernity after 1949 were spearheaded by some of the same individuals active earlier. For example, Jiang became advisor to the Shanghai Qigong Sanitarium (*Shanghai qigong liaoyangsuo*), which played a large role in propagating qigong in the 1950s, while Chen became president of the China Daoism Association (*Zhongguo Daojiao xiehui*), founded in 1957.

5. Ever since the Republican era, when China took its first steps in becoming a modern nation-state, there has been a heated debate among politicians, intellectuals, and medical workers as to whether to continue or end Chinese traditional medicine. Ralph Croizier (1968) has argued that although the debate was ostensibly about a medical issue, it reflected perceptions of modern China in terms of science, progress, modernity, the authority of tradition, and cultural nationalism. In this sense, the continuation of Chinese traditional medicine through its tolerance and even promotion in the People's Republic of China is of great interest in understanding "modernity" as the Party and the new state conceive of it.

6. However, the training program seldom offered licenses as a qigong master. Cheng Zhonglu received a license as a qigong Master (*qigong yishi*) from the Public Health Bureau of Tangshan (*Tangshanshi weishengju*) in October 1954, which was the first state-issued qigong license (*Zhongguo qigong kexue* 1996, 2: 28.)

7. Those involved in propagating qigong were quite aware of this link. According to Chen Tao of the Shanghai Qigong Sanitarium: "Most qigong therapies in the 1950s came from religion" (Chen 1957: 48). He further claimed that "most of the practitioners had some religious connection with Buddhism or Daoism" (Chen 1958: 50).

8. *Huangdi neijing* does not mention qigong but records a bodily cultivation called *daoyin tuna*, which is seen as very similar to the qigong therapy proposed by Liu Guizhen. Thus, the claim that qigong therapy has a history of more than two thousand years mainly lies in the similarity of bodily cultivation methods of the two.

9. Qian Xuesen (b. 1911) studied at the Massachusetts Institute of Technology and the California Institute of Science and Engineering and received Ph.D. degrees in aviation and mathematics in 1939. After returning to China in 1955 he became a leader in developing science, technology, and national defense. He pioneered Chinese research on rockets and missiles and wielded much influence, especially in the military. Following the market reforms in 1979 he took great interest in promoting research on "supernatural power." Zhang Zhenhuan (1915–94) joined the revolutionary movement in the 1930s and directed military actions. After 1949, he became a major general in the People's Liberation Army and a member of the Commission of Science Technology and Industry for National Defense (*Guofang kexue jishu gongye weiyuanhui*). He organized China's first test of a nuclear explosion. In the early 1980s, he became interested in supernatural power and, with his old colleague Qian Xuesen, active in promoting qigong research.

10. This shows how sponsorship by a state organ gives qigong promoters resources controlled by the state while letting the state organ capitalize its public resources to generate income, an increasingly important task for local states in the market economy. A similar example is the opening ceremony of the "Qigong Workshop Series Contributing to the Upcoming Asian Sports Games" (*Ying yayun zuo*

gongxian qigong zhishi xilie jiangzuo) held by the Beijing Qigong Institute in the Capital Stadium in 1990. The vice-mayor of Beijing and other top officials made speeches at the ceremony. The workshops invited well-known qigong masters to give speeches to a large audience of about 100,000 people and then collected donations of RMB 110,000 for the upcoming Asian Sports Game in Beijing. It is clear that the Beijing Qigong Institute had access to state facilities and other resources due to a close relationship with state organizations. It brought together qigong masters and common people in various activities while providing the Beijing municipal government and its officials some extrabudgetary income.

11. Yang Fucheng has observed that many of the qigong practice methods since the 1980s bear some similarities to folk belief in their theories, doctrines, transmission forms, and associations with religions (Yang 1994).

References

Chen Chengren. 1986. "Jiang Weiqiao." In *Minguo renwuzhuan diwujiuan* (Personages in the Republic of China, vol. 5), edited by Yan Ruping. Beijing: Zhonghua shuju.

Chen, N. Nancy. 1995. "Urban Spaces and Experiences of Qigong." In *Urban Spaces in Contemporary China: The Potential for Autonomy and Community in Post-Mao China*, edited by Deborah S. Davis et al., pp. 347–61. Cambridge, UK: Cambridge University Press.

Chen Tao. 1957. "Tuiguang qigong liaofa buneng jiandanhua" (Propagate qigong therapy without simplification). *Xin zhongyiyao* (New Chinese medicine) 10: 48.

———. 1958. *Qigong kexue changshi* (Fundamental scientific knowledge of qigong). Shanghai: Keji weisheng chubanshe.

Croizier, Ralph C. 1968. *Traditional Medicine in Modern China: Science, Nationalism, and the Tensions of Cultural Change*. Cambridge, MA: Harvard University Press.

Guo Lin. 1980. *Xin qigong liaofa chuji gong* (Basic-level new qigong therapy). Hefei: Anhui kexue jishu chubanshe.

———. 1983. "Xin qigong liaofa zhiliao bingli xuanjie" (A collection of examples of new qigong therapy cures). In *Xin qigong liaofa zhongji gong* (Intermediate-level new qigong therapy). Hefei: Anhui kexue jishu chubanshe.

Hishida Masaharu. 2000. *Gendai Chūgoku no kōzō hendō* (Structural change in contemporary China: symbiotic relations of state and society). Tokyo: Tōkyō daigaku shuppankai.

Hua Wenqi. 1916. *Jingzuo sannian* (Three years of meditation). Shanghai: Shangwu yinshuguan.

Hua Zhongfu (ed.). 1995. *Zhongguo zhongyi yanjiuyuan yuanshi* (History of the Chinese Medicine Research Institute Hospital). Beijing: Zhongyi guji chubanshe.

Lei Tongqun. 1920. *Gangtianshi jingzuo xinli* (Okada-style seizahō psychology). Shanghai: Shangwu yinshuguan.

Li Hongzhi. 1994. *Zhuanfalun*. Beijing: Zhongguo guangbo dianshi chubanshe.

Liu Guizhen. 1957. *Qigong liaofa shijian* (Qigong therapy practices). Shijiazhuang: Hebei renmin chubanshe.

Liu Renhang. 1916. *Shenxin tiaohefa* (Harmonization of body and mind). Shanghai: Shangwu yinshuguan.

Liu Yafei. 1984. "Xiang baba nayang reai qigong" (Just like your father, love qigong). *Qigong yu kexue* (Qigong and science) 12: 8–10.

Lü Bingkui. 1980. "Qigong liaofa de yanjiu yu yixue fazhan de daolu" (The path of qigong therapy research and medical development). In *Qigong liaofa jijing* (A collection on qigong therapy), edited by Tao Chengfu. Beijing: Renmin weisheng chubanshe.

Ma Jiren. 1983. *Zhongguo qigongxue* (Chinese qigong studies). Xi'an: Shanxi kexue jishu chubanshe.

Ma Litang. 1985. *Yangqigong jianshenfa* (Qigong fitness methods). Beijing: Renmin tiyu chubanshe.

Ministry of Health, Pavlov Theory Study Association (Zhongyang weishengbu Bafuluofu xueshuo xuexihui). 1954. *Bafuluofu xueshuo xuexi wenji* (Collected works on studies of Pavlov's theory). Beijing: Renmin weisheng chubanshe.

Ministry of Propaganda (Zhongyang xuanchuanbu). 1982. "Guanyu renti teyi gongneng xuanchuan wenti de tongzhi" (On publicizing the supernatural power of the human body). Beijing.

Nanjing zhongyi xueyuan (Nanjing College of Chinese Medicine) (ed.). 1959. *Zhongyixue gailun* (Introduction to traditional Chinese medicine). Beijing: Renmin weisheng chubanshe.

Qian Xuesen. 1988. *Lun renti kexue* (On human science). Beijing: Renmin junyi chubanshe.

She Zhichao. 1999. "Xin Zhongguo qigong shiye de kaituozhe—liu guizhen he tade neiyanggong" (The exonerater of new China's qigong: Liu Guizhen and his neiyanggong). *Zhongguo qigong kexue* (Chinese qigong science) 10: 18–20.

Shen Zhenyu (ed.). 2001. *Zheng yu xie—kexue yu teyigongneng ji xiejiao dalunzhan* (Good and evil: a polemical struggle between science and supernatural power and cult). Beijing: Qunzhong chubanshe.

Song Tianbin (ed.). 1994. *Zhongyi qigongxue* (Qigong study in Chinese traditional medicine). Beijing: Renmin weisheng chubanshe.

Xu, Jian. 1999. "Body, Discourse, and the Cultural Politics of Contemporary Chinese Qigong." *Journal of Asian Studies* 58, 4: 961–91.

Xu Yinggao. 1954. "Yiliao yufangxin 'shenghuxi liaofa'" (Preventive health care "deep breathing therapy"). *Xin zhongyiyao* (New Chinese medicine) 2.

Yang Fucheng. 1994. "Zailun minjian zongjiao qigong" (On qigong in popular religion). *Zhongguo renti kexue* (Chinese human science) 2, 2.

Yao Yushan. 1990. *Chen Yinning (Yuandunzi) qigong lunji* (The qigong collection of Chen Yinning [Yuandunzi]). Beijing: Gaodeng jiaoyu chubanshe.

Yin Shizi. 1917. *Yinshizi jingzuofa* (Yinshizi's meditation method). Shanghai: Shangwu yinshuguan.

Yu Guangyuan. 2000. *Tong weikexue zhishao haiyao dou yibainian* (At least one hundred tears of struggle with pseudoscience). Nanning: Guangxi renmin chubanshe.

Zeng Yiyu. 1954. "Xin Zhongguo yiliaotiyu zhi youyi xingshi—(jingzuo liaofa)" (Another form of sports therapy in new China [meditation therapy]). *Xin zhongyiyao* (New Chinese medicine) 2.

Zhang Honglin. 1996. *Zhengben qingyuan—huan qigong benlai mianmu* (Restore the original features of qigong). Beijing: Zhongguo shehui kexue chubanshe.

Zhao Baofeng. 1987. *Zhongguo qigongxue gailun* (Introduction to qigong in China). Beijing: Renmin weisheng chubanshe.

ahung (ahong) 阿洪
aiguo aijiao 愛國愛教
anli de zhanglao 按立的長老
Bafuluofu xueshuo 巴甫洛夫學說
Bafuluofu xueshuo xuexihui 巴甫洛夫學說學習會
baiqianfo 拜千佛
Baiyunguan 白雲觀
Baiyunshan 白雲山
Baizhang Huaihai 百丈懷海
baizhang qinggui 百丈清規
bangongshi 辦公室
Baoding 保定
baojiangong 保健功
Beijing ditan gongyuan 北京地壇公園
Beijing dongdan gongyuan 北京東單公園
Beijing gongren tiyuchang 北京工人體育場
Beijing kongjiaohui 北京孔教會
Beijing qigong yanjiuhui 北京氣功研究會
Beijingshi kexue jishu xiehui 北京市科學技術協會
Beijingshi zonggonghui 北京市總工會
Beijing yaoersi liaoyangyuan 北京一二四療養院
Beijing yixueyuan 北京醫學院
bude renxin 不得人心
bushi 布施
chaodu 超渡
Chen Tao 陳濤
Chen Yingning 陳攖寧
Chengdu xinqigong yanjiuzu 成都新氣功研究組
Chengdu zhongyi xuehui 成都中醫學會

Chengdu zhongyi xueyuan　　成都中醫學院
Cheng Zhonglu　程忠祿
Chiang Kai-shek　蔣介石
Chongqing zhongyi yanjiusuo　　重慶中醫研究所
Chongsheng pai　重生派
chujia daoshi　出家道士
chuandao ren　傳道人
chuantong　傳統
cuimian xueshuo　催眠學說
dahui　大會
dahuizhang　大會長
daji　打擊
dayan qigong　大雁氣功
Daizu　傣族
dangshi wenshi ziliao　黨史文史資料
Dang zhongyang weiyuanhui　黨中央委員會
Daohuisi　道會司
daojia qigong　道家氣功
daolusi　道路司
daoyinfa　導引法
daoyin tuna　導引吐納
Daozhengsi　道政司
difang chuantong　地方傳通
diyici quanguo qigong
　　fudaozhan peixunban　第一次全國氣功輔導站培訓班
dizang　地藏
Dong Lü　東閭
Dongyuemiao　東嶽廟
Duangong　端公
erduo renzi　耳朵認字
erhui　二會
Falungong　法輪功
faren diaobiao　法人代表
Fan Zhongliang　範忠良
fangyankou　妨煙口
fengjian mixin　封建迷信
fengshui　風水
Fojia qigong　佛家氣功
fucizixiao　父慈子孝
Fudan daxue　復旦大學
fumushi　副牧師

fuqi　服氣
Gangtianshi jingzuofa　岡田式靜坐法
Gangtianshi jingzuoxinli　岡田式靜坐心理
Gonganju　公安局
Gongfa yanjiuzu　功法研究組
Gong Pinmei　龔品梅
Gongshangju　工商局
Gongshang shuiwu　公商稅務
Gong Shirong　龔士榮
Gulishansi　古麓山寺
Gushansi　鼓山寺
gushenlei　古神纇
guanche zongjiao zhengce　貫徹宗教政策
guanguan xianghu　官官相護
Guanli simiao tiaolie　管理寺廟條列
guanpai　官派
Guantong xian　灌雲県
Guanweng　關翁
guanyu renti teyi gongneng xuanchuanwenti
　　de tongzhi　關與人體特異功能宣傳問題的通知
Guanyunxian　灌雲縣
Guangming ribao　光明日報
Guangzhoushi qigong kexue xiehui　廣州市氣功科學協會
Guofang kexue jishu gongye weiyuanhui　國防科學技術工業委員會
guojihua　國際化
Guojia jingji tizhi gaige weiyuanhui　國家經濟體制改革委員會
Guojia minzu shiwu weiyuanhui　國家民族事務委員會
Guojia tiyu zongju　國家體育總局
Guojia zhongyiyao guanliju　國家中醫藥管理局
Guojia zongjiao shiwu ju　國家宗教事務局
Guo Lin　郭林
Guolin xinqigong　郭林新氣功
Guo Morou　郭沫若
Guowuyuan　國務院
Haibin zhonggong zhongyang zhishu
　　xiuyangsuo　海濱中共中央直屬休養所
hajj　哈吉
halifat　哈裏發
Hanafi　哈納肥
hanyu minzu　漢語民族
hefaxing　合法性

Heilongdawang　黑龍大王
Heilongdawang ci　黑龍大王祠
Honganji　本願寺
honghuo　紅火
huxi anmo yundong　呼吸按摩運動
huxi yangshenfa　呼吸養身法
Huabei zongjiao nianjian　華北宗教年鑒
huanyuan　還願
Huangdi neijing　黃帝內經
Huang Huaizhang　黃懷璋
Hui　回
huiliangong　慧蓮功
Huiquan　會泉
huizhang　會長
huoju　火居
jicheng he fayang zuguo yixue yichan　繼承和發揚祖國醫學遺產
jiji　積極
jiating jiaohui　家庭教會
jiating juhui　家庭聚會
Jiangkou　江口
Jiangsu sheng zhengfu gongbao　江蘇省政府公報
Jiang Weiqiao　蔣維喬
jiao　醮
Jiaojing dadui　交警大隊
jiaoshi　教師
Jiaoyuju　教育局
Jin Luxian　金魯賢
Jing'an　敬安
jingshen　敬神
Jingzuofa　靜坐法
jingzuo liaofa　靜坐療法
Jingzuo sannian　靜坐三年
Jiuhuashan Foxueyuan　九華山佛學院
ju　局
juhuidian　聚會點
jushi Fojiao　居士佛教
Kang Youwei　康有爲
kexuexing　科學性
Kotoku Shusui　幸德秋水
laodong gaizao　勞動改造
Laozi　老子

Li Hongzhi　李洪志
lisheng　禮生
Li Yangzhen　李養真
li yi yi qi　禮以義起
liandan　煉丹
lianqi　練氣
Liang Qichao　梁啓超
Linji　臨済
Linshangong　麟山宮
Linyeju　林業局
ling　靈
Lingbao　靈寶
lingying　靈應
Lingyinghou　靈應侯
Liu Guizhen　劉貴珍
liuzijue yangshengfa　六字訣養生法
Longhushan　龍虎山
longwang　龍王
Longwanggou　龍王溝
Longwanggou daoguan guanli weiyuanhui　龍王溝道觀管理委員會
longwanggou shandi shumuyuan　龍王溝山地樹木園
Longwanggou wenwu guanlisuo　龍王溝文物管理所
Lü Bingkui　呂炳奎
Lüshan　閭山
luoma dahui　騾馬大會
Ma Jiren　馬濟人
Ma Litang　馬禮堂
Ma Litang yangqigong　馬禮堂養氣功
Mazu　馬祖
Maoshan　茅山
Mei Gucheng　梅殻成
menhuan　門宦
mifang　秘方
mixin　迷信
mixin dapo yundong　迷信打破運動
mixin zaopo　迷信糟粕
mixiugong　密修功
miaochan xingxue yundong　廟產興學運動
Miaofengshan　妙峰山
miaohui　廟會
Miaozhan　妙湛

minban   民辦
minjian qigong   民間氣功
minjian xinyang   民間信仰
Minnan   閩南
Minnan Foxueyuan   閩南佛學院
Minzhengbu   民政部
Minzhengju   民政局
minzu   民族
Ming Sha Le   明沙勒
moshibie minzu   沒識別民族
Mulian   目連
Nanjing zhongyi xueyuan   南京中醫學院
Nanjō Fumio   南條文雄
nanpian   南片
Nanputuo cishan jijinhui   南普陀慈善基金會
Nanputuosi   南普陀寺
Nanputuosi guanli weiyuanhui   南普陀寺管理委圓會
neibu   內部
neigong   內功
neiyanggong   內養功
nian jing bu chi, chi bu nian jing   念經不吃吃不念經
Okada Torajirō   岡田虎二郎
paichusuo   派出所
pailou   牌樓
pingjing   平靜
Pudu   普度
Putian   普天
Puzhao Laoren   普照老人
qi   氣
qigong   氣功
qigong daducao chuangshiren   氣功大毒草創始人
qigong liaofa   氣功療法
qigong yishi   氣功醫師
Qigong yu kexue   氣功與科學
qiye   企業
Qian Xuesen   錢學森
qing   清
Qingchengshan   青城山
Qinghua daxue   清華大學
Qing shigao   清史稿
Qingsongshan   青松山

Qingwei Lingbao　清微靈寶
Quanfanwei jiaohui　全範圍教會
Quanguo Fojiao daibiao huiyi　全國佛教代表大會
Quanshen　全真
Quan xue bian　勸學編
Quanzhou　泉州
ren　忍
renjian fojiao　人間佛教
Renmin ribao　人民日報
renti kexue　人體科學
renti kexue zhuanjia xiaozu　人體科學專家小組
rujia qigong　儒家氣功
sanbu zhengce　三不政策
sanfang guanli　三方管理
sanjiao heyi　三教合一
sanju　散居
Sanyijiao　三一教
Seizahō　靜坐法
Shaanbei　陝北
Shaanbei xiao Xianggang　陝北小香港
shan　善
Shanghai jiaotong daxue　上海交通大學
Shanghai qigong liaoyangsuo　上海氣功療養所
Shanghai zhongyiyao　上海中醫藥
shehui liliang　社會力量
Shehui tuanti guanli tiaoli　社會團體管理條例
Shenci cunfei biaojun　神祠存廢標準
shenhuxi liaofa　深呼吸療法
Shennong　神農
Shenxin tiaohefa　身心調和法
Shenyueguan　神樂官
shengchan dadui　生產大隊
Shenghui　聖輝
shengzuo　升座
shier duanjin　十二段錦
shifang conglin　十方從麟
shiye　事業
shoulu　受籙
shoushen　守神
Sichuan yixueyuan　四川醫學院
sijiu　四舊

Tadoushan   塔門山
Taiping   太平
Tai Shuangqiu   台爽秋
Taiwanshengzhengfu minzhengting   台灣省政府民政廳
Taixu   太虛
Tanxu   倓虛
Tangshan qigong liaoyangsuo   唐山氣功療養所
Tangshanshi gongren liaoyangyuan   唐山市工人療養院
Tangshanshi weisheng ju   唐山市衛生局
tangwei   堂委
teshu de kexue   特殊的科學
teyi gongneng   特異功能
Tian Ruisheng   田瑞生
Tianshifu   天師府
tiaojian fanshe xueshuo   條件反射學說
Tongyi zhanxian bu   統壹戰線部
tupo kongjian zhang'ai   突破空間障礙
Wan Niwen   萬倪雯
Wang Zhe   王喆
weikexue   偽科學
Wenwu guanli weiyuanhui   文物管理委員會
Wudangshan   武當山
wushu qigong   武術氣功
wuxing   五行
Xi'an wanbao   西安晚報
xitong   係統
Xiamen   廈門
Xiamen daxue   廈門大學
Xiamen Fojiao jushilin   廈門市佛教居林
Xiamen Fojiao xiehui   廈門市佛教協會
Xiamen shi minzu yu zongjiao shiwu ju   廈門市民族與宗教事物局
xiandai   現代
xiandaihua   現代化
xianji wenwu   縣級文物
Xianyou Fengting   仙遊楓亭
Xianxue   仙學
xianzhelei   先哲類
xianggong   香功
xiaozu   小組
xiejiao   邪教
xiexiqian   寫戲錢

Xinjiang wenti guojihua　新疆問題國際化
Xin qigong liaofa zhiliao bingli xuanjie　新氣功療法治療病例選解
Xinya　新亞
xinyongshe　信用社
Xin zhongyiyao　新中醫藥
Xinghua　興化
Xing Wenzhi　邢文之
xiulianfa　修練法
Xu Daozang　續道藏
xuyuan　許願
Xuanchuanbu　宣傳部
xuanchuan zichanjieji yinhui sixiang
　　de daducao　宣傳資産階級淫穢思想的大毒草
Xuantian shangdi　玄天上帝
xuexi Sulian　學習蘇聯
Yan'an　延安
Yanjiujie　燕九節
Yan Xin　嚴新
Yanxin qigong　嚴新氣功
yangge　秧歌
Yang Fucheng　楊福程
yangqi　養氣
yangqigong　養氣功
Yang Wenhui　楊文會
Yao　猺
Yihewani　依黑瓦尼
yihui　壹會
yijia qigong　醫家氣功
yiliao tiyu　醫療體育
yiquan zhanzhuang gong　意拳站樁功
yixueyuan　伊學院
yincilei　淫祠類
Yinshizi jingzuofa　因是子靜坐法
yinsi　淫祀
yinyang　陰陽
Ying yayun zuo gongxian qigong
　　zhishi xilie jiangzuo　迎亞運, 做貢獻氣功知識系列講座
you miao jiu you hui　有廟就有會
Yonglesi　永樂寺
Yu Bin　于斌
yufang yiliao　預防醫療

Yuhuang   玉皇
Yulin   榆林
Yuntaishan faqi si   雲台山法起寺
Yuan Shikai   袁世凱
Zen Ze-kuin   陳日君
zhaigu   齋姑
zhaitang   齋堂
Zhang Daoling   張道靈
Zhang Fu   張付
Zhang Honglin   張洪林
Zhang Yuqing   張宇清
Zhang Zenhuan   張震寰
Zhang Zhidong   張之洞
Zhangzhou   漳州
Zhao Puchu   趙樸初
Zhejiang sheng   浙江省
zhen   真
Zhenchuan   鎮川
zhengdangxing   正當性
zhengdang zongjiao huodong   正當宗教活動
Zhengli cengjia zhidu lun   整理僧伽制度論
zhengli zuguo yixue yichan   整理祖國醫學遺產
zhengshen   政審
Zhengyi Tianshi Dao   正乙天師道
zhengzhi biaoxian   政治表現
zhian   治安
Zhihuan jingshe   祇洹精舍
zhishi   執事
Zhongguo dangdai Daojiao   中國當代道教
Zhongguo Daojiao xiehui   中國道教協會
Zhongguo Fojiaohui   中國佛教會
Zhongguo jiaoyuhui   中國教育會
Zhongguo kexueyuan   中國科學院
Zhongguo minzu zhi   中國民族志
Zhongguo Musilin   中國穆斯林
Zhongguo qigong kexue   中國氣功科學
Zhongguo qigong kexue yanjiuhui   中國氣功科學研究會
Zhongguo renti kexue   中國人體科學
Zhongguo renti kexue xuehui   中國人體科學學會
Zhongguoshi de xiandaihua   中國式的現代化
Zhongguo Yisilanjiao xuehui   中國伊斯蘭教學會

Zhonghua cishanhui　中華慈善會
Zhonghua Fojiao zonghui　中華佛教總會
Zhonghua minguo linshi zhengfu　中華民國臨時政府
Zhonghua quanguo zhongyi xuehui
　　qigong kexue yanjiuhui　中華全國中醫學會氣功科學研究會
Zhonghua quanguo zonggonghui　中華全國總工會
Zhong-Ri-Han Fojiao youhao jiaoliu huiyi　中日韓佛教友好交流会议
zhongxiyi jiehe　中西醫結合
Zhongyang daxue　中央大學
Zhongyang weishengbu　中央衛生部
Zhongyao yaodian　中藥藥典
zhongyi　中醫
Zhongyi qigongxue　中醫氣功學
Zhongyixue gailun　中醫學概論
Zhongyi yanjiuyuan　中醫研究院
Zhongyi yanjiuyuan qigong yanjiushi　中醫研究院氣功研究室
Zhou Enlai　周恩來
Zhouzhice　周智冊
Zhu Hongsheng　朱洪聲
Zhu Yuanzhang (Ming Taizu)　朱元璋 (明太祖)
zichuan　自傳
ziyang　自養
zizhi　自治
zizhu　自主
zongjiao huodong changsuo　宗教活動場所
Zongjiaoju　宗教局
zongjiaolei　宗教額
Zongjiao lisu faling huibian　宗教禮俗法令彙編
zongjiao shiyong changsuo　宗教使用場所
Zongjiao zhengce falü zhishi dawen　宗教政策法律知識答問
Zongli Yamen　總理衙門
zuguo yixue yichan　祖國醫學遺產
zuochan　坐禅

Contributors

YOSHIKO ASHIWA is Professor of Anthropology, Hitotsubashi University, Tokyo. She has conducted research in Sri Lanka, China, and the United States on social structure and values, war and peace, religion and modernity, and cultural policies. She has published *The Search for Peace in Sri Lanka: Complexities of Culture, Politics, and Society* (Center for the Study of Peace and Reconciliation, 2007), and numerous articles (in Japanese) on Buddhism, including "Making 'Religion' and 'Ethnic-nationalism': The Cosmopolitanism of Modern Buddhist Reformists in China and Sri Lanka" (in *Ethnic Movements and Leaders*, Yamakawa, 2007).

TIMOTHY BROOK is a historian of Chinese society from the Ming dynasty to the twentieth century. He is concurrently the Shaw Professor of Chinese at the University of Oxford and the Principal of St. John's College at the University of British Columbia. Recent books include *Vermeer's Hat: The Seventeenth Century and the Dawn of the Global World* (Blomsbury/Penguin/Profile, 2008) and, with Jerome Bourgon and Gregory Blue, *Death by a Thousand Cuts* (Harvard, 2008).

ADAM YUET CHAU is University Lecturer in the Anthropology of Modern China, Department of East Asian Studies, University of Cambridge. He received his Ph.D. in anthropology from Stanford University. He is the author of *Miraculous Response: Doing Popular Religion in Contemporary China* (Stanford, 2006) and articles in *Minsu quyi, Asian Anthropology, Modern China, Ethnology,* and *Journal of Chinese Religions.*

KENNETH DEAN is James McGill Professor and Drs. Richard Charles and Esther Yewpick Lee Chair of Chinese Cultural Studies, Department of East Asian Studies, McGill University. His publications include *Lord of the Three in One: The Spread of a Cult in Southeast China* (Princeton, 1998), *Taoist Ritual and Popular Cults of Southeast China* (Princeton, 1993), *Epigraphical Materials on the History of Religion in Fujian: Xinghua Region, 1995, and Quanzhou Region*, 3 vols. (with Zheng Zhenman, 2004), and *First and Last Emperors: The Absolute State and the Body of the Despot* (with Brian Massumi, 1992).

LIZHU FAN, a native of Tianjin, is Professor of Sociology, Fudan University, Shanghai. She has conducted ethnographic work on contemporary expressions of Chinese traditional religious heritage, and her research includes the role of NGOs/NPOs in China's modernization. She has authored *The Transformational Patterns of Religious Belief Systems in Contemporary China: Case Study of Popular Believers in Shenzhen*, and articles in Chinese and international journals, and has edited several volumes of cross-cultural and cross-disciplinary research papers.

DRU C. GLADNEY is Professor of Anthropology at Pomona College and President of the Pacific Basin Institute. His books include *Muslim Chinese: Ethnic Nationalism in the People's Republic* (Harvard, 1991/1996); *Making Majorities: Constituting the Nation in Japan, China, Korea, Malaysia, Fiji, Turkey, and the U.S.* (editor, Stanford, 1998); *Ethnic Identity in China: The Making of a Muslim Minority Nationality* (Wadsworth, 1998); and *Dislocating China: Muslims, Minorities, and Other Sub-Altern Subjects* (Chicago, 2004).

RICHARD MADSEN is Distinguished Professor of Sociology, University of California, San Diego. He has co-authored *The Good Society* and *Habits of the Heart* (Los Angeles Times Book Award, Pulitzer Prize jury nomination). A former Maryknoll missionary, his authored or co-authored books on China include *Morality and Power in a Chinese Village* (C. Wright Mills Award); *China's Catholics: Tragedy and Hope in an Emerging Civil Society*; *China and the American Dream*; *Democracy's Dharma: Religious Renaissance and Political Development in Taiwan*. He has co-edited *The Many and the One: Religious and Secular Perspectives on Ethical Pluralism in the Modern World*.

UTIRARUTO OTEHODE, originally from Inner Mongolia, is a Ph.D. candidate in Anthropology, Hitotsubashi University, Tokyo. He conducted two years of fieldwork on *qigong* in Henan and Hebei provinces and is writing a dissertation titled "The Formation of Modernity and Restructuring of Traditions in China: Observations on the Institutionalization and Practice of Qigong." He has also co-translated (with Mio Yuko) a publication on folk belief in Hakka villages.

CARSTEN T. VALA is Assistant Professor of Political Science at Loyola College in Maryland. He recently finished his dissertation at the University of California, Berkeley, entitled "Failing to Contain Religion: The Emergence of a Protestant Movement in Contemporary China." He has also co-authored "Attraction without Networks: Recruiting Strangers to Unregistered Protestantism in China" (with Kevin J. O'Brien), *Mobilization*, 2007.

DAVID L. WANK is Professor of Sociology, Sophia University, Tokyo. He has authored *Commodifying Communism: Business, Trust, and Politics in a Chinese City* (Cambridge, 1999), as well as numerous articles on state-business relations, social networks, consumer culture, and institutional change in China, and co-edited *Social Connections in China: Institutions, Culture, and the Changing Nature of Guanxi* (Cambridge, 2002, with Thomas B. Gold and Doug Guthrie), and *Dynamics of Global Society: Theory and Prospects* [in Japanese] (Sophia, 2007, with Tadashi Anno and Murai Yoshinori).

Tsai, Lily, 215
TSPM (Three Self Patriotic Movement)
  churches. *See* Protestantism
Turkey, 156, 171
Turxun, Abulimit, 165
underground Catholics, 77–78, 85–86, 88–92

United Front Work Department (*Tongyi
  zhanxian bu*), 59, 132
United Nations, 143, 158, 165, 171
Utiraruto Otehode, 13, 71*n*9, 241, 279
Uyghurs
  ethnogenesis and indigeneity of, 166–68
  Hui and, 155
  identity politics of, 168–74
  integration into Chinese society, lack
    of, 164
  internal divisions amongst, 169
  international support for, 171, 172, 173
  protest of Chinese representations of, 174
  terrorist threat from, 165–66, 168–71
  Xinjiang resistance movement, 151, 163,
    165–66, 168–74
Uzbekistan, 169, 170
Uzbeks, 153, 164, 168

Vala, Carsten T., 13, 96, 280
Valentine, Daniel, 68–69
van der Veer, Peter, 2
Vatican attempts to control power of
  Sheshan shrine, 83–85, 88, 90

Wahhabism, 162, 169, 173
Wan Niwen, 254
Wang Mingdao, 106
Wang Mingming, 216
Wang Zhe, 179
Wank, David L., 1, 14, 126, 148*n*8, 211, 234,
  280
Watchman Nee, Local Church of, 114–15
Weber, Max, 17, 147, 161
Welch, Holmes, 179
Weller, Robert, 214
Wickeri, Philip L., 99
"world Buddhism," 56
World Parliament of Religion at Chicago
  Exposition (1893), 46, 55
World Uyghur Congress, 170
World Uyghur Youth Congress (WUYC),
  165, 166

Xi Dao Tang, 161
Xiamen City, Buddhism in, 14–15, 126–50
  Bailudong Temple, 136
  Buddhist Association of China and
    Xiamen Buddhist Association
    conflict between Religious
      Affairs Bureau and local clergy,
      involvement in, 63–64, 137–40
    as key organizational actor, 130–33
    Nanputuo Temple, role in revival of,
      134, 135, 136
    shift away from Nanputuo Temple
      involvement, 140–44
    smaller temples, role in revival of, 136
  conflict between local and central
    authorities, 63–64
  development of smaller temples in,
    66–67, 136
  economic and political repercussions,
    62–64
  fieldwork conducted on, 127–28
  historical background, 128–29
  Hongshan Temple, 136
  institutionalization of modern discourse
    on religion, as consideration of,
    126–28, 144–47
  key organizational actors, 130–33
  Nanputuo Temple. *See* Nanputuo Temple
  organizational field, concept of, 127
  political phases of, 133–34
  State Administration for Religious
    Affairs, 130–31
  Xiamen Buddhist Lodge (*Xiamen Fojiao
    jushilin*), 128, 136
  Xiamen Religious Affairs Bureau
    bifurcation of local field by, 140–44
    conflict with Buddhist clergy at
      Nanputuo Temple, 63–64, 137–40
    as key organizational actor, 131–33
    revival of Nanputuo Temple, role in,
      134, 136
    smaller temples, development of, 136
  Yangzhenggong Temple, 136
xianzhelei (sage category), 51
Xing Wenzhi, Joseph, 94
Xinjiang separatist movements
  Chinese nationality policy and, 156, 157
  Sufi networks and mobilization of
    resistance, 162
  Uyghur resistance movement, 151, 163,
    165–66, 168–74